ZERSTÖRER

ZERSTÖRER

THE MESSERSCHMITT 110 AND ITS UNITS IN 1940

JOHN J. VASCO & PETER D. CORNWELL

JAC PUBLICATIONS

CONTENTS

Published by JAC Publications
28 Bellomonte Crescent
Drayton, Norwich
Norfolk, England   NR8 6EJ

Printed in England by:
M F Barnwell
Aylsham
Norfolk NR11 6ET

Cover portrait:
25th September 1940. Oberleutnant Ernst Matthes, Staffelkapitän of 7./ZG 26,attacks a Spitfire, and
seconds later suffered engine damage at the hands of another Spitfire. Matthes managed to get his
damaged Bf 110 C back to the French mainland, and force-landed at Cherbourg.

Page 1:
Messerschmitt 110s of 5./ZG 26 in line astern formation, Battle of France period. The two lower fuselage
apertures for the ejection of spent 20 mm. cartridges can be clearly seen on the nearest aircraft.

Page 2, top:
With the port engine already running, mechanics crank the starboard engine of 3U + CR of 7./ZG 26.

Page 2, bottom:
M8 + DP of 6./ZG 76 taxi-ing. Note the spinner tip in the 6th Staffel colour of yellow.

Page 3:
Excellent air-to-air view of M8 + JK of 2./ZG 76 with the two-tone green upper surface camouflage
extending the full length of the fuselage sides. The third character of the fuselage code 'J' appears to be
red outlined with white.

FOREWORD
BY ERNST MATTHES
FORMER STAFFELKAPITÄN
7th STAFFEL, ZERSTÖRERGESCHWADER 26

It is particularly noteworthy that English military historians have dealt with the subject of the activities of the German Messerschmitt 110 'Zerstörer' units in the Battle of Britain. Although the Zerstörer units were in action on all fronts, there has not been a fully co-ordinated account of their actions up to the present time. That may be due to the fact that the aircraft lacked individuality and served in a variety of different roles such as fighter, night-fighter, fighter-bomber, low-level attack aircraft and reconnaissance, and their organisation was frequently changed.

The Messerschmitt 110 was one of the most eagerly awaited aircraft by German fighter units - a twin-engined fighter with an endurance of two hours and well armed. It was already in service at the outbreak of the war. In the Battle of Britain it was used mainly in the escort role; later as a fighter-bomber and low level attack aircraft. Escort meant ensuring that bombers were protected from attacks by enemy fighters on their way to the target. A thankless task, since it involved defensive duties and no possibility of engaging in long combats, the most important remit being the continuous protection of the bomber units to their target. These duties required strict discipline in rear positions, shadowing those aircraft requiring protection, in order to take up the best position to prevent enemy attacks. This meant, however, that there were few combat victories, and the bomber formations were critical, as it was impossible to totally prevent attacks by enemy fighters. The Messerschmitt 110 aircrew fulfilled their escort duties unto death. Nearly 90% of aircraft committed in the Battle of Britain were lost. The loss of aircraft was not the whole story, since losses over England inevitably meant the loss of flying personnel also. The failure of the fighter and Zerstörer units to com-pletely fulfil their tasks cannot be blamed on the highly-trained crews.

It was a fight between life and death. It was fought honourably by both sides. Crews shot down could expect fair treatment. Between opponents there was no real feeling of hate. Their military duty powered the war effort. Why this war had to happen, and why no other alternative was found is another matter. Former enemies are able to look each other in the eye, and many became friends after the war.

The psychological and physical burden of the war period has shaped the survivors, and has brought to these men a greater understanding for international development within the consideration of national interests. This war generation, which simply did its military duty on either side, doesn't want any more killing, only free competition and a willingness to negotiate. They hope that they can pass on to their children and grandchildren this belief in the importance of life.

The survivors look back in deep sadness on the victims of this unholy conflict.

ERNST MATTHES

FOREWORD
BY WOLFGANG FALCK
FORMER GRUPPENKOMMANDEUR OF I. GRUPPE,
ZERSTÖRERGESCHWADER 1,
AND FIRST GESCHWADERKOMMODORE OF
NACHTJAGDGESCHWADER 1

It is a special honour for me that John Vasco has asked me to write a foreword to his documentation of the Me 110. I am very pleased to do this, since in 1939 the Staffel that I led belonged to the first units that were equipped with the Me 110 and from that time it was the aircraft which I flew exclusively.

The head of the Luftwaffe at that time, Hermann Göring, visited us, Jagdgeschwader 'Richthofen', one day at Döberitz, near Berlin and explained to us that he had selected from his airforce an 'elite band' that would compare to the 'Ironsides' of Cromwell. This meant that these units would act as the main spearhead of the Luftwaffe. They would be equipped with the Me 110, a twin-engined, two-man aircraft, with a large range and heavy, concentrated weapons. The Me 110 would outperform any enemy aircraft. That sounded wonderful, even though two engines and a second man wasn't really what a true fighter pilot wanted. The newly-formed III./Jagdgeschwader Richthofen was equipped with the Me 110 in the summer of 1939; a radio was installed and blind-flying training began for the pilots. Because of the political pressure, the training and re-adjustment to the new model required immediate high level training.

Following the occupation of Czechoslovakia, the Gruppe found itself in Olmütz. There it began to adjust to the new requirements of the aircraft. At the same time the Gruppe was named I./Zerstörergeschwader 76. In comparison with the Me 109, the Me 110 was certainly larger and more clumsy. In August we were stationed at an airfield in Schlesia. From one day to the next we awaited the outbreak of war.

On 1st September it arrived. The attack on Poland began. Our first mission was, coincidentally, the first occasion that I took the complete Staffel into the air. Our orders were to accompany a flight of bombers to Krakow airfield. It was a wonderful, cloudless day. In spite of this we saw no bombers so we flew alone to Krakow in the hope that we would meet them there. Krakow lay in the morning sun far below us, but no bombers - and no Polish aircraft! So, our first trip was really just a stroll, a good practise flight for the Staffel.

In the days that followed, however, we saw more of the enemy and the prophecies of Göring were fulfilled to more than our expectations. We had many successes and no losses. After the end of the Polish campaign we were sent to the French border. Here, there was absolute quiet, such as one might find in peacetime. In the middle of December we were sent to North Germany, to the North Sea. Immediately, on the second day, we were called to action and I was soon in the air with four aircraft on an introductory flight in the region of Wilhelmshafen and Heligoland. There, a group of 22 Wellington bombers were attacking the coast. It was our first engagement with an RAF unit. Here, the complete range of the Me 110's weaponry was needed, also the skill of the pilots. The rear gunner of one of the Wellingtons shot both of my engines to pieces, and the ammunition at the rear of my cockpit caught fire. Thankfully, due to my altitude, a fortunate wind and not too much weight, I managed to glide to the airfield at Wangeroog and make a smooth landing.

In April 1940 the Me 110 was also to find itself engaged in hostilities against Denmark and Norway. Then followed action in Holland, Belgium, France and the Channel coast. The first days ran pretty well much to plan. Then, when we came up against Hurricanes for the first time, and particularly Spitfires, we were suddenly given sharp, hard lessons. Both types of plane were, as regards to speed, climbing ability and turning power, far superior. Should one appear behind its target, its concentrated firepower had a devastating effect. Otherwise, we fought for our lives and suffered many losses. Worst were the engagements over the Channel and those over the south coast of England. At this time there was no more talk of 'Ironsides'. There is never a negative without a positive, however! Here the second engine was our saviour. Often we were able to reach, on one engine, our home airfield or an emergency landing on the mainland when things had really gone badly. The halo of Göring and his 'Ironsides', however, was completely destroyed.

WOLFGANG FALCK

GLOSSARY

Beobachter	Observer
Bf	Bayerische Flugzeugwerke
Bordfunker	Radio Operator
Bordschutze	Rear gunner
Ergänzungsgruppe	Replacement Wing
Erprobungsgruppe	Experimental/Test Wing
Feldwebel (Fw)	Flight Sergeant
Flieger (Flgr)	Aircraftsman
Flugzeugführer	Pilot
Freie Jagd	Free fighter sweep
Gefreiter (Gefr)	Leading Aircraftsman
Geschwader	Roughly equivalent to 3 RAF Wings
Gruppe	Roughly equivalent to a RAF Wing
Gruppenkommandeur	Commanding Officer of a Wing
Hauptmann (Hptm)	Flight Lieutenant
Henaja	Illuminated night fighting (Hell Nacht Jagd)
Jagdbomber	Fighter-bomber
Jagdgeschwader (JG)	Roughly equivalent to 3 RAF Fighter Wings
Kampfgeschwader	Roughly equivalent to 3 RAF Bomber Wings
Kanone	Cannon (designation used for guns of 20 mm. calibre and above)
Kommodore	Commanding Officer of a Geschwader
Lehrgeschwader (LG)	Training Geschwader (in practise these units were on active service)
Luftflotte	Air Fleet
Luftwaffe	Airforce
Leutnant (Lt)	Pilot Officer
Major	Squadron Leader
MG	Maschine Gewehr (Machine Gun)
Nachtjagd	Night fighting
Nachtjäger	Night fighter
Oberfeldwebel (Ofw)	Warrant Officer
Obergefreiter (Ogefr)	Senior Aircraftsman
Oberleutnant (Oblt)	Flying Officer
Oberst	Group Captain
Oberstleutnant	Wing Commander
Ritterkreuz(träger)	Knights Cross (holder)
Schwarm	Section of four aircraft
Stab	Staff (section of a Gruppe or Geschwader)
Staffel:	Roughly equivalent to a RAF squadron
Staffelkapitän	Commanding Officer of a Staffel
Unteroffizier (Uffz)	Sergeant
Werk Nummer (W. Nr.)	Works number (of component, or aircraft)
Wespe	Wasp (unit emblem)
Zerstörer	Destroyer (name given to the Messerschmitt 110)
Zerstörergeschwader (ZG)	Unit of 3 wings of Messerschmitt 110s

Two views of Bf 110s in wintery conditions. The first part of the W. Nr. 30.. can be seen on CF + NP. In the head-on view, the full factory code of CF + NS can be seen on the underside of the wings.

Messerschmitt 110 B, 3U + BC, of the Gruppenstab of II./ZG 26. Note the single lightning flash emblem on the nose. As the improved 'C' version came into service, the 'B' was relegated to a training role.

INTRODUCTION

In 1934 the Reichs Luftfahrt Ministerium (RLM) issued a requirement for a twin-engined fighter capable of combating other aircraft and possessing exceptional range to enable it to escort bombers deep into enemy territory, this new generation of modern fighter-destroyer aircraft for the emergent Luftwaffe being designated 'Zerstörer'.

This introduced a new class of combat aircraft to the military stage, the strategic fighter, the advent of which had long been expounded by air-warfare theorists. However the specification for such an aircraft placed conflicting requirements on its design, its performance as a fighter and manoeuvrability having to be balanced against the weight penalties incurred by the need for extended range and durability. These contradictory factors could only be met by compromise.

The first flight of Willi Messerschmitt's rakish response to the RLM's requirement, the Bf 110 V-1, took place at Augsburg on 12 May 1936 with test pilot Rudolf Opitz at the controls. Two further prototypes joined the flight trials programme before the end of the year, with official trials commencing at Rechlin in January 1937.

Initial results from the official trials were not promising. A level speed of 316 mph. (500 km/h) was attained but flight endurance fell far short of expecta-

tions. There were also reservations as to the Bf 110's controllability, manoeuvrability and acceleration. But despite this inauspicious start, the RLM was sufficiently interested to order 4 more aircraft for service evaluation and these Bf 110 A-0s, as they were designated, were delivered by March 1938.

Arriving too late for combat testing with the Legion Condor during the Spanish Civil War, the first major production model, the Bf 110 C, followed early in 1939. Powered by two redesigned Daimler Benz DB 601 engines each providing 1,100 hp., it carried a heavy forward-firing armament of four 7.9 mm. MG 17 machine guns and two 20 mm. cannon in the nose, and with a single 7.9 mm. MG 17 machine gun for rear defence it was a formidable aircraft for its time.

Large scale reorganisation of the Luftwaffe fighter force implemented on 1st January 1939 resulted in its Schweren Jagdgruppen being redesignated 'Zerstörergruppen' as follows:

I./JG 141 - I./ZG 1	Bf 109 D	Jüterbog-Damm
II./JG 141 - II./ZG 1	Bf 109 C	Fürstenwalde
I./JG 142 - I./ZG 26	Bf 109 C	Dortmund
II./JG 142 - II./ZG 26	Bf 109 C	Werl
III./JG 142 - III./ZG 26	Bf 109 C	Lippstadt
I./JG 143 - I./ZG 52	Bf 109 B	Illesheim
I./JG 144 - I./ZG 76	Bf 109 B	Gablingen

The winter of '39-'40 was particularly severe, but aircraft serviceability still had to be maintained, as evidenced by this view of a 1./ZG 1 Bf 110 C with groundcrew in attendance. Note the W. Nr. on the port side of the cockpit canopy.

These units were all scheduled to take delivery of the Messerschmitt 110 as it became available. The first two Gruppen to do so being I./ZG 1 and I./ZG 76 who re-equipped with the new type immediately.

On 1st September 1939, further reorganisation of the German fighter forces saw those Zerstörergruppen which were still Bf 109-equipped being redesignated as Jagdgruppen pending conversion to the Bf 110. The only exceptions were I. and II./ZG 26, where delivery of the new type was imminent.

Thus, on the outbreak of war on 3rd September 1939, a total of 195 Bf 110 Cs were already in Luftwaffe service, those deployed for the attack on Poland being:

I.(Z)/LG 1	Major Walter Grabmann
I./ZG 1	Major Joachim-Friedrich Huth
I./ZG 76	Hauptmann Gunther Reinecke

During the Polish campaign the Zerstörer proved particularly impressive in the close support role and a most powerful adversary in the air, demolishing all fighter opposition that it met. Its fearsome reputation as a combat machine, largely created by the German propaganda machine, was born here.

The Bf 110 was first encountered by the RAF on 18th December 1939 when Wellington bombers from Nos. 9, 37 and 149 Squadrons sortied to attack German naval units in the Heligoland Bight and at Wilhelmshaven. Tracked by German naval radar as they approached the German coast, they were intercepted by a large force of fighters including the Bf 110s of

I./ZG 76. According to one RAF history, "seven Wellingtons were lost in battle, and others came down in the sea while flying home." Despite enthusiastic claims in the British press that 6 of the 12 enemy fighters shot down were Bf 110s, only 2 were damaged, those of Oberleutnant Falck and Leutnant Uellenbeck. It had been an inauspicious introduction to the new German fighter.

Not until Dunkirk, when the Zerstörer was first opposed by modern day-fighters operating in any numbers, were its limitations exposed. The concept of the heavy twin-engined escort for the day bomber was sorely tried in the skies over southern England in the summer of 1940 and found to be flawed. Once it became evident that the Bf 110 could only continue to operate as a day fighter if provided with escort fighters of its own, the myth was finally exploded.

Nevertheless, and largely due to the failure of its intended successor, the Messerschmitt 210, the ubiquitous Zerstörer soldiered on through the entire war in a variety of guises and over many different fronts including the Mediterranean, North Africa, Russia and the Balkans. Treated with genuine affection by its crews and with grudging respect by its enemies, the Bf 110 rightly established its own unique place in the history of military aviation.

This book relates some of the background to its operational history during the early part of the war and recounts the stories of some of those who flew and fought in it.

Bf 110 D-1/R-1, M8 + SL, a 'Dackelbauch' of 3./ZG 76.

CHAPTER 1

PRELUDE - DENMARK AND NORWAY - APRIL/MAY 1940

With the successful conclusion of the autumn Polish campaign, many of the Luftwaffe units involved returned to their bases in Germany to spend the winter resting, refitting and preparing for the offensive to come. During the long severe winter of 1939/40 little air activity took place beyond occasional fighter skirmishes over the German frontier, attacks on naval targets and armed reconnaissance of ports and coastal shipping movements.

Throughout the winter months an uneasy stalemate persisted as the so-called 'phoney war' or 'Sitzkrieg' ran its grim course. The German planners were, meanwhile, finalising preparations for the Western offensive and the invasion of France scheduled for early in the New Year. But before this could be attempted there had to be one further military intervention aimed at securing Germany's exposed northern flank against possible invasion. The guarantee that Norway would be able, or even prepared, to protect its declared neutrality was considered extremely doubtful. Its territorial waters were regularly infringed by both British and German naval units alike.

As a result, Operation 'Weserübung', the simultaneous invasion of Denmark and Norway, was viewed as an essential pre-requisite if Germany was to have any real chance of launching a successful campaign into mainland continental Europe that spring. The deep-water harbours of Norway also offered the Kriegsmarine attractive bases from which a naval blockade of

Britain could be mounted. Additionally, from airfields along the Norwegian coast, the Luftwaffe could sustain an offensive on British targets and its shipping and sea communications.

The air-sea nature of the intended campaign required close co-operation between every arm of the German forces involved and would be on a scale unlike anything attempted before. It provided for surprise sea-borne and airborne attacks along the whole Norwegian coast from Oslo in the south-east to Narvik in the far north, with simultaneous landings at Arendal, Kristiansand, Egersund, Stavanger, Bergen and Trondheim.

In Denmark, German forces would simply cross the frontier at night with dawn landings taking place at Copenhagen and various other strategic points around the Danish coast and islands. The Luftwaffe's role was tactical and strategic support as well as providing the massive transport resources required to air-lift the necessary troops, equipment and supplies. A total of 571 Junkers Ju 52/3 m aircraft were assembled for this purpose, representing half the total airforces deployed for the entire operation.

Reflecting the predominantly maritime nature of the operation, the OKL (OberKommando der Luftwaffe) allocated Fliegerkorps X, anti-shipping specialists commanded by Generalleutnant Hans-Ferdinand Geisler, to overall operational control of the air component for 'Weserübung'.

Above and below, left: Two views of M8+DH of 1./ZG 76 jacked-up in the firing butts to have its guns aligned. The thinner fuselage cross is of the early 1940 style.

This tethered cockerel's eternal claim to fame is that it was the inspiration for the Staffel emblem of 9./ZG 26.

Lt. Helmut Lent, pilot of 3./ZG 76. Lent moved to the night-fighter forceand had 102 victories to his credit when he was killed in action on 7/10/44.

Major interference by British naval forces was closely monitored by Luftwaffe reconnaissance aircraft for two days immediately preceding the invasion. Also, during the early evening and night before the attack, He 111s of II./KG 26 bombed the British fleet in Scapa Flow losing three of their number to Hurricanes of No. 43 Squadron.

Little opposition from either the Danish or Norwegian armed forces was anticipated and this also helped determine composition of the Luftwaffe forces eventually subordinated to Fliegerkorps X for the operation. A single Gruppe of Junkers Ju 87 Stukas from I./StG 77 was deployed together with three fighter Gruppen: the Bf 109 Es of II./JG 77 and the Bf 110 Cs of the Luftwaffe's two premier Zerstörergruppen, I./ZG 1 led by Hauptmann Wolfgang Falck and I./ZG 76 under Hauptmann Gunther Reinecke.

At dawn on 9th April German troops tossed aside the frontier barriers and marched across the border into Denmark. Given the relative size of the opposing forces, organised military resistance was futile and little or none was offered. Paratroop landings on Ålborg's airfields were rapidly reinforced by airborne infantry airlifted by Junkers Ju 52/3s. The whole operation progressed according to plan and effectively cut off from any outside help, Denmark capitulated the same day.

Taking off from their base at Barth to provide air cover for the paratroop landings at Ålborg, the Bf 110s of 1./ZG 1 led by Oberleutnant Martin Lutz met no opposition and landed at Ålborg almost as soon as the runway was cleared of parachutes.

Lutz, ever mindful of the comfort and well-being of his troops, summoned Oberleutnant Victor Mölders and ordered him to immediately set about finding appropriate accommodation for the entire Staffel - one of the better hotels in Ålborg should do nicely! They were among the first Germans to arrive, but that would not remain so for long. Within the next few hours Ålborg would be teeming with assorted representatives of the victorious Wehrmacht, and it would be a case of first come, first served!

Mölders, still wearing his bulky flying suit, pondered the proposition. There was no transport available and they were some way out of town. How was he supposed to get there? Ever helpful, Lutz took him gently by the arm and turned him towards the distant boundary fence. "Look", he said, pointing beyond the wire, "there is the road. Cars drive on it. Get a lift."

And so it was that soon after setting his Bf 110 down at Ålborg, Victor Mölders found himself sitting in the front seat of a car driven by a Danish milk-machine salesman as it sped past columns of German paratroops marching along the highway towards town.

Pausing for a most welcome breakfast at his driver's home, the less than startling news was announced on local radio that German troops were occupying the country. Suitably refreshed, Oberleutnant Mölders was dropped in town outside a perfect hotel which he promptly commandeered on behalf of the Luftwaffe in general, and ZG 1 in particular. Business concluded and duty done, it only then dawned on him that he must be the first, and probably still the only, German soldier in Ålborg. He had effectively occupied, at least part of, the town single-handed!

Meantime the Zerstörers of I./ZG 76 had a more difficult time. The Gruppe was charged with neutralising the Norwegian Air Force based at Oslo and Stavanger prior to landings there by paratroops. Oberleutnant Werner Hansen's 1st Staffel was allocated to the attack on Oslo-Fornebu airfield while Oberleutnant Gordon Gollob's 3rd Staffel were to cover Stavanger-Sola. The Stabsschwarm, along with Oberleutnant Heinz Gresen's 2nd Staffel, would move forward to Ålborg as a forward base from which to support the continuing air operations over Norway.

Early that morning 8 Bf 110 Cs of 1./ZG 76, led by their Staffelkapitän Oberleutnant Werner Hansen, had taken off from Westerland on the island of Sylt. They were briefed to provide Flak suppression and local fighter defence for the landings at Oslo-Fornebu scheduled for 8:30 am.. Once the airfield was secured by their troops, the Bf 110s were to land, refuel and continue to provide close ground support using Fornebu as a forward base. Their sortie was to be a one-way trip.

Flying with Hansen in the first Schwarm as they groped their way through the heavy fog shrouding the Skagerrak were Leutnant Helmut Lent, Leutnant Erhart Kort and Unteroffizier Helmuth Mütschele. Behind them, a second Schwarm of 4 Bf 110 Cs led by Leutnant Gerhard Böhmel with Leutnant Hans-Ulrich Kettling, Oberfeldwebel Gerhard Herzog and Feldwebel Johan Schonherr.

They encountered increasingly bad weather during the outward flight but ploughed on, their blind-flying experience tested to the full. Unknown to them, II./KGzbV 1, the first wave of 29 Junkers 52/3s carrying the paratroops intended for the initial landings, had

Two groundcrew pose on a Bf 110 of ZG 1. Of interest is the all-white spinner, an uncommon feature, and the sloping demarcation line between the upper and lower surface fuselage.

already abandoned the attack due to the weather and were heading back to the nearest landfall at Ålborg which by now should be in German hands. Without them, the second wave of Ju 52/3 transports, KGzbV 103, would be landing airborne troops on a still well-defended target, and if they didn't establish an early foothold, there would be nowhere for the fighters to land once their fuel was exhausted. The unexpected filthy weather placed the whole operation in jeopardy.

As the fighters flew on, with the second wave of transport aircraft some way behind, orders came through from Hamburg to abandon the attack. But the Bf 110s were already well beyond their limits of range so Hansen had little choice but to continue the mission. They would have to put down at Oslo-Fornebu once their fuel was exhausted, whatever happened!

Hansen's 8 Bf 110s all emerged safely from the fog and cloud which draped the Norwegian coast, bursting through into bright sunlight over Oslofjorden. They were promptly set upon by 7 Gloster Gladiators of the Norwegian Air Force and a short, sharp battle ensued during which two of the Zerstörers were shot down.

Leutnant Erhart Kort and his Bordfunker, Obergefreiter Heinrich Bockheimer, fell almost immediately to one of the Gladiators, possibly that flown by Lt. Tradin. They were both killed when their aircraft impacted at Frogn.

Claiming destruction of one of the Gladiators, but heavily damaged in attacks by others, Unteroffizier Helmut Mütschele somehow managed to survive mur-derous ground-fire from the Norwegian defences before crash-landing near Voyen Gard, outside Oslo. Along with his Bordfunker, Gefreiter Karl Lorey, Mütschele was taken prisoner, but both of them were soon released by German troops and returned to their unit none the worse for their experience.

Closely engaged by the nimble biplanes, Helmut Lent at last managed to latch on to one and opened fire. The crippled Gladiator, piloted by Sgt. Per Schye, fell away to a crash-landing at Bratenjordet giving Lent his fifth victory of the war. Badly hit himself in frenzied attacks by the more agile Gladiators, he was lucky to escape still relatively airworthy.

Two more Gladiators dropped out of the combat over Fornebu, Sgt. Lutken and Sgt. Waaler both falling victim to the superior fire-power of the German fighters. With the advantage steadily slipping away from them, the other Gladiators were soon forced to disengage and retire. They dropped away, vanishing into the ground haze below, to attempt landings on the frozen lakes north and west of Oslo, only one surviving as airworthy.

Oberleutnant Hansen reformed his 6 remaining Bf 110s over Fornebu and began repeated strafing attacks on parked aircraft and airfield defences. Two Gladiators found sitting on the runway were set alight, one of them being Sgt. Waaler's machine damaged in combat earlier. Having subdued the local defences, the Zerstörers circled Fornebu awaiting the paratroops who were to capture the airfield. Their fuel reserves had provided for only 20 minutes combat over Fornebu and this time was now long gone.

After what seemed an eternity, a formation of 'Tante Jus' finally lumbered into view. But to the amazement of the circling Zerstörers, instead of disgorging paratroops, the heavy transports formed a landing pattern and started to make approaches to the runway. What Hansen and his pilots didn't realise was that this was the second wave of Ju 52/3s carrying the airborne troops of II./IR 324 who were to consolidate an area already supposedly captured by paratroops.

The Ju 52/3s had also ignored the recall order and continued their mission, having broken through the worst of the weather and already approaching the target area by the time the signal was received. As the first of them touched down on the runway, they came under heavy ground fire which forced many to open up and take off again. The Kommandeur of KGrzbV 103, Hauptmann Wagner, was killed while attempting to land. Recognising that the airfield was not yet secured, many of the Ju 52/3 transports sheered away and headed back for Ålborg.

By now the Zerstörers were flying on fumes. In every cockpit the red warning lights were on indicating that their fuel was exhausted. Three of them were already flying on one engine. They could no longer stay in the air. Hansen ordered Leutnant Lent first in to land while the others provided covering fire.

Lent ordered his Bordfunker, Gefreiter Walter Kubisch, to strap-in tight. Their starboard engine, damaged in the earlier combat with the Gladiators, was now smoking ominously and sounded increasingly rough. Sizing-up the runway below, Lent could see that the landing was going to be very tight indeed.

Wrestling the controls and only barely conscious of the heavy ground-fire they were attracting, Lent came in low over the threshold but far too fast, and thumped his aircraft down onto the asphalt. He was to be thankful for his high speed which got him to the intersection of the two runways just a few yards ahead of a Ju 52/3 landing ahead of him.

With a fully-laden Ju 52/3 thundering past close behind his tail, Lent began applying the brakes as hard as he dared and watched the end of the runway rush towards him. Lent shouted to Kubisch to brace himself as they careered straight off the end of the runway and headlong down a boundary slope, shearing off both undercarriage legs. They came to rest close to a house beyond the airfield boundary, both miraculously unhurt.

They had been incredibly lucky and good fortune would remain with them through the next five years of war. They were to become one of the Luftwaffe's most successful crews and survive more than 500 combat sorties, most of them at night, during which Lent amassed 113 victories, rising in August 1943 to Geschwaderkommodore of NJG 3. Both awarded the coveted Ritterkreuz, they would eventually meet their deaths when their Junkers Ju 88 hit an HT cable whilst landing at Paderborn on 5th October 1944.

Two more Bf 110s landed almost together. One of them, Hansen, with a damaged starboard engine, end-

ing up within yards of the boundary fence. Leutnant Kettling pulled off a commendable landing despite heavy damage to both engines and one radiator which he had sustained in combat with the Norwegian fighters.

Oberleutnant Hansen marshalled his remaining 5 Bf 110s along the north-west boundary of the airfield and deployed them so that their rear-firing MG 17s could provide some defence. But unknown to him and his crews, the Norwegian forces defending the airfield had already started to withdraw, so Fornebu was effectively already in their hands. It had fallen to a dozen aircrew of 1./ZG 76.

By 9:15 am. a few of the Ju 52/3s had managed to put down, the infantry they carried quickly securing key buildings and installations. Once the situation became clear an urgent signal was sent off to HQ Fliegerkorps X confirming that Oslo-Fornebu was in German hands and ready for landings. It was triumphantly ascribed: '1st Staffel, Zerstörergeschwader 76'.

It was another three hours before the main force of paratroops and infantry started to arrive. But by midday, transport aircraft were disgorging troops at both Oslo-Fornebu and nearby Oslo-Kjeller, where the Ju 87s of I./StG 1, airborne that morning from Kiel-Holtenau, soon established a forward base for their close-support operations for ground troops.

During the afternoon, Fornebu became choked with aircraft as IR 234 deployed its men and equipment and by that evening, Oslo became the first capital city to fall to airborne troops. As Generalleutnant Geisler was to cheerfully confide to Werner Hansen when they met two days later, "But for your Staffel things might have turned out very differently!".

Meanwhile, 8 Bf 110s of 3./ZG 76 led by their new Staffelkapitän, Oberleutnant Gordon Gollob, had also taken off from Westerland early that morning to cover the landings at Stavanger-Sola. Gollob had only just been appointed to command of the Staffel following the death of Hauptmann Gutmann the previous day.

Flying over the Skagerrak further west than Hansen's formation, they met even more appalling weather but pressed on. But when Gollob eventually lost sight

Flying crew of 2./ZG 76. Fourth from left is Wolfgang Falck.

of all his aircraft in the thickening gloom, he was reluctantly forced to call-off the attack and order them all back to Ålborg.

Unaccountably, only the first Schwarm followed this order and turned for the Danish coast, the rest carried on, blindly forging ahead through the thick fog and mist. Inevitably, tragedy followed and the Bf 110s of Leutnant Bodo Habben and Unteroffizier Grams collided in the mist and crashed into the sea with the loss of both crews.

The remaining Rotte, Oberfeldwebel Fleischmann and Oberfeldwebel Hans Gröning, arrived over Stavanger-Sola minutes before the Ju 52/3s of 7./KGzbV 1 dropped the paratroops onto their objective. The attack achieved total surprise and the airfield was secured within 30 minutes, the Bf 110s landing shortly afterwards, their fuel almost exhausted. Apart from 1./ZG 76's reception over Oslofjorden, opposition from the tiny Norwegian Air Force had been negligible; most of their 100 or so aircraft being destroyed on the ground.

Reaction from the RAF, operating from bases in England on the far side of the North Sea, had not been expected to materialise before mid-day at the earliest. By that time the fighters were re-armed, re-fuelled and ready to provide local fighter defence. Light AA had also been installed at Stavanger, Oslo and other key points. In the event, the RAF response on this first day of invasion, and for some days to come, was limited to reconnaissance sorties.

However, the anticipated appearance of the Home Fleet did materialise during the course of the morning when a force of British battleships and cruisers was reported off Bergen. For over three hours they were subjected to almost continuous attacks by the He 111s of KG 26 and KG 30 which Geisler had held in reserve for just this eventuality.

During the course of these well-executed attacks the battleship 'Rodney' was hit; the cruisers 'Devonshire', 'Glasgow' and 'Southampton' damaged and the destroyer 'Gurkha' sunk west of Stavanger. It was a salutary demonstration of the vulnerability of naval forces to air attack, but the Royal Navy had worse to suffer before the end of the Norwegian campaign.

By 10th April, the Germans were consolidating their territorial gains and I./ZG 76 moved to Stavanger-Forbus for operations, the neighbouring airfield at Stavanger-Sola being occupied by the He 111s of KG 26. Despite stout defence by Norwegian forces, Kristiansand and Trondheim-Vaernes also fell into German hands on this day, the Bf 109s of I./JG 77 soon moving into the former.

It was while they were based at Stavanger-Forbus that one of I./ZG 76's most memorable and enduring characters really came into his own. He was universally popular with all of the pilots and aircrew, but particularly attached to Oberleutnant Arno Walter, senior pilot and deputy Staffelkapitän of 1./ZG 76, whom he followed everywhere. 'Puck', or to give him his full name, 'Puck der Peter', was a black Scots terrier and faithful Staffelhund of 1./ZG 76.

Oblt. Walter, Staffelkapitän of 1./ZG 76, with the Staffelhund, Puck. Puck was 'acquired' from an SS officer in a circuitous way, and had to be posted 'missing in action' before the Staffel could lay full claim to him.

He had first met the pilots of 1st Staffel when they started frequenting 'his' bar in Buer-am-Ruhr and soon became a firm favourite of theirs, regularly spending week-ends with them at their airfield. It was during one of these visits that the unit suddenly received orders to move to forward bases for the attack on Norway. Unable at such short notice, or possibly unwilling and certainly reluctant, to return him to the bar, the pilots of 1st Staffel elected to pack him up with the rest of their gear and simply take him along.

Puck accordingly became an honorary member of the Staffel and flew regular sorties, normally happily ensconced in Arno Walter's aircraft, against every standing order known. But this was not his main claim to fame.

Stavanger-Forbus was plagued with hedgehogs, the airfield being practically infested with them. They were of particular interest to Puck, who gave the pilots hours of entertainment harassing the hedgehogs and nuzzling them into spiky balls. Unable to provoke the cowardly hedgehogs into any decent sort of action, and obviously puzzled by their unsporting behaviour, Puck developed the perfect mode of attack. Having cornered one in its normal defensive position, he would simply cock his rear leg and spray the enemy with his full armament, much to the delight of the pilots. He was very soon an 'ace'.

After they had been at Stavanger for some time, the Gruppe received a message requesting that Puck be returned to the bar in Buer. Apparently the barmaid there was not his proper owner and had only been looking after him during his real owner's absence. Now the owner, an SS officer, was keen to have him back and was not a little displeased that he had been commandeered by the Luftwaffe.

Over the next few months, increasingly vague messages from the Staffel and terse signals from the SS were exchanged attempting to determine Puck's future. Meantime Puck, blissfully unaware of the high-level signals traffic of which he was the subject, continued to raise his 'score'. Finally, in an inspired official letter from 1./ZG 76, Puck's owner was advised "with deepest regret" that his faithful friend had gone off in a Bf 110 on a combat sortie and failed to return. He was officially declared 'lost in action', after which all correspondence ceased. Puck remained with 1./ZG 76 throughout the Norwegian campaign, rendering them invaluable service, but regrettably his ultimate fate is not known.

In the far north, the German invasion force which had taken Narvik now formed a pocket, isolated from the rest of the country and blockaded by the Royal Navy. The Luftwaffe kept them supplied by air from Stavanger and Trondheim but on 14th April a British advance party, later followed by landings in strength, came ashore at Narvik, which was recaptured the following day.

Further allied landings down the coast at Namsos and Åndalasnes were made over the next 5 days, despite heavy Luftwaffe attacks on naval transports, escort vessels and ground forces. Two British divisions, plus Polish and French troops, successfully established beach-heads north and south of German-held Trondheim.

From 19th April, the character of the Norwegian campaign changed. While the Luftwaffe increased its attacks on the allied landings which threatened to encircle German positions both at Narvik and Trondheim, it also quietly started to withdraw units back to Germany in preparation for the opening of the western campaign.

The British response to these increased attacks was to intensify its own bombing of Luftwaffe airfields in southern Norway and Denmark, but the increasingly long range at which its aircraft were forced to operate imposed severe restrictions on their efforts. Narvik itself was well beyond the range of any RAF aircraft then based in Britain and could only be reached by Fleet Air Arm aircraft operating from carriers. The need for locally-based RAF support was rapidly becoming a strategic imperative.

On 24th April, Fliegerkorps X was subordinated to the newly formed Luftflotte 5 under Generaloberst Hans-Jurgen Stumpff, who moved from Hamburg to set up his HQ in Oslo. For those units scheduled to remain based in Norway under his control, mine-laying sorties, shipping attacks or long-range reconnaissance

Aircrew of 1./ZG 26 pose before a Bf 110 C in pristine condition sporting the 'Ringelpitz' emblem of the I. Gruppe.

flights over the inhospitable waters of the North Sea were soon to become the established routine.

That same evening, 18 Gloster Gladiators of No. 263 Squadron landed on an improvised airstrip on frozen Lake Lesja, forty miles from Åndalasnes. From here they were to provide air support to their ground troops and local defence against further Luftwaffe bombing attacks. Led by Squadron Leader John Donaldson and guided by two FAA Blackburn Skuas, they had taken off in a blinding snow storm from the aircraft carrier HMS Glorious.

From dawn the next day, they were in continuous action and subject to constant bombing until the lake was no longer tenable as a base. At dusk, their five remaining Gladiators moved to another landing strip at Setnesmoen. But by the following evening, after another day of ceaseless action, No. 263 Squadron was reduced to a single Gladiator and even this was not deemed airworthy.

With the whole of southern Norway already in German hands and the military advantage in central Norway also clearly going their way, the situation deteriorated to a point where immediate British withdrawal was warranted. Thus, on the evening of 28th April, the evacuation of all troops from Namsos and Åndalasnes was ordered; the final withdrawal being completed by 2nd May.

The Wehrmacht's success in central Norway was largely due to the overwhelming level of air support they enjoyed. It was also certainly assisted by the comparative lack of British air support, which was difficult to provide and almost impossible to sustain. The continuous pressure maintained by the Luftwaffe through bombing attacks and close-support of ground troops, tactics they had perfected in Poland, made a critical difference.

The only serious setback to the whole German campaign was at Narvik and this was similarly resolved by increasing the level of air support. This was on the personal orders of Hitler who, with the opening of the Western offensive imminent, felt that the Narvik enclave could become an unwelcome distraction.

On 30th April two Bf 110s of Stab, I./ZG 76 sat at 'Alarmbereitsschaft' at Stavanger-Forbus when two RAF Blenheims put in an appearance. The Bf 110s, piloted by Gruppenkommandeur Hauptmann Günther Reinecke, and his Adjutant, Oberleutnant Hans Jäger, immediately took off in pursuit as the Blenheims disappeared heading due west low over the water.

After a short chase the Zerstörers caught up with one of the Blenheims and began making alternate attacks on it. All three aircraft raced along skimming the waves and exchanging fire when, after about 10 minutes and during one such attack, Hauptmann Reinecke's aircraft was hit by return fire. It veered up sharply to the right, then just as suddenly dropped its nose and dived straight into the sea.

There had been no time for any shouted message, and despite Jäger's frantic search of the area in the deepening gloom, no trace of wreckage nor any sign of the crew was found. Reluctantly, he returned to base

Bf 110s of 4./ZG 26 bank to port. Of interest are the different sizes of the crosses under the wings of the nearest machine, an indication, perhaps, of a replacement wing. Note also the painting-out of a letter on each wing outboard of the cross.

as he supposed, did the Blenheim.

The loss of Reinecke came as a severe blow. Coming as it did on the same day as the loss of another crew, Oberfeldwebel Fleischmann and Obergefreiter Mierke of 3./ZG 76, it was a black day for the whole Gruppe. But there was no time for mourning - the demanding schedule of daily sorties continued unabated.

Werner Hansen, Staffelkapitän of 1./ZG 76, took over as acting-Gruppenkommandeur until 11th May, when Hauptmann Werner Restemeyer arrived to take command. Restemeyer faced a difficult task, his predecessor had been an extremely outgoing, sociable type, well-connected in glamorous society circles. By way of contrast, Restemeyer was a much more reserved, even private, individual. It would take him some time to become fully accepted by some of the 'Alte Hase' in the Gruppe.

On 18th May I./ZG 76 detached an independent Staffel of 8 'Dackelbauch' Bf 110 D-0s to Trondheim, the rest of the Gruppe remaining at Stavanger. Reinecke's old second-in-command, Oberleutnant Hans Jäger, was appointed Staffelführer, relinquishing his Gruppenadjutant role. This was filled by Oberleutnant Gustav Loobes, who joined the Stabsschwarm from 3rd Staffel.

The 'Sonderstaffel' was equipped with Bf 110 D-0s from the establishment of 3./ZG 76 and made up of crews selected from every Staffel in the Gruppe. Hand picked for their blind-flying experience, the pilots included, in addition to Jäger himself, Helmut Lent, Gustav Üllenbeck and Unteroffizier Jänicke. They were to fly standing patrols and provide fighter support for the Luftwaffe's continuing attacks on the British forces around Narvik and Harstad in the far north, well within the Arctic Circle.

The pre-production Bf 110 D-0 presaged development of the long-range 'Langstrecke' D-series. It involved the fitting of a purpose-built, ventral former to a standard 'C' model Zerstörer to which a streamlined wooden fairing was permanently attached. This immense ventral fairing, often fitted as a field modification, enclosed a 1,050 litre fuel tank and gave the aircraft its distinctive belly-dragging appearance; hence the name 'Dackelbauch' or 'Basset Belly'.

This fitment changed the aircraft's appearance considerably and led to many instances of mis-identification by RAF pilots who encountered it, the Bf 110 D-0 often being mistaken for a Dornier Do 17 Z.

Many Zerstörer pilots hated this adaptation because they felt that it ruined the Bf 110s flying characteristics and filled the cockpit with petrol fumes. The loss in performance was, in fact, so severe that the ventral fairing was dropped for the Bf 110 D-1 production model, which made provision for a 900 litre drop-tank under each wing instead, and was much preferred by pilots.

As Oberleutnant Hans-Ulrich Kettling of 1./ZG 76 recalls, "The idea was to use the fuel from the wing tanks first, discard them over the sea and reach the fighting area with the belly-tank as the sole handicap. But this ungainly blister was handicap enough. It made the plane several miles (per hour) slower, the unused fuel slugged around and made steering and aiming unstable, and since the container consisted mainly of plywood, it was dangerously inflammable."

Nevertheless this small group of 'Dackelbauch' Bf 110 D-0s, with their extended range and endurance, represented a significant German fighter presence in the far north of Norway. As Hans Jäger's Flugbuch records, gruelling sorties of up to five hours duration were flown daily in cramped cockpits and frequently hostile Arctic weather conditions. His pilots often took off and landed late at night, or the early hours of the morning, taking advantage of the almost permanent daylight in those high latitudes.

On 20th May an RAF presence was re-established when No. 263 Squadron returned to northern Norway. Re-equipped with a fresh complement of aircraft, they flew 16 Gladiators into Bardufoss airfield from the aircraft carrier HMS Furious. Within four days, two more airfields at Skaanland and Bodø became available for operations; a section of three Gladiators, under Flight Lieutenant 'Caesar' Hull, deploying to Bodø on the 25th to cover the southern sector of operations.

On the following day, further RAF reinforcements in the shape of 18 Hurricanes of No. 46 Squadron, led by Squadron Leader Kenneth Cross, flew off the carrier HMS Glorious. Ten put down at Skaarland, two nosing over on landing due to the poor state of the runway, so the remainder diverted to Bardufoss where the entire squadron collected the next day.

On 27th and 28th May, allied troop reinforcements landed at Narvik, posing an immediate and serious threat to the beleaguered German forces in the area.

This drew a prompt and emphatic response from the Luftwaffe.

At 4:30 am. on the first morning of the landings, 4 Bf 110 D-0s of Hans Jäger's Dackelbauch Staffel were flying escort for 12 Stukas of I./StG 1 attacking Bodø when they tangled with two Gladiators of No. 263 Squadron's detached section. As Caesar Hull later confided to his diary, "Suddenly the balloon went up. There were 110s and 87s all around us, and the 87s started dive-bombing a jetty about 300 yards from the aerodrome.

"Got the Gladiator going and shot off without helmet or waiting to do anything up. Circled the 'drome, climbing, and pinned an 87 at the bottom of its dive. It made off slowly over the sea and just as I was turning away, another 87 shot up past me and its shots went through my windscreen, knocking me out for a little while. Came to and was thanking my lucky stars when I heard a rat-tat behind me and felt my Gladiator hit. Went into a right-hand turn and dive, but could not get out of it. Had given up hope at 200 feet when she centralised and I gave her a burst of engine to clear some large rocks. Further rat-tats behind me so gave up hope and decided to get down. Held off, then crashed."

During his attack on the Ju 87s, Hull had been 'bounced' by the Bf 110s, two Gladiators being claimed: one by Lent and the other by Jäger. This proved to be the last action for No. 263 Squadron's detached flight. With all its aircraft destroyed or damaged, and further heavy attacks throughout the rest of the day which rendered the airfield inoperable, Bodø was declared 'out of action'.

Flight Lieutenant Hull was wounded in the head and one knee but managed to crawl from the wreckage of his fragile fighter and was admitted to a base hospital. Air-lifted back to England by Sunderland flying boat, he was to remain out of action for some time, returning to command No. 43 Squadron for a mere seven days at the height of the Summer battles until his death in action over London on 7th September.

As the tempo of the fighting in the far north quickened and the campaign moved towards its conclusion,

M8 + KK of 2./ZG 76 in the classic 'Kopfstand'.

Oblt. Gustav Üllenbeck of 2./ZG 76.

Hans Jäger's Dackelbauch Staffel was seldom out of the air. In the early evening of 29th May, they were assigned an escort sortie to Bardufoss after which, exploiting the extended endurance of the Bf 110 D-0, they would fly a freelance fighter sweep over Skaanland. Accompanying them on this sortie was the Gruppenkommandeur, Hauptmann Restemeyer, who led the formation with Oberleutnant Jäger flying on his right. High over the Tjelsund, west of Skaanland, they were intercepted by Hurricanes of No. 46 Squadron, whose presence came as a total, and most unwelcome, surprise.

The leading Zerstörers were the main target for the Hurricanes first devastating attack. Somehow surviving the sudden hail of fire from their first pass, Oberleutnant Jäger was forced to break away and shut down one of his engines which was badly damaged. Hauptmann Restemeyer was also badly hit and his Bordfunker, Unteroffizier Werner Eichert, severely wounded.

Fortunately for them, none of the Hurricanes followed up their attack and the damaged Bf 110s swung south towards Trondheim which lay 350 miles across the mountains. The Zerstörer flew perfectly well on one engine so Jäger was fairly confident that he could make it back until, after only a few minutes flying, his other engine suddenly ground to a halt.

Jäger managed to glide down and settle gently on the sea about 100 metres from the shore at Balingen, their aircraft staying afloat just long enough for them to vacate the cockpit and struggle ashore in their heavy flight clothing. At a nearby cottage they were treated like shipwrecked mariners and given hot drinks and dry clothing. They were quietly congratulating themselves on their good fortune when two coastal patrol boats put in to shore.

A landing party of 15 enemy soldiers disembarked and headed straight for the cottage. It was barely 30

minutes since their landing, Jäger and Feick had not even had time to consider their next move, so obviously their landing had been observed and these troops sent to pick them up. There was no chance of escape - they were 'in the bag'.

The landing party turned out to be Poles. Some of the more surly among them were clearly bent on settling the score for the bombing of Warsaw and other so-called German outrages during the Polish campaign. The situation started to turn decidedly ugly, Jäger and Feick being subjected to particularly rough handling, when an officer intervened and ordered them placed in his custody. It was a dangerous moment, emotions were running particularly high, some of the troops still keen to literally beat the life out of the German airmen and the officer too if he got in their way. But fortunately a few wavered, discipline prevailed and begrudgingly they delivered up their prizes.

After a very uncomfortable night spent under guard, Jäger and Feick were dragged off to British HQ at Haarstadt for interrogation the next morning. Here, separated from each other, they remained for the next few days before being shipped to the UK on 5th June. As the interrogators were fond of reminding them, "For you the war is over!". Jäger spent the next 6 years as a prisoner of the British at Grizedale Hall in England and Bowmansville camp in Canada, where he would share a room with other captured Zerstörer pilots: Oberleutnant Victor Mölders of 1./ZG 1 and Oberleutnant Jürgen Möller of 2./ZG 1 amongst them. He was eventually repatriated to Germany in 1946.

Evacuation of the allied North Western Expeditionary Force from Narvik was completed between 2nd and 8th June; continuous standing patrols by No. 46 Squadron's Hurricanes, as well as the atrocious weather, preventing any serious interference by the Luftwaffe. On the 7th, the remaining 10 Gladiators and the 10 Hurricanes took off from their Norwegian bases for the last time and flew off to land on HMS Glorious. This was the first ever deck landing by Hawker Hurricanes, but all of them got down safely.

Tragically, the carrier was sunk late the following evening when she was engaged in a brief but critical action with the German battle cruisers Scharnhorst and Gneisenau. Their second salvo exploded in the Glorious's upper hangar and within two hours she had gone with the loss of almost her entire crew. Of the 20 or more pilots on board only two were saved. It was a potentially crippling blow to British naval power and at the same time a particularly poignant end to the RAF's ill-fated expedition to Norway.

The joint British, French and Norwegian task-force had fought a difficult, isolated campaign, the eventual outcome of which was never in any real doubt. With their final withdrawal, Narvik was re-occupied by German forces on 10th June, effectively bringing the fighting in Norway to an end.

For the Zerstörer crews of I./ZG 76 this meant a welcome break from the hectic regime of sorties they had been flying over the past few weeks. Their main opponent throughout had been the conditions in which

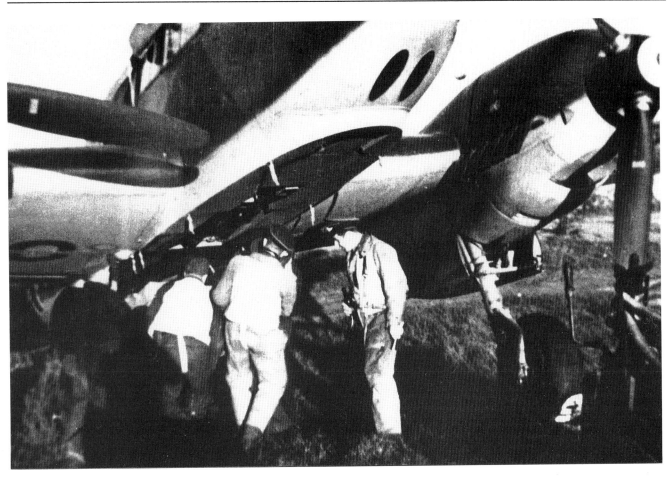

This page and overleaf: Three views of activity centred around fitting the Dackelbauch to a Bf 110 D of I./ZG 76. The two-tone upper fuselage camouflage is clearly evident in these views.

they had been forced to operate, not the enemy. Coping with problems of supply, maintenance and basic accommodation in the often bleak environment had been their major difficulties.

Now they began to settle down to a regular diet of long-range patrols, shipping reconnaissance flights and skirmishes with the odd RAF bomber or Coastal Command aircraft who were to remain fairly constant and regular visitors to Norwegian waters over the coming months.

The Gruppe were to remain based at Stavanger over the coming months, maintaining a long-range fighter presence in Norway whilst the main conflict raged in western Europe and across southern England. In August they would venture across the North Sea as escort to a calamitous attack on the north-east coast of England, as described later.

In September, I./ZG 76 would provide the cadre from which II./NJG 1 would be formed as the emergent German night-fighter force evolved. The wealth of blind-flying expertise amongst its pilots would be put to good use in their new roles, raising many to celebrity status as successful night-fighter pilots later in the war.

Meantime, I./ZG 1 remained at Ålborg where they had been based since opening day of the invasion of Denmark. From here the Zerstörer's long-range fighter capabilities proved invaluable for armed escort and reconnaissance sorties over the North Sea and Heligoland Bight. They were also ideally placed to defend against

incursions by RAF Bomber Command aircraft en-route to naval targets in north-west Germany or industrial targets in the Ruhr.

It was during this period of operations from Ålborg that the Gruppenkommandeur of I./ZG 1, Hauptmann Wolfgang Falck, established the practise of 'twilight sorties' to combat the British bombers who habitually came over just as darkness was falling. His blind-flying experience, along with that of some other pilots in the Gruppe, led him to believe that use of the Zerstörer as a night-fighter was not only a viable proposition but a strategic imperative. His enthusiasm and commitment to this initiative ultimately provided the necessary stimulus for the formation of the Luftwaffe's night-fighter force described later on in the text.

Within the month, I./ZG 1 were transferred from Ålborg back to Germany, where they completed rapid preparations for their part in the next offensive, the invasion of Holland.

So, Operation Weserübung concluded with Germany's northern flank secured. From the very first, it had been ably demonstrated to both sides that the use of paratroops and airborne landings to seize tactical advantage at key points achieved a measure of surprise which paralysed conventional defences. But these lessons came far too late for the Belgian, Dutch and French armies in western Europe, where the same tactics would all too soon be repeated with equally startling and dramatic success.

In the early hours of 10th May flying personnel of 5./ZG 26 receive last minute instructions before taking off for their first mission of the western campaign. On the right of the picture, turning to look at the camera, is Alois Komanns, who was killed in action on 18/5/40.

CHAPTER 2
ASSAULT IN THE WEST - MAY/JUNE 1940

When the attack orders were finally issued by the OKL no-one seemed particularly surprised. Most of the young Luftwaffe airmen based in the west were simply relieved that the long months of waiting and preparation were at last over. Throughout the early months of 1940, Luftwaffe units had been brought to progressively advanced states of readiness, many moving forward to bases closer to the borders with Belgium, Holland and France as tension and expectancies rose. The inevitable outbreak of hostilities was clearly becoming imminent. Aircraft losses sustained in the Polish campaign had been made good over the Winter months and a steady influx of freshly trained aircrews had been arriving at units. These products of the Luftwaffe training system had a wealth of campaign experience gained over Spain and Poland passed on to them through the Zerstörerschulern and Ergänzungsgruppen, where many of the instructors were combat veterans.

Then, before daybreak on 10th May 1940, briefing rooms all over Germany came alive with bustling crowds of excited aircrew. Experiences at most were similar. At Gütersloh the pilots and aircrew of II./ZG1 assembled, the Gruppe Technical Officer, Leutnant Richard Marchfelder, later recalling, "In the small hours of the morning we were ordered to the assembly hut. Minutes later, after we had a short briefing, we taxied

to the take-off point of the runway, following the position lights of the aircraft ahead of us. The C.O. made a wide circle and kept an altitude of 500 feet until all planes were airborne. Then he climbed to 2,000 feet and took up course to the west.

Appearing like a ghost ahead of us was the Rhine. Like a huge silver snake it wound its way to the west. On both sides of the river was farmland. Lights were burning in all the houses. Having been used for months to living under black-out, it seemed very odd to us. Obviously the owner must have considered himself too far away from civilisation and too safe to bother about any precautions. Of course he didn't know that he was in danger, nor that we were invading his country. To my right, and ahead of me, flew Dickoré. I was unable to see him, only his Bordfunker. His goggles reflected the faint light from the east. He looked like Frankenstein's nephew on his nightly haunt. Any minute now something was going to happen. My nerves were like violin strings stretched beyond endurance."

On this their first mission of the campaign, II./ZG 1 were to subdue anti-aircraft positions at Vlissingen airfield, attacking from ground level and roof-top height. Flying as Bordfunker to Hauptmann Rolf Kaldrack, the Staffelkapitän of 4./ZG 1, Feldwebel Erich Hermanski recalls, "We attacked these positions around the airfield and on top of the hangars in three approaches. Helmut Voss was flying too high in the second attack and his Me 110 was hit. He had to make a forced-landing in a field."

From very early that morning increased German air activity over Holland had been reported as Luftwaffe aircraft laid mines in rivers, estuaries and the approaches to the Dutch coast and harbours. Then shortly after dawn the Western front erupted as the greatest concentration of military forces yet assembled in war was finally unleashed. It was a perfect morning, hazy with some high cloud, as co-ordinated attacks on airfields, rail systems and transportation centres across Holland, Belgium and north-east France began.

Without ultimatum or declaration of war, German bombers struck at Dutch airfields at Rotterdam-Waalhaven, Amsterdam-Schiphol, Bergen and de Kooy. These initial attacks being closely followed by parachute troop landings in advance of troop transport landings at strategic points all over southern Holland. By 5:00 am. German troops had attempted landings on the airfields at Ockenburg, Valkenburg and Ypenberg near the Hague, while Fallschirmjägern of III./FJR 1 established a foothold on Waalhaven where Junkers Ju 52/3s began to disgorge the troops and equipment of III./IR 16.

A similar landing at Rotterdam-Waalhaven went less successfully. I./ZG 1 provided 25 Bf 110s as escort for the Junkers 52/3s. Flying with Oberleutnant Martin Lutz's 1st Staffel, Victor Mölders recalls, "We reached our destination, Rotterdam airfield, without meeting any opposition. In a compact group the Ju (52/3)s came in to land. Immediately the first aircraft exploded in a ball of fire, then the second, then the third. Soon the airfield was covered with blazing aircraft, the airborne troops and 80% of the soldiers were eliminated. With our Bf 110 we could merely afford some flak protection."

The Maas bridges at Dortrecht, Moerdijk and Rotterdam were prime objectives, the all-important Moerdijk road and railway bridges falling to II./FJR 1 whose parachutists landed in the wake of precision dive-bombing attack on defence installations.

In the Dutch capital, the Hague, a series of early attacks by Fallschirmjägern on the Royal Palace were fiercely repulsed while military barracks elsewhere in the city were bombed. Later in the morning German aircraft dropped leaflets exhorting the population to surrender.

Simultaneously, attacks were launched on targets across neutral Belgium. Bombs fell on Evere aerodrome and in the capital, Brussels, where many civilian deaths resulted. The Belgian Aeronautique Militaire, taken completely by surprise, lost more than half its aircraft on the ground in the first few hours of the attack. In the air, its Fiat CR 42s and antiquated Fairey Firefly

The tension of flying combat missions was mixed with interminable periods of waiting on the ground for the next order to take off. Here, aircrew of 5./ZG 26 are seen between sorties on the first day of the western campaign on 10th May 1940

3U+CA of the Geschwaderstab of Zerstörergeschwader 26 takes off in a cloud of dust.

fighters proved no match for Messerschmitts, be they Bf 109s or 110s.

In a particularly audacious attack the permanent fort at Eben Emael, which dominated the bridges over the Albert canal at Briedgen, Veldwezelt and Vroenhoven, was over-run by 70 German combat engineers who landed on top of the defences from 7 DFS 230 gliders towed to the target area by Junkers Ju 52/3s. Within 36 hours, in the first ever use of glider-borne troops, these parachute engineers, re-supplied by air and with close support by Henschel HS 123s of II./LG 2 and Junkers Ju 87s of StG 2, had neutralised the defences and secured two of the bridges intact. As forward elements of General Richenau's 6th Army advanced to join them from the East, the Belgian garrison surrendered and Eben Emael fell.

Within an hour of the opening of the German offensive both Belgian and Dutch governments appealed to Britain and France for help, and early that afternoon, British troops crossed the frontier into Belgium whilst French troops advanced into Luxemburg.

Von Manstein's ambitious plan of attack, codenamed 'Fall Gelbe', relied upon massive air support of rapid armoured thrusts into Holland, Belgium and Luxemburg. It effectively side-stepped the Maginot Line, the massive French defensive system facing Germany, thus avoiding a costly frontal attack on fixed fortifications. This risk of a static front developing was something which Wehrmacht strategists, recalling the horrors of World War 1, were keen to avoid.

The demands on the Luftwaffe for the Western offensive were on an unprecedented scale, a total of 3,875 German aircraft being assembled of which 355

were Bf 110s. The Zerstörer-equipped units deployed being as follows:

I./ZG 1	Hauptmann Falck
II./ZG 1	Hauptmann Dickoré
I./ZG 2	Major Gentzen
I./ZG 26	Hauptmann Macrocki
II./ZG 26	Hauptmann von Rettberg
III./ZG 26	Major Schalk
I./ZG 52	Hauptmann Lessmann
II./ZG 76	Hauptmann Groth
V.(Z)/LG 1	Hauptmann Liensberger

The onslaught achieved total surprise, the sheer weight of the German attack overwhelming defences. Little or no fighter opposition was met. Almost half of the total strength of the Royal Netherlands Air Force was wiped out in the initial bombing and strafing attacks on their airfields. Flying with the Stabsschwarm of II./ZG 1, the Gruppe Technical Officer, Leutnant Richard Marchfelder recorded his impressions of one such attack, "Airport ahead! It looked more like a football field with airplanes neatly lined up on one side, two rows deep, resembling soldiers on parade. We opened fire. With fascination I watched the little fountains caused by the bullets hitting the ground, the way they scurry ahead until they hit an object, in this case an airplane. First smoke was pouring out, perhaps produced by tracers, seconds later flames shot up into the air, followed by an explosion just as we were passing over it. The shock waves caused us to jump. Like dominoes the fire leapt from one plane to the next.

"Fighters ahead! I never found out who our lookout was, but sure enough there were a dozen or more airplanes ahead, buzzing around like angry hornets, trying to intercept us. At the beginning we had the advantage of having the rising sun behind us. Soon, however, the battle turned into a circus of dogfights.

"One fellow in front of us panicked; he bailed out without giving a damn about his plane. Another was not quite so lucky, he started to burn and dived away. Never in my life did I see such a crazy performance like the spectacle displayed in front of me. Dickoré ran amok! He dived into the very centre of all the fighting, hardly leaving me sufficient room to pass between. A few times I was very close to crashing into another plane. In spite of navigating around friend and foe in a merry-go-round gone mad, my eyes detected a Me 110 with one of his engines burning. It crossed in front of us, obviously diving for sanctuary. After fighting for seemingly hours, we turned around. On our way home we passed Jochem Schröder (6./ZG 1) in the company of others, all limping along on one engine. Damage to our planes was moderate! They were taken into the hangars for repair. We were well prepared for losses and had enough spares available to fill the gap."

Miraculously some Dutch fighters managed to get into the air, Fokker G.Is of the 3rd JAVA from Waalhaven and Fokker D.XXIs of the 1st JAVA from de Kooy making desperate attacks on successive waves of German aircraft before they were themselves forced down or destroyed. The Luchtvaart Afdeling (LVA) lost 62 aircraft on the first day of hostilities and within 3

An unidentified crew of the 'Haifischgruppe', II./ZG 76, prepare to board their 'Sharksmouth'.

days was reduced to 10 aircraft. By nightfall on 13th May even these had been lost and the Royal Netherlands Air Force, despite heroic resistance, effectively ceased to exist. In France, the Luftwaffe struck at 47 airfields including the Armée de l'Air's main bases at Dijon, Lyon, Metz, Nancy and Romilly. At most, remarkably little damage was caused but there were notable exceptions. At Boulogne-Alprecht the Chance-Vought 156 Fs of Aeronavale Escadrille AB 3 were totally wiped out, while at Tournes-Belval airfield GAO 2/551 lost all its Potez 63-11s to Luftwaffe ground-attack aircraft.

AA fire, where encountered, was largely sporadic and inaccurate. Landing back at their base at Kaarst/Neuss after their first combat mission, a bomber escort sortie over Charleroi, the Bf 110 pilots of 5./ZG 26 were quick to acknowledge that Oberfeldwebel Kurt Rochel and Oberfeldwebel Fritz Herber, veterans of the Condor Legion in Spain, had been right to maintain that you should ignore Flak as 'good for nothing'.

Others had less comforting experiences. Leutnant Richard Marchfelder, flying with Stab, II./ZG 1 recounts, "We had barely time for a smoke when we took off again. This time we met no fighters, only heavy anti-aircraft fire, which was especially scary for us, as we flew at tree top level. Rushing up ahead of us were tall trees theatrically supported by underbrush. Something was moving between them... fragments from my left windshield went buzzing around my head. Passing over I saw the muzzle fire from anti-aircraft

guns between the bushes... fortunately none of us were hit. Oops! We almost took some wires from a radio mast along. It was not Dickoré's fault, he left me sufficient room... but I was jittery and found it hard to concentrate. My nerves were playing tricks with me making it almost impossible to collect myself. We met more and more gunfire, greeting us with their lethal missiles. To reduce the risk of being passed on from one flak battery to the next, Dickoré changed the course of our flight. In spite of it, I felt more and more uncomfortable with every minute."

For other Zerstörers, the morning consisted of routine escort missions for the Heinkel He 111s and Dornier Do 17s bombing targets often deep in enemy territory. Some, like the 30 Bf 110s of III./ZG 26 'Horst Wessel' who sortied to Antwerp, flew completely uneventful missions, returning to their bases in Germany up to two hours later after what many pilots somewhat laconically described as a 'training flight'.

The morning and early afternoon passed quickly as Bf 110s, refuelled and rearmed, sat on their airfields in Germany awaiting further orders. News from the front was encouraging and the German advance continued unchecked. But it was not until late afternoon that many of them were called upon to fly a second sortie which, for most, again passed uneventfully.

That evening's Situation Report from the OKW was disappointingly brief, even terse. For many young Bf 110 airmen, aware that they had been involved in momentous and historical events, the communiqué sum-

An aircraft burns in the distance as groundcrew service Bf 110 C, 2N + FH, of 1./ZG 1 during the French campaign.

marised their feelings all too well - 'The first day of offensive operations in the West went favourably as planned'. It seemed a huge anti-climax after all the months of training and preparation.

Two Bf 110s were lost on this first day of action. A 4./ZG 1 aircraft in the attack on Vlissingen - as previously described. The other, a 3./ZG 26 machine, failed to return from a sortie over Rethel south-west of Charleville. Its Bordfunker, 25 year-old Obergefreiter Heinrich Röwe, from Eutin near Lübeck, thereby becoming the first Bf 110 airman to die in the western offensive.

The weather on 11th May had deteriorated but II./ZG 1 were off early that morning on a freelance sortie in support of the landings at Rotterdam. Flying on his first combat mission of the war, Obergefreiter Herbert Klinke, a 21 year-old Bordfunker with 5./ZG 1, found the ground-fire remarkably heavy. Returning to Gelsenkirchen-Buer on one engine after their 90 minutes baptism of fire over Rotterdam, he and his pilot, Feldwebel Dähne, ruefully examined the damage to their machine as they pondered on the missions to come.

The weather was marginal enough to keep some Bf 110 units grounded until afternoon. II./ZG 26 flew two sorties, an evening attack on Vlissingen bringing Oberfeldwebel Fritz Stahl of 4th Staffel his first claims of the campaign - 2 Potez 63s destroyed.

Fighter opposition over the front remained sporadic and many Zerstörers again returned to base without encountering enemy aircraft. But not so for I./ZG 2 who met up with 5 Hurricanes of No. 1 Squadron's 'A' Flight during an escort sortie over Sedan during the late afternoon.

Flying as No. 3 in the British formation, Pilot Officer Paul Richey later recorded his recollections of what followed in a contemporary diary, "...it was not until the last moment that the Me 110s wheeled, some to the right and some to the left, going into line-astern in their twos and threes.

"We went in tight and in a tight bunch, each of us picking himself an adversary... I selected the rear one of two in line-astern who were turning tightly to the left. He broke away from his No. 1 when he had done a half-circle and steepened his turn, but I easily turned inside him, holding my fire until I was within 50 yards and then fired a shortish burst at three-quarters deflection. To my surprise a whole lot of bits flew off him... and as I passed just over the top of him, still in my left-hand turn, I watched fascinated as he went into a spin, smoke pouring from him. I remember saying, 'My God, how ghastly!' as his tail suddenly swivelled sideways and came right off, while flames poured over the fuselage."

This account, which provides valuable insights into the respective combat performances of the Hurricane and the Bf 110, also makes reference to the Zerstörer's standard formation when attacked, the defensive circle.

"In a moment I was in the centre of what seemed a mass of 110s, although there were in fact only five of them. I knew I hadn't the speed in my wooden-blader

The crew stand alongside Bf 110 C, 2N + AK of 2./ZG 1, the aircraft usually flown by Fw. Erich Puschnerus. Note the covering over the fuselage cross. The individual aircraft letter, 'A', appears to be red outlined white.

to dive away and beat it, so I decided to fight them and make the best of it. Although I was more manoeuvrable at this height (6,000 feet) I found it impossible to get an astern shot in, because whenever I got one almost lined up tracers, would come shooting past from another on my tail. So all I could do was to keep twisting and turning and when a Hun got behind me do as tight a turn as possible, almost spinning, with full engine, and fly straight at him firing a quick burst (before) pushing the stick forward and going underneath him. Then I would pull up in a steep climbing turn to meet the next.

"They used a lot of diving down and then climbing up and taking a full deflection shot. Their shooting was wild and this manoeuvre was easily dealt with by turning towards them and going over their heads, causing them to steepen their climb until they were stalled and had to fall away. But don't imagine for a moment that I was enjoying this performance. Far from it. My mouth was becoming drier and drier and I was getting more and more tired and desperate."

After a furious combat which lasted over 15 minutes, Richey was eventually shot down in a head-on attack on one of the Zerstörers, vacating his aircraft over Remilly when his front header tank was hit by a cannon shell and exploded. I./ZG 2 lost only two Bf 110s

despite accounts which suggested they may have lost up to ten aircraft. Whatever the final tally, Richey returned to No. 1 Squadron the following day bearing a prized souvenir of the action, a Bf 110 rudder and fin, complete with bullet holes.

Most of the Bf 110 losses throughout the day were due to AA fire which was now much better concentrated and becoming more accurate. A total of 7 Bf 110s were lost in action over France and Holland, 8 crewmen being killed or wounded. Another 3./ZG 1 machine returned to base damaged from an escort sortie over Gorinchem with a wounded Bordfunker aboard.

A succession of desperate but unsuccessful air attacks were launched on the bridges over the Albert Canal at Veldwezelt and Vroenhoven during the day. Of 8 Fairey Battles from Nos. 88 and 218 Squadrons who mounted a low-level attack, only one returned to base, the rest never even reaching the target. Similarly, 6 from a formation of 9 Belgian Fairey Battles were also lost to the murderous light flak which surrounded the target.

That night, as Panzer divisions poured across the Albert Canal to threaten Liege, Belgian forces fell back to defensive positions on the Antwerp-Namur line where they were reinforced by British troops the following day. 'Blitzkrieg', the revolutionary form of warfare employed by the Wehrmacht, was bringing them unparalleled successes both on land and in the air. At Condé-Vaux airfield, 6 Blenheims of 114 Squadron were destroyed at a stroke - a low-level bombing attack by Dornier Do 17s of 4./KG 2. It was the same bleak picture all over.

A break in the high cloud on Whit Sunday, 12th May, brought increased air activity over the entire front

The machine guns of a Bf 110 receive attention from a mechanic. Of interest is the aperture in the nose for the gun-camera, and the rim of the lens of the ESK 2000 in position.

The one-time Staffel emblem of 1./ZG 1, "Löwen in den Fängen" needs no explanation!

The Ladybird emblem of 2./ZG 76.

and for the first time enemy fighters were more in evidence. Major Johann Schalk's III./ZG 26 opened their scoring with a Koolhoven falling to Oberleutnant Heinrich, the Staffelkapitän of 7th Staffel, south-east of Ghent shortly after 8:15 in the morning. Five French Moranes were claimed during the next 25 minutes in combats ranging from Ghent to Termonde and Wachtebecke. Oberleutnant Sophus Baagoe of 8./ZG 26, who was to be one of the Gruppe's highest scoring pilots of the campaign, being one who filed claims. Early the same afternoon, in action south-east of Antwerp, 2 French Curtis Hawks rounded off the day's total score of 8 enemy aircraft destroyed for no losses.

Oberleutnant Helmut Müller's 13th Staffel of V. (Z)/LG 1 had a less satisfactory day. They lost 3 Bf 110s , including deputy Staffelkapitän, Leutnant Hans Gaffel, to flak and fighters during escort missions over St. Mihiel and Vouziers respectively.

But allied air attacks continued to suffer even worse from the mobile light flak which invariably accompanied the advancing German columns. Of 11 Bregeut 693s of GBA 1/54 engaged in strafing armoured columns near Tongres, only 2 returned to base at Montdidier and were so badly damaged that they were only fit for spares. It was their first operational sortie of the war.

The vital bridges over the Albert Canal at Vroenhoven and Veldwezelt were again subject to allied attacks during the day. First by 12 Blenheims who lost 4 of their number to flak and fighters. Then later, by 5 Battles of No. 12 Squadron based at Amifontaine escorted by 8 Hurricanes of No. 1 Squadron from Vassincourt. This courageous attack by volunteer crews, pressed home despite heavy flak and intensive small-arms fire, culminated in the first RAF VCs of the war - awarded posthumously to F/O D.E. Garland and Sgt. T. Gray. Four of the Battles were lost with their entire crews but severe damage was caused to the Veldwezelt bridge.

On 13th May the German's main armoured spearhead struck West across the Meuse at Houx, the overwhelming pressure they exerted on the allied line carrying them across the river between Sedan and Mezieres. Close tactical support for this stage of the offensive called for maximum effort by the Luftwaffe and Bf 110s were heavily involved throughout the day, maintaining their bomber escort sorties and strafing attacks on allied airfields.

Vlissingen airfield was again the target for II./ZG 1. Erich Hermanski recalls, "We started long before daybreak from Gelsenkirchen-Buer, flew west almost to the English coast and then east towards Vlissingen. With the dark sky behind us and coming from the west we could easily be mistaken for English planes. As we approached the airfield we could make out quite a few planes on the field and several ships in the harbour...Some of the ships were shooting flares, the code of which we did not have. They started to shoot, but we were flying above the reach of their guns. It was quite funny to see the tracers coming up like a string of pearls and turning just beside your plane."

The entire Gruppe, about 40 planes in all, spread out into line and went into a shallow dive strafing air

Hptm. Roderick Küppers, Staffelkapitän of 5./ZG 1, killed in action on 13/5/40.

Oblt. Eberhard d'Elsa, Staffelkapitän of 5./ZG 26 (left) with Ofw. Danielsen, 'Speiss' (senior NCO) in charge of ground personnel of the Staffel.

craft on the ground with their forward guns. They later claimed over 40 aircraft destroyed but lost one of their number to ground fire, the Bf 110 of Hauptmann Roderich Küppers, the Staffelkapitän of 5./ZG 1, who was killed.

In action over Mauberge, Oberleutnant Kirchoff's 3rd Staffel of ZG 26 lost 2 Bf 110s along with their crews; a 4./ZG 76 machine completing the Zerstörer losses for the day when it failed to return from a combat sortie over Valenciennes. But by 5:00 pm. that evening the unthinkable had happened - Sedan had fallen and a German breakout west to the coast at Boulogne and Calais was fast becoming a reality.

At Rotterdam on 14th May a tragedy of war occurred which hastened the collapse of Dutch resistance. The stubborn defence of the city was causing a severe delay to the German advance and surrender negotiations between the Dutch army garrison and XXXIX. Panzer Corps were making too slow progress - despite Wehrmacht ultimatums.

German plans were to break the deadlock with a concentrated bombing attack on the northern approaches to the Maas bridge's situated in the heart of the city. Tragically, with negotiations on the brink of being finalised, 100 Heinkel He 111s of KG 54 arrived over their targets at exactly the time originally set as a deadline for the Dutch to surrender. Airborne from their bases at Delmenhorst, Hoya/Weser and Quackenbruch some 90 minutes earlier, they had failed to recei-

ve messages advising them of the further delay in talks and ordering them to divert to alternative targets in Antwerp.

Too late some of the bomb-aimers saw ground signals and aborted the attack, but 57 aircraft unloaded their HE bombs onto target - the resultant fires devastating a large section of the old inner city where 900 people died. Rotterdam capitulated and within 6 hours all Dutch forces were ordered to cease resistance - the Dutch army laying down its arms the following day.

Meanwhile the allied air force, at the urgent request of the French High Command, were throwing everything they had at the pontoon bridges at Sedan in a vain effort to stem the German advance. A suicidal attack from 2,500 feet by 12 elderly Amiot 143s of 34e and 38e Escadres typifying the desperation - only one from the 38e returned to base.

The RAF fared no better, for mid-afternoon 62 Fairey Battles despatched against the same targets lost 35 of their number to the lethal mixture of fighters, flak and small-arms fire. No higher rate of loss in an operation of comparable size would ever be experienced by the RAF during the entire war. By the end of the day, the French bomber force effectively ceased to exist and Nos. 105 and 218 Squadrons of the AASF had been reduced to 2 aircraft apiece and were disbanded.

Another 4 Bf 110s were lost on operations during the day, Hauptmann Lessmann's I./ZG 52 suffering its first losses of the campaign with 2 Bf 110s failing to return from a sortie south of Diederhofen.

The next day was to prove one of the most costly in the whole campaign for the Zerstörer units. In an almost constant series of bitter combats over the front west of Sedan, the Bf 110s were heavily committed throughout the entire day. A total of 9 Bf 110s were lost, two 1./ZG 1 machines colliding over Kirchhellen.

Oblt. Martin Lutz, Staffelkapitän of 1./ZG 1, enjoys an alfresco meal of 'gummi Adler' during the French campaign. Lutz was a veteran of the 'Legion Condor' and went on to command Erprobungsgruppe 210 during the Battle of Britain, being killed in action on 27/9/40.

III./ZG 26, 'Horst Wessel', suffered their first loss of the campaign, an 8th Staffel machine which crashed from 100 feet attempting to land on one engine at Kirchberg due to combat damage, both of the crew being killed.

Patrolling over the Meuse valley between Fumay and Givet on the Belgian border, 2./ZG 26 lost two aircraft in combat. Two more of their machines limped back to base damaged with wounded on board, including their Staffelkapitän, Hauptmann Herbert Kaminski. It was a bad day for the Gruppe as a whole, for in a combat further west over Chimay, they also lost their Gruppenadjutant, Oberleutnant Hans-Günther Koch and his Bordfunker, Unteroffizier Wolff. The Hurricanes of No. 1 Squadron based at Berry-au-Bac would seem to have been the main protagonists, recording a total of 13 Bf 110s destroyed on the day, but losing two pilots in the process.

Late in the afternoon, 6 Hurricanes of 'B' Flight led by 'Prosser' Hanks tangled with a formation of Bf 110s from II./ZG 76 west of Laon. As a squadron history records, "Over Laon the Messerschmitts turned, spotted them and swung back into the attack. The Hurricane pilots were quickly aware that they were faced with no ordinary fighter unit. These guys were good, confident and thirsting for a fight.

"Boy Mould managed to shoot down two Huns before running out of ammunition and legging it back to base. Hanks dived on the leader and blew him to bits with one burst, but was then set on by several others. One of them punctured his glycol tank and almost blinded him with the hot fluid. He baled out and landed in open country with eyes like poached eggs. Boot and Lewis had knocked down one each before running out of ammunition. Of Clisby and Lorimer there was no sign."

In the heat of combat the out-numbered British pilots over-claimed by a ratio of 2 to 1 for Hauptmann Heinz Nacke's 6th Staffel only lost 2 Bf 110s, although others returned to base with severe damage. Three Hurricanes were shot down; two of the pilots being killed, the other baling out safely. A fourth machine barely managed to limp back to Berry-au-Bac.

Paul Richey was among the No. 1 Squadron pilots awaiting their return. "Eventually Boy came back alone... We walked over to him as he climbed out, and... examined some fresh bullet holes in his machine... he had (had) a hell of a time getting away. He went right down to ground-level with a couple of Huns on his tail, and it took him some time twisting and

Uffz. Heinz Braunsberger, 20 year-old Bordfunker of Ofw. Waldemar Gerstman of 1./ZG 1. Braunsberger was killed on 15/5/40 when two Bf 110s collided following take-off from Kirchhellen. Braunsberger was unable to vacate the aircraft.

turning through trees and other obstructions to shake them off. 'What my poor bloody engine's like I don't know,' he said. 'I've honestly never been so scared in my life!'."

The intensity of the fighting reduced somewhat on the following day and was reflected in the losses sustained by the Zerstörers. Three Bf 110s went down with their crews in widespread combats ranging from Brussels to Rheims. Many others returned to their bases damaged with wounded and increasingly tired crews aboard.

One of those lucky to return was Leutnant Wolfgang Schenck of 1./ZG 1, who was badly wounded in the leg during a single-handed combat with 9 British Hurricanes north-west of Brussels. Schenck's injuries would keep him grounded until September when he would talk his way back into service with 1st Staffel, Erprobungsgruppe 210 then based at Denain under his old chief, Martin Lutz. Rising to flying command of the unit, 'Bombo' Schenck would go on to finish the war as a highly decorated Oberstleutnant, with over 400 combat sorties, 40 of them in the Messerschmitt 262 jet

Lt. Victor Mölders (left) and Lt. Wolfgang Schenck, both of 1./ZG 1, with flying Staffelhund 'Bourchi'.

A Messerschmitt 110 C, A2 + EK, of 2nd Staffel, ZG 52 carrying the early 1940 camouflage, and the I. Gruppe emblem, which was continued on their aircraft when the Gruppe was redesignated II./ZG 2 in July 1940. Note the small white band around the front of the propellor back-plate.

fighter, and with 18 victories to his credit.

It was on 16th May that Oberfeldwebel Georg Anthony of 4./ZG 76 claimed his first victory. One of 6 Bf 110s on a freelance sortie over Le Cateau, they had stumbled upon a Morane MS 406 attacking a Henschel HS 126 observation machine. Led by their Staffelkapitän, Hauptmann Heinz Wagner, the Zerstörers dived on the unsuspecting French fighter. The first two Bf 110s overshot due to the speed built up in the dive, and steamed past the startled Morane like express trains. Oberfeldwebel Anthony, third into the attack, managed only a short burst before the Morane jinked to port and into a dive. The heavier Zerstörer had a speed advantage in the dive so Anthony, along with one other Bf 110, closed on the Morane down to ground level and chased it west.

Columns of troops threw themselves flat on the ground as the three aircraft rocketed overhead,. Firing continually with his heavy battery of front guns, Anthony was amazed at the punishment the Morane absorbed, its flaps dropping as they approached a French airfield.

The hapless French pilot had little choice; too low to bale out and pursued by 2 Bf 110s he had no chance of a forced landing. Maybe lowering his flaps was a forlorn effort to cause the Zerstörers to overshoot, or

an attempt to signal surrender, or perhaps his aircraft's hydraulics were simply damaged. Whatever the case, Oberfeldwebel Anthony rapidly overhauled the French fighter giving it a final burst at point-blank range before wrenching his aircraft aside to avoid a collision. The Morane burst into flames, its fuel tanks exploding as it cartwheeled into a cornfield like a meteor.

He claimed his second victory the following day during an escort sortie by 8 Bf 110s of 4./ZG 76 for 9 Heinkel He 111s bombing rail targets in Albert. As usual enemy fighter tactics were to wait until the German formation was on its return flight before they put in an appearance, a mixed formation of about 30 Morane MS 406s and Curtis Hawk 75s falling on the Zerstörers from cloud cover.

These French pilots were impressive, their aerobatic antics being very pretty to watch but making them extremely difficult targets. The Zerstörers had their work cut out and a glorious dogfight ensued. Oberfeldwebel Anthony managed to close on one Curtis Hawk which attacked him but it slid away as he delivered a short burst. The MG 15 in the rear cockpit behind him began clattering away as his Bordfunker, Unteroffizier Nordmeier, alerted him to 3 more Curtis fighters closing from behind. Reefing into a tight turn, Anthony glanced back over his shoulder to see two of them

A Bf 110 C of 3./ZG 1 on a non-combat flight. Note the early style fuselage cross, and the Lion's head emblem on the nose.

break away as the third suddenly reared upwards trailing a plume of smoke.

A Morane MS 406 crossed ahead of him attacking another Bf 110. Oberfeldwebel Anthony closed behind it and delivered a concentrated attack which staggered the French fighter, causing it to pull up vertically and fall away on one wing and into a slow turn, smoke and flames issuing from its fuselage.

Suddenly the combat was over and the French fighters were diving away West. The Bf 110s reformed and headed back to base, landing at Philippeville en-route due to fuel shortage. It had been their toughest combat so far and they had acquitted themselves well, claiming six enemy fighters destroyed for no loss or significant damage to themselves.

The next day, on another escort sortie, this time for Dornier Do 17s making a low-level attack on retreating troops, and installations around Cambrai, 4./ZG 76 put up a single Schwarm of 4 Bf 110s under Schwarmführer Oberleutnant Godborg Christiansen and they formed up with their charges over Dinant at 3,500 feet. The Dorniers delivered their attacks from 150 feet causing havoc amongst the retreating allied columns, but not until the return flight did a single Morane MS 406 appear high above them. After stalking the formation for a while it curved into the attack and opened fire on one of the rearmost Bf 110s. It was a bold manoeuvre by a brave pilot but without total surprise it was doomed to failure.

The Schwarmführer immediately took the Bf 110s into a steep turn to form the familiar defensive circle. To their total surprise the Morane, in a superbly executed and supremely confident move, scythed neatly across the middle of their formation and suddenly emerged right on Christiansen's tail. Flying in the second Rotte, Oberfeldwebel Anthony urged his Bf 110 into an even steeper turn, the Morane swimming tantalisingly close ahead of him one second but masked by friendly aircraft the next. Finally, with the Morane firmly in his gunsight, he opened fire. At such close range a short burst was all that was required. The Morane lurched visibly under the impact of the Bf 110s concentrated firepower, its port wing burst into flames and it pulled up into a steep climb, eventually crashing into the ground near the Canadian WW1 cemetery north-east of Cambrai. Of its pilot there was no sign.

It was Georg Anthony's third victory in as many days and he was rapidly becoming one of the Haifisch Gruppe's more celebrated pilots. This 27 year-old Berliner, one of the founder members of 4th Staffel, ZG 76, later being persuaded to recount his experiences for war correspondent Benno Wundshammer who was attached to II./ZG 76 during the French campaign. Regrettably, along with so many of his kind, Oberfeldwebel Anthony's promising career as a combat pilot was soon to be brought to an abrupt and savage end in the forthcoming clashes over England, being killed in action on 30th August.

Formation view of a Schwarm of Bf 110 Cs from 5./ZG 26. All aircraft carry the early-style upper surface camouflage and the Staffel emblem, a black 'Pik-As' (Ace of Spades) in a white diamond.

< 2N + BB, a Bf 110 C of the Gruppenstab of I./ZG 1, seen early in the French campaign. The chevron denotes the aircraft of the Gruppenadjutant. This would therefore normally have been the mount of Oblt. Siegfried Wandam.

Erwin Landgraf and his wife in a later-war photograph, when he had reached the rank of Leutnant. Landgraf was shot down on 18/5/40 and spent time in French captivity.

On 18th May the German advance reached the upper Somme where, over the next two days, they would establish a bridgehead across the river between Abbeville and Amiens. It was a day of maximum effort by the Luftwaffe and proved to be the day on which the Zerstörer units suffered their heaviest casualties of the whole campaign. By nightfall 9 Bf 110s had been lost and another badly damaged in the bitter fighter combats which spilled across the front between Amiens and Valenciennes. Nine crewmen were killed, two wounded and seven taken prisoner, although five of them would later returned to their units.

ZG 26 bore the brunt, its 5th Staffel being the hardest hit. Only that morning many Zerstörer Gruppen had received orders to move to forward bases; II./ZG 1 from Gütersloh to Trier, near the Luxembourg border; II./ZG 26 to Asch in Belgium. Taking-off from Kaarst/Neuss, their home base in Germany, II./ZG 26 was to support bombing attacks on Amiens with

fighter sweeps, landing at St. Trond to take on fuel enroute to the target.

The petrol bowsers which should have been awaiting them at St. Trond failed to materialise, and the whole Gruppe was seriously delayed by the lack of proper refuelling facilities. So, it was already late in the afternoon when a scratch formation of 8 Bf 110s, the first to finish refuelling, were sent off to support the bombers as arranged.

Led by the Staffelkapitän of 5./ZG 26, Hauptmann Eberhard d'Elsa, they gained height and soon reached the allotted area where they commenced to patrol above the thick layer of cloud which now covered Amiens. In the time it had taken them to refuel the weather had deteriorated, a frontal system moving in from the west. There was absolutely nothing to be seen so, after stooging back and forth for a while, d'Elsa decided to take his formation down through the cloud layer to seek out any enemy fighters who might be lurking underneath. Losing height steadily and in loose formation the Bf 110s dropped out of the clouds and straight into a huge gaggle of British fighters. For the briefest moment, before the intercoms sprang into life, it was difficult to judge who was the more surprised.

The odds against the 8 Zerstörers were obviously too great, some estimating the British formation as 40 aircraft, at least three of which were later claimed destroyed in the action which followed. More had to remain unconfirmed as individual Bf 110s fought for their lives, seeking the protection of the clouds above; their numbers too small to even form a defensive circle.

Unteroffizier Erwin Landgraf of 4./ZG 26, coming under heavy fire, craned in his seat to see his Bordfunker, Unteroffizier Fritz Mathis, slumped across his gun in the rear cockpit - a gaping wound in his head. It was Landgraf's 10th war flight and the first time they had flown together as a crew. Using all his strength, he threw the Bf 110 around in a wild effort to avoid further attacks. But suddenly he felt a tremendous blow on his right shoulder blade as a burst of fire shattered the cockpit, wounding him severely. Exactly how he managed to jettison the hood and vacate the cockpit he was to have no clear recollection, only vague impressions of being face-down across the fuselage. However somehow he broke free and fell away from the crippled aircraft, his parachute opening as he passed out.

Back at Asch, the rest of II./ZG 26 had long since landed from their own belated sortie to Amiens where they had encountered enemy fighters above the cloud. The Kommandeur, Hauptmann Ralph von Rettburg, waiting with the other pilots and aircrew, paced back and forth, clearly concerned.

Finally, in the gathering dusk, a Bf 110 joined the landing circuit, its red spinner tips and distinctive 'Ace of Spades' emblem identifying it as a 5./ZG 26 machine, with another close behind it. Oberfeldwebel Rochel was first down, several bullet holes in his aircraft but both he and his Bordfunker, Unteroffizier Schöffler, unwounded. He described the action as the

Hauptmann Eberhard d'Elsa, Staffelkapitän of 5./ZG 26, was shot down in combat on 18/5/40 and became a prisoner of the French. Due to the severity of his wounds he was unable to continue front line action after his release from captivity.

toughest combat he had ever experienced.

Oberleutnant Arthur Niebuhr was next to land, his aircraft mute testimony to the struggle; riddled by bullets and with one engine practically shot to pieces. He was shortly followed by Oberfeldwebel Auer, whose wounded Bordfunker, Feldwebel Nicolay, had to be lifted from the aircraft.

One by one the survivors limped in to land at Asch, but as evening fell Leutnant Heckert, Feldwebel Schöntier and the Staffelkapitän, Hauptmann d'Elsa were still missing. For some hours hope lingered that they may have been forced to land with combat damage elsewhere in German-held territory. But as more time passed and no news arrived, 5./ZG 26 was forced to accept that it had suffered its first real casualties of the war. The loss of d'Elsa was a particularly hard blow for them. He was particulary well-respected and an immensely popular leader, and had lead them from the start. However it was not until the end of the month that his fate and that of the others was to become clear.

His Bordfunker, Unteroffizier Rössler, was the first to return on 31st May, having been released from French captivity by the rapid German advance. He confirmed that d'Elsa was also a prisoner of the French but was seriously wounded. Feldwebel Schöntier, another temporary guest of the French returned on 17th June with more news. His own Bordfunker, Unteroffizier Alois Komanns, had been killed in the action on 18th May and d'Elsa had lost his left arm - shattered by gunfire, it had to be amputated.

Erwin Landgraf, discovered in a French hospital near St. Pol, was more fortunate - despite the ugly wound to his shoulder, he kept his right arm. The customary sympathetic yet hopeful letter from the Staffel, written on 22nd May by the duty officer Oberleutnant Heinz Ihrke, was still on its way to his family. Repatriated to the Marienhospital in Düsseldorf, he would be visited by a succession of comrades over the coming months, including the irrepressible Oberleutnant Bier who, with remarkable lack of tact, gleefully showed him photographs of his burned-out Bf 110. After a year spent recovering from his wounds, Landgraf would return to active service as a ferry pilot, his injuries preventing him from flying any further combat missions for the rest of the war.

Nothing was heard of the other missing crew, Leutnant Heckert and Unteroffizier Berger, until confirmation was eventually received via the International Red Cross in Geneva that they both survived unwounded as

Uffz. Alois Komanns of 5./ZG 26, killed in action on 18/5/40, the first casualty of the Staffel.

prisoners of the British. Despite confusion during the allied withdrawal they had been processed through rear echelons and shipped across the Channel to England for interrogation. Clearly the experience of 5./ZG 26 suggested that, given a choice, it was preferable to spend a short time in French hands than sit out the next few months in the Tower of London awaiting the German invasion.

Co-ordination between the British and French on the handling of German prisoners was understandably haphazard during the offensive, another high-ranking Luftwaffe officer having good cause to bless the fact later the same day. His experiences, related here, can be taken as fairly typical of many of the Luftwaffe aircrew who were taken prisoner only to be released by their own troops and returned to their units during this chaotic period.

Around 6:00 pm. on 18th May, 6 Bf 110s of the 'Haifisch' Gruppe, II./ZG 76, took-off for a low level attack on Douai airfield. Flying with them was the Geschwaderkommodore of ZG 76, Major Walter Grabmann, and the Gruppenadjutant, Leutnant Herbert Peters. Just before the target they met a formation of about 30 enemy fighters, either Hurricanes or Curtis Hawks.

Closing on one of the enemy fighters, Grabmann's aircraft came under heavy attack from another, whose concentrated fire cut off the tail of his Bf 110. With the stick suddenly slack and useless in his hand, and his machine suddenly out of control and in a steep dive, Grabmann instinctively released the cockpit canopy and found himself outside the aircraft reaching for the ripcord. Of his Bordfunker, Feldwebel Richard Krone, there was no sign.. Grabmann had heard nothing from the rear cockpit during the combat, which suggested that Krone had probably been killed in the attack by the enemy fighter.

Grabmann drifted down to land in the middle of a French AA position where he was immediately relieved of all of his valuables by grateful Poilus. Before nightfall, he was taken by truck and under armed guard to the HQ of a French Infantry Division. Here, bombarded by a battery of questions from a panel of senior French officers including a General, he responded curtly to their crude efforts at interrogation with "I'm a German officer not a traitor!"

After this dignified outburst their attitude suddenly changed and he was offered a cigarette. He accepted, reflecting that the French probably realised that their positions could well be reversed in the near future. Sensing a slight impasse, Grabmann took the initiative. After pointing out to all present that the German Army was just outside Arras so there was a good chance he would be released the next day, could they arrange to have his valuables returned? The General who was present immediately convened a conference in a corner of the room, where he harangued his staff for 15 minu-

The fin and rudder of Wolfgang Falck's Bf 110 sporting 8 victory bars, the first three of which were obtained during the Polish campaign in 1939.

Two views 2N + CH of 1./ZG 1 seen during the French campaign carrying the name of the pilot's girlfriend, 'Ilse' on the nose. This aircraft was normally the responsibility of ground mechanic Willi Falkenroth.

tes. Soon afterwards Grabmann was handed his possessions and with more than customary relish took a cigarette from his own case and smoked it under the curious gaze of his guards.

Later that night he was shackled to a guard, bundled into a car and with an escort of two more officers driven off in the direction of Arras where he was eventually delivered into the custody of civilian police. Sitting around a crude wooden table in the early hours of the morning, drinking red wine and enjoying a smoke with the local Gendarmes, Grabmann found himself expounding on the military situation. "The German Army is right outside town but you've no reason to leave," he told them. "Stories of atrocities are all propaganda and lies. On the contrary, they will restore order and security for you." The French police were clearly impressed and seemed quite relieved by this news. Grabmann felt that things were definitely going his way when a squad of British soldiers burst through the door.

They were attached to a RAF squadron based nearby which had now withdrawn and were on their way back to England. They were a friendly mob, offering to dress the scratches he had suffered vacating his aircraft and seemed keen to take him along with them - definitely an unwanted development. They plied him with cigarettes as did the French, putting Grabmann in something of a quandary - which to accept? Cannily, Grabmann voiced a preference for the French brand. Feigning unparalleled satisfaction beyond the wildest dreams of the manufacturer, he inhaled the course black tobacco to the obvious delight of the Gendarmes and the disgust of the Tommies. Shortly afterwards the British left without him, explaining that they had no desire to find themselves overtaken by the German advance.

Early the next morning Grabmann was transferred

An unknown airman poses proudly beside the fin of 2N + AN of 5./ZG 1 which carries seven victory bars, and two souvenirs of its latest encounter with the Royal Air Force.

to the main jail in Arras. Obviously the French military hadn't the proper facilities or the time to deal with him and had simply dumped the problem on the civil Gendarmerie. Grabmann found himself being treated exactly as a common criminal. He was forced to strip, searched and his valuables were again confiscated. Interminable forms then had to be filled in. Voicing his indignation at this outrageous treatment of a Luftwaffe officer, Grabmann soon recognised that he was wasting his breath on the half-wit in charge. He was eventually shown to a dingy solitary cell; its walls covered in obscene pencilled graffiti and with a narrow bed in one corner covered by a filthy straw mattress. That night, as he tried unsuccessfully to sleep, Grabmann brooded on his miserable situation.

Next morning an unexpected visitor arrived in the person of the prison commandant. Gloriously bedecked in the most wondrous uniform, he resembled something out of a comic opera. Grabmann reflected that he made a fantastic hotel porter. "Are you English?", he asked in a friendly tone. This took the Kommodore by surprise - just exactly what sort of allies were the French and British? And how in the name of reason could the French ever treat a RAF officer this way?

He told the commandant his nationality, unprepared for the dramatic effect it would have. Screaming in German, the commandant ranted, "Get up! Every time

I enter the room you must stand immediately!" Suddenly the small cell was flooded with guards and Grabmann was again forced to strip, every article of clothing and the entire contents of the cell being closely inspected. A letter from home and family photographs were confiscated. His fur-lined flying boots were examined for false heels and his flying helmet, with its earphones, throat microphone and long electrical cable, came under extreme scrutiny. "Obviously," declared the commandant, "this is capable of transmitting messages back to Germany." It was too much; Grabmann collapsed in loud bursts of laughter and the search party sheepishly withdrew.

Two or three days passed interminably, a familiar routine soon being established. Bread and water in the morning, a bowl of steaming soup at noon, usually potato and carrot, with more soup in the evening. All meals were taken alone and in total silence. Throughout the night at hourly intervals a guard would throw open the door, switch on the light and check the cell. Grabmann's only view of the outside world was a small patch of sky glimpsed through a narrow window high up on one wall.

The next morning was a Sunday. Grabmann could hear bells outside but interspersed with the sound of a distant machine-gun fire. Around 7:00 am. the commandant arrived in more conciliatory mood: obviously the imminent arrival of German Panzers had made

Oblt. 'Rudi' Rademacher, centre, Technical Officer of I./ZG 76 in casual conversation with two unknown members of the unit.

some impression on him. The Kommodore decided to try to turn the situation to advantage. "Look," he said, "the Germans are already in Arras so by tomorrow latest I'll be free. Improve these conditions now and you have the chance to guarantee your own future treatment." It was a bold effort, but unsuccessful, as was his request to have his wristwatch returned, it being a gift and of great sentimental value. "Impossible," declared the commandant apologetically as he left the cell, "strictly against regulations."

Within the hour he was back, "Would you like a wash?", he asked. "Certainly", Grabmann replied, "can I have some soap?". All through the morning, as the gunfire drew nearer, the Commandant kept up a regular series of visits to Grabmann's cell with solicitous enquiries as to his welfare and constant reminders of how well he had been treated. "Are they here?", was the Kommodore's constant question, to which the Commandant always replied, "No, not yet, but they will be soon." It was farcical.

Around 11:00 am. the Commandant entered the cell and tossed a small packet onto the bed. "Get ready to move immediately", he ordered. Grabmann, who assumed that the package was Red Cross supplies, was delighted to find that it actually contained all

Uffz. Otto Schamberger, in flying gear, in front of a Bf 110 C of I./ZG 1 with ground personnel. This aircraft appears to be in pristine condition and shows to good effect the demarcation line between the upper and lower surface camouflage, as well as the two tone upper surface greens. In the background can be seen a 1st Staffel machine, 2N + GH.

5th Staffel, Zerstörergeschwader 26 in flight. 3U + AP, W. Nr. 3044, a 6th Staffel machine, was brought to 5th Staffel by Oblt. Theodor Rossiwall, who moved from 6th to 5th to take up the role of Staffelkapitän after the loss of Hptm. d'Elsa. 3U + GN was the normal aircraft of Ofw. Rochel and Uffz. Schöffler, one of the most successful crews of 5th Staffel. They were shot down over the Thames estuary on 2/9/40.

his possessions including his precious watch. Snatching up half a loaf of bread, his flying helmet and gloves, he followed the guard out into the prison yard. 40 prisoners were gathered there, mainly Belgian smugglers. To his despair Grabmann found himself handcuffed to a 60 year-old murderer who could barely walk. The French were evacuating the prison and there was no sign of any transport.

The roads west were a nightmare. Packed with retreating troops, transports, tanks and artillery, plus civilians with their cars bicycles animals and belongings - it was pandemonium. The small column of prisoners shuffled along surrounded by a heavily-armed escort of Gendarmes and with the Commandant puttering back and forth on a commandeered motorcycle. Grabmann, dragging his geriatric gangster along behind him, revell-

Bf 110 C, 2N + HH of 1./ZG 1, nosed over during the French campaign.

Two views of the partially burnt-out remains of 2N + EH of 1./ZG 1, seen during the Battle of France period. Note the early style fuselage cross on this and on 2N + CH behind it, and the lack of outline to the individual aircraft letter.

The burial ceremony of Oblt. Fritz Lüdders, Staffelkapitän of 1./ZG 2. He was killed as a result of a landing accident at Neufchâteau following a combat mission on 20/5/40.

ed in the thought that this bore all the hallmarks of a full-blown military rout, not an organised withdrawal. Progress was painfully slow, and the column made many stops, but finally near Avesnes-le-Comte a Panzer reconnaissance unit finally overtook them and Grabmann's sojourn as a criminal was over.

He remained with the Panzers all that day and the next as they advanced towards Montreuil and the coast. En-route, and to Grabmann's mortification, they were bombed by Blenheims and strafed by Spitfires. Reaching Hesdin, the Panzers halted for a day before pushing on for Calais. Grabmann took his leave of them, having confirmed by radio that ZG 76 were still at their old base, where he landed within hours to an emotional reunion with comrades. It had been six days since his last sortie during which time the Geschwader had received no news of him.

Meantime, allied aircraft continued to exact a toll through increasingly despairing and desperate combats over the rolling front line. Also, with bombing attacks on airfields only recently vacated by themselves and now occupied by the Luftwaffe. Low-level attacks on Rouen-Boos on the 19th and 20th May caused several casualties amongst groundcrews of III./ZG 26 with 12 killed and another 15 seriously wounded.

Back at Asch in Belgium early in the afternoon of 19th May, the remnants of 5./ZG 26 could only muster 3 serviceable Bf 110s for an escort sortie to Amiens.

Along with other Staffeln and led by their new Staffelkapitän, Legion Condor veteran Oberleutnant Theodor Rossiwall who had relinquished command of 6./ZG 26 that morning, they were soon embroiled in combat with French Moranes.

During the return flight, Oberleutnant Niebuhr and his Bordfunker, Unteroffizier Theissen, had to abandon their aircraft when it suddenly burst into flames. Lucky enough to land among German forward troops, they were soon returned to their unit, but 5./ZG 26 was now reduced to a mere 2 operational aircraft.

Since their move to Asch the unit had suffered a miserable time and their uncomfortable surroundings did little to relieve their melancholy. Most of the men were billeted in glum blocks of flats in this dingy Belgian industrial hinterland, the officers occupying a small hotel. As if to justify its name, the whole area was constantly shrouded in a choking film of coal dust which percolated everywhere. The order to move forward to St. Trond on 20th May elicited almost universal delight, despite the fact that by the following day they were down to a single serviceable aircraft.

20th May was a costly day for the Zerstörers, not in terms of aircraft lost, but for the loss of two valuable tactical commanders. Oberleutnant Fritz Lüdders, Staffelkapitän of 1./ZG 2, crashed on the approach to Neufchâteau on return from a combat sortie and died in the blazing wreck of his aircraft along with his Bord-

The grave of Ofw. Stegemann and Uffz. Solluch of 13. (Z)./LG 1, shot down in combat on 21/5/40.

funker, Unteroffizier Baron. His replacement was Oberleutnant Gerhard Goetz who came from the Stabsschwarm as Staffelführer, his own role as Gruppe Technical Officer being taken by Oberleutnant Reinhold Messner, who transferred from 3rd Staffel.

Another Staffelkapitän lost this day was Oberleutnant Kurt-Wilhelm Heinrich of 7./ZG 26. Badly wounded in action over Sedan, he managed to get back to base at St. Marie but died of wounds in hospital in Coblenz four days later.

The Zerstörers were beginning to experience increasingly heavy fighter resistance as the ground fighting moved closer to the Channel ports. Over Calais during an afternoon sortie on 23rd May, 12 Bf 110s of II./ZG 76 were providing fighter cover for Stuka attacks on harbour installations and shipping. Suddenly the 'Haifisch' Gruppe was engaged by Spitfires, a series of isolated combats developing as each Rotte of Bf 110s came under separate attack. The Spitfires were probably from No. 92 Squadron on their second sortie over Dunkirk that day. Led by Squadron Leader Roger Bushell, they had moved from their base at Croydon to Hornchurch only that morning for their first combat sorties over the French coast.

Leading one flight was Flight Lieutenant Robert Stanford Tuck whose biography recounts, "Wheeling round in the thick of this confusion, for a time Tuck could see nothing to shoot at. Then a 110 drifted majestically in front of him, startlingly close, in a gentle bank and skidding slightly. It seemed enormous, impregnable. Its rear gunner swung his long barrel round

and Tuck instinctively ducked as the bullets ricocheted off his cowling and canopy."

It was only Tuck's second combat sortie of the war, the first being that same morning, and he was lucky to survive it. In a head-on attack by another Bf 110 his armoured windscreen took two 20 mm. shells, "On the top left and bottom right corners of his windscreen there were ugly, opaque blotches, staring at him like big blind eyes. Two of the Hun's shells had smacked him squarely: if the fitters hadn't installed the new type screen just over an hour before, these hits would have come through and taken off his head." He nursed his crippled Spitfire back to Hornchurch where he landed with his engine seized.

Later, "when the Squadron's losses for the day were known, the whole station was grim and very quiet... the fact that stunned everyone was that in a single day's fighting almost half the squadron had gone." Among the losses was the CO, Roger Bushell, last seen chasing a 110 inland at low level. Tuck was appointed to command the remnants of No. 92 Squadron with only 6 serviceable Spitfires available for operations on the following day.

Months later Roger Bushell's own account of this action filtered through to the squadron from Germany where he was a POW. "I was shot down by Messerschmitt 110s, but managed to get two of them first. My first I got with a full deflection shot underneath. He went down in a long glide with his port engine pouring smoke. I went into a spin, as two others were firing at me from my aft quarter. I only did one turn of

45

The grave of Uffz. Walter and Ogefr. Rothenberger of 1./ZG 1, killed in action on 22/5/40, lies near to the wreckage of their Bf 110 C alongside the Leguin to Roubaix road, south-east of Lille.

the spin and pulled out left and up. I then saw a Messerschmitt below me and trying to fire up at me, so I went head-on at him, and he came head-on at me. We were both firing, and everything was red flashes. I know I killed the pilot, because suddenly he pulled right up at me and missed me by inches. I went over the top of him and as I turned I saw him rear right up in a stall and go down with his engine smoking. I hadn't got long to watch, but he was out of control and half on his back. My engine was badly shot up and caught fire. My machine was pouring glycol. I don't quite know what happened, but I turned things off and was out of control for a while..."

Belly-landing east of Boulogne, Bushell was quickly rounded up and captured. For him it was the start of an entirely different war - a war of escape, evasion and organised resistance. As 'Big X' of the escape organisation at Stalag Luft III, the story of his heroism and death at the hands of the Gestapo in 1944 were later to be immortalised in 'The Great Escape'.

Embroiled in the same combat and suddenly separated from his wingman, Leutnant Werner Guth, one of the original founder members of 6./ZG 76, had good cause to count his blessings. Badly wounded in the right shoulder, his cockpit shattered, instruments damaged, both engines losing power and with coolant temperatures off the clock, he had the satisfaction and intense relief of watching the Spitfire which had attacked him explode as it spiralled down towards the Channel. Another Spitfire dropped out of the combat

and plunged into the Channel on fire, the Gruppenkommandeur, Hauptmann Erich Groth, jubilantly announcing his 8th victory over the radio.

Then Guth's Bordfunker, Unteroffizier Kurt Niedzwetski, was screaming, "Three more Spitfires behind!" With his aircraft flying like the proverbial brick, Leutnant Guth knew they stood little chance of escape. Standing the Zerstörer on its nose he went into a vertical dive down to ground level in an effort to shake off his pursuers. Niedzwetski kept up a steady barrage with his single MG 15 machine gun in the rear but against the combined fire of 24 Brownings it was a futile gesture and after a while it stopped.

Careering across a field near Ardres, south of Calais, Guth made a creditable belly-landing despite his wounds. Somehow he dragged his badly-wounded Bordfunker from the blood-soaked rear cockpit and across the field away from the aircraft. Niedzwetski had suffered a severe head wound and was in a bad way, lapsing in and out of consciousness; in fact Guth had initially thought him dead. Guth hurriedly applied a field dressing before returning to the aircraft which he unsuccessfully attempted to set alight.

Fortunately, they had landed in German-held territory and before long a Luftwaffe Oberstabsarzt and Sanitätsfeldwebel arrived on the scene having watched them come down from a nearby field hospital. They immediately tended to Unteroffizier Niedzwetski, this treatment certainly keeping him alive long enough to be airlifted to hospital at Trier. There he held on for an

Erich Hermanski, Bordfunker of Hptm. Rolf Kaldrack of 4./ZG 1, wounded in action on 24/5/40. Hermanski is seen here in a later-war shot following promotion to Oberfeldwebel.

other 6 days before eventually succumbing to his wounds. Leutnant Guth's injuries were comparatively light and he was soon back with 6./ZG 76 albeit with his arm in a sling.

Two more Bf 110s were badly damaged in the combats which raged over Calais that day. Gruppenadjutant of Stab, I./ZG 26, Oberleutnant Günther Specht, claimed 3 British fighters destroyed before he and his Bordfunker, Unteroffizier Fritz Fischer, were both badly wounded and forced to land. Rudi Proske came from 3./ZG 26 to take Specht's place in the Stabsschwarm and inherited the Adjutant's old aircraft with its distinctive pencil and single chevron emblem.

Specht, who had lost his left eye in an attack on a RAF Wellington the previous December, would recover from his wounds and go on to survive being shot down 6 more times during the course of the war. As Kommodore of JG 11 and a legendary figure in the 'Defence of the Reich', he would eventually go missing in action over Asch, in Belgium, on New Year's Day 1945. Posthumously promoted to Oberstleutnant and awarded the Oakleaves to the Knight's Cross of the Iron Cross, he was credited with 34 victories at the time of his death.

On their final sortie of the following day, 24th May, II./ZG 1 were providing the escort for Heinkel He 111s bombing a convoy in the English Channel. After the attack they escorted the Heinkels into a solid layer of cloud and well on their way home before splitting up into separate Staffeln for freelance activity - the

Stabsschwarm also operating independently.

There were several enemy fighters in the vicinity and the Bf 110s were soon engaged. Flying in his customary position as Bordfunker to the Staffelkapitän, Hauptmann Kaldrack, Feldwebel Erich Hermanski of 4./ZG 1 recalls. "We broke through clouds and saw an English reconnaissance plane about 500 metres in front of us flying east as we were. Before we shot him down the tail gunner hit our left wing and engine. We made it as far as Trier on one engine, touching ground about 300 metres before the landing cross. The left wheel, most likely punctured by a bullet, dug into the grass and flipped the Me 110 upside down. Luckily the plane did not catch fire."

Hermanski awoke the next afternoon in hospital in Trier, his ribs all broken and his right lung punctured. After three weeks languishing in hospital he discharged himself and hitch-hiked back to his unit. Ordered to take immediate sick leave, he was back with them again after only a week. But despite his insistence, his injuries would prevent him from flying any more combat sorties.

Kaldrack also survived the crash and was subsequently to become Kommandeur of the Gruppe, by then redesignated III./ZG 76, following the death of Hauptmann Dickoré on 15th August. A veteran of the Spanish Civil War, where he achieved 3 victories, Kaldrack would be awarded the Ritterkreuz on 2nd November 1940 on gaining his 11th victory.

By 25th May the allied armies were divided, the main British army separated from the French by the rapid German advance. German armoured thrusts now penetrated beyond Arras; they had taken Boulogne, reached the outskirts of Calais, and in the North, were closing on Ghent. But the overwhelming speed of their advance which had given them such spectacular territorial gains also put the front-line at the limit of range for their single-engined fighters and Stukas. So, for the first time in the campaign, allied aircraft began to enjoy a measure of air superiority and wrest control of the skies over the front-line.

This was undoubtedly one of the factors which influenced Hitler's decision, announced on this day, to halt the advance to the coast literally in its tracks. He wished to save the remaining Panzers for the continuing campaign deep into mainland France and, still hopeful of forcing the British to come to terms, he wished to avoid inflicting too crushing a defeat on them.

So, he gave the Luftwaffe free rein for the final assault on Dunkirk. Hadn't Göring himself given assurances that they alone would destroy the enemy now entrapped there? In the event, the first air attacks on Dunkirk would not take place until the following day, Sunday 26th, the main weight of the Luftwaffe being already committed to attacks on Lille, Amiens and Calais. At Calais, no evacuation was planned, Churchill having ordered the British forces there to resist to the bitter end. But concentrated attacks throughout the day by Stukas of StG 2 and StG 77, plus a constant artillery bombardment and final assault by the 10th Panzer Division proved too much for the 20,000 troops defending the town and at 4:45 pm. they surrendered. They had engaged two Panzer divisions for four days, preventing them from interfering with the withdrawal to Dunkirk, but in the words of one historian, it had been "a grim affair".

Despite the lack of airfields within comfortable range, the Luftwaffe threw every available aircraft into preventing the British withdrawal by sea. But over the beaches of Dunkirk and La Panne, they met determined RAF fighter opposition operating in strength. During the morning of 26th May, a continuous air battle was fought over the French coast between Calais and Dunkirk, exhausted pilots returning to base describing "the sky filled with aircraft".

Leading the Stabsschwarm of I./ZG 1 over Calais, the Gruppenkommandeur, Hauptmann Wolfgang Falck, only barely managed to survive a surprise attack by British fighters by diving straight down to ground level. However his Gruppe Technical Officer, Oberleutnant Konrad Martin, and Signals Officer, Leutnant Werner Kleinecke, were less fortunate. They were both shot down bringing the Gruppe's losses for the day to 4 aircraft and crews, two 1./ZG 1 aircraft being lost in action over Ostend.

For many Zerstörer pilots, it was during these early combats over the Channel ports that they had their first encounter with the redoubtable Spitfire operating from bases in England. The experience was mutual, for many of their RAF counterparts would also be meeting Göring's much-vaunted Zerstörer for the first time. However the balance of combat experience was certainly in the Luftwaffe's favour at this stage, for most of these young Spitfire pilots, some of whom would go on to become famous RAF aces later in the war, were flying their first combat sorties of the war.

Flying with Stab, II./ZG 1 on his first sortie over Dunkirk, Richard Marchfelder recalled the "huge column of smoke ascending from ground level way up into the blue sky, serving as a landmark for the battle ground". This evocative image, forever associated with the Dunkirk battle, being the huge plume of smoke from oil storage tanks set ablaze in air attacks around noon.

"As we arrived, one of our Me 109s was engaged in a dogfight with an odd looking aircraft... 'Spitfires!' somebody shouted. There were more, but they turned away from us then headed across the Channel; probably out of ammunition. At this point the first Spitfire broke off the fight with the Me 109 and followed the others. Two Messerschmitts tried to catch it, but it got away.

"Dickoré tried to cut off two Spitfires on their way

Victor Mölders of 1./ZG 1 in a 'liberated' Bugatti. Based at a French château for part of the time during the French campaign, Mölders, Falck and other officers would race the high-powered vehicles around the grounds of the château in the off-duty evening time.

Uffz. Otto Schamberger, Bordfunker of Lt. Werner Kleinecke of Stab, ZG 1, wounded in action on 26/5/40.

Otto Schamberger's Bordfunker pass, showing his entry into military service (Diensteintritt) on 16/4/36 with Flieger Ersatz Abteilung, Neubiberg.

home, but we were too slow. It was then that we found out how vulnerable our Me 110 was. After our first encounter with British fighters it became soberly clear to us that the holidays were over and we had to use all our wits to fight a desperate enemy."

Oberleutnant Victor Mölders of 1./ZG 1 was of a similar opinion. "The Spitfire was considerably superior to our clumsy and slower Bf 110. During the Polish campaign, where we met slow but manoeuvrable fighters, it became clear that the Bf 110 wasn't really suitable for battle where it was single-seater against two-seater, or single-engine against twin-engine aircraft."

Before the war, Victor and his brother Werner had tested the respective merits of Messerschmitt's two fighters - Victor flying a Bf 109 and Werner the Bf 110. In a mock dogfight over Wiesbaden, Werner had found it virtually impossible to stay on the Bf 109's tail, while Victor experienced no difficulty in regularly 'shooting down' his brother.

Victor recalls, "The Bf 110 was not manoeuvrable. The steering was too heavy. In tight turns it slid about and fell out of the sky like a leaf from a tree. Trimming the aircraft or increasing speed didn't help. The Bf 110 was suitable as a night or all-weather fighter, and for low-level attacks on specific targets, particularly later

when armed with bombs or (30 mm. Kanone) as in the Bf 110 C-6."

Not all Bf 110 losses on the day resulted from combat, however. At Neufchâteau, Stab, I./ZG 2 suffered two serious losses in unnecessary and tragic circumstances. Due to adverse weather conditions the Gruppe was stood down, most of its aircraft having overdue routine maintenance and servicing completed. In spite of these conditions, a surprise attack on the airfield by two impertinent Blenheims so incensed the Gruppenkommandeur, Major Johannes Gentzen, that he harangued groundcrew to make two Stabsschwarm aircraft ready immediately - one for himself and another for his Gruppenadjutant, Leutnant Domeier.

Only one machine was fully serviceable so both officers leapt aboard, Domeier settling into the Bordfunker as the Zerstörer took-off in pursuit of the now rapidly vanishing Blenheims. It was a classic 'Alarmstart'.

To save time taxi-ing into position, and to the consternation of spectators gathered around the old bus which served I./ZG 2 as a mobile briefing room, Gentzen took off in the wrong direction across the main runway. With engines straining at maximum boost in a vain attempt to gain sufficient height, Gentzen's Bf 110 ploughed into trees fringing the airfield and cartwheeled into the ground. Neither Gent-

zen, nor Domeier had had time to strap in properly. Both were killed outright.

Remembered as a popular if somewhat excitable commander, Gentzen had received his flying training with the clandestine Luftwaffe at their secret base at Lipezk in Russia between the wars. He was a highly experienced pilot and tactical commander of a type the Luftwaffe could ill afford to lose in this way, and at the time of his death was credited with 10 victories. His successor as Kommandeur, Major Ernst Ott, arrived within days; Oberleutnant Gerhard Granz coming from 1st Staffel to replace the unfortunate Domeier as Gruppenadjutant.

Bad fortune dogged I./ZG 2 throughout that day, for they suffered the loss of two further aircraft in landing accidents at Neufchâteau, the combined effect of exhausted pilots and tired aircraft taking its toll.

That evening the halt command issued to the Panzers was lifted and Dunkirk declared the Luftwaffe's main target. Meanwhile, across the Channel in England, orders were issued to commence 'Operation Dynamo', the evacuation of the British army from France, which began the following morning at dawn.

2N+DH of 1./ZG 1 nosed over in soft ground during the French campaign. 'D' is blue outlined in white. The practice of using blue as a colour for the individual aircraft letter was unique to 1./ZG 1, and it carried this practise forward to Erpr. Gr. 210 when it formed the 1st Staffel of that unit. Note the swastika partly covering the rudder, and the single victory bar on the fin.

The remains of a Bf 110 of ZG 76 showing that certain parts had been salvaged following its demise.

The Luftwaffe was committed to preventing the evacuation but was seriously hampered by lack of suitable airfields within easy range, and the marked deterioration in the weather which set in. On 27th May, I./ZG 52 lost 3 Bf 110s in combat with British fighters north of Calais, including that of their Gruppenadjutant, Leutnant von Neumann.

By nightfall on that day, over 7,500 British troops had been lifted from Dunkirk and over the next four days a constant stream of British ships would manage to rescue another 192,000 men from France.

Weather conditions were certainly in their favour, fog and rain hampering Luftwaffe activity apart from the afternoon of 29th May when heavy attacks were again launched. During the course of the day the Luftwaffe sank 5 large passenger ships and 3 destroyers; 7 more destroyers being damaged.

Shipping proved a more elusive target for the bombers on 31st May due to indifferent weather over the coast. 5./ZG 26 provided a single Schwarm of 4 Bf 110s as escort for one Gruppe of bombers which trailed up and down the coast unsuccessfully seeking targets through the layer of cloud which wreathed the Channel. Led by their Staffelkapitän, Theodor Rossiwall, three of the Zerstörers left the bombers after a desultory hour to fly one last sweep of the coast before returning to St. Trond.

Since the debacle of 18th May, 5./ZG 26 had been thirsting for an opportunity to notch up some victories and redress the balance of their losses. It seemed that they were not to be disappointed on this occasion as about 50 Spitfires slowly emerged from the mist draping the English coast heading for Dunkirk. The odds were decidedly unfavourable but Rossiwall judged that with the Bf 110's advantage of height a single surprise attack was just possible.

Choosing his moment, Rossiwall took the Bf 110s at full speed straight into the attack and fell on the rear of the British formation. Two Spitfires were picked off in the first pass and dropped away smoking towards the Channel as the Zerstörers regained height using the speed built up in their dive. It was a well-executed and bold attack, but against such numbers it was bound to

end in trouble.

To Rossiwall's astonishment, far from engaging his Kette from all sides, the rest of the Spitfires were aimlessly milling around beneath him, getting in each other's way. They gave him the impression of being a complete bunch of beginners.

Needing no second bidding, Rossiwall, closely followed by Oberleutnant Niebuhr and Oberfeldwebel Rochel, dived into a second attack. This time his speed was too great and he overshot his target which managed to swing in behind him. However, the Spitfire was much too slow in reaching a firing position and was easily flushed off by Kurt Rochel.

These novices promised to provide easy pickings and so for the third time the Zerstörers dived straight through the middle of the British formation. Again two Spitfires spiralled down out of formation as the Bf 110s retired, their discretion getting the better of them. Five claims for no loss against such odds was the stuff of heroic sagas! It was exactly the sort of boost the Staffel needed and went far to compensate for their losses on 18th May. Confidence and morale in the unit soared overnight.

1st June dawned clear and sunny and the Luftwaffe once again threw every available aircraft against Dunkirk. This was the day on which the air fighting over Dunkirk reached its climax. Stukas attacked shipping in the Channel and the harbour whilst Heinkel He 111s bombed the main railway station. Escort for one of the main attacks of the day being provided by the Messerschmitt 110s of the 'Haifisch' Gruppe, II./ZG 76.

At that morning's briefing in the farmhouse which served as their Geschwader operations room, the Gruppenkommandeur, Hauptmann Erich Groth, had been blunt. "Very well, gentlemen, for the next few days Dunkirk is the target for our attacks. The enemy is cornered there by our Panzers and has fallen back in rapid retreat to the harbour. Almost the entire British expeditionary force is trapped. Obviously, they will be trying to get as many of their troops back to England as possible while the French fight a rearguard action.

"Our task is first, support for the Panzers and motorised infantry divisions, and second, escort for our bombers and Stukas." And then, glancing around the group of officers crowded around him, he added prophetically, "It will be just like Calais all over again, but this time we can reckon on even stronger British fighter resistance." Before the end of the day nobody would have any cause to doubt it.

Leading 6./ZG 76 over Dunkirk, their Staffelkapitän, Oberleutnant Heinz Nacke, held his aircraft in a shuddering turn, the Spitfire ahead of him swimming slowly into his sights. Opening fire with his cannon, he saw strikes on the Spitfire's rear fuselage and tail heralding a small explosion under its belly. Following it down to see it erupt in flames just above the high-water line in the dunes outside Dunkirk, Nacke came under intense small-arms fire from the mass of troops crowding the beaches but miraculously escaped without damage.

Gaining height he climbed to rejoin the combat rag-

Officers of I./ZG 1 surround their Kommandeur, Hptm. Wolfgang Falck (centre) during the French campaign. Far left - Oblt. Wandam (Gruppenadjutant); 5th from left - Oblt. Jürgen Möller (2nd Staffel); 2nd from right - Hptm. von Scheve (Major beim Stabe); 3rd from right - Lt. Wolfgang Schenck (1st Staffel); 4th from right - Oblt. Martin Lutz (Staffelkapitän - 1st Staffel); 5th from right - Lt. Gerhard Schmidt (1st Staffel); 6th from right - Oblt. Ehle (3rd Staffel); 7th from right - Lt Werner Kleinecke (Gruppenstab).

ing above as the Stukas continued their attacks on shipping crowding the harbour approaches. Then he was engaged by another Spitfire which proved a particularly stubborn and determined opponent. All caution abandoned, they threw their aircraft at each other like some berserk predatory birds, but neither could gain an advantage. Then suddenly they were head-on and Nacke froze as the nose of the Spitfire loomed larger and larger in his windscreen. Narrowly avoiding a collision, the Spitfire rocketed past shaving close under the belly of the Bf 110 and buffeting it hard with the impact of its slipstream. It dived away far below and behind, heading back for the English coast at wave-top height, presumably low on fuel.

While surviving records of the period remain notoriously sketchy, Flying Officer 'Paul' Edge of No. 609 Squadron recorded a strikingly similar experience on this day. He was flying as No. 2 in a section of three Spitfires led by acting-Squadron Leader, Flying Officer 'Hack' Russell, an American who had seen action with No. 607 Squadron during the debacle in France. High over Dunkirk, the No. 3, Gordon Mitchell, who was flying his first operational sortie, became separated and lost them on a turn.

Edge recounts, "I was searching the sky for him and momentarily drew abreast of Hack. In that precise moment an Me 110 must have crept up astern. I saw Hack, surrounded by bursting shells and tracer, pull up in a near vertical climb, then fall off in a stall and commence a long slow spiral into the sea. I followed him down until it was obvious he was not in control, and then climbed hard.

"The Me 110 was still there, flying in a wide circle. I pulled the Spit hard round and tried a deflection shot, but its nose swung violently off target because the four guns in the port wing failed to fire. Suddenly the Me 110 turned sharply and attacked head-on. It seemed he was deliberately trying to ram me, and with a closing speed of at least 400 mph. a collision seemed imminent. I had only a split second to decide whether to pass over or under. Some intuition forced me to ram the stick forward, and he flashed overhead with only feet between us. Feeling less than semi-operational, I went for the sea..."

Also physically shaken and with nerves slowly returning to normal, Nacke ordered his scattered unit to reform and maintain their patrol as the Stukas continued to wreak havoc among the shipping below. However before long more British fighters arrived and the Bf 110s were once again engaged in bitter combats during which he claimed another Spitfire which fell in flames towards the burning oil tanks of Dunkirk, its pilot bailing out.

After more than an hour of almost constant combat

Two views of a Bf 110 of ZG 1 which has come to an abrupt halt at the edge of a field. Note the aperture in the nose for the ESK 2000 gun-camera.

with successive waves of British fighters, the exhausted 'Haifisch' Gruppe finally withdrew, escorting the Stukas away from the carnage on the beaches. Without doubt, it had been their toughest action to date, but they could claim 7 victories without loss to themselves. This was good arithmetic and proper cause for celebration. But despite this, the general feeling back at base that evening was that the RAF were going to prove a more determined and formidable opponent than may have been expected. Somehow, a little of the 'sport' seemed to have gone out of the war in the air - forever. Across the Channel in England, RAF pilots were of a similar mind, Paul Edge feeling, "The war quite suddenly became grim and tragic."

The RAF had maintained a strong fighter presence over the French coast since first light. Shortly after dawn a formation of 48 Spitfires drawn mainly from the Duxford squadrons Nos. 19, 41 and 222, but reinforced by another, were already patrolling the Belgian coast towards Nieuport and 'looking for trouble'. Leading the Spitfires of No. 19 Squadron, acting-Squadron Leader Brian Lane later recounted, "From 5,000 feet we watched the drama being enacted below us. Above was a thin layer of cloud, not more than fifty feet thick, through which the sun was just visible. Suddenly in front of us appeared a twin-engined aircraft, followed by eleven more, all heading

towards Nieuport. I switched on the R/T: 'Twelve Me 110s straight ahead' I said, then opened the throttle and gave chase.

The Messerschmitts evidently saw us coming, for they went into a circle and tried to get into the clouds. For once the odds were in our favour, and four to one at that. I was still out of firing range when, to my astonishment, one of the enemy aircraft staggered and then plummeted down, with a strange pendulum motion as its tail came off. None of my section had fired, and since we were leading and out of range still, I could not imagine how on earth the Hun had been shot down.

"By now we had closed with the enemy and turning right I got on the tail of a Messerschmitt and chased him down as he dived away, the rest of the squadron fighting to get a target! It really was pathetic. By our standards of training those pilots should never have left FTS, yet here they were trying to fight four times their number, and with no idea of how to do it. War is war, but I remember cursing the Hun for a cold-blooded devil in sending out pilots like these to fight us. Even as I cursed I realised what a queer thought this was. We ought to be thankful for cold meat like this!"

This account, originally published during the war, is somewhat coloured and perhaps understandably so. Whilst critical of I./ZG 1 whose pilots were undoubtedly involved, it fails to make adequate allowance for the overwhelming superiority enjoyed by the British in this action. Three Bf 110s were actually lost including the deputy Staffelkapitän of 2./ZG 1, Oberleutnant Jürgen Möller and his Bordfunker Unteroffizier Karl Schieferstein, who both fell into British hands. Another 1st Staffel machine crashed east of Dunkirk, the Bordfunker, Unteroffizier Martin Rutz, receiving a field burial amongst the dunes which bordered the road between Coxyde and Dunkirk-east.

The ferocity of the Luftwaffe attacks throughout the day and the heavy losses inflicted on British shipping forced Vice-Admiral Sir Bertram Ramsey, the officer in command, to conclude that any further evacuation from Dunkirk would only be possible if attempted at night. At least 10 vessels had been sunk, including 3 destroyers loaded with troops. The level of RAF fighter losses sustained in defence of the eva-cuation was also giving cause for concern. Clearly the withdrawal would have to be concluded, one way or another, within the next few days.

By dawn on 4th June the last troops to be evacuated were brought off the beaches and improvised jetties, bringing the total number returned to England to over 338,000 during the nine days of 'Operation Dynamo'. It was a singular achievement, but as Churchill was later to declare to the House of Commons, "We must be careful not to assign to this deliverance the attributes of a victory. Wars are not won by evacuations. But there was a victory inside this deliverance, which should be noted. It was gained by the Royal Air Force."

During the ferocious air battles over the Channel ports between 26th May and 3rd June a total of 87

Above, and opposite: Two views of a Bf 110 of ZG 1 with activity centring on both sides of the instrument panel.

British aircraft had been lost whilst claiming some 377 German aircraft destroyed. The Luftwaffe had suffered its first serious defeat of the war in failing to prevent the withdrawal. But also, and possibly of even greater significance, they had experienced a bitter foretaste of what was to come.

On 3rd June, Paris was the target for the Luftwaffe. Leading the Bf 110s of I./ZG 1 as part of the escort to bombers attacking Le Bourget, Wolfgang Falck recalls massed formations of German aircraft stepped-up above Paris like some pre-war air show. Suddenly, a single Morane appeared from the haze below in solitary defence of the French capital and was promptly set upon "by the whole German Air Force". Falck, enclosed by scores of screaming fighters which crossed above, below and ahead of him as they all converged on the hapless Frenchman, abandoned his attack and warily pulled up and away to one side. It was one of the most dangerous moments he had experienced during the whole campaign.

Others suffered worse from 'friendly' fighters. On 6th June, Oberleutnant Victor Mölders of 1./ZG 1 force-landed his damaged Bf 110 C-6 back at Norrent-Fontes airfield, his tyres shot through and his Bordfunker, Feldwebel Helmut Krappatsch, slightly wounded. Mölders was unsure whether he had just experienced extreme good luck or bad fortune. Engaged on low-level attacks on ground targets around Le Havre with his 30 mm. Kanone armament, he had claimed 2 enemy aircraft destroyed on the same sortie before himself coming under attack by Messerschmitt Bf 109 Es, which he only just managed to shake off by flying into thick cloud.

Two aircraft of this special variant of the Bf 110 had been allotted to 1./ZG 1 for operational evaluation; the effect of its heavy 30 mm. calibre weapon in low level attacks on ground targets being of particular interest to the Luftwaffe General Staff. Along with his Staffelkapitän, Oberleutnant Martin Lutz, Victor Mölders was considered to be one of the unit's most experienced pilots at that time. So, they were chosen to become the only two pilots to fly the 30 mm. Kanone-armed Bf 110 C-6 variant in action during the offensive in France. In attacks on trains, tanks, gasometers and other targets of opportunity, they both flew several missions to evaluate the potential of the weapon during the latter stages of the campaign.

After Dunkirk the Luftwaffe continued in its close support role for the German army in the rapid advance south and west into the French interior. The French army and remaining British forces continued to resist but on 9th June Guderian's armour started to punch through from Sedan towards Dijon and the Saone. On every front resistance became increasingly sporadic and the inevitable final collapse soon followed.

By 11th June, the main German advance had reached Chatres and the population of Paris began vacating the city which was finally occupied by German troops three days later. At long last the Luftwaffe was able to focus its attention on the western Channel and Atlantic ports where the remnants of the allied forces were still being evacuated to England.

Despite recent reinforcement by fresh squadrons from England, those RAF fighter units still operating were pushed back to Nantes and Dinard. From here they would provide cover for the final movement and

evacuation of the Advanced Air Striking Force from France. What remained of the Fairey Battle squadrons had returned to England on 15th June; the last RAF fighter squadrons in France, Nos. 17 and 242 Squadrons following three days later after covering the evacuation of Cherbourg.

Throughout this final phase of the campaign the Zerstörers continued to operate in their familiar role; flying numerous bomber escort, freelance missions and ground attack sorties. But a little-known aspect of the western offensive in which the Bf 110 played a significant part, aside from the mainstream operations, should also be recorded.

Since the outbreak of fighting in Europe, Switzerland had vigorously defended its neutrality - denying its air space to all of the belligerent nations. However, with the opening of the western offensive on 10th May, border violations had become more frequent as Luftwaffe bombers, often damaged, tried to reach their bases in southern Germany by crossing Switzerland. The Swiss Air Force consequently adopted a tougher stance, the Messerschmitt 109 Es of its border surveillance patrols challenging any aircraft found over Swiss territory. A number of German aircraft had been attacked and damaged; three Heinkel He 111s having been shot down.

The German High Command were incensed and issued threats of reprisals which the Swiss ignored. So, on 4th June, Heinkel He 111s again appeared over Swiss territory but this time with a fighter escort of Bf 110s from II./ZG 1. It was a blatant affront, and in the combats which resulted, the Swiss claimed 2 Bf 110s and a He 111 destroyed for the loss of one of their fighters. In fact only one Bf 110 was shot down, a 6./ZG 1 machine which crashed north of Morteau with the loss of its crew. But clearly, and despite being heavily outnumbered, the volunteer pilots of the tiny Swiss Air Force were not going to be easily intimidated.

This was particularly irksome for the Luftwaffe, and Generalfeldmarschal Göring decided to bring matters to a head. So, at mid-day on 8th June, 32 Bf 110s of II./ZG 1 orbited the Jura mountains between France and Switzerland in another deliberate violation of neutral Swiss air space. Their orders were to provoke Swiss fighters into combat and inflict heavy losses in relation to the clashes of four days before.

Reaction was swift, 2 Messerschmitt Bf 109 Es of Fliegerkompagnie 15 arriving first on the scene closely followed by 12 more of the Swiss fighters. One of the first Bf 110s they engaged was a 5./ZG 1 machine flown by Feldwebel Manfred Dähne, who was attacked at 1,500 feet by one of the gaudy red and white striped Bf 109 Es. Dähne's aircraft received hits in the port engine which promptly failed, forcing him to break off combat and head for Freiburg. Separated from the rest of the Gruppe, the Bf 110 was now pursued and under attack by 3 Swiss Messerschmitts; its Bordfunker, Obergefreiter Herbert Klinke, maintaining a steady return fire from his single MG 15 in the rear cockpit. Klinke's spirited defence eventually forced 2 of the Bf 109 Es to break away and caused considerable damage to one which sustained 34 hits and crash-landed due to damaged hydraulics with a badly wounded pilot aboard.

This was the sole casualty suffered by the Swiss, who claimed the destruction of 4 Bf 110s. II./ZG 1 records confirm the loss of 4 aircraft, three of them over Morteau including that of Oberleutnant Gerhard Kadow, Staffelkapitän of 6./ZG 1. The fourth was the

2N + GN, the Bf 110 C of Dähne and Klinke of 5./ZG 1, which was shot down by a Bf 109 E of the Swiss Air Force over Swiss air space on 8/6/40.

Dähne (in the cockpit) and Klinke with their Bf 110 C, 2N + GN.

Bf 110 of Dähne and Klinke which, having finally beaten off repeated attacks from pursuing Bf 109 Es, was hit by flak which caused the remaining engine to fail and forced them to make an extremely hazardous belly-landing in mountain terrain near Laufen, south of Basel. Miraculously they both survived the landing although Klinke broke two bones in his hand and was badly concussed. Rounded up by the local militia they were transported to Lucerne under armed escort. Interned for the next 3 weeks in fairly comfortable surroundings, Dähne and Klinke were eventually taken by bus to Basel/Lörrach and repatriated on 28th June along with 8 other Luftwaffe aircrew; three days after the fall of France.

Due to his injuries, Klinke remained unfit for flying duties for some months, Dähne, unaffected by his enforced leave of absence, returned to 5./ZG 1 within days and was allocated a new Bordfunker, Obergefreiter Fritz Müller. On his own return to the Staffel, Klinke teamed up with Oberleutnant Günther Schmidt, flying numerous flights from Denain to test the operational capabilities of the Bf 110 C as a dive-bomber before II./ZG1 redeployed to Norway in November.

By the 25th June the German armies had reached the Atlantic coast and the Spanish frontier. Hostilities

Feverish groundcrew activity around the port engine of a Bf 110.

ended and the campaign in France was won. For the French people and the armed forces, particularly the Armée de l'Air, it was a devastating defeat. They had fought valiantly over the past 6 weeks, but with obsolescent machines, or more modern aircraft with which they had only barely re-equipped and were inexperienced, they constantly found themselves at a disadvantage.

French airfields and advanced landing grounds had come under continual attack and the speed with which the Germans had overran their bases completely disorganised the French ground supply organisation, which was thrown into total confusion. Meanwhile, Luftwaffe attacks paralysed communications. The Armée de l'Air had to contend with constant shortages of fuel, ammunition and spares, and their fighters were thrown into a ground attack role, one for which they were singularly unsuited, and suffered 70 % losses as a result.

Nevertheless the Armée de l'Air inflicted a heavy toll during the campaign, claiming 935 Luftwaffe aircraft destroyed of which 684 were confirmed victories. These were losses for which the British could have proved more grateful, representing as they did a significant number of aircraft and crews who would not be

continuing the battle against the RAF over the coming months. But it had cost the French dear, 201 of their pilots aid aircrew being killed, another 231 wounded and 31 more taken prisoner.

For the Zerstörer units it was a time of replenishment and for taking stock; Major Johannes Schalk's III./ZG 26 was typical of many. Their overall tally during the western offensive was 79 aircraft shot down and 8 damaged in combat, together with the destruction of 7 aircraft on the ground, 2 trains, 12 petrol bowsers and 23 balloons. They had mounted over 1,200 sorties, including 50 low-level attacks.

The overall contribution of the Bf 110 units had been significant. Repeating their successes in Poland, they had shown themselves to be more than capable opponents but, it had to be conceded, mainly against inferior single-seat fighters or more obsolescent types.

As heavily-armed escort fighters, often operating from bases far behind the front line, their considerable range and endurance time and again proved invaluable in providing vital fighter cover for German bomber raids. Even as a ground attack aircraft the Bf 110 had demonstrated considerable flexibility and potential, its capabilities as a fighter-bomber only recently beginning

Bf 110 C, 2N+DC, of Stab, II./ZG 1 with damage to the leading edge of the starboard wing. Note the rear wheel has a whitewall tyre, still an occasional occurrence in 1940. Aircraft 'D' of the Gruppenstab was usually allocated to the Nachrichtensoffizier; this aircraft, therefore, was probably that of Oblt. Florenz.

June, near Le Havre. Victor Mölders is in the tank, with Oblt. Wandam pointing the stick at him.

to be fully recognised and explored.

In fighter combats over Belgium, Holland and France it had been shown that, particularly when in the hands of an experienced pilot, the Bf 110 could hold its own against most types including the RAF Hurricane. But in the Spitfire, encountered for the first time over Dunkirk, they had more than met their match. Yet certain Zerstörer pilots remained unconvinced of this. Those who flew the Bf 110 with some flair and a certain élan; and in combat situations invariably flat out at full emergency boost, had no such qualms.

The Luftwaffe was again the victor and a fresh generation of its heroes were lauded in the German press. It had played a significant role in support of a new and revolutionary form of warfare which had achieved unparalleled success. Morale and confidence among its combat units was justifiably high. Over the next few weeks they would be reorganising and settling into new bases, replacing personnel losses with fresh crews and refitting with new aircraft for a fresh onslaught against England.

But many had begun to realise that they now had to contend with a fiercely determined and doggedly resolute foe who faced them across 20 miles of English Channel. It was going to be a costly and bloody affair.

Loss returns for the campaigns in Denmark and Norway in April/May 1940 fall outside the main scope of this book. It was not the intention to list all the loss/damage incurred by the Bf 110 units over Denmark and Norway, but the following list for I./ZG 76 gives an idea of the level of casualties experienced by the Bf 110 units involved and may be taken as being representative.

Gruppenstab	Hptm. Reinecke (Gruppenkommandeur)	Pilot	Killed	30th April
Gruppenstab	Ogefr June	Bordfunker	Killed	30th April
Gruppenstab	Oblt. Jäger	Pilot	POW	29th May
Gruppenstab	Uffz. Feick	Bordfunker	POW	29th May
Gruppenstab	Uffz. Eichert	Bordfunker	Wounded	29th May
1st Staffel	Lt. Kort	Pilot	Killed	9th April
1st Staffel	Ogefr. Bockheimer	Bordfunker	Killed	9th April
1st Staffel	Uffz. Jacobi	Bordfunker	Killed	12th May
2nd Staffel	Lt. Stahlbusch	Pilot	Killed	24th April
3rd Staffel	Lt. Habben	Pilot	Killed	9th April
3rd Staffel	Uffz. Wengarz	Bordfunker	Killed	9th April
3rd Staffel	Uffz. Grams	Pilot	Killed	9th April
3rd Staffel	Ogefr. Türke	Bordfunker	Killed	9th April
3rd Staffel	Ofw. Fleischmann	Pilot	Killed	30th April
3rd Staffel	Ogefr. Mierke	Bordfunker	Killed	30th April

A Luftwaffe band plays in the background behind the Bf 110 C, L1 + XB, of the Gruppenkommandeur of V.(Z)/LG 1, Hptm. Horst Liensberger. Taken at St. Marie, in Belgium, this photograph shows a very unusual style of non-standard fuselage cross. It can be clearly seen that part of the standard-sized white area of the cross has been overpainted; the reason for this is unknown.

Two Staffelkapitäne of I. Gruppe, ZG 1, Oblt. Martin Lutz (middle) of 1st Staffel,and Oblt. Walter Ehle (right) of 3rd Staffel pose prouldy beside one of the cars used in the races with the Bugatti shown earlier with Victor Mölders.

From left: Wolfgang Falck; Oblt. Wandam, Gruppenadjutant, I./ZG 1; Albert Kesselring and the airfield commanding officer, at Kirchhellen.

Officers of I./ZG 1 at the Channel coast in June. From left, Oblt. Wandam, Stabsarzt Dr. Sieke and Oblt. Mölders.

LOSS TABLES - MAY/JUNE 1940

Date	Name of crew and rank	Unit	Status	Fate	Aircraft Code & W. Nr.	Damage state	Reason for casualty	Place
10.05.40	Uffz. Helmut Voss Ogefr. Willi Steffen	4./ZG 1 4./ZG 1	P Bf	POW POW	Bf 110	90%	Shot down by AA over Vlissingen Crew captured	Goesche Sas
10.05.40	Fw. Hannes Reimann Ogefr. Heinrich Röwe	4./ZG 26 4./ZG 26	P Bf	POW K	Bf 110	100%	Failed to return from combat mission.	East of Rethel.
11.05.40	Lt. Hans Leickhardt Uffz. Willi Fabian	14.(Z) LG 1	P Bf	U K	Bf 110	100%	Shot down by AA fire during bomber escort mission.	St. Mihiel.
11.05.40	Uffz. Ludwig Leidenbach	3./ZG 1	Bf	W	Bf 110		Damaged by AA fire.	Gorinchen.
11.05.40	Fw. Franz Stadler Ogefr. Kurt Knuth	3./ZG 1 3./ZG 1	P Bf	POW POW	Bf 110	100%	Shot down by AA fire during escort mission.	Gorinchen.
11.05.40	Uffz. Alexander Maske Ogefr. Gerhardt Schulze	6./ZG 1 6./ZG 1	P Bf	W W	Bf 110		Damaged by AA fire. Force-landed.	Leiden, near Bocholt.
11.05.40	Lt. Dietrich Möller Gefr. Günther Kergel	1./ZG 2 1./ZG 2	P Bf	U K	Bf 110	100%	Failed to return from combat mission.	Charleville-Liart-Rethel.
11.05.40	Lt. Walter Maurer Uffz. Stefan Makera	3./ZG 2 3./ZG 2	P Bf	POW* POW*	Bf 110	100%	Failed to return from combat mission.	
11.05.40	Lt. Friedrich Auinger Ogefr. Bernhard Höfeler	1./ZG 26 1./ZG 26	P Bf	POW* K	Bf 110	100%	Crashed and burned out	South-east of Hirson.
11.05.40	Uffz. Willi Weis Uffz. Erich Ebrecht (Pilot escaped from French captivity and returned to unit on 20.5.40.)	1./ZG 26 1./ZG 26	P Bf	POW* K	Bf 110	100%	Failed to return from combat mission.	South-east of Hirson.
12.05.40	Lt. Hans Gaffal Uffz. Aloysius Dierkes	13(Z) LG 1	P Bf	POW* POW	Bf 110	100%	Shot down during escort mission to Mourmelon.	Vouziers.
12.05.40	Lt. Helmut Schultze Uffz. Gustav Wiebe	13(Z) LG 1	P Bf	POW* POW	Bf 110	100%	Shot down during escort mission to Mourmelon.	Vouziers.
12.05.40	Uffz. Kurt Hartenstein Ogefr. Georg Conrad	13(Z) LG 1	P Bf	K K	Bf 110	100%	Shot down during escort mission to Mourmelon.	Vouziers.
12.05.40	Uffz. Herbert Jacobi	1./ZG 76	Bf	K	Bf 110		Killed on combat mission.	Near Bergen.
12.05.40	Lt. Otto Krause Uffz. Fritz Auerbach	4./ZG 76 4./ZG 76	P Bf	K W	Bf 110	100%	Engine and undercarriage damaged by AA fire. Belly-landed.	Zissenheim.
13.05.40	Ogefr. Paul Nick	2./ZG 1	Bf	W	Bf 110		Wounded on combat mission.	Gent.
13.05.40	Hptm. Roderich Küppers (Staffelkapitän) Fw. Erhard Behrend	5./ZG 1 5./ZG 1	P Bf	K K	Bf 110	100%	Shot down by AA fire.	Vlissingen.
13.05.40	Lt. Ferdinand Dunstheimer Ogefr. Heinz Bütehorn	3./ZG 26 3./ZG 26	P Bf	K K	Bf 110	100%		Mauberge.

* = Returned from French captivity following armistice.

Date	Name of crew and rank	Unit	Status	Fate	Aircraft Code & W. Nr.	Damage state	Reason for casualty	Place
13.05.40	Fw. Ulrich Ernst	3./ZG 26	P	K	Bf 110	100%		Mauberge.
	Gefr. Theodor Hoffmann	3./ZG 26	Bf	K				
13.05.40	Uffz. August Pfaff	4./ZG 76	P	K	Bf 110	100%	Failed to return from combat mission.	Valenciennes.
	Uffz. Fritz Radzko	4./ZG 76	Bf	POW*				
14.05.40	Lt. Wolfgang Schenck	1./ZG 1	P	U	Bf 110		Damaged in combat with. fighters.	15 Km. north-east of Braine L'alleud.
	Uffz. Josef Kehren	1./ZG 1	Bf	W				
14.05.40	Lt. Heribert Heisel	2./ZG 26	P	W	Bf 110		Damaged on combat mission.	Chimay, 40 Km. west of Maas.
14.05.40	Oblt. Kurt Brückner	2./ZG 26	P	K	Bf 110	100%	Crashed due to flying accident during combat mission. Cause unknown.	South of Vogelsang airfield.
	Gefr. Eberhard König	2./ZG 26	Bf	K				
14.05.40	Lt. Elmar Josten	6./ZG 26	P	K	Bf 110	100%		Solre le Château.
	Uffz. Josef Stangl	6./ZG 26	Bf	K				
14.05.40	Fw. Otto Weckbach (died 16.5.40)	1./ZG 52	P	POW	Bf 110	100%	Engine set alight in combat with fighters.	South of Diedenhofen.
	Uffz. Karl Klaus	1./ZG 52	Bf	K				
14.05.40	Ofw. Johannes Oertel	3./ZG 52	P	W (POW)*	Bf 110	100%	Shot down in combat with fighters.	South of Diedenhofen.
	Uffz. William Mentzel	3./ZG 52	Bf	K				
15.05.40	Ofw. Waldemar Gerstmann	1./ZG 1	P	W	Bf 110	100%	Pilot injured baling out follow-ing collision with Uffz. Eberlein's Bf 110.	1 Km. south-west of Kirchhellen.
	Uffz. Heinz Braunsberger	1./ZG 1	Bf	K				
15.05.40	Uffz. Helmut Eberlein	1./ZG 1	P	K	Bf 110	100%	Collided with Bf 110 of Ofw. Gerstmann.	1 Km. south-west of Kirchhellen.
	Ogefr. Gerhard Schlender	1./ZG 1	Bf	K				
15.05.40	Lt. Franz Mentzel	3./ZG 2	P	POW*	Bf 110	100%	Shot down on combat mission.	Vouziers.
	Gefr. Wilhelm Oechsle	3./ZG 2	Bf	POW*				
15.05.40	Oblt. Hans-Günther Koch (Gruppenadjutant)	Stab I. ZG 26	P	K	Bf 110	100%	Shot down in combat.	North of Chimay.
	Uffz. Kurt Wolff	Stab I	Bf	K				
15.05.40	Ogefr. Karl-Heinz Brockstedt	2./ZG 26	Bf	W	Bf 110		Wounded on combat mission.	Fumay-Givet.
15.05.40	Hptm. Herbert Kaminski (Staffelkapitän)	2./ZG 26	P	W	Bf 110		Returned damaged from combat mission.	Fumay-Givet.
	Ogefr. Karl-Heinz Brockstedt	2./ZG 26	Bf	W	Bf 110			
15.05.40	Lt. Karl Pertl	2./ZG 26	P	K	Bf 110	100%	Shot down in combat.	Fumay-Givet.
	Gefr. Alois Steiner	2./ZG 26	Bf	K				
15.05.40	Fw. Kurt Friedrich	2./ZG 26	P	K	Bf 110	100%	Shot down in combat.	North of Secheval.
	Gefr. Willi Neuburger	2./ZG 26	Bf	K				
15.05.40	Fw. Josef Kistler	8./ZG 26	P	K	Bf110	100%	Damaged in combat. Crashed attempting to land on one engine.	Kirchberg, Hunsrück.
	Gefr. Kurt Wengler	8./ZG 26	Bf	K				
15.05.40	Oblt. Hans-Jochen Knop	6./ZG 76	P	POW*	Bf 110	100%	Failed to return from combat mission.	Montcornet airfield.
	Uffz. Jakob Neumayer	6./ZG 76	Bf	POW*				

* = Returned from French captivity following armistice.

Date	Name of crew and rank	Unit	Status	Fate	Aircraft Code & W. Nr.	Damage state	Reason for casualty	Place
15.05.40	Lt. Gerd-Ulrich Jaschob Uffz. Friedrich Rigling	6./ZG 76 6./ZG 76	P Bf	K K	Bf 110	100%	Shot down in combat.	Montcornet. airfield.
15.05.40	Uffz. Hans Obert	6./ZG 76	Bf	W	Bf 110		Damaged in combat.	Montcornet airfield.
16.05.40	Lt. Georg Schwarzer Ogefr. Fritz Petrich	15.(Z) LG 1	P Bf	K K	Bf 110	100%	Shot down during escort to reconnaissance mission.	La Fere.
16.05.40	Lt. Wolfgang Schenck Fw. Robert Jaschke	1./ZG 1 1./ZG 1	P Bf	W U	Bf 110		Wounded in combat with Hurricanes.	North-west of Brussels.
16.05.40	Lt. Heinrich Bucksch Gefr. Heinz-Werner Roth	1./ZG 1 1./ZG 1	P Bf	K K	Bf 110	100%	Failed to return from combat mission.	North-west of Brussels.
16.05.40	Fw. Leander Gramann Uffz. Karl Ehemann	8./ZG 26 8./ZG 26	P Bf	K K	Bf 110 3U + FS (3096)	100%	Failed to return from combat mission.	Over Rheims.
16.05.40	Ogefr. Paul Seidel	8./ZG 26	Bf	W	Bf 110		Damaged in combat.	North-west of Rheims.
17.05.40	Oblt. Werner Methfessel (Staffelkapitän) Uffz. Heinz Resener	14.(Z) LG 1	P Bf	K K	Bf 110	100%	Shot down on escort mission for KG 2.	West of Rheims.
17.05.40	Lt. Kurt Schalkhauser Uffz. Joachim Jäckel	14.(Z) LG 1	P Bf	W U	Bf 110		Damaged in combat during escort mission for KG 2.	West of Rheims.
17.05.40	Uffz. Friedrich Schmitt Uffz. Heinz Schmidt	14.(Z) LG 1	P Bf	K K	Bf 110	100%	Shot down on escort mission for KG 2.	West of Rheims.
17.05.40	Lt. Helmut Schwabedissen Ogefr. Wilhelm Chranowski	3./ZG 1 3./ZG 1	P Bf	K K	Bf 110	100%	Failed to return from combat mission.	Douai.
18.05.40	Uffz. Otto Bräutigam	3./ZG 26	Bf	W	Bf 110		Wounded in combat.	South-east of Valenciennes.
18.05.40	Lt. Horst Hensel Gefr. Friedel König	2./ZG 26 2./ZG 26	P Bf	K K	Bf 110	100%	Shot down in combat.	30 Km. south-west of Mauberge.
18.05.40	Uffz. Erwin Landgraf Uffz. Fritz Mathis	4./ZG 26 4./ZG 26	P Bf	W* K	Bf 110	100%	Shot down in combat.	Lens.
18.05.40	Hptm. Eberhard d'Elsa (Staffelkapitän) Uffz. Hermann Rösler	5./ZG 26 5./ZG 26	P Bf	W (POW)* POW	Bf 110 3U + AN	100%	Shot down in combat.	Amiens.
18.05.40	Lt. Lothar Heckert Uffz. Ernst Berger	5./ZG 26 5./ZG 26	P Bf	POW POW	Bf 110	100%	Shot down in combat.	Amiens.
18.05.40	Fw. Hermann Schönthier Uffz. Aloys Komanns	5./ZG 26 5./ZG 26	P Bf	POW K	Bf 110	100%	Shot down in combat.	Amiens.
18.05.40	Ofw. Josef Auer Uffz. Matthias Nicolay	5./ZG 26 5./ZG 26	P Bf	U W	Bf 110		Damaged in combat.	Amiens.
18.05.40	Major Walter Grabmann (Geschwaderkommodore) Fw. Richard Krone	Stab ZG 76 Stab	P Bf	POW* K	Bf 110 M8 + XA	100%	Failed to return from combat mission.	10 Km. north-west of Douai.

* = Returned from French captivity following armistice.

Date	Name of crew and rank	Unit	Status	Fate	Aircraft Code & W. Nr.	Damage state	Reason for casualty	Place
18.05.40	Uffz. Helmut Jörke	4./ZG 76	P	K	Bf 110	100%	Both engines damaged on combat mission.	South of Denain.
	Uffz. Gerhard Schlabowski	4./ZG 76	Bf	M				
18.05.40	Lt. Jurgen Uhlhorn	5./ZG 76	P	K	Bf 110	100%	Shot down on combat mission.	Douai.
	Gefr. Horst Neumann	5./ZG 76	Bf	K				
19.05.40	Fw. Friedrich Helbig	9./ZG 26	P	K	Bf 110	100%	Failed to return from combat mission.	Farguies.
	Uffz. Otto Pirschalek	9./ZG 26	Bf	K				
20.05.40	Oblt. Fritz Lüdders (Staffelkapitän)	1./ZG 2 Stab	P	K	Bf 110	100%	Crashed on return from combat mission.	Outside Neufchâteau airfield.
	Uffz. Leonhard Baron	I./ZG 2	Bf	K				
20.05.40	Uffz. Wilhelm Ross	9./ZG 26	P	K	Bf 110	100%	Shot down in flames; abandoned by crew.	20 Kms. North-east of Beauvais.
	Gefr. Alfred Welzel	9./ZG 26	Bf	W (POW)*				
20.05.40	Oblt. Kurt-Wilhelm Heinrich (Staffelkapitän) (died 24.5.40)	7./ZG 26	P	W	B 110		Wounded in combat.	Over Sedan.
21.05.40	Ofw. Alois Steggemann	13.(Z)	P	K	Bf 110	100%	Failed to return from escort mission for KG 2.	St. Marie.
	Uffz. Georg Solluch	LG 1	Bf	K				
21.05.40	Uffz. Günther von Schemm	7./ZG 26	Bf	W	Bf 110		Damaged in combat.	Guise.
22.05.40	Uffz. Heinz Walter	1./ZG 1	P	K	Bf 110	100%	Failed to return from combat mission Crashed and burned out.	7 Km. south-east of Lille.
	Ogefr. Georg Rothenberger	1./ZG 1	Bf	K				
22.05.40	Lt. Dieter Nülle (Gruppenadjutant)	Stab II. ZG 1	P	M*	Bf 110	100%	Shot down by Morane. Abandoned by crew.	20 Km. south-west of Soissons.
	Ogefr. Alfons Hyrschke	Stab II.	Bf	M*				
23.05.40	Oblt. Günther Specht (Gruppenadjutant)	Stab I. ZG 26	P	W	Bf 110 U8+BB		Damaged in combat.	Between Boulogne and Calais.
	Uffz. Fritz Fischer	Stab I.	Bf	W				
23.05.40	Ogefr Willi Kirberg	3./ZG 26	Bf	W	Bf 110		Wounded in combat.	Calais.
23.05.40	Lt. Werner Guth	6./ZG 76	P	W	Bf 110 M8+GP		Damaged in combat.	Calais.
	Uffz. Kurt Niedzwetski (died 29.5.40)	6./ZG 76	Bf	W				
24.05.40	Hptm. Rolf Kaldrack (Staffelkapitän)	4./ZG 1	P	W	Bf 110		Crashed due to undercarriage failure on landing.	Trier-Euren.
	Fw. Erich Hermanski	4./ZG 1	Bf	W				
24.05.40	Fw. Heinz Supke	9./ZG 26	P	K	Bf 110	100%	Suffered engine failure during combat mission; abandoned by crew.	South-east of Amiens.
	Gefr. Karl Schödl	9./ZG 26	Bf	U				
24.05.40	Lt. Lothar Hagen	3./ZG 52	P	K	Bf 110	100%	Crashed during routine test flight.	Metlach/Saar.
	Ofw. Heinrich Hein.	3./ZG 52	Obwmstr.	K				
25.05.40	Lt. Hans-Joachim von Rochow	2./ZG 26	P	W	Bf 110		Damaged on combat mission.	Emptinne.
	Uffz. Josef Benkelmann	2./ZG 26	Bf	W				
25.05.40	Lt. Herbert Peters (Gruppenadjutant)	Stab II. ZG 76	P	K	Bf 110	100%	Shot down in combat.	Calais-Ardres-Gravelines area.
	Uffz. Anton Stumpf	Stab II.	Bf	K				

* = Returned from French captivity following armistice.

Date	Name of crew and rank	Unit	Status	Fate	Aircraft Code & W. Nr.	Damage state	Reason for casualty	Place
26.05.40	Oblt. Konrad Martin (Gruppe Technical Offizier)	Stab I. ZG 1	P	K	Bf 110	100%	Failed to return from combat mission.	Calais.
	Fw. Herbert Kräft	Stab I.	Bf	W				
26.05.40	Lt. Werner Kleinecke	Stab I. ZG 1	P	W*	Bf 110	100%	Failed to return from combat mission.	Calais.
	Uffz. Otto Schamberger		Bf	W*				
26.05.40	Lt. Georg Wölfle	1./ZG 1	P	K	Bf 110	100%	Shot down in combat.	Ostend.
	Fw. Robert Schulze	1./ZG 1	Bf	W*				
26.05.40	Uffz. Erich Michi	1./ZG 1	P	W*	Bf 110	100%	Shot down in combat.	Ostend.
	Ogefr. Otto Hoffmann	1./ZG 1	Bf	K				
26.05.40	Major Johannes Gentzen (Gruppenkommandeur)	Stab I. ZG 2	P	K	Bf 110	100%	Crashed on take-off following RAF bombing attack on airfield.	Neufchâteau.
	Lt. Hartwig-Borris Domeier (Gruppenadjutant)	Stab I.	BS	K				
26.05.40	Lt Hans Rosenkranz	3./ZG 2	P	K	Bf 110	100%	Crashed into parked Ju 52 landing cross-wind and exploded.	Neufchâteau. airfield.
26.05.40	Ogefr. Heinz Schröter	3./ZG 2	Bf	W			Control surfaces damaged when cockpit jettisoned prior to force-landing. Crashed into a truck.	Neufchâteau airfield.
27.05.40	Gefr. Hans Nickel	5./ZG 1	Bf	W	Bf 110		Damaged in combat with with Spitfires.	10 Km. north-west of Dunkirk.
27.05.40	Uffz. Karl Berndt	1./ZG 26	Bf	K	Bf 110		Killed on combat mission.	Dunkirk.
27.05.40	Lt. Christian-Friedrich von Neumann (Gruppenadjutant)	Stab I. ZG 52	P	K	Bf 110	100%	Shot down in combat with RAF fighters.	North of Calais.
	Uffz. Hermann Laudemann	Stab I.	Bf	W*				
27.05.40	Lt. Gerhard Borrmann	2./ZG 52	P	K	Bf 110	100%	Shot down into the Channel by RAF fighters.	Off Calais.
	Uffz. Hans Riebesell	2./ZG 52	Bf	K				
27.05.40	Uffz. Karl Kübler	2./ZG 52	P	K	Bf 110	100%	Shot down in combat with RAF fighters.	North of Calais.
	Ogefr. Fritz Günther	2./ZG 52	Bf	K				
29.05.40	Hptm. Werner Restemeyer (Gruppenkommandeur)	Stab I. ZG 76	P	U	Bf 110 M8 + AB		Damaged in combat with fighters during sortie over Bardufoss.	Over the Tjelsund, west of Skaarland.
	Uffz. Werner Eichert	Stab I.	Bf	W				
29.05.40	Oblt. Hans Jäger (Gruppenadjutant)	Stab I. ZG 76	P	POW	Bf 110 M8 + LL	100%	Shot down by Norwegian fighter fighter during sortie over Bardufoss.	Over the Tjelsund, west of Skaarland.
	Uffz. Helmut Feick	Stab I.	Bf	POW				
29.05.40	Uffz. Albert Links	5./ZG 76	Bf	I	Bf 110		Damaged in combat; force-landed.	20 Km. north-west of St. Omer.
30.05.40	Lt. Engelbert Eichler	5./ZG 1	P	K	Bf 110	100%	Crashed on take-off on cross-country flight to Trier-Euren. Cause not known.	
	Gefr. Hermann Book	5./ZG 1	Bf	K				
	Uffz. Josef Schmitt	5./ZG 1	1. Wart	K				

* = Returned from French captivity following armistice.

Date	Name of crew and rank	Unit	Status	Fate	Aircraft Code & W. Nr.	Damage state	Reason for casualty	Place
01.06.40	Oblt. Jürgen Möller Uffz. Karl Schieferstein	2./ZG 1 2./ZG 1	P Bf	POW POW	Bf 110	100%	Abandoned after being damaged by wreckage from RAF aircraft attacked.	5 Km. east of Dunkirk.
01.06.40	Uffz. Martin Rutz	1./ZG 1	Bf	K	Bf 110		Damaged on combat mission.	East of Dunkirk.
01.06.40	Uffz. Gerhard Richter	1./ZG 1	Bf	W	Bf 110		Damaged on combat mission.	Dunkirk.
01.06.40	Uffz. Richard Müller Uffz. Hans Dietsch	3./ZG 1 3./ZG 1	P Bf	K K	Bf 110	100%	Failed to return from combat mission.	Over Dunkirk.
02.06.40	Uffz. Emil Flug	1./ZG 52	P	W	Bf 110		Force-landed on combat mission.	
02.06.40	Oblt. Hans-Jürgen Kirchhoff (Gruppe Nachrichtens-offizier) Ofw. Herbert Mette	Stab I. ZG 26 Stab I.	P Bf	W W	Bf 110		Damaged on combat mission.	Transloy.
02.06.40	Oblt. Godborg Christiansen	4./ZG 76	P	W	Bf 110		Crashed on landing following damage to both engines in combat.	Haynecourt.
03.06.40	Uffz. Ewald Ahrens Gefr. Alfred Fiedler	9./ZG 26 9./ZG 26	P Bf	K K	Bf 110	100%	Crashed on landing due to combat damage.	St. Marie.
04.06.40	Uffz. Albert Killermann Uffz. Gottfried Wöhl	6./ZG 1 6./ZG 1	P Bf	K K	Bf 110	100%	Shot down by Swiss Bf 109 E. Aircraft abandoned by crew.	North of Morteau.
04.06.40	Oblt. Herwarth Ziebarth (Gruppenadjutant) Uffz. Johann Sisterhenn	Stab I. ZG 52 Stab I.	P Bf	M* K	Bf 110	100%	Engine damaged during combat mission. Believed force-landed.	Pont a Mousson.
05.06.40	Fw. Fritz Duensing Uffz. Reinhard Ander	1./ZG 1 1./ZG 1	P Bf	U K	Bf 110	100%	Abandoned following collision with Bf 110 of Uffz.Rinke during fighter combat.	10 Km. north of Rouen.
05.06.40	Uffz. Josef Rinke Uffz. Heinrich Meyer	3./ZG 1 3./ZG 1	P Bf	K K	Bf 110	100%	Collided with Bf 110 of Fw. Duensing during fighter combat.	10 Km. north of Rouen.
06.06.40	Uffz. Maximilian Maske Ogefr. Erhardt Schulze	6./ZG 1 6./ZG 1	P Bf	K K	Bf 110	100%	Shot down in combat during escort sortie.	Meaux.
08.06.40	Fw. Otto Beiter Ogefr. Robert Hink	4./ZG 1 4./ZG 1	P Bf	K U*	Bf 110	100%	Shot down in combat with Swiss Bf 109s.	Morteau.
08.06.40	Uffz. Alois Scholz Ogefr. Walter Hofmann	4./ZG 1 4./ZG 1	P Bf	K K	Bf 110	100%	Shot down in combat with Swiss Bf 109s.	Morteau.
08.06.40	Fw. Manfred Dähne Ogefr. Herbert Klinke	5./ZG 1 5./ZG 1	P Bf	U W	Bf 110 C 2N + GN		Crash-landed following fighter combat with Swiss Bf 109s	Laufen, south of Basle.

* = Returned from French captivity following armistice.

Date	Name of crew and rank	Unit	Status	Fate	Aircraft Code & W. Nr.	Damage state	Reason for casualty	Place
08.06.40	Oblt. Gerhard Kadow (Staffelkapitän)	6./ZG 1	P	W	Bf 110	100%	Shot down in combat with Swiss bf 109s.	Morteau.
	Uffz. Fritz Wunnicke	6./ZG 1	Bf	K				
10.06.40	Fw. Wilhelm Klöpping	5./ZG 76	P	K	Bf 110	100%	Shot down by own AA fire during combat mission.	Verneuil.
	Uffz. Willy Görlitzer	5./ZG 76	Bf	K				
11.06.40	Oblt. Günther Schmidt (Staffelkapitän)	5./ZG 1	P	W	Bf 110	100%	Crashed during return flight following combat mission.	Haslach, Black Forest.
	Uffz. Arthur Lotz	5./ZG 1	Bf	W				
13.06.40	Fw. Willi Weis	1./ZG 26	P	K	Bf 110	100%	Failed to return from combat mission.	La Houssoye.
	Uffz. Hans Bornkessel	1./ZG 26	Bf	K				
14.06.40	Lt. Werner Kuhlke	9./ZG 26	P	M	Bf 110	100%	Failed to return from combat with fighters.	Between Conches and Rugles.
	Gefr. Paul Eckert	9./ZG 26	Bf	POW*				
14.06.40	Uffz. Karl Wissmann	9./ZG 26	P	K	Bf 110	100%	Failed to return from combat with fighters.	Near Marbeuf.
	Ogefr. Willy Bülow	9./ZG 26	Bf	K				
16.06.40	Uffz. Heinrich Wilkering	1./ZG 26	1. Wart	W	Bf 110		Damaged during combat mission.	30 Km. south-west of Quevauvillers.
19.06.40	Lt. Werner Hoffmann	1./ZG 52	P	W	Bf 110		Damaged in low level attack on troop concentrations.	
19.06.40	Oblt. August-Wilhelm Bier (Staffelführer)	6./ZG 26	P	W	Bf 110		Damaged in RAF bombing attack	Boos-Rouen airfield.
	Uffz. Georg Schulz	6./ZG 26	Bf	W				
20.06.40	Uffz. Erich Michi	1./ZG 1	P	W	No aircraft involved		Low level attack on base by fighters.	Boos-Rouen airfield.
22.06.40	Fw. Martin Thier	2./ZG 1	P	K	Bf 110	100%	Crashed during non-combat flight. Cause unknown.	1 Km. east of Paderborn. airfield.
	Fw. Adolf Brutsche	2./ZG 1	Bf	K				

* = Returned from French captivity following armistice.

KEY TO INFORMATION IN THE LOSS TABLES

The following information is relative to the above loss tables, and those which follow later in this book.

1. All ranks are abbreviated. See glossary section for full German ranks.
2. In the 'status' column:
> P = Pilot
> Bf = Bordfunker
> BS = Bordshutze
3. In the 'fate' column:
> K = Killed
> W = Wounded
> M = Missing
> U = Unhurt
> I = Injured
> POW = Prisoner of War

With regard to the latter category, it should be noted that at the end of the Western campaign, many Luftwaffe aircrew who were prisoners of the French and the Swiss were returned to their units. Occasionally, as in the case of Oblt. Jäger and Uffz. Feick, they became prisoners of the British, and were promptly shipped over to England.

1. Wart Uffz. Grübener on the cockpit sill of a Bf 110 C of 1./ZG 1 which carries the final Staffel emblem of 1st Staffel. This emblem has always been ascribed to the night-fighter force; in fact it was designed by Victor Mölders, who took it with him into NJG 1 when he moved from 1./ZG 1 to night fighters at the end of June.

CHAPTER 3

NACHTJAGD : FORGING OF A WEAPON
JUNE-DECEMBER 1940

German night-fighting can trace its origins back to the First World War. But back in 1916 successful interceptions were ad-hoc affairs by fragile aircraft lacking adequate instruments and equipped with fairly rudimentary navigational aids. However these pioneer sorties proved beyond doubt that an aircraft stood out quite clearly against the night sky, particularly on bright moonlight nights, making interceptions quite possible. Under certain conditions, visual contact of enemy aircraft was not as impossible as had been supposed.

By the spring of 1918, the German Luftstreitkräfte had developed a system by which their night-fighters were operating in conjunction with searchlights and AA guns. These early trials achieved a fair measure of success and presaged, by more than 20 years, tactics to be re-employed with telling effect during World War Two.

However these techniques were overlooked or largely forgotten between the wars, no real effort being put into exploring or further developing the capabilities of the night-fighter by any of the major military powers. A generally low opinion of the practicability of this form of warfare was held by most military strategists of the period.

Prevailing wisdom was that 'the bomber will always get through'. The concept of an ultra-modern day-bomber, fast and well-armed, operating in large formations which rendered them virtually invulnerable to fighter attack, was widely endorsed.

The doctrine of subjugating an enemy through air attack alone originated in the theories advocated by General Giulio Douhet (1869-1930). His book, 'Air Power', published in 1921, was a major influence on the strategic thinking and air policy of many countries between the wars. Germany, along with most other military powers of the day, saw no military advantage to be gained from diverting scarce resources into a largely unproved and unnecessary weapon like the night-fighter.

Air defence of Germany by fighters was considered of secondary importance, most serious development work by the Luftwaffe before the Second World War concentrating on the dive-bomber and the AA gun. Defence against the night bomber was to be the exclusive preserve of the Flak forces who were considered to be the elite arm of the Luftwaffe. Certainly their guns, searchlights and prediction systems were by far the best in the world at the time.

The Luftwaffe's excellent 88 mm. AA gun was more successful in engaging and destroying targets at night than any aircraft then flying. But the belief that its further development could keep pace with, or even exceed, future aircraft performance proved to be a fallacy which resulted in serious over-dependence on the Flak forces as Germany's main defence against the night bomber.

Thus, at the outbreak of war, 40% of the Luftwaffe's total strength comprised bombers and dive-bombers. Fighters represented only 30% of the complement, and even this included fighter-bombers fulfilling a dual role. Only after the outbreak of war did the Luftwaffe General Staff even begin to consider seriously the need for, and potential value of, a dedicated specialised night-fighter arm.

Yet as early as May 1936 Hauptmann Blumensaat's II./JG 132 was involved in night sorties over Berlin acting in co-operation with searchlights and re-learning the lessons from 1918. These trials were later extended by JG 134 and JG 137 who flew within specified 'control zones' and operated as an adjunct to the Flak. No dedicated night-fighter units were formally established as a result of these experiments but operational trials were continued.

Hauptmann Blumensaat was a committed advocate of the night-fighter, but it was not until 1st February 1939 that the Luftwaffe's first night-fighter unit was activated with the formation of 10./JG 131 at Döberitz equipped with Arado Ar 68s. A second was formed on 1st June, 10./JG 132, but several other Nachtjagdgruppen formed at the same time switched to day-fighter status shortly before the opening of the Polish campaign, exchanging their Ar 68s for Messerschmitt Bf 109 Ds.

In the early months of the war, to counter increasing British and French night-bomber incursions over the Reich, three additional night-fighter Staffeln were formed: 10.(N)/JG 26 at Bonn-Hangelar; 10.(N)/ZG 26 with detachments across Northern Germany and 10.(N)/JG 53 based at Heilbronn. Formed to support the Flak protecting Cologne and Stuttgart, these units flew twilight sorties but, lacking any proper ground control, they were not very successful in intercepting enemy bombers. Their failure to do so almost certainly influenced Luftwaffe policy, determined around that time, not to extend the night-fighter force.

Before the end of 1939, these units were all amalgamated to form IV.(N)/JG 2 commanded by Hauptmann Blumensaat. From his HQ at Jever, Blumensaat's night-fighters operated as detached flights, spread across most of north-west Germany directly in the path of RAF bombers. They operated elderly Messerschmitt Bf 109 Ds and acted in conjunction with local searchlights who provided the necessary ground control. But again, results were disappointing, their first and only success coming on the night of 9th July

when Feldwebel Paul Förster shot down a No. 10 Squadron Whitley over Heligoland; its pilot, Flight Lieutenant Ffrench-Mullen, and his crew all being captured.

It was a start, and April 1940 found elements of Blumensaat's Gruppe based at Ålborg and Gardemoen where they joined the Bf 110s of I./ZG 1 and I./ZG 76 against the British bombers crossing Norway and Denmark on most nights.

The Zerstörers, plus the Bf 109s of JG 77, had achieved some notable successes, intercepting and shooting down several RAF bombers during the late evenings and early mornings when twilight conditions were favourable. The fighters were assisted in these interceptions by a German 'Freya' radar station based on the coast which gave them information on the bearing and range of an enemy aircraft but, given the available technology, could not yet determine altitude.

This initiative was the brainchild of Hauptmann Wolfgang Falck, Gruppenkommandeur of I./ZG 1, who, along with pilots selected for their blind-flying experience, pursued the RAF bombers as they returned over the North Sea shortly before daybreak. In addition to Falck himself, Oberleutnants Werner Streib, Walter Ehle, Martin Lutz, Victor Mölders and Feldwebel Martin Thier were among those involved in these pioneering sorties.

Falck takes up the story: "We were ordered to Ålborg in the north of Denmark. There it was that, at dusk, the British bombers, returning from their targets in Germany, would drop any unused bombs, or they would fly low and attempt to shoot-up our aircraft standing on the ground. Each time, we would get a warning from the radar: 5 minutes to go; 3 minutes etc., and we pilots sat in slit-trenches. That was simply too much! I looked for three particularly good crews to join me in finding out whether or not one could also fly the Me 110 by night. Three of us thought that it was possible if certain modifications to the instrumentation and exhaust were made. Only one of us had certain misgivings - Oberleutnant Streib, one of the most experienced night flyers. I made arrangements with the radar people and the local searchlight units, that, on being told about the approach of enemy aircraft, we would fly out to sea. We waited out there until the aircraft were returning and the radar station had given us locational information. We hoped then at the first light of dawn to be able to see the high-flying aircraft against the light morning skies and be able to attack them. That was the plan."

Falck, encouraged by these early successes, found that visual contact was relatively easy to achieve given the support of even fairly rudimentary ground control. On 30th April, along with two 2./ZG 1 pilots, Oberleutnant Streib and Feldwebel Thier, Falck managed to engage some homeward-bound Hampdens which were lost in fog over the North Sea after exchanging a few bursts of fire.

"One day, suddenly the bombers were over us again. In spite of them dropping several bombs, four of our planes took off without airfield lights and flew out to sea. Certainly each one of us had seen a target.

Two of us managed to fire shots, but at such a range neither caused any damage and the bombers disappeared into the sea mist. The result was, therefore, that it was advisable to consider a night attack only with the co-operation of all three weapons systems, airmen, flak and air information, in order to plan a successful mission.

"With urging from all sides I now wrote of my experiences and at the same time recommended equipment, instrumentation and composition of the recommended ammunition. Amazingly, this report reached the highest levels, since shortly afterwards, General Milch came to see me to discuss these experiences and recommendations."

But shortly afterwards I./ZG 1 was ordered back to Germany to support the opening of the Western campaign and so, for the time being at least, Falck's theories on night-fighting had to wait.

During this hiatus, on the nights of 15/16th May, the first RAF bombing attack on Germany was launched after months of ineffectual leaflet raids. The weather was good but ground haze prevented the German Flak from mounting an effective defence and although efforts were made by Blumensaat's night-fighters, on this and subsequent nights, they failed to make any contact.

So, on 22nd June, shortly after the end of the campaign in France, Falck was again summoned to a high-level meeting, this time at General Christiansen's HQ at Wassenaar, near the Hague. At this meeting a bemused Falck was ordered by Göring to immediately transfer part of his Gruppe to Düsseldorf to form a 'Nacht-und-Versuchs Staffel' and trial his night-fighting techniques. They were expected to be operating that very night.

This urgency cost dear. During the hurried transfer of 23 Bf 110s, a 2./ZG 1 machine crashed just outside the eastern boundary of Paderborn airfield with the loss of one of their most experienced crews, Feldwebel Martin Thier and his Bordfunker, Feldwebel Adolf Brutsche.

Some aircraft (including the 30 mm. cannon-armed Bf 110 C-6s) and personnel of 1./ZG 1, including their Staffelkapitän, Oberleutnant Martin Lutz, went off to the newly-formed Erprobungsgruppe 210, the rest of the Staffel going to form the nucleus of 1./NJG 1 led by Oberleutnant Victor Mölders. This level of upheaval resulted in the inevitable splitting-up of some crews. Mölders lost his own long-time Bordfunker, Feldwebel Helmut Krappatsch.

This was to have unusual repercussions just over 3 months later when Mölders, by then a Staffelkapitän flying a Bf 109 fighter-bomber in his brother Werner's Jagdgeschwader JG 51, force-landed in England and became a POW on 7th October.

Ignoring standing orders on the subject, Krappatsch evidently had his Flugbuch with him when he and his pilot, Feldwebel Fritz Duensing, were shot down and killed two days earlier on 5th October. This document, which fell into British hands, was a boon to RAF Intelligence Officers, for it detailed every sortie Mölders and

Krappatsch had ever flown together all through Poland, Denmark and France. It was most unsettling for Mölders to find that his RAF interrogators seemed to know a great deal more about his combat flights than he did himself! That is, until they revealed their source.

Many Zerstörer pilots resented the sudden switch to night-fighting, particularly as they had just won a successful campaign and were looking forward with some confidence to increasing their scores in combat with the RAF. While more fortunate comrades continued to collect victories and awards, as Nachtjägern they stood a better than excellent chance of killing themselves in this dangerous sport of night-flying.

Virtually the entire Wehrmacht was on the offensive with victory almost in their grasp. Nachtjagd was a purely defensive and, as yet, unproven weapon which lacked operational experience, ground organisation and control systems. It couldn't be taken seriously and was considered by many as a bit of a military backwater.

Yet many Zerstörer crews adapted to the change very well and soon settled into their new roles. Teams such as Kollak and Hermann with 1./NJG 1, Reinhold Nacke and Kurt Bundrock with 2./NJG 1, and Hans-Dieter Frank with Stab, I./NJG 1 emerged to become celebrated Nachtjägern during the war. Meanwhile, many of their contemporaries who remained in the Zerstörergeschwadern died over England during the bloody battles to come.

On 26th June, in a further 30-minute audience with Göring, Falck was formally appointed Geschwaderkommodore of NJG 1 with full authority to choose his own staff. Subordinated to Kesselring's Luftflotte 2 and coming under Luftgau VI for administrative purposes, Falck was given the daunting task of creating an effective night-fighter force from scratch. It was an unprecedented appointment for a humble Hauptmann, but a position he would make his own and hold until 30th June 1943 when he was transferred onto the staff of Luftflotte Reich.

"From that time onwards there began the systematic building-up of the night-fighter arm, with all the necessary modifications to the Me 110. As a night-fighter the Me 110 was re-born. Even with the minimal of testing, the aircraft performed outstandingly in this role and remained until the end of the war the backbone of the German night-fighting force. From the once 'Ironsider' there developed the excellent 'Nightfighter'". As 'Father of the Night-fighters' Falck was awarded the Ritterkreuz on 1st October for his 8 victories at that time and his leadership and achievement in forging the Luftwaffe's premier night-fighter unit, NJG 1. By 1944 he would rise to Oberst and Chief of Staff to the Luftwaffe General for Training and survived the war to pursue a successful career in commercial aviation.

But on 1st July 1940 Falck's reorganised command stood as follows:

I./NJG 1 Gruppenkommandeur - Hauptmann Günther Radusch
1. Staffel Staffelkapitän - Oberleutnant Victor Mölders
2. Staffel Staffelkapitän - Oberleutnant Werner Streib
3. Staffel Staffelkapitän - Oberleutnant Walter Ehle

Simultaneously, Blumensaat's IV.(N)/JG 2 was subordinated to Falck's command to form the cadre of a second Gruppe in NJG 1. Blumensaat, clearly unhappy with this development, was replaced by one of his own Staffelkapitäne, who acted as Kommandeur until a successor could be appointed.

Falck selected Conrad von Bothmer to command his second Gruppe and had the pleasurable task of telling von Bothmer's commanding officer the news in person. More than a little annoyed by the arbitrary manner in which a subordinate officer could be spirited away by an upstart Kommodore of a non-existent Geschwader, he started to tell Falck, in no uncertain terms, just where he could go. Maintaining the dignity for which the German Officer Corps is justifiably renowned, Falck awaited a slight pause in the tirade to calmly announce that the transfer had already been sanctioned 'with the compliments of Reichsmarschall Göring'. It was a swift, stunning and eminently satisfying conclusion to the meeting.

As Gruppenkommandeur, von Bothmer was a popular and effective leader. But his subsequent career was to take an unfortunate turn and end in tragedy. He was unfairly disgraced when, in his absence, a particularly boisterous party in his officers' mess at Schleswig got out of hand leaving busts of Hitler and Göring festooned with fish. This heinous insult, duly reported by civilian cleaning staff, quickly rocketed up through official channels and, blown out of all proportion, left Kammhuber, and ultimately Falck, no option but to relieve von Bothmer of command and arrange his transfer to the Western front. He never got over it and shot himself in a hotel room in late 1941.

Before the end of June, Falck's emergent night-fighter force was expanded by the addition of Zerstörerstaffel KG 30 who were redesignated 4./NJG 1 and, by incorporating an influx of crews from various units including III./KG 54, soon developed to full Gruppe status, being formally designated II./NJG 1.

This new Gruppe was based at Amsterdam-Schipol and commanded by Hauptmann Karl-Heinrich Heyse. They were to operate as a long-range night-intruder unit and the different Staffeln were equipped with Junkers Ju 88 C-2s and Dornier Do 17 Z-10s. The bulk of its pilots were very experienced airmen and included many former reconnaissance and transport pilots, blind-flying instructors and senior Lufthansa aircrew. II./NJG 1 included such pilots as Paul Semrau, Heinz Strüning, Wilhelm Beier, Hans Hahn and Alfons Köster - all to become well-known night-intruders and Ritterkreuz holders later in the war. The command structure was as follows:

II./NJG 1 Gruppenkommandeur - Hauptmann Karl-Heinrich Heyse
4./NJG 1 Staffelkapitän - Oberleutnant Herbert Bönsch
5./NJG 1 Staffelkapitän - Oberleutnant Rolf Jung
6./NJG 1 Staffelkapitän - Oberleutnant Karl Hülshoff

This development resulted in von Bothmer's Bf 109s being designated III./NJG 1 from 1st July.

To co-ordinate the activities of the night-fighters, searchlights and Flak, and establish proper control systems, a Night Fighter Division was activated on 17th July with its Headquarters in Brussels - a command post being established in August at Zeist, near Utrecht in Holland. Nachtjagd Division I was commanded by Oberst Josef Kammhuber, who, as Geschwaderkommodore of KG 51, had been shot down on 1st June and only recently released from French captivity.

As pre-war Chief of the Luftwaffe Organisation Staff, Kammhuber was justly renowned for his great organisational skills and his name, possibly more than any other, would become irrevocably linked with the development of the night-fighter defence of the Reich. Many of the revolutionary innovations and counter-measures introduced during the war were as a direct result of his energetic support of the foundling arm. The award of his Ritterkreuz would be announced on 9th July 1941 following the 500th victory for Nachtjagd Division I. But as Inspector-General of night-fighters later in the war, he was to have serious differences with Göring and Hitler over defence against allied bombers and was, for a time, out of favour. He survived the war as General der Flieger, in command of all jet aircraft.

With no ground control system yet in place, Falck's Zerstörer's were forced to adopt the simplest of tactics. On receipt of the radio message 'Fasan', the Bf 110s would take off and circle within defined 'stand-by' zones which lay adjacent to the searchlight belt. There they would simply wait for a bomber to be illuminated by searchlights before attempting to intercept and attack.

This so-called 'Helle Nachtjagd', or 'Illuminated Night-fighting' had its limitations, for even if a target was sighted, the Bf 110s had just about 3 minutes to engage before the enemy bombers flew out of searchlight range. It was a tedious and frustrating business, pilots often spending three hours or more circling around without success.

Meantime, RAF Bomber Command's own targets, the industrial centres of the Ruhr, were prohibited areas for the night-fighters. These areas lay within concentrated flak zones which remained the Flak's sole preserve. NJG 1 had to content themselves with seeking out targets on the bombers' main approach routes.

On 20th July, Oberleutnant Werner Streib, Staffelkapitän of 2./NJG 1, scored the first victory using the 'Helle Nachtjagd' tactics. He had taken off from Gütersloh shortly before midnight and finally sighted his first target after circling in the stand-by zone for almost two hours. His Bordfunker, Unteroffizier Lingen, identified it as another Bf 110 so Streib approached with some caution and closed right up on it until they were flying almost wingtip to wingtip.

It was a Wellington! "I never saw an enemy plane so close and clear," he recorded later. "Not wishing to be shot point-blank by the rear gunner, I darted away in a 90 degree turn to starboard." Coming in to the attack from astern and one side, Streib was met by fire from the rear gunner. He closed in and concentrated his aim on one of the Wimpey's engines which burst into flames after only two short bursts from the Bf 110's machine guns and cannon.

"His starboard engine was burning. Two dots detached themselves and two parachutes opened out and disappeared into the night. The bomber turned on a reciprocal course and tried to get away but the plume of smoke from its engine was still clearly visible even by night. I attacked again, aiming at the port engine and wing, without this time meeting return fire. Two more bursts and engine and wing immediately blazed up. Close behind, I turned sharply away..."

The Wellington, flown by Squadron Leader Moneypenny of No. 9 Squadron, crashed and exploded near Münster, its bomb-load still on board. It was later formally acknowledged as the first victory for Falck's embryo night-fighter force.

Their second and third victories soon followed, coming on the very next night. Oberleutnant Walter Ehle, Staffelkapitän of 3./NJG 1, and Oberleutnant Siegfried Wandam, Gruppenadjutant of Stab, I./NJG 1, claimed a brace of Wellingtons between them - one over Münster and the other over Borken. No. 37 Squadron lost Pilot Officer Muirhead and his crew who crashed near Kleve that night and may well have been the subject of one of these claims. Another of No. 37 Squadron's Wellingtons survived a night-fighter attack which killed the rear gunner, but returned to base at Feltwell severely damaged.

More night-fighter victories followed in quick succession as Falck's pilots found their feet, Streib claiming a Whitley destroyed over Münster at 02:00 am. on 22nd July: Sergeant Monkhouse and his crew of No. 78 Squadron all being killed.

Meanwhile, Feldwebel Otto Wiese and Feldwebel Gustav Schramm of II./NJG 1 engaged a Wellington over the North Sea on the night of 23rd July, and filed the first claims for the Fernnachtjägern. Their target, from No. 149 Squadron based at Mildenhall, actually managed to limp back to England severely damaged - its navigator, Pilot Officer Sterling, killed in their attacks.

As if to establish a sense of balance, NJG 1 suffered their own first casualties on the night of 25th July when the Bf 110 of Leutnant Wilhelm Pack of 3./NJG 1 crashed at Coesfeld during an attack on an RAF Wellington. He died along with his Bordfunker, Unteroffizier Hans-Jürgen Hildebrandt. Before the end of the month, Walter Ehle's 3./NJG 1 would lose another Bf 110 when Feldwebel Werner Hahn and his Bordfunker, Unteroffizier Karl Huber, plunged into the ground near Ennigerloh, hit by return fire from a RAF bomber they had unsuccessfully attacked.

By the end of August I./NJG 1 had moved to Vechta, closer to RAF Bomber Command's approach routes and Werner Streib had raised his score to four, with a 'Doppel' scored on the night of 30/31st; a Wellington over Emmerich shortly before midnight and a Whitley over Arnhem barely an hour later. While surviving records are incomplete, these claims are believed to correspond with a No. 50 Squadron Hampden loss of Pilot Officer Smetton and his crew which crashed at Angerlo, and a No. 214 Squadron Wellington down at

Zelhen in Holland, piloted by Flying Officer Craigie-Halkett.

Maintaining a high level of activity and sorties flown, 3./NJG 1 were unfortunate to lose another aircraft on the night of 1st September when Leutnant Rudolf Schmitz and his Bordfunker had to abandon their Bf 110 over Lippborg when they suffered engine failure due to problems with the fuel system. Schmitz was injured on landing.

However more successes soon followed, Feldwebel Paul Gildner of 3./NJG 1 opening his score in the early hours of 3rd September claiming a Whitley over Sittard. Reflecting the difficulties of correct identification at night, his victim was in fact a No. 144 Squadron Hampden flown by Pilot Officer Churchill, which fell near Maastricht.

Two weeks later, on the night of 18/19th, Gildner would chalk up a 'Doppel', claiming a pair of Hampdens - one over Groenlo and the other over Zwiuwent. But again, he confused his Whitleys and Hampdens, for it was a No. 58 Squadron Whitley, piloted by Sergeant Crossland, which crashed at Groenlo. His second victim that night, another Whitley, was one of two aircraft from No. 77 Squadron that failed to return to its base at Linton-on-Ouse.

Later rising to deserved prominence among Nachtjägern and eventually succeeding Reinhold Nacke as Staffelkapitän of 1./NJG 1, Gildner had claimed his first daylight victories during the French campaign with an RAF Blenheim on 10th May and a French Morane on 5th June. He would go on to score another 42 victories, all at night, until his death in action on the night of 24/25th February 1943 when his Bf 110 G-4 crashed near Gilze-Rijen due to an engine fire.

On 7th September more changes were made to the embryo night-fighter force as it continued to grow and evolve. Heyse's II./NJG 1 was re-organised to form the first Gruppe of a new Geschwader, NJG 2. This unit were to continue specialising in long-range night-intruder missions, 'Fernnachtjagd', and I./NJG 2 moved from Amsterdam-Schipol to Gilze-Rijen to form the basis of the new Geschwader and carry on with its sorties over England.

Simultaneously, a new II./NJG 1 was formed at Deelen-Arnhem, equipped with Bf 110 D-1s and commanded by Hauptmann Graf von Stillfried. Formed from a nucleus of aircraft and crews from I./ZG 76, they had moved to Deelen from Norway apart from 1./ZG 76, who changed designations with the existing 3./NJG 1 in a move designed to spread night-fighting expertise around both Gruppen.

Around this time, and on Falck's insistence, von Bothmer's III./NJG 1 re-equipped with the Bf 110 which resulted in a spate of accidents as pilots came to terms with the handling characteristics of the new type. One Staffel, 10./NJG 1 under Oberleutnant Waldhelm, retained the Bf 109 until their disbandment the following month.

By mid-September a whole series of developments were being trialled aimed at improving the detection and ground control systems for night-fighters, 'Helle

Nachtjagd', as already described, having severe limitations. On 17th September Kammhuber ordered a Freya radar set to be coupled to a searchlight site near Arnhem. This arrangement, which was code-named 'Parasit', enabled the searchlight to locate a target and ground control to guide the night-fighter onto it through an integrated system. It effectively reduced the night-fighter's run onto the target and proved much quicker and more effective than earlier methods. Within two weeks, a second installation at Zutphen had assisted in the first 'Parasit' kill. It was a significant technological advance in the defence against the night bomber.

Meantime, the Bf 110 Nachtjägern continued to gain in both experience and ability, many growing increasingly confident in their new role. One reaching top form was Oberleutnant Werner Streib, Staffelkapitän of 2./NJG 1, who, on the night of 30th September, claimed no less than three RAF bombers destroyed within the space of 40 minutes.

It was a particularly successful night for I./NJG 1 with a fourth bomber, a Wellington, falling at Löningen. This was the second victory for Oberleutnant Heinrich Griese of 1./NJG 1 who had claimed his first, another Wellington, over Bramsche on the previous night - Pilot Officer Dingle and his crew of No. 37 Squadron all being killed.

The night's events were only marred by an unfortunate error when a Junkers Ju 88 of 9./KG 30 was also engaged and shot down near Kloppenburg, the crew bailing out unhurt.

Streib's first of three victims that night was a Wellington which fell at 22:49 over Bersenbrück. He then managed to infiltrate a bomber stream to claim a No. 10 Squadron Whitley flown by Sergeant Snell at 23:19 am. over Badberge and a Wellington two minutes later over Menslage. This increased his total victories at night to seven, but three in one night was a notable accomplishment which had a significant impact on the growing morale of the whole night-fighter force.

In recognition of this achievement, 29 year-old Streib was awarded a well-merited Ritterkreuz on 6th October and later promoted to Hauptmann, succeeding Günther Radusch as Gruppenkommandeur of I./NJG 1. New names started to appear on the Gruppe's 'Abschußtafel' as more and more pilots started to gain in experience and confidence. Typical of many, 21 year-old Leutnant Hans-Georg Mangelsdorf of 2./NJG 1 claimed his first night victory with a Whitley over Arnhem on the night of 2nd October - a No. 58 Squadron aircraft flown by Flying Officer Estley, which failed to return to its base at Linton-on-Ouse.

Mangeldorf's next victim fell at Röwitz shortly after 3:00 am. on the 15th, but it proved to be his last. Approaching too close to his target, Mangelsdorf was hit by return fire from the crippled bomber and was killed along with his Bordfunker, Unteroffizier Hubert Winter, their Bf 110 crashing near Gardelegen.

Their victim was also reported to have crashed and was one of three victories claimed by I./NJG 1 that night. Oberfeldwebel Herzog of 3./NJG 1 opened his score with a Hampden at Gardelegen just before 1:00

am. and Oberleutnant Streib added to his growing tally with another downed at Kolbe. According to contemporary records, two Hampdens did fail to return that night, a No. 50 Squadron aircraft flown by Pilot Officer Davis and Sergeant Burt's crew of No. 44 Squadron. The only other loss reported by RAF Bomber Command being Squadron Leader Hinks of No. 9 Squadron whose Wellington failed to return to Honington, its crew being reported 'missing'.

Losses among the Zerstörer night-fighter units, due to flying accidents, mechanical failures, and in some cases over-confidence, rose sharply during October as the level of sorties flown increased. Hauptmann Graf von Stillfried, Gruppenkommandeur of the recently-formed II./NJG 1, was killed in a crash at Koenen on the 6th when an engine of his Bf 110 D caught fire during a routine flight.

His successor as Kommandeur was Walter Ehle, promoted from Staffelkapitän of 3./NJG 1, which was inherited by Werner Hansen. Ehle was to command II./NJG 1 for more than three years until his death on 17th November 1943 when his Bf 110 G-4 crashed on a night-landing approach to Horpmoel in Belgium when the airfield landing lights failed.

Development of night-fighter tactics and procedures continued apace throughout October, new Würzburg-A ground control radar sets being linked to the searchlights of the 'Kammhuber line'. These new radar sets now accurately determined direction, range, and, most important of all, altitude.

Experienced crews had long insisted that the enemy bomber and the night-fighter should be tracked by the same radar. Now it was possible, and, utilising the new equipment, three dedicated night-fighter zones were soon established covering the Zuider Zee and the Rhine estuary. Now separate ground control centres could track both aircraft within their own defined zones, each of which measured 30 Km. by 20 Km, and which pilots immediately dubbed 'Himmelbett', or 'Four-poster bed'.

The new system was rapidly extended to cover the strategically-important ports of Bremen and Kiel, adopting control procedures which, it was claimed, could vector the Bf 110s to within 400 yards of their target. But the tactics imposed by Kammhuber were considered too restrictive by some pilots and even less successful than existing 'Henaja' methods.

On his own initiative, Hauptmann Günther Radusch, Gruppenkommandeur of I./NJG 1, ordered his crews to revert to the old tactics, and with some success. 'Fips' Radusch, one of Falck's original Zerstörer pilots, made a very successful transition to night-fighting and would survive the war a highly-decorated Oberstleutnant and Geschwaderkommodore of NJG 3 with a total of 65 victories.

Meanwhile Walter Ehle's crews in II./NJG 1 persevered with the new system but failed to score a single victory. These constant failures proved very frustrating to some tyro Nachtjäger pilots, who weren't enjoying the successes they felt they would have had as day-fighter Zerstörers.

Oberleutnant Helmut Lent, Staffelkapitän of the new 6./NJG 1, went as far as submitting a formal request for a return to day-fighters. As Geschwaderkommodore, Falck gave the request serious consideration but turned it down, urging Lent to stick at it for another month or so when they would talk about it again. It was sage advice, for Lent later went on to become one of the most successful and highly-decorated pilots of the entire Nachtjagd.

On 16th October, Leutnant Ludwig Becker of 4./NGJ 1 and his Bordfunker Feldwebel Josef Staub, claimed their first night victory with a Wellington engaged over the Ijsselmeer. The Wellington, a No. 311 Squadron aircraft flown by Pilot Officer Landa, crashed at Oosterwolde. It has the dubious distinction of being the first victory gained by a Bf 110 guided by Freya radar operating in conjunction with AN direction finding.

Ludwig Becker had transferred to night-fighters from 14.(Z)/LG 1 early in July and teamed up with Staub to form one of the most successful of the pioneer night-fighter crews. Rising to the rank of Hauptmann and Staffelkapitän of 12./NJG 1, Becker would amass a total of 44 victories before their deaths on 26th February 1943 when their BF 110 G-4 crashed into the sea off Schiermonnikoog during a daylight sortie against American bombers.

On the night of 21st October, Oberleutnant Arno Walter, Staffelkapitän of 8./NJG 1, crashed on take-off from Stendal and was killed along with his Bordfunker, Unteroffizier Horst Hoffmann. Whether 'Puck' (mentioned in an earlier chapter) had followed him on transfer to 'Nachtjagd' or remained the scourge of Stavanger's hedgehogs is not clear. It was the end of a chapter and another pioneer Zerstörer pilot was lost.

The final victory to be credited to a Bf 110 night-fighter pilot before the end of the year occurred on the night of 24th October. Oberleutnant Walter Fenske of 1./NJG 1 took the honours claiming a No. 75 Squadron Wellington over Bremervoer at 22.40 hours, Pilot Officer Sanderson and his crew crashing into the sea off the coast of Denmark.

For the reminder of the year, it fell to the aircraft and crews of NJG 2 to continue the attrition of the RAF at night, most of their claims over England or far out over the North Sea. But as the end of 1940 approached, with Falck's Bf 110s now firmly established at Venlo, Leeuwarden and St Trond, Nachtjagd Division I absorbed more Zerstörer units as RAF Bomber Command's night offensive gathered momentum and the pressure for new Bf 110 night-fighter units increased.

What remained of V.(Z)/LG 1 was disbanded in October, shortly after the death of their Kommandeur, Horst Liensberger. The remnants were withdrawn from the carnage over England to Vechta where they immediately commenced re-training as night-fighters. They formed the nucleus of I./NJG 3 to be commanded by Hauptmann Günther Radusch, who relinquished I./NJG 1 to Werner Streib.

Similarly, the remnants of I./ZG 2 started re-training for 'Fernnachtjagd' early in October, its Bf 110 Ds forming a 4th Staffel in Karl-Heinrich Heyse's I./NJG 2.

Their first victory was claimed in the early hours of the 17th November when Oberleutnant Prinz Egmont zur Lippe-Weissenfeld shot down a Wellington over Medemblik. Born in Salzburg on 14th July 1918, zur Lippe-Weissenfeld transferred from the Austrian Army to the Luftwaffe in 1938, initially as an army reconnaissance pilot. After re-training as a Zerstörer pilot, he joined 3./NJG 1 from II./ZG 76 in August 1940 and soon became established as one of the Luftwaffe's most distinguished night-fighter pilots. Rising to the rank of Major, he died on 12th March 1944 when his Bf 110 G-4 crashed in bad weather at St. Hubert in Belgium. At the time of his death he was Geschwaderkommodore of NJG 5 and credited with 51 night victories.

As winter took hold, strength and serviceability in the Nachtjagdgeschwadern dropped sharply due to the constant losses from flying accidents and through increased enemy action. By the end of the year, less than 60% of their total establishment of 195 aircraft were serviceable, and, on average, each Staffel could only muster 4 crews. Units were spread perilously thin and had to be moved from one part of Germany to another in a desperate effort to counter the growing threat from RAF Bomber Command.

With the exception of I./NJG 2, all were Zerstörer-equipped, operating basic Bf 110 C-2s, C-4s and D-1s in exactly the same trim as their day-fighter counterparts - apart from the removal of the ventral fuel tank from the latter sub-type. By the close of the year, the Nachtjagd had accounted for at least 42 enemy bombers against a mere 30 credited to the Flak during the same period. And while the majority of these victories had fallen to the Fern-Nachtjägern, the Bf 110 had more than compensated for its failings as an escort-fighter and was proving itself most effective operating in its new role as a night-fighter.

Other aircraft types, some of them specifically designed for the task, were to be employed as night-fighters during the war but the Bf 110, in a bewildering variety of sub-types and equipped with increasingly sophisticated devices, would remain the backbone of the Luftwaffe's night-fighter arm throughout. It was mainly as a result of this new lease of life, originated in 1940, that the Zerstörer remained in production until March 1945 with the total number built exceeding 6,000 aircraft.

So, from fairly modest beginnings, Falck's vision of a night-fighter force would, by the War's end, have developed into six full Geschwadern representing close to 700 specially equipped aircraft, with six attendant searchlight regiments and 1,500 radar stations stretching from Bodø to Bordeaux, and beyond.

In the course of the war, they underwent greater technical and tactical advances than any other branch of the German armed forces, with over 7,000 enemy aircraft ultimately falling to their guns. They had flown a long, hard and glorious course since those twilight sorties from Ålborg.

Köln-Ostheim airfield in the early days of July. Personnel of Erprobungsgruppe 210 are in the middle distance, with a Bf 110 of the unit in the right foreground awaiting the application of unit codes.

CHAPTER 4

'KANALKAMPF' - THE CHANNEL BATTLES - JULY/AUGUST

Immediately following the fall of France, there was a period of consolidation and reorganisation for the Zerstörer units as the Luftwaffe marshalled its forces for the coming attack on Britain. Whilst many Bf 110 units settled into their new bases in northern France making good their losses in men and materials, some were reorganised to establish new units. Other moved back to Germany.

On 26th June, in a move to rationalise the tactical organisation of the Zerstörergeschwadern, two units were redesignated. Hauptmann Karl-Heinz Lessmann relinquished command of I./ZG 52, which became II./ZG 2, Major Harry Carl moving from Stab, I./ZG 1 as the new Kommandeur.

Simultaneously, Hauptmann Friedrich-Karl Dickoré's II./ZG 1 was redesignated III./ZG 76, moving to its new base at Laval on the 30th. Their Technical Officer, Richard Marchfelder, recorded his impressions of the move, "The airport crept into view to the east of the town, along the road to Château-Gontier. The runway was camouflaged by mobile haystacks, but they didn't fool us. The power lines gave the place away."

Laval was well-equipped with the usual assortment of hangars, offices and buildings, plus camouflaged revetments for the aircraft around the perimeter. "Included in the scenery were the usual abandoned aircraft tucked safely away from the area of traffic. Some planes were without wings. Four Potez 63s, in the company of an invalide Morane-Saulnier MS-406 stood in one corner...it was difficult to visualise that this ghost of a plane had given us such a hard time during the battle over France."

Ground crews were housed in barracks adjacent to the airfield, the NCOs being billeted among private houses locally. The officers found a 200 year-old château packed with period furniture and antiques and set in parkland, not too far from the airfield, near the small town of Entrammes. Leutnant Marchfelder shared a suite on the second floor with Hauptmann Max Graf Hoyos, Staffelkapitän of 8./ZG 76, one occupying the salon while the other took the adjacent boudoir!

Within days of moving into Laval, III./ZG 76 received orders to prepare a forward base at Lannion, 130 miles away on the coast, as a jump-off point for operations against England. Here, the officer's accommodation was to be much less imposing - a simple hotel on the beach at Plage de Tresmeur, their first floor bedrooms with balconies overlooking the sea. Somehow, the war seemed very far away.

The formation of Germany's fledging night-fighter force generated more sweeping organisational changes to the Zerstörer forces during this period. Those Bf 110 units earmarked as Nachtjagdgruppen set about the arduous task of reforming and retraining for their new role.

Hauptmann Wolfgang Falck's I./ZG 1 suffered by far the biggest upheaval. Most of the Gruppe's aircraft and personnel transferred to Düsseldorf on 22nd June to form the nucleus of I./NJG 1, while the 1st Staffel was split. Those 1./ZG 1 pilots with blind-flying experience accompanied the rest of the Gruppe to Düsseldorf under their senior pilot, Oberleutnant Victor Mölders, and formed the cadre of 1./NJG 1. The rest of the Staffel, apart from Leutnant Horst Marx who moved to the Bf 109 E-4/B - equipped 3rd Staffel of Erprobungsgruppe 210, transferred to Köln-Ostheim under Staffelkapitän, Oberleutnant Martin Lutz, and reformed as 1st Staffel, Erprobungsgruppe 210.

Erprobungsgruppe 210 was a specialist unit created to test, under operational conditions, the dive-bombing and low-level tactical support capabilities of the Zerstörer and the Bf 109 E. This advancement of the fighter-bomber concept being of particular relevance to the eventual deployment of the Bf 110's successor, the Messerschmitt 210, then still under development.

As a result of these changes, by early July, the Zerstörer units based in northern France for the opening attacks on Britain were deployed as follows:

LUFTFLOTTE 2

Stab, ZG 26 based at Lille - Oberst Joachim-Friedrich Huth
I./ZG 26 based at Yvrench - Hptm. Wilhelm Makrocki
II./ZG 26 based at Crécy - Hptm. Ralph von Rettberg
III./ZG 26 based at Barley - Major Johann Schalk

Stab, ZG 76 based at Laval - Hptm. Erich Groth
II./ZG 76 based at Abbeville - Hptm. Friedrich-Karl Dickoré

Erpr. Gr. 210 based at Denain - Hptm. Walter Rubensdörffer

LUFTFLOTTE 3

Stab, ZG 2 based at Toussous - Obstlt. Friedrich Vollbracht
I./ZG 2 based at Amiens-Glissy - Major Ernst Ott
II./ZG 2 based at Guyancourt - Major Harry Carl

V.(Z)/LG 1 based at Alençon - Hptm. Horst Liensberger

Initially, the prime objective of the Luftwaffe was to sweep the Channel of British shipping and attack its coastal ports. This, it was planned, would have a two-fold effect. It would prevent the passage of convoys carrying essential goods and supplies between the east and west coasts of England, thus tightening the blockade on Britain. It would also soften up the coastal defences and force the withdrawal of Royal Navy des-

'Freed' from the fire station at Denain on 10th July, these musical instruments and helmets were given an impromptu airing by groundcrew of Erpr. Gr. 210 while a bemused Lt. Karl-Heinz Koch, Gruppe TO, in peaked cap, looks on. Koch and his Bordfunker, Uffz. Rolf Kahl, became POWs when shot down following the attack on Croydon airfield in the early evening of 15th August.

The machine guns of this Bf 110 of 4./ZG 26 receive attention from a lone mechanic while his colleagues discuss something below. Note the ZG 26 clog emblem, and the unfinushed Staffel emblem on the nose.

troyers from their bases at Dover and Portsmouth.

This effectively cleared the Channel for a possible invasion, the lack of German supremacy at sea being substituted by complete mastery and control of the air over the Channel and landing points on the coast of southern England.

As a first step towards achieving this objective, a tactical battle group was formed under Oberst Johannes Fink, Kommodore of Kampfgeschwader 2, for attacks on shipping targets. In addition to the Dornier Do 17s of his own Geschwader, he was given additional control of the Junkers Ju 87s of II./StG 1 and IV. (Stuka)/LG 1. Fighter protection was to be provided by the Messerschmitt Bf 109 Es of Theo Osterkamp's JG 51, the first Jagdgeschwader to be installed on the Channel coast.

Fink's role was to secure air superiority over the Channel and to close the straits of Dover to shipping. From his command post on the cliffs at Cap Gris Nez, he would maintain pressure on the British while the rest of the Luftwaffe readied itself for the major assault to follow. Meantime, further west, Generalmajor von Richthofen's VIII Fliegerkorps was to attack shipping targets between Portsmouth and Portland.

While not subordinated to Fink's command, ZG 26 often flew fighter cover for his bombers. With its long range, heavy fire-power and endurance, the Bf 110 was ideal for armed-reconnaissance, anti-shipping strikes and escort duties over the Channel. Operating in the pure fighter role, it would also contribute to the

Luftwaffe's prime objective: the elimination of the RAF as a fighting force. Certainly, early clashes between the Zerstörers and RAF Hurricanes and Spitfires high above the English Channel tended to vindicate this policy, although during the first week of July, Luftwaffe activity was largely confined to scattered night raids and mine-laying sorties.

By 9th July, air activity off the English coast and over the Channel had started to increase as the Luftwaffe probed the English defences. Late that morning, 3 Hurricanes of No. 43 Squadron's Red Section, led by Squadron Leader Lott with Pilot Officer Miller and Pilot Officer Carey, were ordered off from Tangmere to investigate RDF plots approaching the coast. The weather was bad but, guided by ground control, the Hurricanes broke cloud 10 miles south-west of St. Catherine's Point and instantly sighted 6 Bf 110s of V.(Z)/LG 1 ahead of them and flying south.

Unfortunately for the British pilots, these particular Zerstörers were wide awake and spoiling for a fight. They immediately seized the advantage, turned about and attacked the Hurricanes head-on. George Lott's aircraft was well and truly clobbered, a cannon shell exploding on his armoured windscreen which splintered, lacerating his right eye with shards of perspex. Reefing away from the Zerstörer's attack, he sought refuge in cloud, radioing the others to return to base independently. Blinded, bleeding profusely, and with his aircraft on fire, he struggled back to Arundel Castle through the low cloud covering the area. He had de-

L1 + AK of 14.(Z)./LG 1 at the firing butts having its machine guns aligned. Note the light camouflage on the fuselage side, and the even lighter area either side of the fuselage cross where the factory codes had been oversprayed in preparation for the application of unit codes.

scended to 700 feet when flames finally forced him to abandon his aircraft which crashed on Fontwell racecourse. In the meantime, the other Hurricanes managed to extricate themselves from a brief skirmish with the Bf 110s and return safely to base, V.(Z)/LG 1 subsequently claiming all 3 Hurricanes destroyed.

Later that same evening, 3 Spitfires of Green Section, No. 609 Squadron were ordered off from Warmwell in pouring rain to patrol Weymouth. Here they sighted some Junkers Ju 87s diving through the clouds about 15 miles off the coast. Flying last in line, Pilot Officer David Crook had "settled down to enjoy a little slaughter of a few Ju 87s, as they are rather helpless machines...when I happened to look round behind. To my intense surprise and dismay, I saw at least nine Me 110s about 2,000 feet above us. They were just starting to dive on us when I saw them, and...they were overtaking us rapidly. This completely altered the situation. We were now hopelessly outnumbered, and in a very dangerous position...if we were not jolly quick we should all be dead in a few seconds." This contemporary account, though inaccurate, does give a vivid first-hand impression of those early clashes over the Channel when small formations of relatively inexperienced British pilots found themselves opposed by vastly superior numbers of, apparently, supremely confident and well-handled German fighters.

"I immediately called up Peter (Flying Officer Drummond-Hay) and Michael (Pilot Officer Appleby) and

shouted desperately 'Look out behind, Messerschmitts behind' - all the time looking over my shoulder at the leading enemy fighter, who was now almost in range. But though I kept shouting, (they) both continued straight on at the bombers ahead." Unknown to Crook, both Drummond-Hay and Appleby had their radios on 'transmit' so hadn't heard his warning.

"I have never felt so helpless in my life...at that moment the leading Messerschmitt opened fire at me and I saw his shells and tracer bullets going past just above my head. They were jolly close too. I immediately did a very violent turn to the left and dived through a layer of cloud just below. I emerged from the cloud going at very high speed - probably over 400 mph.."

The two rear Spitfires were lucky to survive this initial attack. Pilot Officer Appleby had switched his radio over just in time to hear Crook shout 'Messerschmitt!' and whipped his aircraft around to find himself under attack by three of the German fighters. He barely managed to escape by spinning, first one way and then the other, and expended most of his ammunition on various targets without result. About a mile away he noticed a great flurry of machines which was Flying Officer Drummond-Hay's valiant effort against the bulk of the Messerschmitts who had fallen on him from behind.

Crook emerged unscathed but badly shaken from this, his first combat, and turned back for the coast. "I

Zerstörers of 4./ZG 26 in a close formation low-level flight.

saw another Spitfire flying home on a very erratic course, obviously keeping a very good look behind. I joined up with it, and recognised Michael, and together we bolted for the English coast like a couple of startled rabbits. I made a perfectly bloody landing on the aerodrome and overshot so badly that I nearly turned the Spitfire on her nose in my efforts to pull up before hitting the hedge. I got out to talk to Michael and found my hand was quite shaky, and even my voice was unsteady."

The Sector Controller's practise of sending up what Squadron Leader George Darley of No. 609 Squadron called 'penny packets' of fighters to intercept often large enemy formations was bitterly resented by pilots. A feeling which was echoed across every coastal Sector of Fighter Command at the time.

Many of the more experienced British pilots then in squadrons, some of them pre-war regulars, fell victim to this policy. But striking the proper balance between an effective response to impending attack while holding back a level of reserve, against a possible feint, was a hard lesson the RAF had yet to learn. Such ignorance of proper tactics by both Sector Controllers and, it must be conceded, formation leaders themselves, was another factor.

Luftwaffe policy of sending over small formations of bombers with large fighter escorts was proving successful in drawing RAF fighters into combat at a disadvantage. The British fighters were extremely vulnerable to attack as they climbed to combat level, and the close format-ion fighting tactics they employed also put them at serious risk.

Major Johann Schalk's III./ZG 26 also flew its first bomber escort sortie over the Channel on this day, losing an 8th Staffel crew, Feldwebel Hans Langbein and Obergefreiter Walter Franzke in a brief skirmish with British fighters. But early in the afternoon of the following day, they would clash with much larger numbers of RAF fighters over the west-bound convoy 'Bread' as it steamed past Dover and Folkestone. The

Bf 110s were to provide fighter cover for Dornier Do 17s of III./KG 2 detailed to bomb the convoy, high level protection being provided by Bf 109s of III./JG 51.

'B' Flight of No. 56 Squadron was scrambled from Manston to intercept the incoming raid which, plotted by RDF as it formed up over Calais, had been accurately reported as a formation of 20 aircraft flying at 6,000 feet with another group of 70 plus at 12,000 feet. Flying in Blue Section, Pilot Officer Geoffrey Page found himself thinking that "six against ninety was hardly fair odds for someone going into his first fight. Why didn't they send up another squadron to give them a hand?"

For once, the Sector Controller had done exactly that. Correctly identifying this as a major raid, elements of three more squadrons from neighbouring sectors had already been scrambled to intercept.

Leading No. 56 Squadron's Hurricanes, Flight Lieutenant 'Jumbo' Gracie detached Green Section to attack the Dorniers while he took his three Hurricanes into a climb towards III./ZG 26 above. As Geoffrey Page recalls, "Out of the corner of my eye I spotted three machines of the other section diving to intercept the now clearly visible formation of twenty bombers. Then I saw the fighter escort we were to engage. There was no mistaking the ugly outlines of the thirty Messerschmitt 110s and above these another formation of about forty Messerschmitt 109s. My mouth went completely dry."

Gaining sufficient height, Gracie led his section into an attack on Schalk's formation. As they gathered speed in their dive, Page noticed that the Bf 110s were forming a defensive circle "to protect themselves from...our three British planes."

This circular formation adopted by Bf 110s and often referred to by British pilots was not always an entirely defensive manoeuvre. The idea that 30 Zerstörers would automatically protect themselves from attack by 3 Hurricanes in this way reflects the relative naivety of some of the younger, more inexperienced, RAF pilots of the time. Yet this notion clearly improved their confidence when facing such odds.

First observed by British pilots in France earlier in the war, the defensive circle often adopted by Bf 110s, or 'Abwehrkreis' as it was termed in Luftwaffe parlance, had two potential purposes. It was certainly a defensive manoeuvre, the forward guns of each aircraft protecting the tail of the aircraft ahead. But it also allowed a formation to effectively take possession of an extensive area of sky which they could occupy and defend for as long as necessary - when covering the approach or withdrawal of another formation, for example. Used in this fashion, it lured enemy fighters to attack at disadvantage a potentially lethal formation.

This more provocative use of the defensive circle gave rise to it being renamed the 'Angriffskreis' or 'attack circle' which, it was argued, had a more confident ring to it. Later, with the grim humour commonplace in any airforce, some Zerstörer pilots came to call it the 'Angstkreis' or 'circle of fear', their schoolgirl shrieks down the radio as they circled around prompting angry rebukes from the Kommandeur.

Uncertain of the best method of attack, Page decided to spray his guns in the general direction of two Bf 110s before diving through the middle of the circle. Opening fire on an enemy aircraft for the first time, the young British pilot was having the time of his life - until reality dawned. "The enjoyment ceased the instant half the enemy gunners opened fire at my diving fighter. Fascinated for a second by the appearance of orange glowing electric light bulbs suspended in the air, I suddenly ducked my head at the frightening realisation that the pretty little balls of fire were hundreds of machine gun bullets aimed at Geoffrey Page personally."

Collecting his thoughts, Page regained height and decided on an alternative method of attack which he hoped would be more effective and slightly less suicidal. "I positioned myself for the second attack. This was executed with more discretion, and I dived at the circling formation again, but this time almost head-on, and in the opposite direction of flight to the enemy. Through lack of experience I began shooting wildly at the Me 110s but nonetheless achieved the object of making the enemy break formation."

Throughout this furious action, the Bf 110s and Bf 109s were successful in protecting Fink's Dorniers from any serious loss, but the RAF fighters were more effective in thwarting their attacks, which were not successful, only one small ship being sunk.

In the space of 35 minutes frenzied combat off the coast of Kent, Major Johann Schalk's III./ZG 26 claimed a total of 5 Hurricanes and 7 Spitfires destroyed; Feldwebel Sindt of 8th Staffel and Leutnant Roemer of 7th Staffel both opening their scores. Leutnant Erich von Bergen, an 8th Staffel pilot flying with the Stabsschwarm, claimed two Spitfires, while Major Schalk notched up his own fourth victory, a Hurricane south-east of Dover.

Fast-rising star of 8./ZG 26, Oberleutnant Sophus Baagoe also scored twice, both Spitfires, raising his tally to six victories and maintaining his position as top scorer in the Gruppe. This popular 25 year-old from Flensburg was to claim a total of 9 victories during the Battle of Britain and would ultimately meet his death over Heraklion on 14th May 1941 while flying with 5./ZG 26. He would be awarded the Ritterkreuz posthumously having completed 95 war flights and destroyed a total of 14 enemy aircraft.

III./ZG 26's claims were wildly over-enthusiastic, and especially when added to those filed by III./JG 51, who claimed another 11 RAF fighters destroyed. Of the 5 British squadrons involved, only one Hurricane was lost, and this in a collision with a Dornier, whilst another was wrecked in a crash-landing at Manston. Three more RAF fighters returned badly damaged.

The equally exuberant RAF pilots were only slightly less optimistic in their own claims, a total of 7 Bf 110s being claimed destroyed with another 4 damaged. In fact III./ZG 26 lost 3 aircraft, another Bf 110 returning to Barley damaged. Of the 3 crews lost, only Ober-

Bf 110s of 7./ZG 26 move out for take-off on an escort mission. Nearest the camera is 3U + HR.

The Gruppenkommandeur of III./ZG 26, Major Schalk, takes a close-up photograph of the fin and rudder of one of the Gruppe's Zerstörers - no doubt one displaying an impressive tally of victories. Looking on is the Gruppenadjutant of III. Gruppe, Oblt. Barschel, who was killed in action on 27/9/40 along with his Bordfunker, Uffz. Hans Klose, in Bf 110 C-4, 3U + BD.

feldwebel Willi Meyer of 8th Staffel survived.

Busy attacking an RAF fighter, Meyer had been hit by fire from behind; probably from the Spitfire flown by Sub-Lieutenant Dawson-Paul, a Fleet Air Arm pilot flying with No. 64 Squadron. This attack destroyed Meyer's port engine which promptly seized, and also put his flying controls out of action. Struggling to keep his crippled Zerstörer in the air, but realising a crash was imminent, Meyer was half out of his seat when the aircraft hit the waters of Wear Bay east of Folkestone. Thrown clear of the aircraft on impact with the sea, he was eventually picked up and spent the rest of the war as a prisoner. No trace of his Bordfunker, Gefreiter Willi Rohde, was ever found.

The most notable aspect of this combat, deemed a significant engagement by the British, was the way in which III./ZG 26 had gone into a defensive circle when attacked by three Hurricanes and had to be 'rescued' by the Bf 109s. This led them to believe that, as one respected authority puts it, "This was early tacit acceptance of the fact that the Luftwaffe's long-range fighter, flown by the pick of the fighter arm, was as defenceless as a bomber and equally in need of fighter protection."

Eager British strategists seized on the fact that this meant that escorted bombers could only penetrate as far as London, the limit of flying range of the Messerschmitt Bf 109 E. Whilst undoubtedly true, the simple fact remained that German air superiority over the Channel and invasion landing points on the south coast of England was still a viable proposition.

This somewhat over-simplistic assessment of the Zerstörer's limitations also failed to acknowledge its other capabilities. Its turning circle may have been wider and its acceleration poor compared to the British fighters opposing it, but the Bf 110 still remained almost as fast as a Spitfire and even at cruising speed much faster then any Hurricane. When used as a high escort fighter, the Bf 110 proved a formidable opponent and a burst from its considerable forward armament usually proved fatal. It was to be another month, during which time the Zerstörergeschwadern became seriously depleted and demoralised, before Göring was reluctantly forced to concede that his much-vaunted Zerstörers could only continue to operate over England when themselves escorted by Bf 109s. However, in

Aircrew of 7./ZG 26 relax in the sunshine with Bf 110 C, 3U + CR forming a backdrop.

Groundcrew of 1./Erpr. Gr. 210 about their daily tasks, with a Bf 110 of the Staffel in the background.

Excellent head-on view of the 30 mm. Kanone installation under a Bf 110 C-6 of 1./Erpr. Gr. 210.

practise pure Bf 110 fighters were never given direct escort by their slimmer, faster stablemate - all available evidence shows that Bf 110s continued to provide fighter escort to bombers right to the end of the Battle of Britain period.

III./ZG 76 flew their first Channel sortie on the morning of 11th July. They were detailed to provide escort for Junkers Ju 87s of III./StG 2 in a follow-up attack on a convoy. The Zerstörers moved forward to Dinard and Lannion on the French coast as jump-off points, for, as with most convoys, the enemy ships were hugging the English coast.

Flying with the Stabsschwarm, Leutnant Richard Marchfelder recalls, "After take-off Dickoré made a wide circle to give all units a chance to take up their position. Sharp 10:35 we followed our course, direction England. We could see the Stukas in the distance struggling to gain altitude. They all arrived from the island of Guernsey." In addition to their bomb loads, they carried auxiliary petrol tanks under the wings to extend their range. "With every metre we gained in altitude the British coastline crept above the horizon by one inch, with the land behind peeping peacefully across the Channel. The whole damn thing seemed so ridiculously unreal, as if we were on our way to a picnic on a lovely Sunday.

"There was something very uncanny about this mission; it was too quiet. In contrast, on our previous missions, we didn't have to cross water, only anti-aircraft batteries shooting their garbage at us. This silence, and the lack of activity, was worse than a bunch of belching artilleries."

This tranquillity was disconcerting for, as the German pilots well knew, their approach would be monitored by the British defences and RAF fighters despatched to meet them. The Tommies also maintained standing patrols of fighters over their convoys which, although only small formations, could be quickly reinforced if any serious attacks developed. The tension in the cockpits increased the closer they got to the English coast, the German formation loosening as pilots and Bordfunkers scanned the sky for the first tell-tale signs of British fighters.

The strange absence of RAF fighters, so unnerving to the German pilots, was due to a simple plotting error. Unaccountably, this raid had been reported as a single aircraft and six Hurricanes of No. 601 Squadron from Tangmere diverted to investigate. As soon as they sighted the German formation and reported the true position, more RAF fighters were sent up but far too late to prevent the Stukas reaching their targets. They sank the 530-ton patrol vessel 'Warrior', losing one of their number, a 9./StG 2 machine, to No. 601 Squadron's Hurricanes.

But when the RAF reinforcements did arrive, they came literally out of the blue. Flight Lieutenant Walch, leading 'B' Flight, No. 238 Squadron, 'bounced' the Zerstörers south of Portland, his Hurricanes slamming sive.

Following two other Hurricanes into the attack, Dewar singled out one of the Bf 110s and concentrated his fire on the port engine which exploded under his attack. Obviously badly damaged, the Bf 110 went into a vertical dive towards the sea 4 miles east of the Shambles. Forced to break off his attack due to other enemy fighters, Dewar was unable to follow it down, but soon latched on to another which, already crippled, was gradually losing height and flying towards land.

This was Oberleutnant Gerhard Kadow, Staffelkapitän of 9./ZG 76, whose aircraft was severely damaged in the first terrifying bursts of fire from Green Section, No. 238 Squadron: Flying Officer MacCaw, Pilot Officer Mann and Sergeant Parkinson. Kadow, caught flat-footed, had not even been able to return fire. Now, with both engines disabled and his aircraft barely controllable, he was shadowed by two enemy fighters and desperately needed to put down somewhere quickly, before he was shot out of the sky.

Jettisoning his cockpit roof in the hope that it would hit one of his pursuers, Kadow ordered his Bordfunker, Gefreiter Helmut Scholz, to do likewise. Scholz radioed back that his cockpit release mechanism refused to work - it must have been damaged by gunfire. This meant that baling-out or ditching were both out of the question and decided Kadow that a belly-landing was their only real option.

Meanwhile, the rest of III./ZG 76 collected themselves and started to fight back. Marchfelder again, "We closed in at high speed. I corrected my position until the target was centred in my gun-sight, but before I was able to fire the Spitfire pulled up and away." (His recollection is at fault here for there were no Spitfires involved.) "For a split second I had his belly in my sight, and fired my cannons. There was no time to look around to see if he was hit. Dickoré was just ahead of me attacking the wing-man."

"I followed Dickoré who banked so tight I almost blacked out. Some of our squadron formed a large defence circle (which) a Spitfire and his wing-man attacked. Both were met by concentrated cannon fire and had to quit. Others were smarter: they attacked from below, hitting the unprotected belly of the Messerschmitts and scored hits."

Flying Officer Glyde of No. 87 Squadron, together with his wing-man Pilot Officer Jay and at least two other Hurricanes, was among those who managed to break through the Zerstörers' defensive formation and engage targets.

Glyde started hammering away at one Bf 110 gently banking directly ahead of him. After what seemed an eternity, it started quietly smoking and slipped slowly away on one wing. Gathering speed in its dive, the Bf 110 plunged vertically into the sea at incredibly high velocity close to the Shambles lightship. When the waves subsided there was no trace of aircraft or crew, the pilot probably killed instantly in the Hurricanes first attack.

From analysis of German losses, this must have been Leutnant Friedrich-Wolfgang Graf von und zu

Uffz. Joachim Robel, Bordfunker to both Herget and Nacke of II./ZG 76, leans against M8 + XE wearing his newly-awarded Iron Cross, II. Class. II./ZG 76 were unique in 1940 using 'X' as the fourth character fuselage code - the correct letter should have been 'C'.

into Gerhard Kadow's 9th Staffel as they covered the Stukas withdrawal. Although operational for a little over one week, No. 238 Squadron achieved a notable measure of surprise and would notch up their first victories during this action which rapidly spilled out across Weymouth Bay.

Kadow's Staffel, which was reduced to only 7 serviceable aircraft, was detailed to fly at 4,000 metres and cover the right flank of the German formation, another Staffel protecting the left while the third flew close escort for the Stukas. Their orders had been explicit, a pre-flight briefing by none other than the Geschwaderkommodore, Major Grabmann himself, had stressed the need to protect the Stukas whatever the cost - and he meant it!

Battle was soon joined by Blue Section of No. 87 Squadron, led by Squadron Leader John Dewar, whose 3 Hurricanes ploughed into the startled Zerstörers as they attempted to form a defensive circle, their radios suddenly alive with alarm calls. Circling with the others, Richard Marchfelder noticed that the British pilots already seemed to have learned one valuable lesson - they were avoiding head-on confrontations with Bf 110s. Kadow, meantime, managed a front-gun attack on one of the British fighters, but it proved inconclu-

Luftwaffe officers at rest. From left: Oblt. Hans-Joachim Göring, 9./ZG 76, killed in action 11/7/40; unknown; Lt. Friedrich-Wolfgang von-und-zu castell, 7./ZG 76, killed in action 11/7/40 and Oblt. Hans von Boltenstern, Staffelkapitän of 14.(Z)/LG 1, later Gruppenkommandeur of Erpr. Gr. 210, killed in action 4/9/40.

Castell who along with his Bordfunker, Gefreiter Heinz Reder, failed to return from this sortie. As well as Glyde and Jay, both Flight Lieutenant Walch of No. 238 Squadron and Pilot Officer Lindsey of No. 601 Squadron also claimed a Bf 110 shot down in the sea in this area.

Flying Officer Glyde, veteran of the air battles over France, climbed back into the battle raging above him and engaged another Bf 110 but almost immediately came under very heavy attack from behind. This was from either Hauptmann Rolf Kaldrack, Staffelkapitän of 7./ZG 76, or Oberleutnant Günther Tonne of 9./ZG 76 who both claimed Hurricanes destroyed during this action.

Cannon fire struck the armour plating behind Glyde's seat and, narrowly missing his head, shattered the central panel of his cockpit hood. He immediately threw his aircraft into a vicious turn and spiralled violently out of harms way. Eventually regaining control far below the main battle, he returned to Exeter with his aircraft damaged.

Many of the hard-pressed Zerstörer crews were less fortunate. Suspecting that his Bordfunker, Gefreiter Franz Sorokoput, might be critically wounded, Leutnant Schröder of 9./ZG 76 was forced to set his crippled

aircraft down on the water just off the Ney Breakwater, ditching deliberately close to a boat. This turned out to be the Weymouth lifeboat 'William and Clara Ryland', on station since early that morning, which picked him up almost immediately. But despite a wide search they found no trace of his young gunner, who must have been killed in the fighter attacks.

Schröder was landed at Weymouth and handed over to the military after a choppy journey to shore during which he ruefully reflected that at least his dog 'Ihla' would be well cared for. Richard Marchfelder had promised to look after her should Schröder ever fail to return, the TO. being by far the best person in the Gruppe to adopt his beloved 'Schäferhund'.

Meantime, Gerhard Kadow was crossing the English coast, still harried by two Hurricanes; Squadron Leader Dewar of No. 87 Squadron and Flying Officer Riddle of No. 601 Squadron. The Bf 110 was gliding down so slowly that both Hurricanes had to throttle back to avoid overshooting. After a cautionary final squirt from Flying Officer Riddle, Kadow pulled-off a good forced-landing on Grange Heath near Lulworth, Dewar circling the downed Zerstörer long enough to see both crew emerge apparently unscathed.

As Kadow recounts, "After our crash-landing I could

Two views of 2N+EP of Oblt. Gerhard Kadow, Staffelkapitän, pilot, and Gefr Helmut Scholz. of 9./ZG 76, which force-landed at Grange Heath, near Lulworth on 11/7/40. Both pilot and Bordfunker survived the crash.

not leave the aircraft immediately because I found that a bullet had hit my seat and caused a big hole." The bullet had penetrated the back of his aluminium seat leaving ragged edges which snagged his parachute pack and uniform, effectively pinning him to the seat. Wrenching himself free, Kadow got out and tore away the rear cockpit hood to allow Scholz to get out. They barely had time to clamber out of the aircraft, take off their life-jackets and exchange a few words before British troops started to appear in the distance.

Hurriedly gathering up their maps and papers and placing them in a small pile, Kadow attempted to set fire to them before the soldiers arrived. "The first thing to do was to destroy the Me 110. So we opened the fuel tanks and with the muzzle flash of my pistol I tried to ignite the petrol fumes, firing up to eight shots without success. Had I been successful I think the aircraft would have exploded and we would be dead."

To their astonishment, this prompted a rapid volley of shots from the leading group of soldiers. "During the time we tried to destroy our aircraft I heard shots around us. I went around the aircraft to find out where they were coming from and in doing so I was hit in the heel. The bullet entered the rubber heel, was turned aside, and my foot was hurt only by a flesh wound. After this, we both left the aircraft alone. About 20 soldiers stood up and an officer ordered 'Hands up!' I told him that it was unfair to shoot at flyers (who were) shot down. He said that we had tried to destroy our aircraft and he tried to prevent this. 'Be glad', he said, 'that you have not been shot in the belly.'" Mentally accepting that 'Tommy' had a valid point, Kadow resolved that if the Tommies didn't learn anything from them, then a flesh wound was a small enough price to pay.

A crater and scattered fragments are all that remain of the Bf 110 of Oblt. Hans-Joachim Göring, the nephew of Hermann, and his Bordfunker, Uffz. Albert Zimmermann, of 9./ZG 76. Both perished in the crash at The Verne, Portland, on 11/7/40.

Adding considerable insult to his injury, at his subsequent interrogation at Cockfosters in London, Kadow was startled to be greeted by the fact that RAF Intelligence already knew his unit plus the fact that he was the Staffelkapitän. Similarly, they had soon identified Joachim Schröder as coming from the same Staffel; but his deliberately terse responses to their questions failed to add anything to their files.

Unknown to them both, at this stage in the war RAF Intelligence was well ahead of the game and had correctly deduced this information from Kadow's aircraft, the first Zerstörer to land in England. Its code letters, servicing and maintenance documents plus his identity disc number yielded the British valuable intelligence data. Insignificant receipts from shops in Laval, found in their pockets, also suggested to the interrogators their likely base. Rattled, Kadow retained some small satisfaction in the knowledge that at least the RAF didn't know everything; they were clearly unaware that II./ZG 1 had been recently redesignated.

As the Zerstörers of III./ZG 76 withdrew from their first action over the Channel, emotions were mixed. Richard Marchfelder reflected, "A lot has been written about the elated feeling after a battle. Of course this relates to fit, healthy survivors and not crippled aircraft, with the pilot blessing every foot he got nearer to the

sanctuary of France. For those who had to ditch their plane, they had to face a different fate! The more the gap between them and the coast increased, the less the chance to be picked-up. In most cases they had to face a horrible ordeal of dying from thirst, caused by the blazing summer sun, in spite of floating in the midst of an ocean of water. Some corpses were washed ashore, some of them found a resting place in an unknown grave in France. Wounded crew members returning by plane, had no option but to suffer until the plane touched down."

Unteroffizier Alois Haas of 7./ZG 76 also flew on this mission, his 23rd war flight, landing back at Dinard physically and emotionally drained by the nervous strain of an hour and 40 minutes flying miles over water and the effects of combat.

III./ZG 76 had suffered a severe blow, but only when they had got back to Laval and pieced together an account of what had occurred did a true picture start to emerge. Richard Marchfelder recalls, "Our losses were heavy! They included Jochen Schröder, Graf zu Castell and that boisterous nephew of Herrn Reichsmarschall who stupidly tried to take on the whole RAF. Leutnant Graf zu Castell made a desperate effort to rescue him ... The old uncle stirred up quite a fuss after he had been informed that his infallible nephew was missing in action. He was naturally taking it for granted that Hauptmann Dickoré was guarding (him) like a mother hen."

Oberleutnant Göring's Bf 110 had dropped out of the combat over Weymouth Bay in a screaming dive and exploded with considerable violence on the Verne heights overlooking Portland Harbour. It left little more than a smoking crater and no trace of him or his Bordfunker, Unteroffizier Zimmermann, was ever found.

Back at Laval the airfield was a hive of activity as groundcrews and technicians swarmed over damaged aircraft trying to ready them for the next sortie. Officer-pilots with Staff responsibilities were given no time to relax after such a gruelling flight and combat. Leutnant Florenz, Gruppe Signals Officer, summoned all the Bordfunkers together for de-briefing while Leutnant Marchfelder, the Technical Officer, rushed around supervising repairs. Hauptmann Dickoré reported to HQ while his Adjutant, Leutnant Dieter Nülle, began the onerous task of filing casualty reports and drafting letters to next-of-kin.

Staying busy helped to keep everyone's minds off their losses. "Of course we had encountered casualties in the past, but not (so many) on a single raid!" recounts Marchfelder. "Perhaps another reason for our low spirit was our underestimated sense of reality; France was a comparative walk-over for us (and) we

took it for granted that this was to continue. Up to that point we considered ourselves to be seasoned fighters with moderate battle experience. Most of us had no appetite, instead we consumed unusually large quantities of hard liquor and wine."

Two days later, it was again the turn of Liensberger's V. (Z)/LG 1 to take on the British fighters in a mid-afternoon skirmish over the same area south of Weymouth. Twenty of his Bf 110s had taken off from Alençon as close escort for two Dornier Do 17 Ps from I. (F)/123 who were engaged on a photo-reconnaissance mission to Portland. As they approached the English coast, a squadron of Hurricanes suddenly appeared and, like a pack of wild dogs, fell on the German formation from all sides.

This was No. 238 Squadron from Middle Wallop who split into separate sections for the attack. Leading them, Flight Lieutenant Kennedy, took Red Section after one of the Dorniers who were both nose down and heading for home as fast as their over-strained engines could take them. Getting too close on his first pass, Kennedy was hit by return fire and broke away. He nursed his aircraft back to the coast but, probably badly wounded, stalled and crashed attempting to avoid HT cables near Littlemore and was killed. Meantime, the Dornier fell to the other Hurricanes who tipped it into the sea off Chesil Beach.

L1 + XB of the Gruppenkommandeur of V.(Z)/LG 1, Hptm. Horst Liensberger. The nose carries the wolf's head unit emblem against a very light camouflage. On the rear fuselage there is a slightly darker camouflage 'wash'.

Bf 110, M8 + CM of 4./ZG 76 undergoing an engine change. The white 'N' on the engine cowling denotes the fitment of the uprated DB 601 N engine.

The Zerstörers now became heavily engaged with the Hurricanes who were reinforced by three Spitfires of Yellow Section, No. 609 Squadron who had been patrolling west of Swanage.

In the course of a brief but hectic combat, several Bf 110s were badly damaged and Leutnant Hermann Eisele's aircraft fell out of formation. With both engines shot up and smoking badly, it slowly turned over and went into an inverted glide towards the sea south of Portland. One of the crew, Eisele or his gunner Unteroffizier Kurt Lochow, managed to bale out but their parachute fouled on the aircraft which dragged them down with it as it crashed upside down in the sea, breaking up on impact. Only pitifully small pieces of wreckage, the parachute and a life-jacket remained floating on the surface.

Liensberger's Gruppe returned to Alençon and reckoned the cost. In addition to the loss of Leutnant Eisele, two 14 Staffel aircraft barely managed to stagger back severely damaged and with wounded aboard, Leutnant Krebitz being rushed to hospital in Valognes. Back at HQ the Major beim Stabe, Oberleutnant Haarmann, quietly made a note of those killed or wounded on the day in an old exercise book. Over the next month this running tally would go on to record the loss of 9 aircraft with 16 killed and 5 wounded in the course of 34 missions.

For once, both sides claims were more realistic. In addition to the destruction of the Dornier, RAF pilots claimed 2 110s destroyed plus another 3 probably destroyed. V. (Z) /LG 1 submitted 2 claims in all but apart from the loss of the Flight Lieutenant Kennedy, as described earlier, there were no other RAF casualties or aircraft damaged.

By 17th July, the Luftwaffe had completed their preparations and were brought to full readiness. Air activity increased accordingly and during the latter part of the month and into early August, attacks on shipping and ports in St. George's Channel, the English Channel, the Thames Estuary and off the east coast were intensified.

The requirement for detailed reconnaissance on a daily basis now became a strategic imperative. For some time past certain photo-reconnaissance Staffeln based in France had been re-equipping with the Bf 110 as a faster alternative to their Dornier Do 17 M machines.

These reconnaissance Bf 110 C-5 Zerstörers were in action on a regular basis throughout the battle, but theirs was an entirely different type of sortie to the Bf 110s in other units. Not for them missions in Staffel strength, but rather a solo experience, or at best two aircraft. While single aircraft did not attract the same reaction as formations, when intercepted, the pilot of a reconnaissance machine had to call upon all their flying skills and abilities to avoid being shot down.

Instances of reconnaissance Bf 110s falling into British hands during the battle were rare, but the oppor-

Bf 110 C-5, 5F + CM of Oblt. Friedrich-Karl Runde, pilot, and Fw. Willi Baden, Bordfunker, of 4.(F)/14, shot down on 21/7/40, finally coming to rest in a cabbage field at Home Farm, Goodwood.

tunity for RAF Intelligence to examine a relatively intact example occurred on 21st July when Oberleutnant Friedrich-Karl Runde, together with his Bordfunker, Feldwebel Willi Baden, one of several crews attached to 4.(F)/14, became prisoners of war.

On 21st July, Runde and Baden were charged with undertaking a high altitude reconnaissance sortie over England. Runde takes up the story, "We...took off from Villacoublay, an airfield near Paris. According to the weather forecast we could expect clear skies and were ordered to fly high altitude reconnaissance (about 8,000 m.). For this purpose we had heavy photographic equipment installed. Before crossing the Channel we landed at Cherbourg to refuel and then headed for the British Isles, flying extremely low, between 10 m. and 50 m. to avoid the radar, finally climbing to the ordered altitude shortly before arriving at the British coast."

At the coast, they encountered a cloud layer at 2,000 metres, which negated all attempts to carry out the mission. Visual reconnaissance was also out of the question, so Runde returned to Cherbourg. The weather at Cherbourg improved, so with the Bf 110 re-fuelled, Runde took off once again to try to complete the mission. Arriving over south-east England, the weather once again proved adverse, so Runde pressed on further inland in the hope that matters would im-

prove. "We penetrated deeper and ran into a training aircraft and shot it down. Both of us felt very sad when we noticed the parachute of the young fellow didn't open."

The aircraft attacked by Runde was a Hawker Hart from No. 1 FTS being flown by acting-Leading Airman J.A. Seed, RN. The action took place over Old Sarum, and the Hart burst into flames following the Bf 110's attack. Seed jumped from the aircraft, but died of gunshot wounds and multiple injuries.

Following this encounter, Runde next engaged a Fairey Battle training aircraft, converted to an instructor/trainee configuration for training purposes. Willi Baden fired off a burst at this Battle, which received hits and was forced to make a wheels-up landing just outside Shrewton. Two 'Abschüße' for a reconnaissance Zerstörer was indeed good going!

However, things soon changed when three Hurricanes of Red Section of No. 238 Squadron appeared on the scene. Flight Lieutenant Turner, and Pilot Officers Davis and Wigglesworth immediately posed a serious threat to Runde and Baden's chances of returning to France, but once combat was joined, the Hurricanes did not find the Zerstörer easy prey. "It was a running engagement with E/A adopting most peculiar evasive tactics", Pilot Officer Davis noted in his Combat Report, "the E/A did most unusual manouevres, stall turns, half rolls, etc." In spite of his attempts to avoid the Hurricanes, Runde could not prevent hits being scored on his aircraft. "I thought we would be able to escape into the clouds, but they turned out to be some kind of summer fog that dissolved as the sun rose. That's how they got us. Both engines got hit and in spite of managing to get away from them...I had to make a belly-landing as both engines stalled, and we became POWs."

Runde and Baden's Bf 110 C-5, came down at Home Farm, Goodwood and, once repaired to full flying status with parts from Gerhard Kadow's 2N+EP brought down on 11th July, it was test flown on handling and performance trials by the RAF at the Royal Aircraft Establishment in Farnborough. Its last known repository was No. 47 Maintenance Unit, RAF Sealand, in November 1945. Its ultimate fate, however, is unknown.

Signifying the change in pace, westbound convoy CW8 which sailed from Southend was decimated by heavy and continuous attacks by dive-bombers as it entered the Straits of Dover towards midday on the 25th July. Half of the colliers and coasters which formed the convoy failed to round Dungeness and only two of its ships reached port undamaged. The Royal Navy destroyers 'Boreas' and 'Brilliant' who formed the escort were forced to retire back to Dover. Further merchant sailings' through the Channel were promptly forbidden and all convoys stopped - only destroyers and minesweepers continuing to maintain a presence.

It was a turning point, for two days later the entire Dover destroyer flotilla was forced to withdraw,

with HMS Codrington sunk and HMS Walpole badly damaged by air attacks. The Luftwaffe had achieved its objective and had gained effective control of the Channel. The Wehrmacht's invasion path was cleared - at least in daylight.

The Zerstörer units remained fully committed throughout this period with regular escort missions and armed reconnaissance sorties off the south east coasts of England. Apart from Rubensdörffer's Erprobungsgruppe 210, whose aircraft ventured ever closer to the enemy coast in search of shipping targets, Bf 110 losses were minimal. Not until 29th July were they again involved in any significant combat when the Luftwaffe, ominously, began to probe further inland.

Late that afternoon, Major Schalk's III. /ZG 26 provided 30 Bf 110s as fighter escort for 11 Bf 110s of Erprobungsgruppe 210 detailed to dive-bomb the convoy 'CAT' steaming 12 miles off Harwich. In addition to dive-bombing, Erprobungsgruppe 210 included in its formation three Bf 110 C-6s from Martin Lutz's 1st Staffel whose role was sea level attacks and flak suppression with their 30 mm. cannon.

The Zerstörers took-off from their bases on the French coast shortly after 1630 hours and arrived over the convoy 40 minutes later without incident. However as they commenced their attack they were engaged by 9 Hurricanes of No. 151 Squadron, based at North Weald but operating from Rochford as forward base, who were on convoy patrol. Diving on the lower formation of dive-bombers before Schalk's high-level escorts could intervene, Flying Officer Blair closed on one of the Bf 110s whose starboard engine burst into

Bf 110 fighter-bomber of 2./Erpr. Gr. 210 on 21/7/40 after a heavy landing back in France. Pilot Oblt. Alfred Habisch, brought this Zerstörer back, Bordfunker Uffz. Ernst Elfner poses on the port wing root. Note the word 'Jaguar' on the nose, a reference to the propaganda name given to the fighter-bomber version of the Bf 110.

A Zerstörer of ZG 26 after a force-landing. Note the single victory bar on the fin.

Bf 110 fighter-bomber of 2./Erpr. Gr. 210 with the inscription 'Uffz. Hermann' above the unit emblem. The inscription was placed on one aircraft of 2nd Staffel as a mark of honour to Uffz. Paul Hermann, the first pilot of the unit to be killed in action.

Lt. Erich Beudel, pilot of 1./Erpr. Gr. 210, who nursed his damaged Bf 110 C-6, S9+RH, back to St. Omer on 29/7/40 following an attack on a convoy around the south-east coast of England.

flames under his attack. While surviving records are incomplete, this was probably the Bf 110 C-6 of Leutnant Erich Beudel of 1./Erprobungsgruppe 210 which suffered damage consistent with Blair's account. Beudel's aircraft took hits in the cockpit which wounded his gunner, Obergefreiter Heinrich Diemer, damaged the W/T and exploded an ammunition drum. With wings and landing flaps riddled and tyres shot

through, Beudel struggled back to crash-land near St. Omer. Surveying his ravaged aircraft, he may well have acknowledged the accuracy of Flying Officer Blair's claim for a Bf 110 'probably destroyed'.

Orbiting above, III./ZG 26 detached Oberleutnant Mayer's 8th Staffel to take on the Hurricanes, the rest of the Gruppe maintaining height to counter any additional threat which may yet develop. Timing their dives to perfection, Mayer's Zerstörers claimed three Hurricanes destroyed in the space of two minutes in a single dive and zoom attack; the Bf 110s immediately going into a climb to regain height.

Oberleutnant Mayer claimed his fifth victory and Unteroffizier Walter Scherer his fourth, both east of Southend and within a minute of each other. Simultaneously, Sophus Baagoe radioed-in his 7th victory south of Harwich.

The reality was somewhat different, only two Hurricanes being hit but No. 151 Squadron were extremely lucky to have avoided more serious loss, the presence of 8./ZG 26 only being recognised at the very last moment. Had the Zerstörers followed up their attacks the Hurricanes would have been at a serious disadvantage. As it was, Flying Officer Milne urged his severely damaged Hurricane back to Rochford, whilst Flying Officer Whittingham forced-landed at Martlesham Heath, his airframe well and truly peppered. Both British pilots escaped unharmed.

That evening, the Admiralty issued orders prohibiting British destroyers to sail the Channel by day. So, from Portland to Harwich, England's moat was largely dominated by the Luftwaffe, an unpalatable situation for the British who determined to force the issue, and with a vengeance, on 8th August.

Feldmarschall Albert Kesselring, head of Luftflotte 2, visits Erpr. Gr. 210 at Denain on 30/7/40.

LOSS TABLES - JULY 1940

Date	Name of crew and rank	Unit	Status	Fate	Aircraft Code & W. Nr.	Damage state	Reason for casualty	Place
03.07.40	Oblt. Hermann Erbprinz zu Solmslich	6./ZG 26	P	K		No aircraft damage	He 111 crashed into barracks on take-off.	Neuruppin.
06.07.40	Lt. Otto Brix Lt. Ewald Kösters Uffz. Hans Beganau	1.(F)/ Aufk. Ob. d. L.		K M M	Bf 110 D-0 K9+AH 3164	100%	Failed to return from reconnaissance mission to Scotland.	
09.07.40	Oblt. Joachim Glienke Ogefr. Karl Hoyer	13.(Z)/ LG 1	P Bf	U W	Bf 110 C	100%	Shot down by RAF fighters. Crew rescued by Seenotdienst.	Off Portland.
09.07.40	Fw. Hans Langbein Ogefr. Walter Franzke	8./ZG 26 8./ZG 26	P Bf	M K	Bf 110 C-2	100%	Failed to return from combat mission.	South coast of England.
10.07.40	Uffz. Max Brannath Gefr. Hans Geidenberger	3./ZG 2 3./ZG 2	P 1. Wart	K K	Bf 110 C	100%	Crashed due to undercarriage failure during ferry flight from Boblingen in bad weather.	Near Eltsch. 20 Km. SW of Pirmasens.
10.07.40	Oblt. Leo Siegmund Ogefr. Günther Linke	Stab III. ZG 26	P Bf	K M	Bf 110 C-2	100%	Shot down by RAF fighters and AA fire during escort mission for Do 17s of KG 2.	Folkestone.
10.07.40	Ofw. Willi Meyer Gefr. Willi Rohde	8./ZG 26 8./ZG 26	P Bf	POW M	Bf 110 C-2 3U+GS	100%	Shot down by RAF fighters and AA fire during attack on convoy 'Bread'.	Off Folkestone.
10.07.40	Lt. Siegfried Kuhrke Uffz. Heinz Brinkmann	8./ZG 26 9./ZG 26	P Bf	K M	Bf 110 C-4	100%	Shot down by RAF fighters.	Folkestone.
10.07.40		III./ZG 26	P Bf	U U	Bf 110 C-2	5%	Damaged in combat with RAF fighters.	Channel.
11.07.40	Lt. Friedrich-Wolfgang Graf von und zu Castell Gefr. Heinz Reder	7./ZG 76 7./ZG 76	P Bf	M M	Bf 110 C	100%	Shot down by RAF fighters.	Channel, off Portland.
11.07.40	Oblt. Gerhard Kadow (Staffelkapitän) Gefr. Helmut Scholz	9./ZG 76 9./ZG 76	P Bf	POW POW	Bf 110 C-4 2N+EP 3551	100%	Shot down by Green Section of 238 Sqdn. Also attacked by S/L Dewar of 87 Sqdn. and F/O Riddle of 601 Sqdn.. Force-landed.	Grange Heath near Lulworth.
11.07.40	Oblt. Hans-Joachim Göring Uffz. Albert Zimmermann	9./ZG 76 9./ZG 76	P Bf	M M	Bf 110 C-4	100%	Shot down by RAF fighters, possibly S/L Dewar of 87 Sqdn..	The Verne, Portland.
11.07.40	Lt. Joachim Schröder Gefr. Franz Sorokoput	9./ZG 76 9./ZG 76	P Bf	POW K	Bf 110 C	100%	Shot down by RAF fighters, probably F/O Glyde of 87 Sqdn. and P/O Lindsey of 601 Sqdn..	Channel, near the Ney Breakwater.
13.07.40		I./Erpr. Gr. 210	P Bf	U U	Bf 110	45%	Crash-landed due to supercharger failure following attack on convoy in Thames estuary.	Near Ghent.

Date	Name of crew and rank	Unit	Status	Fate	Aircraft Code & W. Nr.	Damage state	Reason for casualty	Place
13.07.40	Uffz. Fritz Donath	14.(Z)/ LG 1	P	W	Bf 110 C-2	50%	Damaged in combat with RAF fighters.	South of Portland.
13.07.40	Lt. Kurt Krebitz Uffz. Hans Koch	14.(Z)/ LG 1	P Bf	W U	Bf 110 C-4	60%	Damaged in combat with RAF fighters.	Off Portland.
13.07.40	Lt. Hermann Eisele Uffz. Kurt Lochow	15.(Z) LG 1	P Bf	K K	Bf 110 C-4	100%	Shot down by RAF fighters.	15 Kms.south of Portland.
15.07.40	Oblt. Ernst Tiefenbrunner	7.(F)/ LG 2	P	K	Bf 110 C-5	100%	Crashed on non-combat flight.	Wunsdorf, near Hohenholz.
18.7.40	Gefr. Ludwig Spreitzer	3./Erpr. Gr. 210	P	K	Bf 110	100%	Right wing broke off during flight.	Antwerp.
21.07.40	Oblt. Friedrich-Karl Runde Fw. Willi Baden	4.(F)/ Auf. Gr. 14	P Bf	POW POW	Bf 110 C-5 5F + CM 2177	100%	Shot down by F/L Turner, P/Os Davis and Wigglesworth of 238 Sqdn.	Goodwood Home Farm, near Chichester.
21.07.40	Oblt. Alfred Habisch Uffz. Ernst Elfner	2./Erpr. Gr. 210	P Bf	U U	Bf 110 S9 + CK	Not known.	Damaged in combat with RAF fighters.	Over the Channel.
21.07.40	Fw. Horst Würgatsch Uffz. Wilhelm Harder	14.(Z)/ LG 1	P Bf	K K	Bf 110 C-4	100%	Damaged by P/O Considine of 238 Sqdn.; Crashed attempting belly-landing at Cherbourg-Theville.	Off Portland.
24.07.40	Uffz. Paul Hermann Uffz. Heinz Meinhardt	2./Erpr. Gr. 210	P Bf	K K	Bf 110	100%	Shot down by AA fire during shipping attack.	30 Km. east of Harwich.
25.07.40	Lt. Wilhelm Pack Uffz. Hans-Jürgen Hildebrandt	3./NJG 1 3./NJG 1	P Bf	K K	Bf 110	100%	Crashed during attack on Wellington.	Coesfeld.
25.07.40		NJG 1	P Bf	U U	Bf 110 C-4	100%	Crash-landed following collision with parachute flare.	Near Gütersloh.
27.07.40	Oblt. Franz Fallenbacher Fw. Friedrich Oberland	2./Erpr. Gr. 210	P Bf	K K	Bf 110	100%	Starboard wing shot off by AA fire during shipping attack.	55 Km. north-east of Harwich.
27.07.40		V.(Z)/ LG 1	P Bf	U U	Bf 110 C	10%	Flying accident. Hit the ground during local flight.	Theville.
29.07.40	Lt. Erich Beudel Ogefr. Heinrich Diemer	1./Erpr. Gr. 210	P Bf	U W	Bf 110 C-6 S9 + RH	35%	Damaged over convoy by 151 Sqdn. Hurricanes.	Off Orfordness.
29.07.40	Fw. Werner Hahn Uffz. Karl Huber	3./NJG 1 3./NJG 1	P Bf	K K	Bf 110 C	100%	Hit by return fire from RAF bomber.	Ennigerloh.
30.07.40	Lt. Hans Herold Ogefr. Lotar Lilienthal	1./Erpr. Gr. 210	P Bf	K K	Bf 110 C	100%	Shot down by F/L Hamilton and Sgt. Allard of 85 Sqdn. during attack on convoy 'Pilot'.	40 Km. east Harwich.
31.07.40		II./ZG 76	P	U U	Bf 110 C	50%	Crashed on take-off due to engine failure.	Le Mans airfield.

Bf 110 C-5 of 4.(F)/14 carrying the 'Baron Münchhausen' emblem.

CHAPTER 5

THE MAIN ASSAULT

During the mid-afternoon of 7th August, a west-bound convoy of 25 ships numbered CW9 and code-named 'PEEWIT', sailed from Southend in a combined naval and air operation deliberately aimed at forcing the Straits of Dover. Escort was provided by two Royal Navy destroyers who joined them at Sheerness, whilst the Hurricanes of No. 145 Squadron were put on 'immediate readiness' to counter air attacks throughout the entire day.

Preparations were particularly thorough. The convoy would disperse off the Isle of Wight with additional protection from the Royal Navy destroyers based at Portsmouth. Their precise time of sailing was calculated so they would pass through the Straits of Dover at midnight and the convoy included barges towing barrage balloons as a mobile deterrent to the inevitable Stukas.

However, the Germans were equally well prepared, for CW9 had been closely monitored by reconnaissance aircraft ever since the ships had started to collect. At 3:00 am. in the morning, as it rounded Beachy Head, waiting German E-boats pounced and created havoc. As dawn broke on a perfect day of brilliant

sunshine, the now scattered ships of convoy 'PEEWIT' were wide open to air attack as they pounded toward St. Catherine's Point.

The first wave of dive-bombers materialised as the ships reached a point some 5 miles south-east of St. Catherine's Point. Shortly after 9:00 am. the Stukas of Hauptmann Helmut Mahlke's III./StG 1 arrived overhead and started their screaming dives on the ships which were now strung out in small groups for miles down the Channel.

This raid was broken up by strong RAF fighter opposition which included No. 145 Squadron up from Tangmere on the first of three missions they would fly in defence of CW9 throughout the day. In the course of a brief but vicious action, the Hurricanes lost two aircraft and pilots to the escort Bf 109s of Hauptmann Eduard Neumann's I./JG 27.

Zerstörers went into action during the second major attack on 'PEEWIT' which developed in the early afternoon as the scattered remnants were sailing south of the Isle of Wight. Elements of three RAF squadrons opposed them and bitter combats resulted, the Bf 109s of Neumann's I./JG 27 and Hauptmann Joachim

Groundcrew watch attentively as the engines of this Bf 110 of 7./ZG 26 are run up. Note the tips of the spinners in the Staffel colour of white.

Schlichting's III./JG 27 again being involved.

First on the scene, six Spitfires of 'B' Flight No. 609 Squadron led by Squadron Leader Darley arrived to find Bf 110s methodically shooting down the balloons, still being towed by the barges, to clear the way for another attack by Stukas. The Spitfires steamed into the attack, Darley subsequently claiming one Bf 110 shot down into the sea and another damaged.

The Zerstörers gave a good account of themselves and presented fleeting targets which the Spitfires found difficult to nail with any certainty. Pilot Officer Appleby, busily re-engineering a Bf 110 which obligingly shed engine panels and parts of the cockpit hood, was forced to break off the attack when his Spitfire was badly hit by accurate return fire from a particularly stubborn and determined rear-gunner. He returned to Warmwell with his aircraft badly damaged.

Pilot Officer Curchin managed to silence return fire from the Bf 110 he attacked before engaging another which gave off a lazy puff of smoke before it turned onto its back and dived clean away from him. With its heavier weight and fuel injection this standard evasive manoeuvre by the Bf 110 was almost impossible for British fighters to follow.

Meantime, No. 238 Squadron's Hurricanes also joined the fray and engaged the Bf 110s. During the hectic and confused engagement which followed, No.

238 Squadron would claim the destruction of two Bf 110s plus another two unconfirmed but suffered the loss of two of their own aircraft and pilots in the process.

Three more Hurricanes of Blue Section No. 145 Squadron, led by Flight Lieutenant Boyd, also engaged the Zerstörers. Two days later he would record his impressions of this combat for the BBC in a broadcast aimed at bolstering an anxious British audience starved of good news. It was a masterpiece of British understatement.

Unable to contact the rest of his Squadron due to a faulty radio, Boyd had circled for a while with his section of three Hurricanes 12,000 feet above two huge formations of Zerstörers who were forming a circle below them. "I was curious to know why they were circling round like that, and we decided to have a crack. We went down on them. The Meserschmitt which was at the end of the circling line of fighters was shot down into the sea immediately.

"Well we broke up the happy little circle quite effectively. All three of us got at least one, and I think we must have taken them by surprise. I was attacked by a Messerschmitt 110 which I suppose I had overlooked. I skidded round and climbed for him, but he broke away to the left. I was still turning and at above 1000 feet I stalled. He was right in my gun-sights. I

Aircrew of 6./ZG 2 at an open-air briefing. The Bf 110 behind them, A2 + AL, was the machine of Hptm. Heinlein, Staffelkapitän of 6th Staffel, who crashed to his death in it on 28/9/40.

just gave him a quick burst, he heeled over, and went straight into the sea and broke up. He was really a sitting bird."

The stilted language of the British pilots' Combat Reports reveals a different story. It had been a particularly fast and furious combat with the Hurricanes darting in and out of the German formation taking snap shots at fleeting targets, whilst the overwhelming numbers of Bf 110s simply got in each other's way.

Flying at maximum boost and with his protesting Hurricane shuddering in a turn, Flight Lieutenant Boyd flushed one Bf 110 away from Flying Officer Dunning-White's tail before opening fire on another of the Zerstörers which staggered and fell off on one wing. It plummeted down towards the sea, one of its crew bailing out. Dunning-White claimed another Bf 110 down into the sea before all three Hurricanes eventually managed to extricate themselves from the melee and returned to base without damage.

The rest of the squadron were not so lucky, losing two pilots to the free-ranging Bf 109s of Schlichting's III./JG 27. The Hurricanes of No. 257 Squadron, who had flown into Tangmere from Northolt that morning as reinforcements, were even less fortunate. They lost three aircraft and pilots to the predatory Bf 109s.

Four hours passed before the remnants of 'PEEWIT' came under further attack from a huge raid estimated at over 100 aircraft. This attack was mounted by Stukas from Mahlke's III./StG 1 and Walter Sigel's I./StG 3

with a massive fighter escort provided by the Messerschmitt Bf 109s of Hauptmann Werner Andres's II./JG 27, Joachim Schlichting's III./JG 27 and Major Günther von Maltzahn's II./JG 53.

This time it fell to the Hurricanes of No. 43 Squadron from Tangmere to meet them, three sections diving to attack the dive-bombers while a fourth section of three Hurricanes climbed to engage the German fighters above.

Leading Yellow Section, Pilot Officer 'Wombat' Woods-Scawen, was surprised to find himself outclimbed by a Schwarm of Bf 110s who promptly laid into No. 43 Squadron's Hurricanes with supreme confidence. Lucky to get back to Tangmere with his aircraft only slightly damaged, but wounded by shell splinters in both legs, he managed to claim one of the Zerstörers down in the sea.

Meantime, the detached section of Hurricanes, led by Flight Lieutenant Carey, reached a height of about 15,000 to 20,000 feet where they found "formations of ME 110s executing roughly oval patrol flights eventually stretching from the French coast to the Isle of Wight."

Brushing off attacks by German fighters, Carey became separated from his flight and was stalking a formation of 109s he had originally taken for friendly fighters. As he closed on the rearmost machine and positioned himself for an attack, all hell broke loose. As he later recorded, "a very large explosion nearly

Groundcrew pose with a Bf 110 C-6 of 1./Erpr. Gr. 210. Note the multi-coloured spinner. The light coloured overalls identify the groundcrew as radio mechanics.

9./ZG 26's open air kitchen.

blew me upside down. A Me 110 had seen what was happening, had come down and was sitting about 30 yards behind me and his explosive 20 mm. shots had blown up all the ammunition in my port wing, leaving a hole big enough for a man to crawl through."

He had fallen victim to a classic dive and zoom attack by a Bf 110. Wounded in the arm, Carey righted his aircraft with some difficulty and gingerly set about testing the controls and assessing the damage; all the time craning his neck for other German machines behind. Happily, there were none and finding that the Hurricane still just about answered the controls, he laboriously climbed back over the scattered convoy. Such perseverance deserved to be well-rewarded, but it was not to be - he was again jumped by Bf 110s.

It was to be another demonstration of the devastating fire-power of the Bf 110, "This time they blew one elevator and the rudder off and the aircraft did a half 'bunt' before I collected my senses. Having only about three quarters of an aircraft to control, I thought discretion was the better part of valour and slowly brought the remains back to base." Rounding off the perfect sortie, the Tangmere defences, obviously confused by the unfamiliar appearance of Carey's tattered aircraft, opened fire on him as he came in to land. Fortunately, their fire was wild and inaccurate and he sustained no further damage, although this may have been somewhat difficult to achieve under the circumstances. His comments on landing are not recorded.

It had been a furious combat and No. 43 Squadron had lost two pilots killed, another four of its aircraft returning to Tangmere with varying degrees of damage; two more pilots, Woods-Scawen and Carey being slightly wounded. They were not alone, for No. 145 Squadron also lost another three pilots during this melee whilst Spitfires of No. 152 Squadron lost one aircraft and another damaged to the Bf 109s of Hauptmann von Maltzahn's II./JG 53.

Throughout the day, it had been No. 145 Squadron's Hurricanes who had borne the brunt of the action over the convoy and their tally of victories reflected the fact. By night-fall they stood with the highest score of any Squadron in Fighter Command, but it was at great cost to themselves, for five pilots, almost half the squadron, went 'missing in action' over the Channel that day. It was a chastened crowd in the bar at Westhampnett that evening.

As dusk fell, with smoke from burning and crippled ships wreathing the Channel, small rescue craft and solitary aircraft scoured the darkening sea for survivors. Debris, wreckage and cargo littered the water for mile upon mile. It had been the Luftwaffe's heaviest effort yet against a British convoy, only four of its entire complement of ships reaching port undamaged.

According to that night's communiqué from the OKL, a total of 47 RAF aircraft had been destroyed in action over the Channel during the day - 18 of them being credited to the Zerstörers.

Horst Liensberger's V.(Z)/LG 1 took the honours, claiming a total of 11 Hurricanes plus a couple of Spitfires destroyed over the Isle of Wight. However, five of their Bf 110s struggled back to France with varying

The Bordfunker of this Bf 110 D of I./ZG 2 looks on with concern as his pilot struggles to free himself from the cockpit of their crash-landed machine. Note the early style kapok-filled life jackets.

degrees of damage, three of them almost total write-offs.

Oberleutnant Helmut Müller's 13.(Z)/LG 1 suffered a particularly gruelling sortie, Leutnant Karl Götze being one of the few pilots in the Staffel to file claims on their return. Somewhat less successful, Leutnant Günther Beck got back with his aircraft badly shot-up; his wounded Bordfunker, Unteroffizier Paul Busch, being whisked off to hospital in Caen. Beck soon paired-up with a replacement Bordfunker, Unteroffizier Karl Hoyer, who had previously flown with Oberleutnant Glienke but only recently returned to duty since being wounded on 9th July. But as a crew, Beck and Hoyer were not destined to last too long and would perish together in action over the Channel west of Bournemouth only five days later.

Feldwebel Gerhard Jentzsch nursed his crippled Zerstörer all the way back across the Channel to Cherbourg but, finally succumbing to wounds and loss of blood, he crashed attempting to land at Theville and was killed. His South African-born Bordfunker, Unteroffizier Alfred Dieckmann, survived badly wounded in hospital at Valognes.

One of the early members of 14.(Z)/LG 1, Feldwebel Alfred Sturm, was another of Liensberger's pilots to score. "Abschuß Hurricane! Viktor!" - his victory witnessed by other pilots. But it was to be his last action, as he failed to return and was posted 'missing' along with his Bordfunker, Feldwebel Helmut Brunner.

Major Ernst Ott's I./ZG 2 had also seen action and claimed 2 Spitfires and 3 Blenheims over the Channel south of the Isle of Wight, but Unteroffizier Siegfried Becker of 1st Staffel found himself reflecting that, once again, their close escort tactics had prevented them from scoring more decisively. Along with other pilots in the Gruppe, Becker much preferred to fly freelance rather than 'shackled' to a formation of bombers, but normally orders forbade it. He recalled two over-enthusiastic pilots who had broken formation during the French campaign to engage RAF fighters. They landed 20 minutes after the rest of the Staffel with slight battle damage and had only narrowly avoided an immediate court-martial. It was a salutary lesson to them all.

Typical of many Zerstörer pilots of this period, this 25 year-old from Hamburg felt inhibited by the tactics imposed on him and considered them a complete waste of time. His growing impression was that the Luftwaffe was far too regimented and RAF fighter pilots were allowed much greater freedom to operate as individuals.

8th August had proved to be a decisive day in a pivotal period, and a turning point. Certainly, during these early clashes over the Channel, the Luftwaffe lost twice as many aircraft as the RAF and for a relatively small amount of merchant shipping sunk. But while such losses were sustainable, they were not inflicting sufficiently heavy casualties on Fighter Command, which still remained an effective fighting force.

It was becoming increasingly clear to German strategists that it would be necessary to penetrate further inland in order to engage the RAF more decisively.

Also, and despite Göring's vigorous denials, the Bf 110 had begun to show itself to be something of a disappointment as an escort fighter. It was proving to be too vulnerable, particularly against the Spitfire, when operating without fighter support of its own. It was little consolation that the RAF's own two-seater fighter, the Boulton-Paul Defiant, had suffered similar painful exposure in action with Bf 109s over the Channel.

From a British perspective, RAF Fighter Command had learned some valuable lessons. Their radar warning system and fighter control network had been thoroughly tested in action and this experience led to the introduction of even more effective operating procedures. Similarly, British pilots who had survived had gained invaluable combat experience during the Channel battles and had been quick to adopt fresh tactics in readiness for the onslaught to come.

Luftwaffe planners had estimated that three successive days of good weather were all that would be required for the final assault on the RAF after the losses inflicted over the Channel. But, launch of the heavy attacks heralding the opening of this next phase of the campaign, originally scheduled for 10th August and duly nominated 'Adler Tag', had to be postponed due to thundery squalls over the Channel.

However, continuing their attacks on coastal targets, the Luftwaffe took full advantage of an unexpected improvement in the weather to mount a large-scale attack on Portland harbour the following morning. This took place after some initial feints over Dover which included an unopposed attack on the harbour by Hauptmann Walter Rubensdörffer's Erprobungsgruppe 210.

Shortly before 10:00 am. a huge raid, tracked by British RDF stations as it formed up over the Cherbourg peninsula, reached mid-Channel heading for the Dorset coast. This formation, over 150 aircraft strong and approaching on a five mile front, comprised Junkers Ju 88s of I. and II./KG 54 and Heinkel He 111s of KG 27, escorted by Zerstörers of I. and II./ZG 2 - Bf 109s of JG 2 and JG 27 providing additional fighter cover.

Conservatively reported as '100 plus', it was the largest raid yet launched against England and, accurately assessed as a major attack, was met by 74 Spitfires and Hurricanes from eight British squadrons.

Flying with his Gruppenstabsschwarm, the Kommandeur of I./ZG 2, Major Ernst Ott, arrived at a predetermined point five miles south-east of Portland well ahead of the bombers. Here he ordered his Bf 110s, along with those of Major Harry Carl's II. Gruppe, a force totalling 60 Zerstörers, to form a huge, towering

Bf 110 C, A2 + KL, of 6./ZG 2. Note the fuselage and wing crosses covered for camouflage purposes, and the third character of the fuselage code, 'K', red without any outline. This aircraft does not appear to carry the Gruppe emblem on its nose.

Abwehrkreis.

Their aim was to attract British fighters and divert them away from the incoming bombers, a tactic which proved highly successful. Soon the whole expanse of sky over Weymouth Bay was filled by a spiralling mass of aircraft as the British fighters and Zerstörers clashed.

Flying with No. 609 Squadron, Pilot Officer David Crook recorded, "Some Hurricanes were already attacking the Messerschmidts (sic) and the latter had formed their usual defensive circle... We came right down on top of the enemy formation, going at a terrific speed, and as we approached them we split up slightly, each pilot selecting his own target.

"I saw an Me 110 ahead of me going across in front. I fired at him but did not allow enough deflection and my bullets passed behind him. I then closed in on him from behind and fired a good burst at practically point-blank range. Some black smoke poured from his port engine and he turned up to the right and stalled. I narrowly missed hitting the port wing. It flashed past so close that instinctively I ducked my head".

Flying with 1./ZG 2 on this sortie, Leutnant Wolfgang Münchmeyer recalls a similar experience: "I was guarding 2 Messerschmitt 110s in front of me, suddenly a Spitfire was nearing from aside, pursued by a Bf 109. I tried to avoid a burst of tracer bullets by lifting my left wing...but then smoke was pouring from my left engine and I could not keep up. I suddenly found myself surrounded by Spitfires left and right. So I tried to escape by diving almost vertically at full engine power knowing that our Messerschmitts...could gain faster and have more speed in diving. I calculate (that I) reached 900 to 1,000 Km./h, far beyond instrument limits." Only just managing to pull out at sea level, Münchmeyer feathered the port engine, which had seized solid, and limped back to France none the worse for his adventure.

Meanwhile another No. 609 Squadron pilot, Flight Lieutenant MacArthur, was about to experience something of the same. Leading Green Section, he saw the hood fly off one Bf 110 he fired at, but found himself surrounded and under attack from others. He only managed to escape by throwing his aircraft into such violent evasive manoeuvres that he went into a spin, losing about 5,000 feet. After some trouble restarting his engine, he returned to Warmwell feeling distinctly unwell.

Writing affectionately of his Flight Commander, David Crook thought that 'Mac', who had scored some early victories in the fighting over the Channel, was in danger of becoming over-confident. "He regarded the German Air Force rather as an organisation which provided him with a little target practise and general harmless amusement. He soon learnt better! From now onwards he was a very wise and successful Flight Commander, and never went out looking for unnecessary trouble!"

RAF pilots involved in this action were quick to point out the Bf 109s apparent failure to react immediately to their attacks on the Bf 110s. This was indeed the case, the Bf 109s were late in joining the battle,

but rather than suggest any hesitancy on their part, it merely tends to refute the oft-made assertion that Zerstörers needed escorts of their own at this stage of the battle. Clearly, the Bf 109s had different orders.

Meanwhile, the bombers had successfully penetrated the defences to hit the oil storage tanks at Portland, which they left ablaze. In reality, the Bf 110s tactic of drawing off the British fighter presence and engaging them in combat allowed the bombers to get through relatively unscathed. It also resulted in heavy fighter casualties on both sides - honours being almost even.

On return, ZG 2 claimed a total of 17 victories, Unteroffizier Siegfried Becker of 1./ZG 2 claiming two Spitfires and Leutnant Schmid of II./ZG 2 a Hurricane as his 8th victory. But they had been hard hit themselves, for six crews failed to return, among them Kommodore Vollbracht's Geschwaderadjutant, Oberleutnant Günther Hensel, who went into the Channel 25 Kms. north of Cherbourg.

Worse was yet to come, for another pilot missing was Major Ott, Gruppenkommandeur of I./ZG 2, whose aircraft had also been seen going down towards the Channel. On return, the German air-sea rescue services immediately sprung into action, but despite extensive searches only the body of his Bordfunker, Feldwebel Otto Zimehl, was recovered by German E-boats later that evening. Oberstleutnant Vollbracht appointed Hans-Peter Külbel, Staffelkapitän of 2./ZG 2, as temporary Kommandeur of I. Gruppe - little realising just how temporary a position it would prove to be.

Oblt. Gerhard Granz, Gruppenadjutant of I./ZG 2, smiles and waves for the camera from the port wing root of his Bf 110.

Above, a bomb is loaded onto the bomb rack of a 'Jabo' of Erpr. Gr. 210, and below, the bomb in place. Note the two rectangular chutes for the ejection of spent 20 mm. cartridge cases.

Every Staffel in I. Gruppe lost a crew, the first casualties recorded by the Gruppenadjutant, Oberleutnant Gerhard Granz, in over a month. Four more of their Bf 110s, including Leutnant Münchmeyer's staggered back to France with varying degrees of damage. Major Carl's II./ZG 2 fared better, losing a single aircraft and crew from 4th Staffel, and one machine damaged.

British casualties in this action were more serious, a total of 15 fighters being lost and another 9 damaged - almost a third of the total force committed. Fourteen RAF pilots were lost and four more wounded, Nos. 238 and 601 Squadrons suffering by far the worst casualties, each of them losing 4 Hurricanes with pilots killed

or missing. It was a loss rate the RAF could not sustain.

But even before these losses had been counted, the Zerstörers of Erprobungsgruppe 210 were again in action, striking at convoy 'BOOTY' as it sailed off the Essex coast shortly before mid-day.

This was the first attack in which their 1st Staffel operated a mix of the 30 mm. cannon-armed Bf 110 C-6s and the Bf 110 D-0 fighter bombers. As usual, fighter escort was supplied by ZG 26. - 20 Bf 110s of Hauptmann Wilhelm Makrocki's I./ZG 26 being scheduled to accompany them. Makrocki was not flying with them on this mission, which was being led by Hauptmann Johann Kogler, the Staffelkapitän of 1./ZG 26. Arriving late for their rendezvous over Gravelines, the escort Bf 110s were a few minutes behind Erprobungsgruppe 210 as they flew in over the Thames estuary.

Using the prevailing cloud cover to good advantage, Erprobungsgruppe 210 located the convoy and pressed home their attacks, claiming an 8,000 ton vessel sunk, as the first British fighters appeared on the scene. These were 'A' Flight of No. 17 Squadron whose 6 Hurricanes were on convoy patrol.

They were soon joined by 11 Spitfires of No. 74 'Tiger' Squadron, up from Manston on their third and what transpired to be their toughest combat of the day, who were vectored onto the Bf 110s 30 miles off Harwich. Pilot Officer Freeborn, leading them in the absence of Squadron Leader 'Sailor' Malan whose aircraft had been slightly damaged in a previous sortie, took them straight into the attack.

In a sharp, furious combat, the 'Tigers' were to

Officers of Erpr. Gr. 210 seen in the early stages of the battle at Denain. From left: Hptm. Walter Rubensdörffer, Gruppenkommandeur, killed in action 15/8/40; Oblt. Otto Hintze, Staffelkapitän, 3rd Staffel, POW 29/10/40; Oblt. Wilhelm-Richard Roßiger, Staffelkapitän, 2nd Staffel, missing in action 27/9/40; Oblt. Martin Lutz, Staffelkapitän, 1st Staffel (later Hptm. and Gruppenkommandeur), killed in action 27/9/40; Lt. Horst Marx, 3rd Staffel, POW 15/8/40; unknown behind Marx, and Oblt. Horst Fiedler, Gruppenadjutant, shot down 15/8/40, died of his wounds on 18/8/40.

claim 11 Bf 110s plus 5 more damaged for the loss of Pilot Officers Cobden and Smith, who both failed to return. Equally optimistic, No. 17 Squadron also claimed a number of 'shared' victories but lost Pilot Officer Manger, DFC, with two more of their Hurricanes returning to Debden damaged.

Flying in 'B' Flight of No. 74 Squadron, Pilot Officer Stephen, awarded the DFC for the destruction of 5 enemy aircraft on this day, later recounted, "The German aircraft were going round in steep turns. Imagine them, forty light bombers - very manoeuvrable and fast, the famous Messerschmitt Jaguar 110 fighter-bombers. We were chasing them and they were chasing us in and out of the clouds.

"In a few minutes they started to form one of their well-known defensive circles. By this time several Germans were lying smashed up in the water with the crews swimming around. The Spitfires were now diving in and out of the circle and never letting them complete it. I got my sights on one bomber and gave him a long burst and one of my tracer bullets must have hit his petrol tank, as in a few seconds he went down flaming into the sea.

"I climbed into the clouds just as another bomber darted at me and we passed each other so closely that I do not know how we avoided a smash. Turning on his tail, I silenced his rear gunner with a burst, and as I closed the range the Messerschmitt rolled over and fell upside down in the sea".

Suddenly under attack from all sides, 1./Erprobungsgruppe 210 lost two Bf 110 C-6s before the Zerstörers of I./ZG 26 could intervene. Leutnant Kurt Bertram, meeting enemy fighters for the first time, fell victim to the superior performance of the Spitfires and fell into the sea off Harwich. Meantime, Gefreiter Christian Weiss survived their attacks but suffered serious damage and was forced to glide down and ditch his crippled aircraft on the water. Witnessed by other pilots, a rubber dinghy was dropped to him and his Bordfunker, Obergefreiter Richard Keilhaupt, but tragically neither of them was ever rescued.

Makrocki's Zerstörers tangled with the British fighters 40 Kms. north-east of the Thames estuary, subsequently claiming 9 destroyed, two of them being credited to Leutnant Martin Meisel. Hauptmann Johann Kogler's 1./ZG 26 saw most of the action, losing two Bf 110s to the British fighters. One was the irrepressible Austrian himself, who suffered the indignity of being shot down into the sea off Felixstowe. After a few days in the water, he was fortunate enough to be

Uffz. Rudolf Krause, Bordfunker of 1./ZG 26, killed in action on 11/8/40 with his pilot, Fw. Erich Puschnerus.

picked up semi-conscious by a far-ranging German E-boat and delivered, along with his Bordfunker, Unteroffizier Adolf Bauer, to hospital in Brügge.

Another of Kogler's recently-formed crews, Feldwebel Puschnerus and Unteroffizier Krause, was also seen to drop out of this fighter action and plunge towards the sea, but no parachutes were observed from their aircraft as the other Bf 110s disengaged and withdrew back to Yvrench. Over a week later, a letter of regret from Leutnant Wolfgang Graf von Hoensbroech, leading 1./ZG 26 in Kogler's absence, was sent to Rudolf Krause's father in Westphalia. It offered little hope.

Typical of the more experienced Bordfunkers in Zerstörer units at this time, 20 year-old Rudolf Krause had already flown over 80 sorties before the opening of the Western offensive back in May. Posted to 3./ZG 26, with his pilot, Unteroffizier Mail, Krause survived 22 war-flights during the fighting over France and was awarded the Iron Cross, 2nd Class, on 8th June. He transferred to the newly-formed 2./NJG 1 at Düsseldorf early in July where he flew a number of night sorties

with Leutnant Reese before teaming-up with Feldwebel Erich Puschnerus, who had requested a transfer back to day-fighters. They both transferred to 1./ZG 26 later that month and were on their fourth combat sortie together when shot down on 11th August.

In addition to the losses suffered by Kogler's Staffel, two Bf 110s of Hauptmann Herbert Kaminski's 2./ZG 26 also struggled back across the Channel with serious combat damage, one of them barely making it back and crash-landing at St. Omer.

It had been a hard day's fighting for the Zerstörer crews and 10 were absent from the mess tables that evening. But those that remained, and no doubt drank a toast to 'absent comrades', knew that they had inflicted serious losses on their British counterparts. At this rate, the RAF would soon be beaten.

The following day, British RDF stations and forward airfields were attacked as a prelude to 'Adler Tag' which, with the promise of more settled weather, had now been rescheduled for 13th August.

Operating as independent Staffeln plus the Stabsschwarm, Rubensdörffer's Erprobungsgruppe 210 delivered simultaneous attacks on the RDF stations at Dover, Dunkirk, Pevensey and Rye during the morning leaving three sites temporarily out of action. The aircraft returned to Calais-Marck without loss.

Then, towards mid-day, a major raid of almost 100 Junkers Ju 88s of KG 51 was launched against Gosport, Portsmouth harbour and Ventnor RDF station. Zerstörers formed a prominent part of the escort and again it was the Bf 110s of Oberstleutnant Vollbracht's ZG 2, this time supported by II. and III./ZG 76. Additional fighter protection was provided by the Bf 109s of JG 53, who were to cover the withdrawal.

Hauptmann Friedrich-Karl Dickoré's III./ZG 76, operating out of Jersey for this sortie, flew 'Freiejagd'. Flying in his customary position as the Kommandeur's wingman in the Stabsschwarm, Leutnant Richard Marchfelder, the Gruppe TO recalled, "Far to the left of us I could see Graf Hoyos' plane, followed by Schlafer and his gang. To the right was Kaldrack leading the rest of our Gruppe. Way above us was the British reception committee, Spitfires... However, they didn't know Dickoré.

"At first we thought the Old Man had gone barmy, he banked and at the same time started to climb... to meet the Spitfires head-on. And meet them head-on we did! Some of them turned, obviously inexperienced, but their leaders met us gun for gun!"

Meantime the bulk of ZG 2, in a repeat of the successful tactics they had adopted on the previous day, were forming an enormous Abwehrkreis aiming to entice more British fighters into combat. Orbiting east of the Isle of Wight, and stacked by Gruppen, Vollbracht's Zerstörers towered high above the Nab and held their formation - expectantly awaiting the RAF's reaction.

Once again, No. 609 Squadron's Spitfires were among the 58 RAF fighters sent up to meet this raid, that indefatigable commentator, Pilot Officer David Crook, one of them. As he later recorded, "I saw a big AA barrage going up over Portsmouth, so I turned slightly in that direction. The dockyard at Portsmouth had been hit and I could see one or two big fires going.

"A powerful force of German aircraft was circling over the east end of the Isle of Wight, and I went out towards them, climbing all the time. As I got nearer, I was staggered by the number of Huns in the sky... here, circling and sweeping all over the sky, were at least 200 Huns! 'My God', I muttered to myself, 'what a party'. Later we got used to seeing these enormous formations, but this first occasion certainly made us think a bit".

Rash, bordering on the foolhardy, Crook approached the three formations of Bf 110s who were circling between 20,000 and 28,000 feet and made a solitary attack on the middle layer. He dived through the centre of the German formation at terrific speed, narrowly missing a collision with one Bf 110, and pulled out at over 500 mph. only with enormous difficulty.

"I looked round to see what was going on, and at that moment an Me 110, enveloped in a sheet of flame, fell past within 200 yards of me. I don't know if this was my victim or not, but I definitely think it was...". Crook returned to base where his aircraft was found to be unserviceable. It had been so severely over-stressed pulling out from his high-speed dive that it had to have two new wings fitted.

Meanwhile, the Ju 88s had split into two groups to attack their respective targets. Marchfelder clearly had no inkling of the bombers' plan of attack. "It seemed that our bombers couldn't make up their minds where to go. One Squadron turned towards Portsmouth, the rest scrambled around on the east side of the Isle of Wight, near the radar station at Ventnor. Since this was closer to us, we stayed with the Ju 88s while the Me 109s continued on to Portsmouth".

With all-too-apparent ease the main formation, comprising I. and III./KG 51, penetrated the Portsmouth balloon barrage and delivered a devastating attack on harbour installations in the teeth of intense AA fire. Equally successful, II./KG 51, accompanied by the Geschwaderstab, attacked the Ventnor RDF site with pin-point accuracy and flattened the entire complex, rendering it inoperable. It would be out of action for three crucial days.

It was an impressive display of determined precision bombing. As one eye-witness, Alexander McKee would later write, "In short, what was happening in coastal areas on this day and during subsequent weeks, was that the German fighter escorts, much larger than the numbers sent up early to oppose them, were able to 'hold the ring' for the bombers; so that fighter interference with the actual bombing was negligible. Nevertheless, the spectacle of 12th August over Portsmouth was never repeated - the brassy impudence of the bombers in apparently unchallenged occupation of the sky over the whole area for some twenty minutes".

Their job done, KG 51 attempted to withdraw but

An unknown pilot poses in the cockpit of this Bf 110 C-6 of 1./Erpr. Gr. 210. Note the multi-coloured spinners, a feature of aircraft of this Staffel, and the aperture in the nose for the ESK 2000 gun-camera.

immediately came under heavy attack from British fighters, who had been prudently waiting outside the naval AA zones. Also, learning from their bitter experience of the previous day, the vast majority of the Spitfires and Hurricanes had not rushed into attacks on ZG 2's circling Bf 110s. Now, with their formations still largely intact, the British fighters started to exact a heavy toll on the retreating bombers.

Marchfelder again, "Fascinated, we watched them diving with Hurricanes swarming around like African bees. It was almost impossible to catch them while diving, but the bombers were savagely attacked as they levelled out".

Despite valiant efforts on the part of the German escort fighters, KG 51 lost 8 aircraft, including that of the Geschwaderkommodore, Oberst Dr. Johann-Volkmar Fisser, which crashed at Godshill Park on the Isle of Wight. Two more Ju 88s struggled back to Melun with serious damage and wounded crew members on board, including that of Major Walter Marienfeld, the Gruppenkommandeur of III./KG 51.

Yet despite these losses, the attack was an unqualified success and the day had again gone in favour of the Luftwaffe. Pilot Officer Crook's Spitfire may well have been one of those included in that evening's communiqué from the OKL which claimed over 70 British fighters destroyed. This wildly optimistic assessment included a whole squadron of Spitfires claimed destroyed on the ground in a bombing attack on Manston early in the afternoon by Bf 109s and 110s of Erprobungsgruppe 210 and Dornier Do 17s from KG 2.

It was the first heavy attack on Manston, which received precious little warning of the raid, due, in part, to earlier attacks which had knocked out the British RDF stations. No. 65 Squadron's Spitfires, caught on the ground, were fortunate not to be wiped out. On his return, Oberleutnant Martin Lutz, Staffelkapitän of 1./Erprobungsgruppe 210, reported, "The fighters were all lined up. Our bombs fell right amongst them".

Other German crews were equally convinced, recording, "Four SC 500 (bombs) amongst fighters taking off. Result: four Hurricanes (sic) and five other aircraft destroyed on the ground...". In fact, only one Spitfire was damaged - its engine stopped by bomb blast as it tried to take off. A Blenheim of No. 600 Squadron was also damaged.

In all 22 victories were credited to Zerstörer pilots on the day, I./ZG 2 led by Hauptmann Hans-Peter Külbel claiming a grand total of 10 British fighters destroyed in combat over Portland during an escort sortie for Junkers Ju 88s. This included a notable double for Leutnant Wolf Münchmeyer and his Bordfunker, Unteroffizier Labusch, who claimed a Spitfire apiece. They lost only 2 Bf 110s, another 2 returning damaged.

But on this, his first and only mission as acting-Gruppenkommandeur, Külbel failed to return - his Bf 110 D-0 shot down into the Channel by British fighters. The body of his Bordfunker, Unteroffizier Fritz Budig, was subsequently recovered by HMS Excellent and reported buried at sea, but arrangements must have been hurried, for he was later washed-up on the English coast and finally interred at Gosport.

Major Harry Carl's II./ZG 2 were less successful, only chalking up three Spitfires, Leutnant Schmid claiming one for his 9th victory. But they also lost 2 Bf 110s, both of them from Hauptmann Adolf Schuldt's 5th Staffel. Two more aircraft returned to France damaged.

Hauptmann Erich Groth's II./ZG 76 claimed three Spitfires for no loss, while Dickoré's III./ZG 76 claimed six Hurricanes. One of these was the 5th victory for 22 year-old Leutnant Rolf Hermichen of 9th Staffel, who would later transfer to single-engined fighters and survive 629 war-flights to end the war as Gruppenkommandeur of II./JG 104 with a total of 64 victories to his credit.

The Gruppe suffered two casualties, both from 8th Staffel. One was their Staffelkapitän, the Silesian Count, Hauptmann Max Graf Hoyos, and his Bordfunker, Unteroffizier Siegfried Krommes, whose bodies were both washed ashore on the French coast almost two weeks later and within days of each other.

During the return flight to Lannion, low on ammunition and at a serious height disadvantage, some of III./ZG 76 had been 'bounced' by British fighters, which they had mistaken for Bf 109s. The Tommies singled out Graf Hoyos for attack and the Stabsschwarm went to assist. Richard Marchfelder caught a last, garbled, message, "I have no control, my..." being the last words he picked up as he watched his friend's aircraft going down.

"Graf Hoyos' plane was now a burning mass. Approaching a speed close to Mach 1, it began to disintegrate, losing rudder and elevator with the stabiliser trail-

Below, and overleaf: Two views of a 'Haifisch' Bf 110 of II./ZG 76. This sharksmouth emblem is unusual in that the teeth are much closer together than normal, and an eye has been painted above the mouth.

ing behind, before finally hitting the water. Part of the aircraft continued to burn below the surface, belching geysers of steam and water. A thin thread of waving smoke was rising above the point of impact..."

This loss affected the whole unit badly for, although sometimes difficult to get on with, they had all got to know 'the Count' since he had joined them at Gütersloh shortly after their re-equipment with Bf 110s. Along with Kaldrack, who was probably his closest friend in the Gruppe, Graf Hoyos was a veteran of the war in Spain, having flown bombers with K/88. He was one of only 27 officers in the entire Luftwaffe to have been awarded the Spanish Cross in Gold with Diamonds.

Like many pilots, he had a superstitious streak and flew with a vintage 'floating compass' fitted to his cockpit panel. This had 'brought him luck' throughout the war in Spain and had been handed down to him by an uncle who had salvaged it from his Albatros after he was shot down and crash-landed during the 1914-18 war.

Marchfelder was stunned. Graf Hoyos must have had a premonition of this. "I have a feeling that I'm not going to make it," he had said, in a brief conversation they had shared immediately prior to take-off that morning. "Take care of yourself, I'm glad that we became good friends". Then he had shaken hands, turned around and walked off without another word, leaving Marchfelder standing there as if struck by lightning. Of all people, Max was the last one he had expected to get 'Channel sickness'.

Another 8th Staffel machine barely made it back to a forced-landing on the French coast, badly mauled by British fighters - its wounded crew, Unteroffizier Pet-

ersen and Obergefreiter Heinze, both rushed to hospital in Caen. Others were more fortunate: Alois Haas of 7th Staffel landing back at Caen exhausted after almost 2½ hours in the cockpit but triumphant - his 25th war-flight completed!

The final major action of the day again involved Bf 110s and was the third sortie for the energetic crews of Erprobungsgruppe 210. It was another precision dive-bombing attack on one of RAF Fighter Command's forward airfields. Shortly after 5:30 pm. they struck at Hawkinge, causing sufficient damage to qualify the attack as the airfield's first major raid. Once again, the Bf 110s returned without loss to celebrate the most successful day in their operational history so far.

It had been another day of relentless fighting but the Luftwaffe had exacted a heavy toll on the RAF. Eighteen British fighters had been destroyed and 11 of their pilots killed - 9 of these in action over Portsmouth and the Isle of Wight. Another 8 British pilots were out of action, either injured or wounded. With 'Adler Tag', now scheduled to be launched the next morning, another hectic and punishing day was in store for the Zerstörers, whose crews, despite their losses, remained optimistic and confident.

The long-awaited 'Adler Tag' got off to a poor start and got steadily worse as the day went on. Displaying a hesitancy not evident on previous days, senior Luftwaffe commanders, possibly suffering an overwhelming sense of occasion, botched an early morning attack on Sheerness and Eastchurch.

At the last moment, due to indifferent weather conditions, and on the personal orders of Reichmarschall Göring himself, all attacks were postponed until early afternoon. But 74 Dornier Do 17s of Oberst

Hptm. Horst Liensberger, Gruppenkommandeur of V. (Z)/LG 1, whose Gruppe lost 5 Zerstörers and had 5 more return to base damaged in the mid-day action on 13/8/40.

Fink's 'Holzhammer' KG 2, with an escort of 60 Bf 110s from 'Horst Wessel' ZG 26 led by Oberstleutnant Joachim Huth, were already en-route to the target and had to be recalled.

Unaccountably, increasingly frantic 'Angriff beschränken', or 'Attack cancelled' radio signals from Kesselring's HQ were not picked up by KG 2, who forged ahead with the attack oblivious of the fact that they were bereft of an escort. The Zerstörers, obeying the recall message, turned back at the English coast. With no direct radio contact between the bombers and the fighters, some of Huth's pilots attempted to warn-off the Dorniers by flying across their noses in a series of jinking manoeuvres. Fink was merely outraged by their lack of flying discipline and put it down to high spirits.

Assisted by the cloudy weather, the Dorniers pressed home their attacks causing severe damage at both Eastchurch and Sheerness. But they came under heavy attack from No. 74 Squadron's Spitfires and the Hurricanes of Nos. 111 and 151 Squadrons over the north Kent coast. Five Dorniers were shot down, another seven returning damaged with wounded crew

aboard, but in the event KG 2 had been extremely fortunate. Incorrectly reported by radar as a small formation, they only had three RAF squadrons ordered up to intercept them; had there been more, the Dorniers would have been decimated. On his return to base, Fink was justifiably furious at what had happened, but, ironically, this was to prove to be by far the most successful attack of the whole sorry day.

Zerstörers went into action again towards mid-day when another attack misfired - this time the Bf 110s suffering the consequences. The plan was for Liensberger's V.(Z)/LG 1 to go in ahead of a bombing raid on Portland and bring up the RAF fighters. The Junkers Ju 88s of KG 54, who were to follow, would arrive over the target just as the British fighters were being forced to land to re-fuel and re-arm.

In a reversal of the earlier attacks on Sheerness and Eastchurch, the bombers had received the news that all attacks were delayed, but not the Bf 110s, who went ahead as planned. They were met by 23 Hurricanes of Nos. 238 and 601 Squadrons and a fierce battle was fought, during which 5 Bf 110s and a Hurricane fell into the sea, as the Zerstörers attempted to withdraw back across the Channel.

Liensberger's Gruppe claimed a total of 9 Hurricanes and a Spitfire destroyed, one Hurricane falling to Oberleutnant Otto Weckeiser of 15.(Z)/LG 1, but the Zerstörers returned to base minus five aircraft and crews. Five more of their aircraft were seriously damaged, three of them force-landing almost total wrecks. The planned bombing attack didn't follow until mid-afternoon - it had been a total debacle and a criminal waste.

Reichmarschall Göring was furious and highly critical of the senior commanders for such a serious tactical blunder. Two days later, in an appraisal of the conduct of the battle, he cited them, "The incident of V./LG 1 on August 13 shows that certain unit commanders have not yet learnt the importance of clear orders. I have repeatedly given orders that twin-engined fighters are only to be employed where the range of other fighters is inadequate, or where it is for the purpose of assisting our single-engined aircraft to break off combat. Our stocks of twin-engined fighters are not great, and we must use them as economically as possible."

It was a telling rebuke which indicated Göring's ongoing commitment to his beloved Zerstörers. He was still not prepared to accept any criticism of their capabilities or discussion on their limitations.

Despite the adverse weather which persisted over southern England and the Channel, 'Adlerangriff' was finally launched mid-afternoon with co-ordinated mass raids on the naval bases at Portland and Southampton, approaching the coast shortly before 4:00 pm. The airfields at Detling, Middle Wallop and Andover were also targeted in a well-planned and executed series of attacks.

In the west, attacks on the British No. 10 Group's area were met over St. Alban's Head by RAF fighters from Warmwell, No. 152 Squadron's Spitfires and No. 238 Squadron's Hurricanes, who were joined by the Hurricanes of No. 213 Squadron up from Exeter. Add-

This page and opposite: Three views of a crash-landed Bf 110 of 4./ZG 2, A2 + IH. Note the wide spacing between the 'I' and the 'H' on the fuselage code.

itional support was provided by the Spitfires of No. 609 Squadron from Middle Wallop who orbited Warmwell, while No. 601 Squadron's Hurricanes, from Tangmere, patrolled the Isle of Wight protecting the eastern flank.

Led by acting-Kommandeur, Hauptmann Christians, I./ZG 2 provided escort for the Junkers Ju 88s of III./LG 1 bound for Andover. All too soon, they once again found themselves in the thick of the fighting but claimed 7 Hurricanes destroyed in a confused combat during which they lost 2 Bf 110s.

Flying with 1./ZG 2, 20 year-old Leutnant Wolfgang Münchmeyer from Hanover recalls, "The bombers were diving and disappearing in the clouds to seek their targets. So, we were free to look for possible adversaries and by chance, we found them in the form of Hurricanes flying at a lower altitude. I was flying as rearguard of our formation and as we dived on them with increasing speed, I was hit from below."

He had fallen victim to a No. 601 Squadron Hurricane, flown by Sergeant Guy, which delivered a classic attack from under the Zerstörer's tail. "I received two gun shots in my right foot from beneath and another one must have set (the) elevator steering out of control. Unable to clear the situation, we had to bale out. Baling out, I hit the elevators of my plane with both legs and landed with both legs fractured and suspended by my parachute in a tree." Wolf Münchmeyer came down in a wood at Hursley Park and was rescued from his tree by another 20 year-old, Home Guard Roy Mead, before being whisked off to the Royal Hampshire County Hospital in Winchester to have his legs set.

Both Wolf Münchmeyer and his Bordfunker, Unteroffizier Fritz Labusch, were observed baling out of their crippled aircraft by other pilots in the Staffel, but the unfortunate Bordfunker fell to his death. Their Bf 110 dived vertically into the ground at Knightwood Farm, North Baddesley, where the crater burned well into the next day.

The other loss to the Gruppe was a Stab, I./ZG 2 machine abandoned during the return flight over the Channel. The crew were both later rescued, but the Bordfunker, Unteroffizier Müller, was badly injured when baling out. Another 1./ZG 2 aircraft returned to Barley damaged with a badly wounded Bordfunker, Obergefreiter Maul, on board.

Meantime, Major Harry Carl's II./ZG 2 claimed 5 Hurricanes, one going to Leutnant Schmid - his third victory in as many days. The Gruppe returned to base without loss.

Zerstörers of III./ZG 76 also flew escort on this sortie, having moved forward from Laval to Jersey early that morning. Expectantly awaiting orders throughout the day, they were eventually ordered off in mid-afternoon, Richard Marchfelder flying with the Stabsschwarm in his customary position as wingman to the Kommandeur, Hauptmann Dickoré.

Flying as rearguard to a Stuka Geschwader who had a close-escort of Bf 109s, the Bf 110s came under heavy attack from the Hurricanes of No. 238 Squadron as they neared the English coast. Marchfelder recalls, "Like a madman Dickoré banked sharply to the left to face the attackers. Regrettably this was not what the Spits (sic) had in mind, they changed their position abruptly and proceeded to attack an easier target in the shape of two Me 110s seemingly on a sight-seeing tour.

"Dickoré and I hastened to help them; others appeared on the scene. After a heated dog-fight one of us got the wingman of the second 'Schwarm', but it was too late to intercept the others. Both Messerschmitts were hit! Both planes dragged a tail of fire, then burst into flames. Slowly one Me 110 started to turn belly-up, a typical sign that the pilot was hurt or killed, then plunged straight down... The second Me 110 didn't fare any better, it went into a spin from which it didn't recover until it crashed. There were no parachutes!"

Both of these aircraft crashed into the Channel and despite Marchfelder's somewhat pessimistic account, one crew was later picked up by the German Seenotdienst. The rest of the Gruppe returned to Lannion after almost 2½ hours in the air, claiming 11 'Spitfires' destroyed. Many Bf 110s had sustained combat damage, Marchfelder's among them.

"We all returned to Lannion. Ursula had a neat row of bullet holes spread across the right rudder. This, however, was merely peanuts compared with the damage done to Kaldrack's plane. Its fuselage looked like a sieve! It must have been quite draughty for the navigator on their way back."

While the raids over Portland were still being dispersed, more Bf 110s were in action further east over the Thames estuary. Erprobungsgruppe 210 were operating again that afternoon, having taken-off from Calais-Marck at 15:15 hours for an attack on Southend aerodrome. As usual, their escort was provided by Bf 110s from Hauptmann Wilhelm Makrocki's I./ZG 26.

Heavy cloud prevented the attack, which was aborted over Canterbury, but as the formation withdrew, the escort Bf 110s were engaged by No. 56 Squadron's Hurricanes, ordered up from their forward base at Rochford to counter the threat.

The Hurricanes claimed 3 Bf 110s destroyed and another 6 damaged in a running combat which spread back along the entire north Kent coast. This was a serious over-estimate for, in fact, only one Zerstörer was lost. This was a 3rd Staffel machine which exploded over Warden Bay, Isle of Sheppey, the remains of its pilot, Oberleutnant Karl Fuchs, only identifiable by labels on shreds of clothing recovered from the wreckage over three days later.

However, a number of Makrocki's' Bf 110s were damaged, Leutnant Martin Meisel's of Stab, I./ZG 26 being one. Severely damaged and with a wounded Bordfunker aboard, he staggered back to a hair-raising landing at Clairmarais, crashing into a parked Bf 110 and writing-off his aircraft. His unfortunate Bordfunker,

2N+BN, a Bf 110 C of 8./ZG 76. The 'B' is black, outlined in white. Note the relatively wide spacing between the characters either side of the fuselage cross.

The Zerstörer of Lt. Joachim Koepsell, U8 + BH, after a force-landing at 'sHertogenbosch on 13/8/40. Note the slight variation in the 'Ringelpitz' emblem shown here to the one shown on page 17.

Feldwebel Fritz Fischer, only recently recovered from wounds received on 23rd May, was taken to the field hospital in St. Omer. Yet Meisel's mood remained jubilant; he was one of six pilots in the Gruppe to claim a 'Spitfire' destroyed in this action.

Leutnant Joachim Koepsell of 1st Staffel was equally lucky to return from what was his 13th war flight. Lost and completely disorientated during the return flight, he eventually crash-landed near Vught in Holland, 165 miles from base. The Staffelkapitän himself, Graf von Hoensbroech, came over to collect him the following day and flew him back to Clairmarais.

The Zerstörer pilot's claims were more accurate than their adversaries on this occasion, No. 56 Squadron losing four Hurricanes during the combat with I./ZG 26. Pilot Officer Joubert's aircraft exploded under attack over Faversham, but he managed to bale out wounded in the leg by cannon shell splinters. Flying Officer Davies abandoned his blazing Hurricane high over Seasalter, landing by parachute badly burned. Sergeant Hillwood, shot down in an ambitious head-on attack on another Bf 110, was forced to bale out off Sheerness and swam two miles to shore. Severely damaged, Flying Officer Brooker tried to put his Hurricane down safely, but wrote it off in a forced-landing at Hawkinge.

So, the long-awaited assault on England was at last underway and the campaign moved into a new phase. In the course of almost 1,500 sorties, their heaviest day to date, the Luftwaffe claimed 92 RAF aircraft destroyed, a total which included 18 Blenheims. Thirteen Zerstörers were among the 44 Luftwaffe aircraft lost on operations throughout the day.

Perversely, both sides were well satisfied with the outcome of the day's action. According to Luftwaffe Intelligence assessments, five of the nine British airfields attacked during the day had been put out of action, striking a serious blow to the RAF. But this interpretation was seriously flawed, for while three airfields had been badly hit, not one of them was a Fighter Command base. Unlike the attacks on previous days, little or no material damage to the RAF defences had been achieved.

By way of contrast, Zerstörer activity on 14th August was limited, their main involvement being confined to a dive-bombing attack on Manston shortly after mid-day by the Bf 110s of 1st and 2nd Staffeln of Erprobungsgruppe 210. Delivering their customary well-disciplined precision bombing attack, they destroyed four hangars and cratered the main runway. Oberleutnant Rößiger's 2nd Staffel lost two aircraft to ground fire, both crashing on the airfield, with one crew member, Gefreiter Ewald Schank, surviving a low-level bale-out.

After the lull of the previous day, and with clear weather forecast, 15th August saw a return to a high scale of effort with the Luftwaffe mounting 1,786 sorties throughout the day - their greatest effort of the whole campaign. Most of these were directed against RAF airfields, which were to remain the main targets for attack over the coming week.

Hawkinge and Lympne were the first to be attacked late that morning, but it was early afternoon before the Zerstörers were back in action as part of an ambitious series of attacks launched against targets in both the north-east and south-west of England. This double

Above, Fw. Hans Datz (centre) of 13.(Z)/LG 1 with groundcrew in front of his Bf 110. Datz, also seen below, was shot down on 13/8/40 and entered British captivity.

blow was intended to smother the British defences and divide, what by now had to be, a seriously depleted RAF Fighter Command.

Banking on tactical surprise, Luftflotte 5 launched two attacks from Norway and Denmark against the north and north-east of England. From Ålborg, 50 Junkers Ju 88s of KG 30 approached Spurn Head bound for the RAF Bomber Command airfield at Driffield. Unescorted, they met heavy fighter opposition from the Hurricanes of No. 73 Squadron from Church Fenton and the Spitfires of No. 616 Squadron from Leconfield, who engaged them off Flamborough Head. About half of the bombers fought their way through to their target, which they left badly damaged, losing 7 of their number to British fighters. Another 3 Ju 88s limped back to airfields in Denmark, Germany and Holland with varying degrees of damage and carrying wounded crews.

Meanwhile, a larger formation from Stavanger, 63 Heinkel He 111s of I. and III./KG 26 escorted by 21 Bf 110s of I./ZG 76, made for the airfields at Dishforth and Linton-on-Ouse. Tracked by British radar for almost an hour as they crossed the North Sea heading for the Farne Islands, they were surprised to be met by unexpectedly heavy fighter opposition.

Four British fighter squadrons were deployed to greet them, the first to engage being 11 Spitfires of No. 72 Squadron from Acklington who met the German formation well out to sea. Momentarily nonplussed by the size of the enemy formation, which radar had incorrectly reported as 30+, the Spitfires hesitated. Flying with 'A' Flight, Pilot Officer Deacon-Elliott

Lt. Hans-Ulrich Kettling, pilot of 1./ZG 76, who was shot down and taken prisoner on 15/8/40.

shared in the surprise, "There were at least 200 enemy aircraft at about 40 miles out to sea, made up of every type we knew. Led by He 111 and Ju 88 bombers with a long range escort of Me 110s well to the rear. None of us had ever seen so many aircraft in the sky at one time.

"There was a gap between the lines of bombers and the Me 110s coming up in the rear so in there we went. I do not think they saw us to begin with. When they did, the number of bombs rapidly jettisoned was fantastic." As the Spitfires slammed into the flank of the enemy formation, many bombers jettisoned their loads and sought cloud cover while the Bf 110s immediately started to form defensive circles.

Harried by the Spitfires, the German formation split into two before veering south-west for Tyneside and the Sunderland area. RAF reinforcements in the shape of Hurricanes of No. 79 Squadron, also from Acklington, engaged the northerly group just off the coast and joined in the attack on the Bf 110s which most of their pilots wrongly identified as Dorniers.

Their confusion was understandable. The Zerstörers were fitted with the 'Dackelbauch' auxiliary fuel tank to extend their range and this altered their configuration significantly, making identification by relatively inexperienced British pilots, particularly in the heat of combat, quite difficult. Only Flying Officer

Elsdon of No. 72 Squadron seems to have correctly identified them, later describing them in his combat report as Bf 110s with 'bulbous tanks under the fuselage'.

It was the same story in every British squadron involved. In addition to claims for Heinkel He 111s destroyed, the Hurricanes of No. 607 Squadron from Usworth also claimed 2 Dornier Do 17s destroyed, 1 probable and 1 damaged. No. 41 Squadron's Spitfire pilots from Catterick were equally confused, claiming several Junkers Ju 88s.

Victims of their own faulty Intelligence, and clearly surprised to find so many British fighters covering the north-east of England, the Zerstörers found themselves at a serious disadvantage and in imminent danger of being overwhelmed.

Oberleutnant Hans-Ulrich Kettling, Staffel weapons officer of 1./ZG 76, recalls, "Our formation dissolved into the usual small groups of four, attacking the Spitfires and distracting them from the bombers. I followed my No. 1, Oberleutnant Lent, who went in pursuit of two Spitfires. I heard (my Bordfunker), Obergefreiter Volk, work his MGs and looking back, I stared into the guns of four Spits in perfect formation."

Wrenching his aircraft to one side to avoid the fire from Green Section of No. 41 Squadron led by Pilot Officer Shipman, Kettling still took hits in the starboard engine, which started losing coolant, the oil temperature rising rapidly. He immediately cut the ignition and feathered the propeller. "I tried to reach the protection of the bombers, which were overhead in close formation, but without success - the plane was slow now and not able to gain height. Over the radio I heard the boys in the bombers talking about my plane, so I gave my 'Mayday', which nobody acknowledged, as the Spits came in for a second attack."

Flying on one engine and encumbered by the 'Dackelbauch', Kettling was unable to avoid this next devastating attack from Pilot Officer Bennions of No. 41 Squadron, which hit the port engine, wounded Obergefreiter Volk, and shattered the windscreen - tracer bullets missing his head by inches. Volk slumped down onto the floor of the rear cockpit, unconscious and covered in blood, Kettling unable to tell whether his Bordfunker was alive or dead.

With both engines now out of action, but with his flying controls still functioning and the belly tank empty, Kettling decided on a belly-landing. If Volk was still alive, it would be his only chance. "I dived out of the fighting level, down and down, leaving the lethal Spits behind and looking for a suitable landing field. I eased the plane carefully down over a very large meadow, but on touching ground I found the speed still rather high."

Kettling's Bf 110 hit the ground at Streatlam, near Barnard Castle, careered across the field on its belly, and crashed through a low stone wall hidden by a hedge, breaking off the rear fuselage and tail just aft of the cockpit. As the cockpit section and wings continued on across the field, Kettling looked back over his shoulder to see their rubber dinghy, fully inflated but still fixed to the aircraft by a long length of cable, gro-

Lt. Helmut Woltersdorf, pilot of 2./ZG 76, claimed two Spitfires in the action of 15/8/40, although none of that type were lost. Woltersdorf later moved to the night-fighter arm, and was killed in action on 6/6/42 while flying with NJG 1.

tesquely bouncing along behind them like a dog on a lead.

"The plane came to a halt at last. I jumped to the ground, freed Volk and carried him to a safe distance, fearing fire and explosion of fuel and ammunition. I disabled the radio set by some shots from my pistol. I tried to set the plane on fire, but the two ignition bombs we carried for this purpose did not work as expected. One of them burned my hand badly and that was the only honourable wound I had during the whole adventure."

A large group of obviously belligerent workmen from a nearby construction site were first on the scene but kept their distance while Kettling emptied his pistol at the radio. Military police and troops soon appeared who took Kettling and Volk, whose wounds were not serious, to Barnard Castle Police Station to await initial interrogation by local RAF Intelligence Officers. Ironically, the incendiary charges eventually worked, for 30 minutes after the crash the Bf 110 burst into flames, some bystanders being wounded by the exploding ammunition.

Kettling was not the only one to fall victim to fighters. Hauptmann Werner Restemeyer, the Gruppenkommandeur of I./ZG 76, and his Adjutant, Oberleutnant Gustav Loobes, also failed to return, both being shot down into the North Sea by British fighters.

On return to Stavanger, every Staffel in the Gruppe was found to have suffered losses. But the fight had not been entirely one-sided, with Oberleutnant Heinz Gresens' 2nd Staffel filing most claims.

One of his pilots, Leutnant Helmut Woltersdorf, claimed two Spitfires. Another, Oberleutnant Gustav Uellenbeck, scored hits on another, which dived away through cloud trailing smoke, before he had to break

off as his wingman, Oberfeldwebel Leo Schuhmacher, picked a Spitfire off his tail, claiming it destroyed east of Blythe at 12:50 pm.

Schuhmacher, who did not switch to night-fighters with the rest of the Staffel later in the year, would transfer to single-engined fighters after a period as an instructor. Later in the war, he flew as wingman to Heinz Bär in II./JG 1 and would survive some 250 warflights with 23 victories - one of the last while flying Me 262 jet fighters with JV 44.

Another 'Experte' in 2./ZG 76, Oberleutnant Reinhold Eckhardt, claimed a Hurricane off Flamborough at 13:14 pm. and a Spitfire in the same area 16 minutes later. Eckhardt was to make a very successful transition to night-fighting, being awarded the Ritterkreuz on 30th August 1941. He achieved 22 victories before his death on 30th July 1943 when Staffelkapitän of 7./NJG 3.

But it was not all good news. Gresen's Staffel had lost Oberfeldwebel Klaus Ladwein, whose 'Dora' was seen to plunge into the North Sea, and they almost lost another Bf 110 very early in the combat. This was Unteroffizier Bernhard Richter, who was struck in the head by a burst of machine-gun fire during the first withering fighter attacks and momentarily lost consciousness. Out of control, his aircraft went into a steep dive. Miraculously, Richter regained consciousness just in time to regain control of the aircraft and gingerly nursed it all the way back across the North Sea, at wave-top height, to crash-land at Esbjerg in Denmark. Not sharing in this good fortune, his Bordfunker, Unteroffizier Hans Geishecker, had baled out during their vertical dive towards the sea and was lost.

Fending off repeated attacks by the persistent British fighters, Oberleutnant Gollob's 3./ZG 76 had stuck

Unusual view of a Bf 110 fighter-bomber of 1./Erpr. Gr. 210 seen over the sea returning from a raid on England. The bomb-rack, and multi-coloured spinners of 1st Staffel can be clearly seen.

close to the bombers and, as a consequence, they suffered the heaviest losses. Two of their Bf 110s were missing, another two returning damaged with Unteroffizier Zickler's Bordfunker, Gefreiter Josef Pudlick, badly wounded. Gollob himself, who claimed a Spitfire shot down east of Blythe, was another to return with damage and with his own Bordfunker, Feldwebel Friedrich Meyer, wounded in the British fighter attacks.

Another of his pilots, Oberfeldwebel Lothar Linke, was even more fortunate. Stalking a Spitfire which was busily attacking a Heinkel, Linke closed to 50 yards before he opened fire - the Spitfire rearing up then spiralling down in a vertical dive. Suddenly attacked by two more Spitfires, Linke's Bf 110 was hit in the port wing and engine which started to pour smoke and promptly seized. "I pushed the stick and dived vertically through the clouds with the two Englishmen on my tail. After 2-3,000 feet I pulled out below the upper layer, having meanwhile altered course. Going down through the lower layer, I saw two Spitfires hit the water."

Linke was subsequently credited with two Spitfires destroyed during this combat, eventually landing back at Jever after a tortuous return flight back across the North Sea on one engine.

In fact, British losses during this action were minimal. One Hurricane of No. 79 Squadron returned to Acklington damaged, while a Blenheim of No. 219 Squadron force-landed at Driffield damaged by return fire from an enemy aircraft it had engaged off Scarborough. Only one Hurricane was actually lost, a No. 605 Squadron machine which crash-landed near Usworth, the pilot, Flying Officer Passy, unhurt. Two more of their aircraft returned to Drem damaged, one pilot being badly injured.

In addition to the loss of their Gruppenkommandeur, I./ZG 76 had lost a third of the Bf 110s deployed for this attack; 6 'Doras' failing to return and another 3 returning damaged. KG 26 had lost 8 Heinkels in this ill-fated attack. It came as both a heavy blow and a salutary lesson for Luftflotte 5, who never repeated such attacks - it was a turning point in the battle.

Early in September, the rest of I./ZG 76 were withdrawn from Norway and transferred to Deelen-Arnhem, where they re-trained as night-fighters to form the basis of a newly-constituted II./NJG 1 under Hauptmann Graf von Stillfried.

But on 15th August, attacks continued, with the Zerstörers fully committed. At 3:00 pm. that afternoon the seemingly inexhaustible Erprobungsgruppe 210 delivered a precision dive-bombing attack on Martlesham Heath. They returned without loss, but Leutnant Erich Beudel's Bf 110 of 1st Staffel sustained damage.

Two more carefully co-ordinated raids developed

A line-up of Zerstörers of 4./ZG 26 partly hidden among bushes. The nearest aircraft is coded 3U + AM.

The original 'Wespe' emblem of II./ZG 1, three wasps above a cloud, designed by Richard Marchfelder of that Gruppe, can be seen on this Bf 110 C in a very securely-built blast pen. This emblem was carried over to III./ZG 76 when the Gruppe was redesignated at the end of June. The emblem would later evolve to a single large 'Wespe' on the nose of aircraft of ZG 1 on the Russian and Mediterannean fronts.

Fw. Jakob Birndorfer of ZG 76 displays to good advantage the Luftwaffe pilot's headgear and sunglasses.

Jakob Birndorfer, pilot of 6./ZG 76, with M8 + DP as a backdrop. Birndorfer was killed in action on 15/8/40 in Bf 110, M8 + BP.

later in the afternoon, when at around 5:30 pm. nearly 50 Stukas of I./StG 1 and II./StG 2 from Lannion approached Portland with heavy fighter escort of Bf 109s of JG 27 and JG 53 plus the Zerstörers of Liensberger's V.(Z)/LG 1 and III./ZG 76 led by Hauptmann Dickoré.

Simultaneously, a formation of 60 Junkers Ju 88s of LG 1 attacked Worthy Down, causing little damage, and Middle Wallop, where they added to the damage caused there on the previous day. Their escort included the Bf 110s of Erich Groth's II./ZG 76 who had moved forward from Le Mans to Rennes where they were specially fitted with under-wing fuel tanks to extend their range for this sortie.

Flying as Bordfunker for Feldwebel Birndorfer in 6./ZG 76, Unteroffizier Max Guschewski recalls, "Soon after 16:00 we took off, heading for our assembly point at Guernsey, where we were to escort 40 Ju 88 bombers, but owing to so many losses only 18 came. We flew over Cherbourg for England at 4,000 metres. As we flew over the Channel we climbed to 12,000 metres. Our target was an airfield at Salisbury. As we neared the English coast, the skies were clear, not a cloud could be seen between Portland and the Isle of Wight. Only the condensation trails streaming behind our aeroplane's engines."

Had the German pilots known it, they were to be met by no less than 8 RAF fighter squadrons ordered up to counter these raids, which they engaged on a front extending from south of Portland, over the Isle of Wight, to a point south of Swanage.

II./ZG 76 fell foul of No. 609 Squadron's Spitfires who were defending their home base. As Max Guschewski recalls, "We reached Salisbury and prepared to attack the airfield. It was then the battle commenced. Spitfires appeared to be everywhere. We flew away from the target, but the bombers had not released their bombs, so we returned again. They dropped them, but not all fell on the target. We turned to fly back to our base."

As Groth's Zerstörers fought their way out, badly outnumbered by British fighters, a determined rearguard action took place - Hans-Joachim Jabs of 6./ZG 76 claiming two Spitfires and a Hurricane destroyed. Their route was littered with the blazing wrecks of aircraft, but three of their Bf 110s failed even to reach the coast.

Hauptmann Groth's Stabsschwarm was badly

Sharksmouth Bf 110 C of 5./ZG 76 during the Battle of Britain displaying an unusual white machine gun cowling. Note the victory bars on the port fin.

mauled. Flying with them on this sortie, Unteroffizier Röhrich, ploughed into the ground at Broadlands, near Romsey, probably falling to the guns of Flying Officer Edge of No. 609 Squadron. Both Röhrich and his gunner, Unteroffizier Neymeyer, were killed outright. Leutnant Siegfried Hahn, the Gruppe NO, and his gunner, Unteroffizier Lehner, were both wounded but struggled back to a crash-landing at Cherbourg-West. Oberleutnant Wrede, the Gruppe TO, also crash-landed back at Barneville; his Bordfunker, Unteroffizier Kukawka, only slightly wounded.

From 5. Staffel, Oberleutnant Gerhard Bremer's Bf 110 exploded alongside the Farley Road at Slackstead, literally blown apart in attacks by the Hurricanes of Flight Lieutenant Barton and Pilot Officer Meaker of No. 249 Squadron. This Zerstörer exploded with such violence that neither Bremer nor his Bordfunker, Unteroffizier Leo Pauli, were ever identified. What little of them remained was buried as two 'Unknown Airmen' in the little village churchyard at Hursley.

The same fate also awaited Feldwebel Franz Wagner and Unteroffizier Fritz Spörl of 6./ZG 76 who were shot down by Flight Lieutenant MacArthur of No. 609 Squadron. Their Bf 110 exploded on impact at Furzley, West Wellow causing a heath fire which burned for several hours. They were both buried as 'Unknowns' in Devizes Road Cemetery, in Salisbury.

Meanwhile, Feldwebel Birndorfer had made it back as far as the coast with an alert Guschewski in the rear cockpit managing to keep the ever-present British fighters at bay. "We reached the Solent, but then we were attacked by four Spitfires, two attacking us from the front and two from the rear. Our right motor was hit and started to burn, then our left one was hit and the propeller on it stopped. I tried to bale out, but could not get out."

Flying flat out and at a suicidal low level, Birndorfer threw his badly damaged fighter around, even reputedly circling the proverbial church steeple, in his attempts to shake-off two pursuing Spitfires. Coincidentally, these were both flown by Polish pilots in RAF service, Flying Officer Ostaszewski-Ostoje of No. 609 Squadron and Pilot Officer Zurakowski of No. 234 Squadron. In a final desperate bid to escape, Birndorfer dived straight through the Southampton balloon barrage - closely followed by the Spitfires.

Guschewski was hit by machine-gun fire and passed out as Birndorfer pulled-off a hair-raising belly-landing at North Ashey Down on the Isle of Wight, "I came to as we landed in a field and again I went unconscious for a few minutes." Exactly what happened next is unclear, but what is certain is that Jakob Birndorfer died and unsubstantiated stories persist that he was shot dead by troops after landing.

Badly wounded in the head and back, and paralysed down his left side, Guschewski's next recollection was being released from the cockpit and lifted from the aircraft by soldiers. He spent the night In a local Police cell and was admitted to the British Military Hospital at Parkhurst the following morning after initial interrogat-

Hptm. Dickoré (left) and Oblt. Kaldrack of III./ZG 76. Dickoré was Gruppenkommandeur of III./ZG 76 when killed in action on 15/8/40. Kaldrack, Staffelkapitän of 7./ZG 76, succeeded Dickoré as Gruppenkommandeur of the Gruppe and was himself killed in action on the Russian front with II./ZG 1 on 3/2/42.

Uffz. Alois Haas, pilot of 8./ZG 76, who was killed in action on 15/8/40.

ion by an RAF Intelligence Officer. On recovery, he was shipped to Canada where he would remain a prisoner of war until his eventual repatriation to Germany in 1946.

Groth's Gruppe lost a total of 8 Zerstörers on this sortie with 11 crewmen killed or missing and 3 more wounded. Two Bf 110s crashed in the Channel on the return flight, one of the crews being rescued and the body of another, Oberleutnant Max Wien of 4./ZG 76, being washed ashore over five weeks later.

Dickoré's Gruppe fared little better. They lost 4 aircraft, including that of young Alois Haas of 7./ZG 76 on his 27th mission. From these crews, only Dickoré's Bordfunker, Unteroffizier Herbert Templin, would survive - a prisoner of the British, rescued from Weymouth Bay, the victim of a tragic collision.

Flying on the Kommandeur's left as usual, Marchfelder saw it all. "Dickoré was pumping a round of hardware into the tail-end of a Spitfire. As soon as the old man saw smoke oozing from the Spit's tail, he pulled up, as was his habit ... A second Spitfire, the wingman of the one he hit, passed by mistake in front of my cannons. A few of the bullets damaged his elevator, he lost control of his aircraft and crashed into Dickoré! All three baled out! Ursula had a hard time keeping her nose out of that mess."

Obviously hit by some wreckage, Marchfelder's

starboard engine temperature climbed dangerously high so he cut the ignition and fuel supply, operated the fire extinguisher, and dived out of combat into a blanket of cloud. "Finally, perspiring with pent-up tensions, we left the sanctuary of the clouds. To our relief we were halfway across the Channel. Herbert (Obergefreiter Jentsch) reported that no enemy plane was following us. Shortly afterwards we landed safely in Lannion. Kaldrack took over command of our Gruppe, or what was left of it."

Many of III./ZG 76's survivors remained optimistic for quite a while; after all, three parachutes had been seen and there was still enough daylight remaining for the rescue services to operate. But as more and more time dragged on, well into the next day, their hopes began to fade.

It was a crushing blow for the Gruppe. Dickoré was a well-respected and extremely popular Kommandeur, fondly remembered as an outstanding and extremely capable officer. It was a double tragedy for his family back in Prien am Chiemsee, as his younger brother Rolf had already fallen with the Legion Condor in Spain. Eventually, on 20th September, the sea surrendered Dickoré's body, which was washed ashore near Le Touquet.

Ten British fighters were lost in these combats, 6 of

A 'Wespe' of III./ZG 76 prepares for another mission. Note the Bordfunker sitting facing forward for the take off.

the pilots killed or missing and 2 more being wounded. Another 7 RAF fighters returned seriously damaged. Two pilots of No. 234 Squadron were captured by the Germans, indicating the enthusiasm with which they had pursued enemy aircraft back across the Channel, only to fall victim to predatory Bf 109s who hovered over the coast covering the withdrawal.

As evening fell, a final attack involving 22 Bf 110s and Bf 109 'Jabos' of Erprobungsgruppe 210 penetrated the British defences, escorted by a Gruppe of Bf 109s from JG 52. Leading the attack, their fifth sortie of the day, Hauptmann Walter Rubensdörffer failed to locate their target, Kenley airfield, possibly due to ground haze, and attacked nearby Croydon airfield instead.   In a devastating dive-bombing attack they caused considerable damage to the airfield and destroyed the Rollason and Redwing aircraft factories. Some bombs overshot the airfield causing damage to houses adjoining the airfield and inflicted civilian casualties of 62 killed and 37 seriously injured. It was the first recorded raid on Greater London.

Completing their attacks, Rubensdörffer's formation found themselves in a grave situation. At the bottom of their dives, around 2,400 feet, they came under attack by 9 Hurricanes of No. 111 Squadron, defending their home base, and 9 Hurricanes of No. 32 Squadron from nearby Biggin Hill. The escort Bf 109s from JG 52 for some reason had withdrawn. Now, only the 8 Bf 109s of 3./Erprobungsgruppe 210, led by Oberleutnant Otto Hintze, remained to cover the Bf 110s as they attempted to disengage and retire south.

Gefr. Ernst Hoffmann, Bordfunker of 8./ZG 76, killed in action on 15/8/40.

Lt. Erich Beudel of 1./Erpr. Gr. 210, killed in action on 15/8/40 flying the only Bf 110 C-6 to crash on mainland England.

Ogefr. Ludwig Kretzer, killed in action on 15/8/40 when flying as Bordfunker for the Gruppenkommandeur of Erpr. Gr. 210, Hptm. Walter Rubensdörffer.

As Hintze recalls, "After the attack I made a so-called 'defence circle' between the English fighters. In this position I saw 2 or 3 Me 110s below us who soon disappeared in the thin mist."

They suffered terrible casualties. To be caught at such low level was a serious disadvantage, and the Gruppe Stabsschwarm was decimated as it attempted to break away low across the southern counties harried by Hurricanes, the Bordfunkers desperately maintaining a constant, but unequal, clatter of return fire. Gruppenkommandeur, Gruppenadjutant and Gruppe TO were all shot down, Leutnant Willi Benedens, who joined the unit 5 days before, being the only pilot to survive from the Stabsschwarm. Exhausted, he landed back at Calais-Marck with his aircraft riddled to spend the next two months in hospital. He recalls, "As we dived down onto the target, we were already being attacked by Hurricanes. I think every pilot was as nervous as I was. A terrible dogfight started, during which I was wounded, but I didn't realise I was wounded until I was in the 'Abwehrkreis'. In the awful confusion after the combat everyone had so much to do, in order not to be shot down. I will never forget this raid on Croydon in my entire life."

Oberleutnant Horst Fiedler, Gruppenadjutant, broke from the circle over Croydon and dived away due south closely pursued by two Hurricanes: Sergeant Dymond of No. 111 Squadron and Sergeant Pearce of No. 32 Squadron. Under simultaneous attack by both Hurricanes, Fiedler's port engine burst into flames and he crashed on Redhill aerodrome. Captured along with his Bordfunker, Unteroffizier Johann Werner, who had baled out, Fiedler died of his injuries three days later.

Rubensdörffer, believed already damaged in an attack by Squadron Leader Thompson of No. 111 Squadron, also broke from the melee over Croydon and headed south. Over the radio, he reported that he was wounded and his Bordfunker was dead, so a Bf 109 E-4/B of his 3rd Staffel, flown by Leutnant Horst Marx, dived after him to act as escort. They were spotted by Pilot Officer Flinders of No. 32 Squadron who delivered a beam attack on the Bf 109, "I fired for about two seconds and a stream of white smoke came from his engine. The aircraft dived towards the ground... A minute later I saw a parachute open." Marx was forced to abandon his crippled aircraft over Frant, leaving Rubensdörffer still heading south, but now alone.

His Bf 110 soon came under attack from another

123

Bf 110 C-6 of 1./Erpr. Gr. 210 with the under-fuselage fairing and 30 mm. Kanone clearly seen.

Hurricane, Pilot Officer Duckenfield of No. 501 Squadron, who along with the rest of his unit had intercepted the scattered Bf 110s as they retired south. Duckenfield chased the Bf 110 for several minutes before closing the range sufficiently to open fire with the last of his ammunition. He saw one engine burst into flames before he had to break off his attack due to fuel shortage.

It was enough for Rubensdörffer's Bf 110, now well ablaze and shedding wreckage, spreading itself across a field at Bletchinglye Farm, Rotherfield. He was killed outright, his body and that of his Bordfunker, Obergereiter Ludwig Kretzer, being recovered and buried in nearby Tunbridge Wells cemetery. Four days later, Swiss-born Rubensdörffer was awarded a posthumous Ritterkreuz, the first 'Zerstörer' pilot to receive the honour, and only the 5th of the 'Jagdwaffe', for his tireless leadership of his Gruppe. A veteran of the Spanish campaign, where he had flown with the Stab of Jagdgruppe 88, he had been an early advocate of the dive-bombing concept which his unit had done so much to further since their formation on 1st July.

Celebrating his 100th sortie, Leutnant Karl-Heinz Koch, the Gruppe TO, was another pilot forced to break from the harassed circle of Bf 110s over Croydon. "During this circling and climbing my left engine was hit - presumably by AA - and shortly afterwards my rear gunner was also hit and became unconscious. After reaching about 6,000 feet I decided to leave this unfriendly area and found myself on my own. My left engine was less than windmilling and therefore the airspeed lower than normal; my rear gunner was partly conscious. Approaching the coast west of Hastings I was suddenly attacked by two fighters... Both engines

died immediately. I dived simultaneously to the right to break off from the fighters and looked for a reasonable belly-landing field."

Despite this final attack by Flight Lieutenant Russell of No. 32 Squadron, Koch managed a creditable forced-landing at School Farm, Hooe. There, he was taken into custody by the local LDV, and delivered in handcuffs to Battle Police Station. His Bordfunker, Unteroffizier Rolf Kahl, was taken by ambulance to the military hospital at Hellingly - his wounds so serious that he would be repatriated to Germany in 1943.

The rest of the Gruppe fared just as badly. Leutnant Erich Beudel of 1st Staffel, his Bf 110 damaged on the earlier sortie against Martlesham Heath, was shot down by Flight Lieutenant Connors, and possibly also Sergeant Wallace, of No. 111 Squadron. His Bf 110 crashed at Broadbridge Farm, Smallfield, near Horley, Beudel and his Bordfunker, 19 year-old Obergefreiter Otto Jordan, both being killed.

The mangled wreckage of his Bf 110 C-6, the only variant of its kind to fall into British hands, did not go un-noticed and proved to be the subject of close inspection by RAF Intelligence experts who soon correctly identified its weapon system. Another 1st Staffel machine returned damaged, Unteroffizier Werner Neumann and his Bordfunker, Obergefreiter Karl Stoff, both unhurt.

Two 2nd Staffel aircraft were also lost to swarming British fighters as they tried to withdraw back across Kent. The pilots of both were captured, Oberleutnant Alfred Habisch force-landing near Hawkhurst and Leutnant Helmut Ortner baling out over Ightham; the latter shared by Squadron Leader Worrall and Flight Lieutenant Crossley of No. 32 Squadron.

The 30 mm. Kanone installation on a Bf 110 C-6 of 1./Erpr. Gr. 210.

Erprobungsgruppe 210 lost 6 Bf 110s in this ill-fated attack, another 2 returning to Calais-Marck badly damaged. It was a salutary blow to the unit who, it had to be admitted, had fared relatively well over the preceding weeks given their scale of activities and the specialist nature of their attacks. Oberleutnant Martin Lutz took over as Acting-Gruppenkommandeur of the now sadly-depleted Gruppe.

That evening, as the grim tally was reckoned, both sides knew that it had been a costly day. But what neither side could know was that they would never again lose as many aircraft in a single day during the whole period of the Battle of Britain.

Fighter Command had lost 35 fighters, 11 of the pilots missing or killed, and another 16 wounded. Every German fighter serviceable had been used in an all-out effort to bring the RAF to combat and destroy its fighters in the air, while their airfields were being laid waste by bombing. It proved an expensive strategy.

German losses, on what they subsequently dubbed 'Black Thursday', were disastrous. In all, 128 Luft-waffe aircrew failed to return and 76 aircraft were lost, although the exaggerated British claim made at the time, that 182 German aircraft had been destroyed, actually exceeded the true figure by over 100.

This included the sacrifice of the equivalent of an entire Zerstörer Gruppe - 27 Bf 110s lost, or damaged to such an extent that they had to be written-off, with another 6 suffering lesser damage. By the end of the day's fighting, 46 officers and men of the Zerstörer units were either dead, missing or captured, with another 9 seriously injured or wounded in action.

It was, by far, the worst day in the operational history of the Bf 110. This scale of losses has prompted some commentators to conclude that 15th August saw the demise of the Bf 110 as an escort fighter and it was only able to fly future operations when escorted by Bf 109s. No firm evidence for this assumption has been found and, as shall be seen, Zerstörers continued to operate unescorted over England in their role as long-range escort fighters for some time to come, although never on the same scale.

Attacks during the day had covered the length and breadth of England, finding no gap in the British defences, and yet, despite some damage to RAF airfields, no significant success was achieved. On both sides, exhausted yet determined pilots resigned themselves to 'more of the same' over the days and weeks to follow.

On 16th August, RAF airfields were again the main targets when, towards mid-day, three simultaneous raids totalling some 350 German aircraft, approached the Thames estuary, Dover and Portland. All fought their way through to their targets in spite of heavy fighter opposition from 12 RAF squadrons.

West Malling was heavily bombed and put out of action for four days. Further attacks were made on the naval airfields at Gosport and Lee-on-Solent, and Ventnor RDF station was hit again, rendering it inoperative until the 23rd of the month. RAF Tangmere was also singled-out, many buildings there, along with 14 aircraft on the ground, destroyed or badly damaged in an attack by Junkers Ju 87s of I./StG 2 who lost 5 of their number to the Tangmere squadrons.

Despite their crippling losses of the previous day, Zerstörers were again in evidence and when not restricted by close-escort duties they showed they still packed a considerable punch. As the raids in the Gosport area developed, No. 249 Squadron from Boscombe Down was patrolling a line from Ringwood to Poole, and detached their Red Section, led by Flight Lieutenant Nicholson, to investigate some aircraft spotted in the distance. Seeing that a squadron of Spitfires were already dealing with these, the three Hurricanes were climbing over Southampton to rejoin the rest of the squadron when they were 'bounced' by Bf 110s.

All three Hurricanes were hit simultaneously. Squadron Leader Eric King, who was flying with the squadron for some combat experience prior to taking command of No. 151 Squadron, was hit and badly damaged but managed to get his Hurricane back to base. His namesake, Pilot Officer Martyn King, baled out only to fall victim of a damaged parachute which collapsed at 1,500 feet plunging him to his death.

Leading Red Section, Flight Lieutenant Nicholson's Hurricane took four cannon shells in the cockpit. He was wounded in the leg and thigh by cannon-shell splinters, and the gravity tank, containing 28 gallons of

Bf 110 of II./ZG 2 behind a Renault tracked vehicle, summer 1940.

Officers of II./ZG 76. From left: Jabs; Herget; Groth and Nacke.

high-octane fuel and located directly behind his instrument panel, exploded in flames.

He was preparing to bale out when a Bf 110 flashed past him - probably overshooting the attack. So, in a singular act of stubborn heroism, and despite the inferno now raging in the cockpit, Nicholson stayed in his seat and delivered an attack on the Bf 110 before the searing heat and enveloping flames finally forced him to abandon the aircraft. Severely burned, Nicholson's agony was further compounded when he was peppered by shotgun pellets by an over-zealous LDV sergeant, as he drifted down in his parachute over Millbrook.

For this act of undoubted bravery, Nicholson was subsequently decorated with the first and only Victoria Cross awarded to Fighter Command - the VC being the highest award for gallantry his country could bestow. The official entry in the London Gazette, dated 15th November, cited the destruction of the Bf 110 he had attacked, but this is doubted. Post-war research of contemporary records cannot confirm the loss of a Bf 110 in circumstances which tally with Nicholson's combat.

Nicholson's own combat report of the action, which he dictated while in hospital, is more accurate, and simply details the enemy casualties as 'Inconclusive 1 ME. 110 prob.'. In his own words, couched in the stilted form beloved of officialdom, "Saw ME. 110 diving at same angle and converging - opened fire at approx. 200 yds., and fired till I could bear heat no more. Reflector sight was on but cannot swear whether firing button was at 'safe' or 'fire'. Eye witnesses on ground state that ME. 110 zigzagged and dived steeply after Hurricane opened fire.".

Meantime, the rest of No. 249 Squadron had landed

Bf 110 C, 2N + AP, of 9./ZG 76, whose pilot, Oblt. Schlaffer made a very successful belly-landing on 16/8/40 at Lee Farm, Clapham, near Worthing. The upright, undamaged propeller blade on the port engine indicates that it had been feathered before the landing. This aircraft carried the '3 wasps above a cloud' emblem.

without incident. Among them was Pilot Officer 'Ginger' Neil, still keen for his first sighting of an enemy aircraft, 'let alone an interception', since their move south two days earlier. He vividly describes the trauma and the tension. "Squadron Leader Whizzy King was among us. Excited. Garrulous. Hurrying about. His face creased by sweat and the lines of his oxygen mask. Yes, he'd been hit and damaged. No, he wasn't wounded, but the others had gone. Both shot down. In flames. The blighters had come down and caught them unawares. Down from behind. Me 110s. Whizzy was in a highly emotional state and kept talking about tactics. We'd have to do things differently. Talking quickly and gesticulating."

Six days later, having apparently gained all the combat experience he required, Squadron Leader King assumed command of 151 Squadron at North Weald. He would lead them for only 9 days before his own death in action on 30th August.

Over at Westhampnett, No. 602 Squadron, another 'replacement' squadron which had only recently moved down south into the battle zone, received the order to scramble when officially 'released'. They were extremely lucky to get their Spitfires off the ground just as the Stukas commenced their dives on nearby Tangmere.

Later that afternoon, a strong force of Zerstörers were deployed to form part of the escort for heavy bombing raids which developed around 5:00 pm. that afternoon; aircraft of II./ZG 2, II./ZG 76 and III./ZG 76

all operating as independent Gruppen.

No. 602 Squadron were better warned but still a little unprepared for the hectic pace of combat in their new sector of operations. Squadron Leader Sandy Johnstone recalls, "The air was a kaleidoscope of aeroplanes swooping and diving around us, and for a moment I felt like pulling the blankets over my head and pretending I wasn't there! I had no idea it could be as chaotic as this! I selected a gaggle of 110s and dived to attack. Out of the corner of my eye I caught sight of a Spitfire having a go at another 110 and blowing the canopy clean off it. A Hurricane on fire flashed by and I was momentarily taken aback when the pilot of the aircraft in front of me baled out, until I realised he had come from the 110 I had been firing at! Then it was all over. No one else was about."

Despite some anomalies in their respective accounts, the Bf 110 attacked by Squadron Leader Sandy Johnstone could well have been flown by Leutnant Richard Marchfelder, the Gruppe TO of III./ZG 76. He and his Bordfunker, Obergefreiter Herbert Jentsch, are the only Zerstörer crew known to have abandoned their aircraft in the area at this time.

III./ZG 76 were on the return leg of their escort sortie for the Heinkel He 111s of KG 55, when Kaldrack detached Marchfelder from the Stabsschwarm and ordered him to hang behind, at safe altitude, to keep an eye out for crippled bombers. 'Rima' was to radio the Gruppe for help in the event of any trouble.

As Marchfelder recalls, "Far to the east, about ten

Bf 110 'Sharksmouth' of II./ZG 76 crash-landed in a field in France.

miles ahead...there appeared four Heinkels on their way home. Like scared rabbits they hedgehopped from one batch of clouds to the next, desperately looking for cover. Just then a single aircraft appeared at eleven o'clock! It popped out from the clouds into the sky like a cork from a champagne bottle. As it ignored the Heinkels it was obviously a Me 109, like us guarding the bombers...Relieved that someone else was keeping a watch on the bombers, there was no reason to hang around any longer. I changed course five degrees to the right, to beam in on our home run to Lannion via Portsmouth. The other plane must have seen us because he too changed his direction, turning away from the Heinkels, now facing us. As he banked into position, he exposed for a moment its elliptical shaped wings. It was a Spitfire."

Marchfelder immediately swung into the attack, pushing both throttles wide open and diving head-on at the Spitfire which was climbing to reach them. The British pilot, realising that the Zerstörer was coming straight for him, showed signs of becoming nervous and opened fire too early. Seconds later, with the Spitfire squarely framed in his gun-sight, Marchfelder opened fire with his cannons.

Quickly laying-off a head-on attack, the Spitfire's only chance was to try passing below the Bf 110 but, according to Marchfelder, he miscalculated. "Something went wrong! We both pulled away, unfortunately in the same direction. There was a thud, Ursula shuddered like a car hitting its wheel against a big stone. Nothing happened, except Herbert landed on the floor, together with his harness."

The Bf 110 was damaged, crabbing hard to the right, and demanding all Marchfelder's strength to keep her under control. "With great effort I... managed to move my right leg over to the left rudder to help reduce the pressure (and) keep Ursula on her course. Although we were unable to see anything, out position must have been north of Portsmouth.

"Then, unexpectedly, the starboard engine burst into flames, its propeller paddling in a ball of fire. Closing the fuel line didn't seem to have any effect... Nor did the fire extinguisher show any results. In the distance, the Channel appeared. But to get there and cross it seemed hopelessly remote! Ignoring my silent prayers, flames were creeping through the wall, eating into the cockpit."

Reluctantly accepting the inevitable, Marchfelder gave the order to bale out: 'Aussteigen!' "Herbert couldn't get out! The cover of the 'greenhouse' was jammed! He pushed against it with all the strength he could muster, but it did not budge! Fumes of burning rubber mixed with oxygen were filling my lungs making me cough violently. Fighting for breath, I was getting dizzy."

Struggling to maintain control, Marchfelder tried to turn the aircraft onto its back but the smoke and fumes were affecting his sense of orientation. "I was getting engulfed in flames. Only then it occurred to me that I was turning over the burning engine. Fighting desperately to move away from the heat, I jerked Ursula to the left! As a result Herbert fell out, into the fresh atmosphere, together with his (cockpit) cover!

Marchfelder then tried to lift himself out of the

Lt. Walter Lemmer, pilot of 5./ZG 76, killed in action on 16/8/40.

Uffz. Wilhelm Maier, Bordfunker of Major Harry Carl, Gruppenkommandeur of II./ZG 2. Both were killed on 16/8/40 when their Bf 110 crashed in France following damage in combat over the Channel.

cockpit, but his parachute pack got caught under the rear cockpit frame. It was impossible to move, let alone jump - he was trapped! Struggling to release himself, and desperate to avoid the agony of being roasted alive, he finally managed to pull his parachute clear of the framework and fell clear. "I was free! But not before passing through a ball of fire. What a relief it was to be greeted by the soothing cold air at seven thousand metres."

Jentzsch and Marchfelder both survived, landing safely near Amberley, but 'Rima' wrenched his knee badly on landing. Their aircraft crashed 6 miles away at Droke, near Upwaltham, north-east of Brighton - one of three Bf 110s lost by III./ZG 76 during the late-afternoon fighting.

Oberleutnant Urban Schlaffer, Staffelkapitän of 9./ZG 76, was shot down by another No. 602 Squadron Spitfire, possibly Pilot Officer Moody, and force-landed at Lee Farm, Clapham, where he was captured along with his Bordfunker, Obergefreiter Franz Obser. The third Zerstörer lost by the Gruppe crashed into the Channel, its fortunate crew rescued by the Seenotdienst.

Back at Lannion, Kaldrack assessed the situation in the Gruppe. Moving Oberleutnant Walter Schiller from the Stabsschwarm to take over as caretaker Staffelkapitän of 7th Staffel, and appointing Leutnant Helmut Florenz, the Gruppe NO, as Staffelkapitän of 9th Staffel, left the Stabsschwarm sadly depleted. Now, with the loss of Marchfelder, only Leutnant Dieter Nülle, the Gruppenadjutant, remained of Dickoré's old team. III./ZG 76 were long on experience but suddenly short of officers.

Hauptmann Groth's II./ZG 76 also got embroiled with British fighters north of Brighton, and lost 22 year-old Leutnant Walter Lemmer of 5th Staffel who is believed to have crashed into the grounds of Shopwhyke House, a mansion near Tangmere used as an officer's mess by the Westhampnett squadrons. No trace of the unfortunate Lemmer or his young 19 year-old Bordfunker, Obergefreiter Josef Lewandowski, was ever found.

Major Carl's II./ZG 2 also lost one of their Bf 110s to British fighters, possibly Flying Officer Salmon of No. 1 Squadron, in a short series of bitter combats which erupted over the Sussex coast. The Zerstörer, with a relatively new crew from Oberleutnant Eberhard Heinlein's 6th Staffel, lost its tail and broke up in mid-air, spreading a mile-long trail of debris across Eastbourne. Its pilot, Oberleutnant Ernst Hollekamp, baled out too low for his parachute to deploy and was killed, smashing into the roof of a house in Gaudick Road. His Bordfunker, Feldwebel Richard Schurk, also baled out and landed just off-shore, clearly visible from the esplanade. But no effort was made to rescue him and he drowned, his body coming ashore at Eastbourne on 4th September.

Major Harry Carl, Gruppenkommandeur of II./ZG 2,

Two views of the burial ceremony of Major Harry Carl, Gruppenkommandeur, and his Bordfunker, Uffz. Wilhelm Maier, of II./ZG 2, who were killed while attempting a force-landing on return from a combat mission on 16/8/40. The impassive grave digger in the background in the upper photograph awaits his final instructions.

This page and overleaf: Three views of the wreckage of Bf 110 C, A2 + GL, of Oblt. Ernst Hollekamp and his Bord-funker, Fw. Richard Schurk, of 6./ZG 2 in the grounds of Aldro School, Eastbourne on 16/8/40. In the view over-leaf, the individual aircraft letter can be seen outboard of the wing cross. Hollekamp and Schurk were both killed.

also had his Bf 110 damaged on this sortie but managed to nurse his crippled aircraft all the way back across the Channel. But the effort of landing proved too much, for he crashed just south of Beauzeville and died in the aircraft along with his Bordfunker, Unteroffizier Wilhelm Maier. Carl, well over 37 years of age and maybe somewhat old for combat flying, was a highly experienced Zerstörer pilot previously with the Stabsschwarm of I./ZG 1. His successor was Hauptmann Heinlein, the Staffelkapitän of 6./ZG 2, who took over as acting-Gruppenkommandeur.

By the end of the day, another 44 German aircraft had failed to return, a total which included 8 Bf 110s and added to the heavy cumulative losses suffered by the Zerstörers over the preceding days. But the RAF had also lost 24 aircraft and 11 more pilots - the same human price as exacted on the previous day. In the war of attrition being waged over southern England the advantage was swinging in favour of the Luftwaffe.

After a lull on the 17th, British airfields were again the main targets on 18th August but the attacks scheduled for the morning were delayed by hazy conditions over southern England. Mid-morning, a high-flying weather-reconnaissance sortie by a solitary Bf 110 of 7.(F)/LG 2 was intercepted and shot down into the sea by 5 Spitfires of No. 54 Squadron. Then, shortly after mid-day, the RAF fighter airfields covering the southern approaches to London were targeted by 108 bombers and 150 fighters of Luftflotte 2.

The ambitious plan was for a forward fighter sweep by Messerschmitt Bf 109s of III./JG 26 and JG 3, who would blanket the target area, ahead of 12 Junkers Ju

88s of II./KG 76, who were to dive-bomb Kenley. This attack would immediately precede a ground-level strike by 9 Dornier Do 17s from 9./KG 76, a unit which specialised in such 'Tiefangriff' attacks. Meanwhile, Biggin Hill would be targeted by 60 Heinkel He 111s from KG 1. Finally, high altitude bombing by I. and III. KG 76 would complete the devastation at Kenley, their 27 Dornier Do 17s enjoying a close-escort of 20 Zerstörers from ZG 26 'Horst Wessel'.

The 'Horst Wessel' Geschwader had suffered relatively few losses since attacks on England had begun in earnest. Apart from some minor losses to I. Gruppe over the preceding days, III./ZG 26 had experienced no serious combat losses since 10th July, and II./ZG 26 since 18th May. Today, a bitter balance would be struck and with a vengeance. Flying as a Bordfunker in Hauptmann Hubert Lüttke's 4./ZG 26, Unteroffizier Theodor Rutters remembers, "On this mission we had the first losses of planes and some casualties in my Gruppe."

As this massive German formation approached across the Channel, five RAF squadrons, Nos. 17, 54, 56, 65 and 501, were already airborne over the north Kent coast to cover the approaches to the Thames estuary. Four more squadrons, Nos. 32, 64, 610 and 615, were scrambled from Kenley and Biggin Hill to defend their bases as the German intentions became clear.

As they neared the English coast, feelings among the Zerstörer crews were mixed. Leutnant Joachim Koepsell of 1./ZG 26 was in a quandary - with one engine labouring should he break off the flight or see it

Messerschmitt 110 C-4 of 7th Staffel, Zerstörergeschwader 26
Pilot – Oberleutnant Ernst Matthes(Staffelkapitän) Bordfunker – Oberfeldwebel Franz Santel
Crash-landed at Cherbourg on 25th September 1940

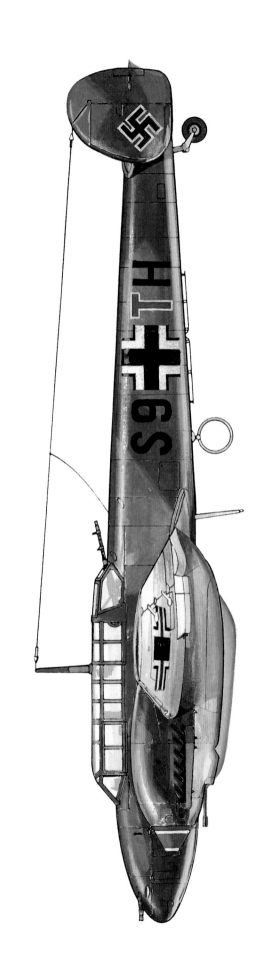

Messerschmitt 110 C–6 of 1st Staffel, Erprobungsgruppe 210
Pilot–Leutnant Erich Beudel Bordfunker–Obergefreiter Otto Jordan
Crashed at Broadbridge Farm, Smallfield, Horley on 15th August 1940

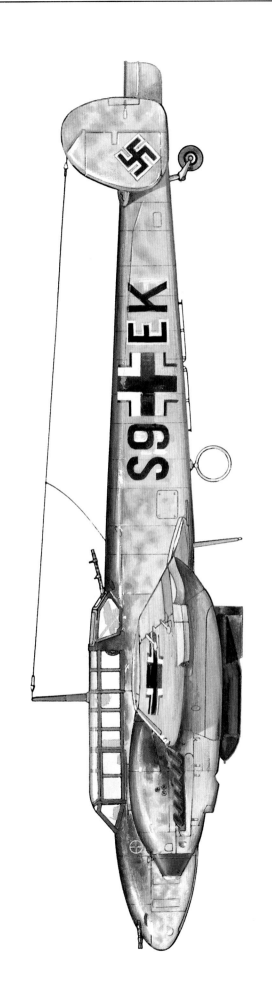

Messerschmitt 110 D-0 of 2nd Staffel, Erprobungsgruppe 210
Pilot-Unteroffizier Balthasar Aretz Bordfunker-Gefreiter Rolf Schilleng

Messerschmitt 110 C of Gruppenstab, II. Gruppe, Zerstörergeschwader 76
Pilot–Oberleutnant Hermann Weeber   Bordfunker–Unteroffizier Max Michael
Force–landed at Little Butts Farm, Cousley Wood, on 4th September 1940

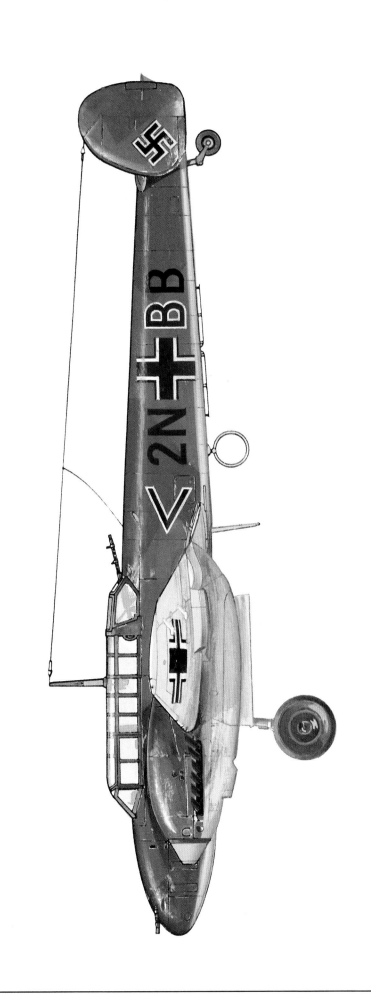

Messerschmitt 110 C of the Adjutant, Gruppenstab, I. Gruppe, Zerstörergeschwader 1
May/June 1940

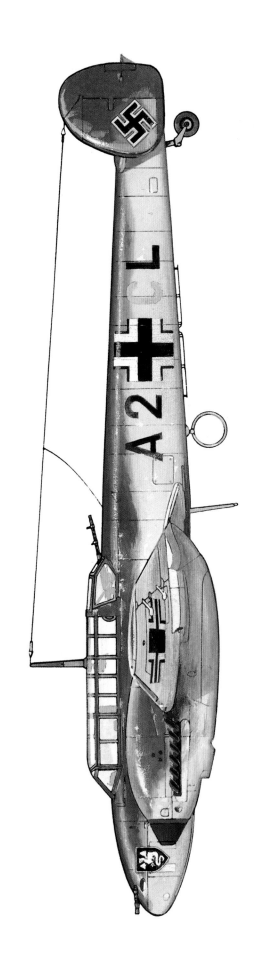

Messerschmitt 110 C of 6th Staffel, Zerstörergeschwader 2
August 1940

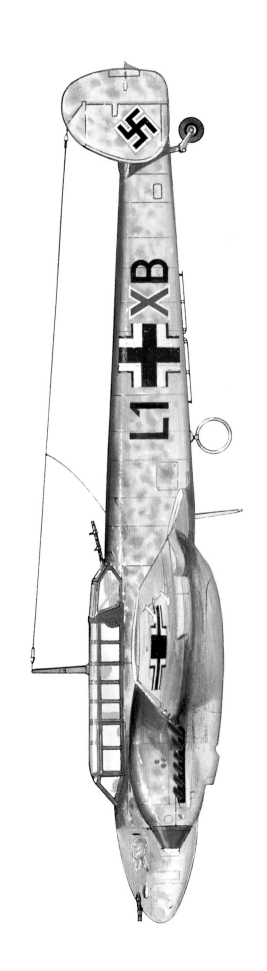

Messerschmitt 110 C of the Gruppenkommandeur of V.(Zerstörer), Lehrgeschwader 1
Pilot–Gruppenkommandeur, Hauptmann Horst Liensberger

Messerschmitt 110 D of 1st Staffel, Zerstörergeschwader76

Lt. Hans-Ulrich Kettling (left), POW 15/8/40, and Lt. Rüdiger Proske, POW 18/8/40.

through? But after nursing the troublesome engine along for 30 minutes, common sense prevailed and he turned back for Clairmarais.

Firing a short burst to check his gun, a pensive Unteroffizier Rutters recalls, "We reached the coast at a height of about 7,000 metres and when I looked up I saw Me 109s, Spitfires and Hurricanes circling."

With No. 615 Squadron's Hurricanes keeping the Bf 109 fighter cover occupied, No. 32 Squadron slipped through the escort to attack the Dornier Do 17s as they forged inland. Squadron Leader Mike Crossley led 'A' Flight into an attack on the bombers, as Flight Lieutenant Peter Brothers took 'B' Flight into a steep climbing turn to meet the Bf 110s head-on - the Zerstörers diving down and attempting to turn in behind the Hurricanes. But unknown to the Bf 110s as they closed on the Hurricanes, Squadron Leader 'Don' MacDonnell was bringing 8 Spitfires of No. 64 Squadron down behind them from 20,000 feet.

Among the leading Zerstörers, Oberleutnant Rüdiger Proske, the Gruppenadjutant of I./ZG 26, dived with the Stabsschwarm clean through the Hurricanes and positioned himself between the British fighters and the Dorniers. As the fighters tangled, Flight Lieutenant

Gruppenadjutant, Oblt. Rüdiger Proske, of Stab, I./ZG 26 force-landed this Bf 110 C-4, U8+BB, W. Nr. 3102, at Dering Farm, Lydd on 18/8/40. As well as carrying the 'Ringelpitz' emblem of I. Gruppe, and the chevron denoting the adjutant's aircraft (the pencil through the chevron in this instance was a sardonic comment on the amount of paperwork heaped on an adjutant on top of flying duties), this aircraft also carried the 'Horst Wessel' Geschwader emblem of the letters H and W intertwined on a red and black quartered shield. Proske and his Bordfunker, Uffz. Hans Mobius, survived the landing.

'Humph' Russell, on his first operational sortie with No. 32 Squadron after a period in the Operations Room, was surprised to be hit by extremely accurate and concentrated return fire from the Bf 110s and was forced to bale out over Edenbridge wounded in the left arm and right leg. First blood to the Zerstörers!

Completing their headlong dives, the Spitfires of No. 64 Squadron curved behind the German fighters, Squadron Leader MacDonnell's scything attack on Proske's Bf 110 hitting both engines and wounding the Bordfunker, Unteroffizier Hans Möbius. Acting instinctively, Proske immediately pushed both throttles wide open and deliberately took his hands and feet off the controls, allowing the heavy aircraft to go into a violent spin. It was a risky manoeuvre but it worked, for it threw off the British fighters who were convinced that the Bf 110 was done for. Proske's comrades who witness his dive were equally convinced and gave him up for dead.

Spinning through 6,000 feet before regaining control, Proske set course for the coast and home. Both engines were smoking heavily but still running, but as he crossed the coast at Dungeness, first one, and then

Three views of the remains of the Bf 110 C-2 crewed by Uffz. Rudolf Mai and Uffz. Josef Gebauer of 1./ZG 26, which came to grief at Rough Common, Harbledown, on 18/8/40. Both crewmen were declared 'missing in action'.

the other, ground to a halt and caught fire. Mobius was badly wounded in the legs and unable to move, so Proske quickly decided against ditching in the Channel and turned back inland seeking a suitable landing place.

With both engines now dead but burning merrily, Proske just managed to clear some HT cables before slamming the aircraft down on its belly at Dering Farm, Lydd. It was a heavy landing which cost him a few teeth but, quickly releasing his seat harness, he pulled Möbius out of the cockpit and dragged him away from the aircraft and the danger of explosion. Seeking cover, they slid down into the bottom of an irrigation ditch where, within a few minutes, they were found by troops from a nearby AA site. They were 'in the bag'.

Meantime the battle raged above. Snatching bursts at fleeting targets, Unteroffizier Theo Rutters of 4./ZG 26 recalls, "The bombers were eager to drop their loads and on our way home we were attacked by a group of English fighters. Our orders were to protect the bombers, so we accepted combat, giving them the chance to escape home."

As the German formation started their withdrawal, Pilot Officer 'Polly' Flinders of No. 32 Squadron out-manoeuvred one of the Bf 110s and chased it east from Kenley. It was a scene reminiscent of 'Hells Angels', for in Flinders' own words, "He immediately dived towards the ground. At 3,000 feet he levelled out and I found that I was gradually closing in. We passed to the north of West Malling and over Detling. I was at about 600 yards. A running fight then ensued, (the Bf 110) doing barrel rolls and half-rolls in an attempt to get rid of me. We were now down to 200 feet and as I knew that I had very little ammunition left I refrained from firing until I had a certain target."

This exhibition of low-flying was testament to the increasing desperation of Unteroffizier Rudolf Mai of 1./ZG 26 to escape Flinders' unwelcome attentions, while his equally desperate Bordfunker, Unteroffizier Josef Gebauer, tried to keep the Hurricane at a respectful distance.

As the two fighters roared low over Dunkirk in Kent, the Zerstörer was hit by ground-fire, causing it to slow up and allowing Flinders to close the range. He emptied his remaining ammunition into Mai's crippled aircraft which promptly burst into flames, dipped its nose, and spread itself across Rough Common, at Harbledown, exploding on impact.

Now, as the Germans retired back across Kent, fresh British squadrons which had been patrolling the north Kent coast were released to join the fray, No. 56 Squadron's Hurricanes falling on the Bf 110s over Ashford as they covered the retreating bomber's left flank. In the unequal running fight which quickly developed, more and more British fighters poured into the area, and 6./ZG 26 was all but wiped out.

Attacking one of the Zerstörers, Pilot Officer Maurice Mounsdon found himself overhauling his target so fast that he was forced to throttle back to avoid overshooting. Probably already damaged, the Bf 110 reared up under his attack and fell away on one wing, diving vertically into a copse at Elmstone Hole, near Lenham, where it blew up.

The crew, Oberleutnant Heinz Hellmuth and Feldwebel Franz Winter, were both killed on impact. Yet three days later, Hauptmann Graf von Stillfried, writing on behalf of the Staffel to Winter's father back in Teublitz, offered the hope that there was 'every indication that he was a prisoner'. He promised more news as soon as it was received, but not until 13th October did the Staffel confirm, via the International Red Cross in Geneva, that Franz had 'died in English captivity' - by which time Stillfried himself had been dead a week.

Sergeant Robinson of No. 56 Squadron singled-out another 6./ZG 26 aircraft which, after a few sustained bursts of fire from the Hurricane's guns, went into a shallow inverted glide. He followed it down to see it crash and burst into flames among open fields at Pluckley. The crew, Oberfeldwebel Adolf Kiefel and Unteroffizier Josef Hemmersbach, were both killed.

Simultaneous take-off of five Bf 110s of 4./ZG 26 from a French airfield during the Battle of Britain.

Bf 110 C, 3U + EP, of Lt. Hans-Joachim Kästner and his Bordfunker, Uffz. Walter Kaffenberger following the force-landing at Blackstone, Newchurch, on 18/8/40. Note the early-style solid two-tone camouflage down the fuselage sides, the spinner tips in the Staffel colour of yellow, and the 6th Staffel emblem.

Leutnant Hans-Joachim Kästner was more fortunate. He managed to shake off the Hurricanes after their initial attacks, but his aircraft had been badly damaged. Unable to reach the Channel, he was forced to make a belly-landing at Blackmanstone, near Newchurch, and he and his Bordfunker, Unteroffizier Walter Kaffenberger, were both captured unhurt.

Pilot Officer George Goodman of No. 1 Squadron also managed to get into the action, chasing another of 6th Staffel's damaged Bf 110s out over the Channel off Felixstowe. Already heavily damaged in the attacks by No. 56 Squadron's Hurricanes, and with smoke streaming from its port engine, it was all that Feldwebel Herbert Stange could do to jink his aircraft from side to side to avoid Goodman's fire. But then the overstrained engine finally burst into flames, closely followed by the other.

Closing for the kill and concentrating on his target, Goodman was very lucky to survive a sudden attack from behind by a Bf 109 and was forced to break away, but he was confident that the Bf 110 was finished. So it was, and the Bf 110 hit the sea heavily, Feldwebel Stange later being picked up and taken into captivity, but his Bordfunker, Unteroffizier Gerhard Wollin was killed - his body subsequently recovered from the sea and buried at Hawkinge.

The carnage was not limited to 6th Staffel, however. Flying Officer 'Squeak' Weaver of No. 56 Squadron shot down a 3./ZG 26 machine which fell just short of the coast at Bonnington, a blazing shambles. What little remained of the pilot, coincidentally another Stange, Oberfeldwebel Willi Stange, and his Bordfunker, Unteroffizier Hans Hesse, defied identification and they were both buried as 'Unknown Airmen' in the nearby churchyard of St. Stephan at Lympne.

Yet the Zerstörers seemingly gave as good as they got, with Theo Rossiwall's 5./ZG 26 returning to base with 2 British fighters destroyed without loss to themselves. Major Schalk's III. Gruppe filed claims for a total of 14 Spitfires and a single Hurricane destroyed, Leutnant Botho Sommer of the Stabsschwarm scoring his 5th victory.

Oberleutnant Meyer's 8th Staffel took the honours claiming 6 of these, with the Staffelkapitän himself scoring his 6th victory. Leutnant Wehmeyer and Unteroffizier Schupp opened their personal scores, while Sophus Baagoe maintained his position as top scorer in the Gruppe with his 9th victory. Feldwebel Scherer notched up his 5th, with the balance being evenly split between Oberleutnant Matthes' 7th Staffel and Oberleutnant Montag's 9th Staffel, who claimed 3 victories apiece.

The reality, as usual, was somewhat different, a total of 16 British fighters actually being lost during these early-afternoon combats; 4 of the pilots being killed. Another 9 Hurricanes and Spitfires were rendered unserviceable due to combat damage.

The pressure was maintained, with ZG 26 back in action later that afternoon when, at around 5:00 pm., the Geschwader provided 25 Zerstörers as close escort for Heinkel He 111s of KG 53 bound for North Weald. Simultaneously, Hornchurch was the target for 58 Dornier Do 17s of KG 2; additional escort for both attacks coming from over 100 Bf 109s.

Unteroffizier Theo Rutters of 4./ZG 26, like most in his Gruppe on their second sortie of the day, felt most uncomfortable at the prospect of another mission shackled to the bombers. "Our mission was almost the same as before. We were under strict orders to fly close escort and this was the reason for the disaster which followed."

No less than 17 RAF fighter squadrons were ordered to readiness as this huge raid, numbering almost 250 aircraft, started to develop. A total of 47 Spitfires and 96 Hurricanes were eventually ordered to intercept and were largely successful in repulsing both attacks.

First to engage, and completely unscathed in the morning fracas, the 12 Hurricanes of No. 56 Squadron met the incoming raid when it was still some miles off the Essex coast. Squadron Leader 'Minnie' Manton led Red Section into the attack on the Bf 110 escort, leaving the rest of the squadron to take on the bombers. Dangerously outnumbered, his 3 Hurricanes could only make snap attacks before breaking away to select other targets. But their niggling attacks left at least one Bf 110 streaming glycol from both engines and leaving formation in a shallow dive towards Sheppey as more British fighters arrived.

This may well have been a 4./ZG 26 machine piloted by Unteroffizier Heinz Jäckel, at 19 years of age one of the youngest pilots in the unit. His Bordfunker, Theo Rütters recalls, "After we had flown through cloud cover at about 4,000 metres, we were attacked by at least 25 Spitfires."

With the rest of the escort already engaged by British fighters above the clouds, Rutters unit, flying close to the bombers as ordered, had received no warning before coming under direct attack. "We had no chance to go into fighting formation. Our only chance of defence was to avoid presenting easy targets. But it didn't work for long. Eventually we were hit in both engines. Without engine power we had to try an emergency landing wherever we could. It became a crash-landing because all (the) fields were blocked by obstacles. Our plane caught fire and I scrambled through the hole behind the cockpit to the bottom (of the fuselage) to avoid the flames."

The crippled Zerstörer crossed Eastchurch airfield, where it came under fire from AA but avoided further damage, and hit the ground at Leysdown in a shallow glide. Unfortunately, they were not flying their usual aircraft on this sortie as it was unserviceable, and the pilot's harness straps had not been adjusted to suit

Uffz. Theodor Rütters of 4./ZG 26 wearing the standard Bordfunker's headgear for the Battle of Britain period. Rütters was shot down into captivity on 18/8/40.

Jäckel, who was quite tall. Consequently, he flew this mission without being strapped in properly and was thrown forward onto the instrument panel on landing, and was badly injured and knocked unconscious as a result.

Despite Rütters' increasingly desperate efforts, he was unable to rescue the unconscious pilot from the burning aircraft largely because Jäckel had not jettisoned his cockpit hood prior to landing. Finally beaten back by increasing heat and flames, the distraught Rütters retreated to a safe distance. "A few seconds after I had left the wing of the plane it blew up in a column of fire." Badly burned on his face and hands, he would spend over a week in the Royal Navy Hospital at Chatham before starting his long period as 'a guest of King George VI'.

Meantime No. 56 Squadron's Hurricanes had become separated after their initial attacks and were now prone to attacks from the hordes of German fighters. Flying Officer Innes Westmacott found himself alone and under attack from all sides by Zerstörers. "There were a lot of Messerschmitt 110s about and they all seemed to be picking on me! Whichever way I turned, there seemed to be one shooting at me. I made for cover of a small cloud. Unfortunately the cloud was too small and I kept popping out of it, to find the Messerschmitts flying round outside. I had a shower of tracer about my ears and was frequently hit. No friends were in sight and it was clear I had to get away - fast!"

Desperate to escape, Westmacott rammed the throttle through the emergency gate, rolled his aircraft onto its back and pulled the stick hard back into his stomach. With the Hurricane standing on its nose, he went into a screaming vertical dive, plunging straight down out of the cloud and soon reaching a paralysing indicated airspeed of 350 mph. "I almost blacked-out when I pulled out of the dive, praying that the aircraft would stay in one piece. I was as terrified as I have ever been in my life!"

Flying with the Stabsschwarm of II./ZG 26, Feldwebel Josef Radlmair was in his usual position as Bordfunker to the Gruppenadjutant, Oberleutnant Walter Henken. Ahead of them flew the Kommandeur, Hauptmann Ralph von Rettberg, and off to one side the Bf 110 of the Gruppe NO, Leutnant Thüring. Behind them came the rest of the Gruppe, or at least all that could be made available - which was fewer and fewer machines. Radlmair had not flown on the morning sortie, but this afternoon's action would more than compensate. On return to St. Omer on completion of his 31st war-flight, his terse Flugbuch entry: 'Luftkampf', would hardly do it justice.

Leading the Hurricanes of No. 85 Squadron from Debden, Squadron Leader Peter Townsend emerged from cloud over the Thames estuary to be greeted by the sight of "a massive column about a mile and a half high, stepped up wave upon wave.

Fw. Friedhelm Gierga of 4./ZG 26 and his wife. Gierga survived into captivity when his Bf 110 was shot down on 18/8/40.

"As we closed in on the bombers, ...a dozen Me. 110s cut across us and immediately formed a defensive circle. 'In we go', I called over the R/T, and a moment later a Me. 110 had banked clumsily across my bows. In its vain attempt to escape, the machine I was bent on destroying suddenly looked pathetically human. It was an easy shot - too easy."

Hauptmann Hubert Lüttke's 4./ZG 26 were particularly hard-pressed as more and more British squadrons joined the battle. Pilot Officer Colin Gray, piloting one of No. 54 Squadron's Spitfires, attacked one of their Bf 110s, which stall-turned, rolled onto its back and went into a steep dive from 15,000 feet. Not wishing to sacrifice too much height, Gray left it slowly spiralling towards Clacton, where it dived deep into some waste ground at Smith's Sandpits, in Alton Park Road. No trace of the pilot, Lüttke himself, nor his Bordfunker, Unteroffizier Herbert Brillo, was found.

Another 4./ZG 26 pilot, Feldwebel Friedhelm Gierga, was attacked simultaneously by three Hurricanes of No. 85 Squadron and forced to ditch his aircraft in the sea off North Foreland. Gierga was rescued later that evening and became a prisoner, but no trace of his Bordfunker, Unteroffizier Gerhard Baar, was ever found, and he is presumed to have gone down with the aircraft.

A fourth 4th Staffel machine managed to extricate itself from the combat and staggered back to land at Wizernes, but the Bordfunker, Unteroffizier Willi Völlinger, was so severely wounded that he died within hours of admission to hospital in St. Omer.

On his 15th war-flight, and last sortie with Graf von Stillfried's 1./ZG 26, Leutnant Joachim Koepsell found himself hounded by a particularly dogged Hurricane which seemed to have an answer for every flying trick he knew. He eventually had to resort to violent bunts whenever his Bordfunker, Unteroffizier Johann Schmidt, shouted the warning that the Hurricane was opening fire. Avoiding four attacks in this way, Koepsell finally had to dive vertically for the sea knowing that now it was simply a question of whose nerve would last out. To his immense relief, with the waves below them rapidly drawing into ever sharper focus, the Hurricane pulled out a split second before him, the Bf 110 levelling out a bare hundred feet above the waves. He got back to Clairmarais after a flight lasting 2¼ hours, astonished to find only 5 hits on his aircraft.

However the sea would lay claim to another Zerstörer pilot. Herbert Kaminski, Staffelkapitän of 2./ZG 26, severely damaged in combat with the British fighters, was forced to ditch during the return flight when both engines failed about 12 miles east of Foulness.

Due to an unhealed shoulder wound from 15th May, Kaminski was flying without harness straps, and was thrown forward violently by the force of impact with the sea, breaking his nose on the instrument panel. His Bordfunker, 20 year-old Westphalian Unteroffizier Heinrich Strauch, also suffered a head injury but got out and deployed the dinghy.

Unaccountably, he failed to connect the oxygen bottle properly, and the dinghy failed to inflate. This

Flying personnel of 9./ZG 26 at readiness during the Battle of Britain.

prompted an enraged Kaminski to place the abject Strauch under 10 days close arrest as they both trod water and pondered their situation, which was dire. Later, when they found that the dinghy was shot through and wouldn't have inflated anyway, Kaminski reluctantly rescinded this punishment

Stripping off their bulky flying clothing and heavy boots, they were relieved to be circled by a returning aircraft which obviously radioed their position, for as twilight fell a welcome Heinkel He 59 rescue floatplane of the Seenotdienst appeared. They watched with growing despair as it tried to land on the choppy sea, but the waves were too high and it was forced to leave them after dropping another dinghy which they reached with considerable difficulty and boarded with even greater effort.

They spent a miserable night bobbing around in the North Sea, singing desultory songs and reciting interminable snatches of Goethe before being rescued by a German Navy minesweeper the following morning. In a joint inter-service search and rescue mission organised by the Geschwaderkommodore himself, Oberst Huth, it was guided to them by four Zerstörers of their unit. Kaminski and Strauch were both admitted to hospital in Dunkirk, Kaminski subsequently flying over 50 sorties against England and claiming two British fighters destroyed before his transfer to the Zerstörerschule at Schleissheim the following October. He would later return to combat duties, and would ultimately be awarded the Ritterkreuz on 6th August 1941.

As darkness gathered, both sides retired to count

the cost of another day of relentless combat. Rossiwall's 5./ZG 26 claimed 4 more victories during this late-afternoon action, once again avoiding any loss or damage to themselves. III./ZG 26 claimed another 7 Spitfires and 3 Hurricanes destroyed, their 7th Staffel enjoying a particularly successful sortie with Feldwebel Franz Sander notching up his second and third kills and making it three for the day. Leutnant Konopka also claimed a 'doppel' on this sortie and Oberfeldwebel Josef Bracun chalked up his second victory, the 30th for the Staffel, with a Spitfire over mid-Channel.

In fact no Spitfires were lost, RAF casualties all being Hurricanes. Nine were shot down, most of them during combat with the Bf 110s, another 3 aircraft returning with damage. Four more British pilots were killed, bringing their total losses for the day to 33 aircraft and 10 pilots.

The Luftwaffe had lost twice as many aircraft, 67 in all, although the RAF reckoned to have destroyed more than double this amount, with 153 claimed. This total included the loss of 16 Bf 110s, at current operating levels the equivalent of two Staffeln, and 27 of their crewmen, another severe blow to the Zerstörers.

As one young Spitfire pilot, Pilot Officer Colin Gray, commented, "a colossal raid...after this scrap they weren't so free with their 110s." An indisputable fact, but not for the reason so often assumed, which was that the Bf 110, like the Stuka, had finally met its match and was at last recognised to be outclassed and out-gunned by British fighters. The facts were far more simple: there weren't enough airworthy Zerstörers left

This Bf 110 of ZG 26 is fully jacked-up for a thorough servicing, with groundcrew working on the starboard undercarriage leg.

in the units to sustain such a level of operations any longer.

At a conference at Karinhall the very next day, Reichsmarschall Göring, in a further resumé of the conduct of the battle, reiterated his firmly held view that, "Twin-engined fighters are to be employed where the range of single-engined aircraft is insufficient, or where they can facilitate the breaking-off from combat of single-engined formations. The protection of returning bombers and fighters over the Channel must be assured by specially designated fighter formations." Evidently, Göring felt that the Zerstörer was still far from finished as a front-line fighter.

But even as the sad tally was taking place that evening, some Zerstörer pilots were adapting to their unexpected change in circumstances. Nervously enjoying a drink in the Officers' Mess of an RAF station where he had been deposited, Proske's sketchy English was being stretched to the limit: "Where do you come from?", one seemingly solicitous enquiry about his home town. Wishing to be polite, but still alert and security-conscious, he replied, "The other side!" - it brought the house down. 'Things could be a lot worse' he pondered.

He remained a guest of the RAF for some time, before being transported to Cockfosters for processing and interrogation. Here, he shared a room with 'Uli' Kettling of 1./ZG 76, who had been captured on 15th August. Suspecting concealed microphones in their cell, they hatched a scheme to contrive long and tantalising conversations for the benefit of the listening RAF. It was all total rubbish, of course, but it kept them amused, and was clearly intriguing enough for the Brit-

Rolf Schilleng, Bordfunker, of 2./Erpr. Gr. 210.

Uffz. Erhard Reinhold relaxes outside the improvised airfield command post of 9./ZG 26 during the battle.

towards Portland, Weymouth and Warmwell, which was bombed and severely damaged.

Guaranteeing overwhelming German fighter superiority, they were escorted by over five times their number of fighters, including two full Geschwadern of Bf 109s: 'Richthofen' JG 2 and 'Pik-As' JG 53, plus those of Hauptmann Schlichting's III./JG 27 from Carquebut.

Zerstörers again provided the close escort and consisted of I./ZG 2, now led by Hauptmann Eberhardt Heinlein, and II./ZG 2, commanded by Major Karl-Heinz Lessmann. Kaldrack's III./ZG 76 and Liensberger's V.(Z)/LG 1 added to the complement.

Both of the Exeter Hurricane squadrons scrambled to meet them, Wing Commander Dewar flying with No. 87 Squadron, with No. 213 Squadron guarding their rear. They first met the enemy formation as it came west over Lulworth, and leading 'A' Flight of No. 87 Squadron, acting-Flight Lieutenant Ian Gleed recalls, "The Jerries seem miles above us; lines of smaller dots show where the 109s are ready to pounce. Beneath them, about our height, circles of 110s turn, chasing each other's tails, moving as a mass slowly towards us. Far below, the bombers are in tight formation. Johnny (Dewar) and 'B' Flight have dived, heading for the bombers. The 110s continue circling. They seem to make no attempt to dive."

Gleed started 'A' Flight in a dive towards the nearest circle of 110s but was forced to change direction to avoid an attack by ferociously-vigilant 109s who, finding themselves outmanoeuvred, deliberately overshot the Hurricanes and climbed steeply back out of reach. Gleed seized the opportunity, "Now's our chance. I straighten out and go for the closest 110. He turns away from me. I turn the firing button on to fire; at exactly 250 yards I give him a quick burst. White puffs are flashing past the cockpit. Another burst. Got him! A terrific burst of fire from his starboard engine, a black dot and a puff of white as the pilot's parachute opens."

In the resulting pandemonium Gleed managed to hit another Bf 110 before the ever-present Bf 109s forced him to take evasive action and return to base.

From Westhampnett, No. 602 Squadron's 12 Spitfires also joined the action as the German formation crossed the coast, two red flares being fired by the leading Bf 110 as the Spitfires curved into the attack. The significance of this is unknown, but it was possibly a pre-arranged signal calling down the 109s who were likely to be operating on a different radio frequency.

Squadron Leader 'Sandy' Johnstone took 'A' Flight at the bombers while 'B' Flight engaged the escort. He recalls, "Our initial attack split up the bomber formations and it soon became a case of every man for himself. Fighters were down among us in no time at all. Earphones filled with shouting. I could only leave the boys to it and hope for the best. Climbed after a 110 and nailed him from below, when the entire tail unit blew off and the pilot baled out in front of me. I dived below the melee to take stock..."

Twelve more Spitfires of No. 609 Squadron, led by Squadron Leader Darley, also steamed into the attack

ish to keep them there in relative comfort, for almost 6 weeks. This was exactly what they had hoped, for it was guaranteed to be infinitely better than their next destination - a permanent POW camp.

They were absolutely right and thoroughly enjoyed their joke at the 'Tommies' expense. But it back-fired on them, for on arrival at Grizedale Hall they had to work equally hard to convince some of their comrades that they weren't stool-pigeons or collaborators, having spent a suspiciously long time in routine processing and interrogation.

After the sustained blood-letting of the previous week, the welcome lull in activity on the 19th came as a blessed relief to both sides. It also heralded a spell of indifferent weather which restricted Luftwaffe operations and allowed for a period of relative respite which lasted until the 24th. But it was 25th August before Zerstörers were again involved in any significant action.

After a quiet morning and afternoon that Sunday, a heavy attack by over 250 aircraft took place around 5:00 pm.. This was delivered by 28 Junkers Ju 88s of II. and III./KG 51, plus 9 from I./KG 54, who approached the coast at Swanage before veering west

Château Brumare, near Brestot, the residence for officers of II./ZG 2 during the Battle of Britain.

Bf 110s of 6./ZG 2 preparing to take-off for an escort mission to England, late August.

on the Zerstörers before the marauding packs of Bf 109s could intervene. Flying as rear-guard, or 'Holzauge', for I./ZG 2, Unteroffizier Siegfried Becker, one of the few pilots remaining of the original Staffel, was caught flat-footed.

When it came, such was the speed of the British attack that Becker's first inkling was when his Bordfunker, Obergefreiter Walter Wötzel, suddenly opened fire and called on him to 'break' starboard into the Spitfires. Becker made the turn, but too quickly for his wingman, Oberfeldwebel Heilmeyer, whose own Bordfunker was less experienced and probably hadn't warned him of the danger.

Suddenly separated from the rest of the Staffel and under close attack by two Spitfires, Becker had to use all his flying skills to stay out of trouble. Using the torque from his two engines he spiralled upwards, then dived straight between another pair of Spitfires manoeuvring below him, inviting the British fighters to collide. But although he was able to open up a slight lead, he was unable to shake off his pursuers, Pilot Officers Agazarian and Gaunt of No. 609 Squadron, who hounded the Zerstörer as it dived for the coast.

Wötzel, meantime, maintained a steady clatter of return fire from the rear cockpit, while idly wondering how long they could continue to manoeuvre like this when both rudders and elevators were already beginning to look like sieves.

Realising that the coast was still some distance away and that the Spitfires were going to catch them even

tually, Becker put the aircraft into a climb to gain precious height. It was not a second too soon, for in the very next attack their port engine exploded in flames. Even as Becker went through the emergency shutdown procedures, another attack destroyed the cooling system to the starboard. Wötzel, however, staunchly kept up a constant return fire through it all.

Enough was enough. "Aussteigen!". Becker gave the order to bale out and started unbuckling his straps. But Wötzel's response was not exactly as expected. "Why?", he radioed back, still clattering away with his machine gun.

Time seemed to stand still in the next few seconds. Becker, momentarily stunned by the question, slumped back in his seat and peered about him in genuine confusion. Every part of the aircraft visible was riddled with bullets, the port engine was a smoking, molten ruin and the starboard engine, on the verge of seizing, was windmilling to a halt - the engine temperature off the clock. Then reality kicked-in and with it came anger, "Just take a look at the engines", Becker roared and repeated the order, "Aussteigen!".

There was an awful pause. Ever the non-committal type, terse even, Wötzel had always been economic with speech. It had bothered Becker at first, but he had soon come to realise that a quiet Bordfunker had its advantages. True to form, Wötzel's response, when it came, was a single word: "Moment" was all he said, 'Just a second'.

'The fellow clearly has no proper sense of urg-

Bf 110 of III./ZG 26 in its camouflaged revetment. Note the panel on the ground which covered the ejection chutes for spent 20 mm. cartridges.

Army personnel in front of a Bf 110 fighter-bomber of 1./Erpr. Gr. 210. Note the multi-coloured spinners, a feature of 1st Staffel aircraft of this unit, light fuselage camouflage and unit emblem.

ency' seethed Becker, 'what the devil is his problem?' Desperate now, for the next Spitfire attack would likely see their last seconds on earth, and wrestling with the controls to keep the aircraft as level as possible to facilitate the bale-out, he repeated the order, trying to keep the rising hysteria from his voice, "Aussteigen!" It brought exactly the same response, but this time measured as if to an impatient child, "Moment." 'To hell with it,' thought Becker, as he jettisoned the hood, rolled the aircraft onto its back and dropped out into space.

At about this time Pilot Officer David Crook of No. 609 Squadron was another pilot experiencing his own personal drama. "I saw an Me. 110 below me and dived down on him going very fast indeed. Unfortunately I was going too fast...with the result that I came up behind him at terrific speed and overshot him badly. I had a good burst of fire at practically point-blank range as he flashed by and then I had to turn away very violently or I should have collided with him.

"His rear gunner took advantage of my mistake and fired a short burst at me, and put several bullets through my wing, very close to the fuselage and only a few inches from my leg. I returned to base absolutely furious with myself for having missed that Me. 110. He was right in front of me, and if only I had not gone at him so wildly I should have had him so easily."

A further 12 Spitfires of No. 152 Squadron, who got away from Warmwell as the bombers approached,

also tangled with the escort fighters west of Portland. In the turbulent dog-fight which was now raging they lost two aircraft and pilots shot down into the Channel.

One of the last British squadrons to engage, the Hurricanes of No. 17 Squadron from Tangmere, led by Squadron Leader Cedric Williams, met the enemy formation as it closed on Warmwell from the south. In a steep climb towards the Bf 110s, with the Hurricanes hanging on their props., they were flying at full throttle with the entire squadron in line astern formation. Last in line, Sergeant Len Bartlett thought that these bloody stupid formation attacks were a thing of the past and invited disaster. He was right!

"They broke straight at us. I can't really remember what happened from then on, except that the sky seemed full of flaming aircraft." Leading the squadron, Squadron Leader Williams met the leading Bf 110 head-on, both aircraft opening fire almost simultaneously. The rest of the squadron could do little but act as horrified observers, including Bartlett, "I was...watching the two aircraft flying towards each other, head-on and both firing hard. At about 400 yards they both appeared to stop in mid-flight and flutter gently to pieces."

Squadron Leader Williams fell into the sea off Portland and was killed; another No. 17 Squadron pilot, Flight Lieutenant Bayne, also forced to abandon his aircraft over Weymouth Bay, was rescued from the sea unhurt.

Lt. Rolf Hermichen, pilot of 9./ZG 76, in the cockpit of his Zerstörer.

The Exeter squadrons suffered badly in clashes with the Bf 109s. No. 87 Squadron lost Sergeant Wakeling, believed to have crashed somewhere near Dorchester, while No. 213 Squadron lost three Hurricanes and two pilots to Hauptmann Mayer's 1./JG 53, the third pilot being rescued from the Channel badly burned. A fourth Hurricane dropped from the combat and crash-landed at Burton Bradstock, its pilot surviving unharmed.

Meanwhile, the Spitfires fared a little better. In addition to No. 152 Squadron's losses, two of No. 602 Squadron's Spitfires also fell to the ravaging German fighters, both pilots baling out unhurt. No. 609 Squadron escaped lightly, two of their aircraft returning to base damaged.

One of these, as described, was Pilot Officer Crook, who witnessed the arrival of the other damaged Spitfire back at Warmwell. As Crook relates, "Osti (Flying Officer Ostaszewski-Ostoje) had an amazing escape in this fight. An Me. 110 got on to his tail and put one cannon shell into his engine, where it blew out most of the induction system, while another shell hit the armour plating behind his head, and the explosion almost stunned him. He managed to get back home with a big hole in his wing as well, but had to land very fast

as his flaps were damaged and he ran through the hedge. His machine was a complete 'write-off', but he was quite OK, apart from a headache."

Ostaszewski was almost certainly one of the three Spitfires claimed by I./ZG 2, who lost four aircraft and crews during this combat, another of their Bf 110s returning damaged.

But these losses were all by 1st Staffel, who had been badly mauled by 609 Squadron's Spitfires and whose Staffelführer, Oberleutnant Gerhard Goetz, was among the pilots who failed to return. With an engine already on fire following an attack by Sergeant Feary of No. 609 Squadron, Goetz was finally shot down by another Spitfire, probably that flown by Flying Officer Webb of No. 602 Squadron. His Bf 110 crashed at Creech Barrow, near Wareham, Goetz and his Bordfunker, Unteroffizier Karl Haupt both baling out. At a stroke, 1st Staffel was reduced to 7 aircraft and crews.

Swinging in his parachute high above East Holme, Unteroffizier Becker was relieved to see another parachute slightly above him. He rightly took this to be his Bordfunker, Obergefreiter Wötzel, who had obviously decided to vacate the aircraft after all. Landing on opposite sides of a railway cutting, Becker freed himself of his parachute harness and set off in the general di-

Uffz. Erhart Reinhold, pilot of 9./ZG 26, killed in action on 26/8/40.

The grave of Uffz. Erhart Reinhold. The date of death shown on the grave marker is incorrect, as it shows 19/9/40, the date his body was washed ashore on the French coast.

rection of Wötzel, who had broken his ankle on landing and was going nowhere.

As Becker doubled towards the railway, some soldiers appeared on the far side of the field behind him and shouted in his direction, presumably ordering him to stop and surrender, which he ignored. Then, as he neared the cutting, one of the troops fired a warning shot which passed close above his head. Almost without thinking, Becker, never one to give up without a fight, drew his pistol and returned fire. A few rounds back across the field in the general direction of the troops caused them to scatter like rabbits and drop out of sight. It made him feel better.

Then he realised what he was doing and quickly holstered his weapon. He must be insane, he decided; there was no point in exchanging fire with the whole British army. The best he could hope to do was to keep them at bay long enough to seek cover until nightfall.

Scrambling down the cutting, he ran off down the track which was running due south. The railway sleepers made the going easier in his clumsy flying boots and he soon put a respectable distance between himself and the troops behind him. But after a while, he was reduced to a shambling trot and soon a steady walk.

Rounding a bend, he came upon a small bridge crossing the track and realised too late that there were several figures leaning on the parapet watching him approach. Nearing them, he could see that some were armed and in uniform, while others wore civilian clothes. His own flying clothes simply identified him as a downed airman, there was nothing obviously German about them, so Becker decided to brazen it out.

Not missing a stride, and with a studied air of nonchalance, he reached the bridge and, glancing up to meet the curious gaze of his audience, he tossed them a hearty "Good evening!" as he passed under the bridge and carried on tramping down the line towards the coast. They caught him up within ten yards.

Becker was disarmed and taken to a nearby farmhouse where he was treated to tea and cake, and allowed a wash. Regular troops from an artillery regiment then collected him and took him back to their HQ, from where he was taken by train, under armed escort, to London. At Cockfosters, he was kept in isolation for what seemed a very long time before his interrogation by an RAF Intelligence Officer who, as more than they lost. II./ZG 2 was an exception, claiming a single Hurricane for the price of one Zerstörer written-off on return and two more damaged, but mercifully without crew casualties.

III./ZG 76 claimed the destruction of five British fighters but lost one crew, Feldwebel Manfred Dähne and Unteroffizier Fritz Müller of 8th Staffel, who plunged with their aircraft deep into the ground at North Farm, Buckland Ripers, where they would remain undiscovered for 41 years.

Liensberger's V.(Z)/LG 1 claimed three British fighters shot down in this action but lost two of their own, those of Oberleutnant Joachim Glienke and Unteroffizier Horst Hamann, who were both posted missing. Another of their Bf 110s crash-landed at Barfleur, while Feldwebel Karl Röhring crash-landed back at Roquancourt, his aircraft a total wreck and his Bordfunker, Obergefreiter Herbert Grosse, wounded.

In fact, RAF Fighter Command lost only 10 fighters during this action, another 3 of their aircraft returning badly damaged, but 6 more British pilots had been killed. At this point in the battle, the attrition rates in the British fighter squadrons and their counterparts in the Zerstörer units were both nearing the critical.

Over the next few days, the scale of activity involving Zerstörers reduced somewhat, although sorties were still flown and a number of losses occurred. But on 30 August they were once again thrown into action with a vengeance, on a day which saw some of the heaviest fighting of the entire campaign to date.

After some early probing attacks during the morning, another huge raid against the RAF airfields to the south of London developed around 11.00 am., during which the Biggin Hill area was heavily bombed, but the airfield itself escaping serious damage. Then, throughout the afternoon and well into early evening, successive waves of Luftwaffe aircraft flew in over the southern counties in a effort to swamp the British defences.

Shortly before mid-day, Heinkels of KG 1 attacked Farnborough, the Bf 110s of Kaldrack's III./ZG 76 forming part of the escort. Flying in Oberleutnant Schiller's 7./ZG 76, Unteroffizier Georg Bierling wondered how much longer they could continue these missions for, apart from his old friend Willi Schultis, Bierling was one of the last pilots left of the original Staffel. Had he but known it, the answer was exactly 10 days before his own death in action, by which time his old friend Willi Schultis would already be a prisoner of war.

The main raid of the day involving Zerstörers came in at around 5:00 pm., when the Vauxhall works at Luton was the target for 30 Heinkel He 111s of KG 53. They were closely escorted by a large force of Bf 110s drawn from II./ZG 2 led by Major Karl-Heinz Lessmann, Hauptmann Ralph von Rettburg's II./ZG 26 and Hauptmann Erich Groth's 'Haifisch' Gruppe II./ZG 76. Bf 109s provided additional fighter protection. Ten RAF Squadrons countered the raid as it battled its way inland from Sheppey over the southern Home Counties, the Bf 110s being mainly opposed by Hurricanes of Nos. 56 and 242 Squadrons.

Uffz. Paul Nick, Bordfunker, of 9./ZG 26, killed in action on 26/8/40.

usual, knew more about 1./ZG 2's history and personalities than Becker did himself. After a few days, he was transferred with others to a camp near Oldham where he finally caught up with Wötzel again.

"Why the hell didn't you bale out when I kept telling you to?" he demanded, "What was your problem?" "Well," said Wötzel, "I guessed that we were going to be captured and I wanted to look my best. I was just trying to find my uniform cap." 'Of course,' thought the dumbstruck Becker, 'I should have known.'

Following this raid, a success in German eyes and a reprise of the massive attacks of previous weeks, the Luftwaffe claimed 35 RAF fighters destroyed for the loss of 17 of their own aircraft, 6 of them Bf 109s. The bombers had reached their target and caused serious damage at Warmwell, for the trifling loss of two Ju 88s, both of them 6./KG 51 machines. But possibly of greatest significance was the disturbing fact that over half the Luftwaffe aircraft lost in this attack were Bf 110s, 9 Zerstörers failing to return.

The balance sheet was not entirely one-sided, however, most of the Zerstörer units involved claiming

Excellent in-flight view of 3U + CA, the Geschwaderadjutant's aircraft from the Geschwaderstab of ZG 26. Note that this Bf 110 also carries the single chevron marking, denoting Adjutant, on the nose.

A Bf 110 of III./ZG 26 moves towards its take-off point as other aircraft move out behind it.

Lt. Wilhelm Herget, pilot of 6./ZG 76, posted as Staffelkapitän of 4./ZG 76 on 29/10/40. Herget moved to night-fighters after the Battle of Britain, and survived the war as one of the most successful pilots in that role, achieving a total of 73 victories, including 58 at night.

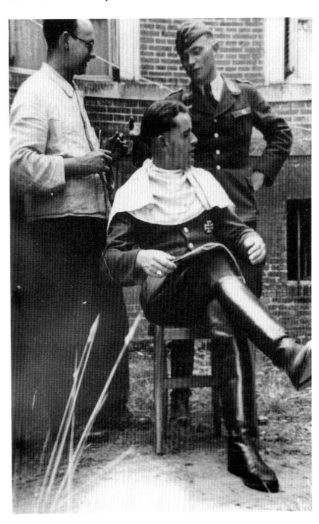

Aircrew of 9./ZG 26 wait, fully prepared, for the order to take-off on their next escort mission.

Fourteen Hurricanes of Douglas Bader's No. 242 Squadron, who had moved down from Coltishall to Duxford for the day in support of the hard-pressed No. 11 Group squadrons, were patrolling North Weald as KG 53 approached. They were perfectly positioned and fell on the Zerstörer escorts as the German formation neared the Enfield - Hatfield area.

Bader ordered his Green Section, led by Flight Lieutenant Christie, to attack the top layer of Bf 110s while he took the rest of the squadron into the attack on the main formation below. But very soon all semblance of order was lost as formations clashed and spilled all over the sky.

Christie made a head-on attack on the leading Zerstörer which promptly pulled over on one wing and dived, followed by the Hurricane. Keeping up a steady fire as both aircraft dived all the way down to 6,000 feet, Christie noticed that return fire from the Bf 110 ceased and the starboard engine let go streaming gouts of oil, just before its fuel tanks exploded and it went over the vertical.

Three views of the wreckage of Bf 110 D-0, A2 + HK, of Hptm. Schuldt and his Bordfunker Uffz. Dyroff, of 5./ZG2 at Durrants Road, Ponders End, Enfield on 30/8/40. Schuldt and Dyroff were killed in the crash.

The crew didn't get out and Hauptmann Adolf Schuldt, Staffelkapitän of 5./ ZG 2, and his gunner, Un-teroffizier Karl Dyroff, both died when the Zerstörer exploded amongst the greenhouses at Rochfords Nursery, Ponders End. Little remained of their machine but a shattered engine sitting in a suburban back garden and , nearby, an enormous crater which slowly filled with muddy, oil-stained water.

Within five minutes of this crash and less than 3/4 of a mile away, another Zerstörer came down carrying another Staffelkapitän, Hauptmann Heinz Wagner of

Two views of the remains of Bf 110 C, M8+BM, W.Nr. 3257, of 4./ZG 76, which came to grief at the Enfield Sewage Farm, Ponders End, Enfield on 30/8/40. The crew of Hptm Heinz Wagner, Staffelkapitän, and Bordfunker Stabsfw. Heinrich Schmidt were killed. '8' of the unit code can be seen on the fuselage wreckage, and the individual aircraft letter of 'B' can be seen outboard of the port wing cross.

Lt. Kawatsch, pilot of 7./ZG 26, who joined the Staffel on 15/8/40

Karl-Heinz Boock flew as Kowatsch's Bordfunker in 7./ZG 26 for the second half of 1940.

4./ZG 76, to his death.

This fell victim to another of Bader's pilots, Pilot Officer McKnight, although the Hurricanes were all over the Bf 110s and many duplications and shared claims resulted. Flying as wingman to Bader, McKnight had already attacked one Bf 110 and a Heinkel before engaging the Bf 110 flown by Wagner. The two aircraft locked in a furious combat all the way down to 1,000 feet, McKnight all the while receiving heavy and accurate return fire from Wagner's Bordfunker, Stabsfeldwebel Adolf Schmidt.

Finally closing to a murderous 30 yards range, the Hurricane fired a last withering burst of fire which riddled both crew and set the Zerstörer on fire. It crashed heavily alongside one of the filter tanks at Enfield Sewage Farm, a passing cyclist quickly making off down Conduit Lane with a pair of flying boots removed from one of the dead crewmen.

Another veteran pilot of 4./ZG 76 fell on this sortie, Oberfeldwebel Georg Anthony, dying when his Zerstörer crashed on Barley Beans Farm, Kimpton. He first came under attack from Flying Officer Paszkiewicz of No. 303 Squadron, whose 'B' Flight had literally stumbled on the German raid in the course of a routine training flight. It was the first combat engagement for the Polish unit which was promptly declared 'fully operational'.

With his starboard engine put out of action in Paszkiewicz's initial attack, Oberfeldwebel Anthony disengaged and dived away south out of combat area. But he was not able to shake off the stubborn Pole who was soon joined by another Hurricane flown by Pilot Officer Wicks of No. 56 Squadron. As the two British fighters closed-in and Wicks opened fire, both pilots saw the stricken Zerstörer's gunner, Unteroffizier Heinrich Nordmeier bale out. But Anthony, probably already dead or dying, stayed with the aircraft as it started its final plunge to earth.

Nordmeier's parachute opened late as he plummeted down over the Hertfordshire countryside and he landed very heavily. Troops who arrived to take him prisoner found that he had broken his back and was completely paralysed.

But not every Zerstörer crew suffered such 'Pech', or hard luck, Unteroffizier Rudolf Franke having good cause to count his blessings. Franke, the youngest pilot in 5./ZG 26, and his regular Bordfunker, Unteroffizier Willi Hübner, were not flying their usual aircraft on this sortie. Their 5th Staffel machine was unserviceable, and so they made use of a spare aircraft from 6th Staffel. Once in the air, Franke understood the reason why this Bf 110 was available - he had his work cut out keeping in touch with the rest of his Staffel due to the below-average performance of the engines! The whole Gruppe was flying close escort for the Heinkels

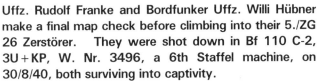

Uffz. Rudolf Franke and Bordfunker Uffz. Willi Hübner make a final map check before climbing into their 5./ZG 26 Zerstörer. They were shot down in Bf 110 C-2, 3U + KP, W. Nr. 3496, a 6th Staffel machine, on 30/8/40, both surviving into captivity.

of KG 53 on this, their second sortie of the day, but were turned back before reaching the target area by the sheer weight of the British fighter attacks.

Going into their familiar defensive circles, Franke had been startled to see at least one British fighter flying in the opposite direction on the inside of their circle making snap head-on attacks on each Zerstörer as they came around into his sights. Hit by one of these bursts, his starboard engine damaged and losing power, Franke was relieved when the Staffel finally turned east and headed back for St. Omer. They were flying at about 10,000 metres and as far as he could see there was no convenient cloud cover to dive into.

With every second that passed and every mile flown, Franke's optimism grew but somehow he knew that it was too much to hope. Suddenly, Hübner's voice filled his earphones, "Six Spitfires behind!" Franke could do very little but maintain height and course. "So what!", he radioed back fretfully, sitting there waiting for the inevitable attacks to start. But miraculously the next message was "Two Spitfires behind!" 'Things are definitely improving', thought Franke, 'but we're not out of trouble yet', and there was still nothing to be done. Again he responded with "So

what!" and flew on.

Once again, the long-expected attacks didn't materialise and Franke began to convince himself that the 'Tommies' must be out of ammunition. Obviously, that was why the others had broken off the chase - they might make it back yet. Then, shattering his nervous calm, Hübner suddenly opened fire with his single machine gun, which provoked an immediate reply from the 16 British machine guns behind them!

Somehow they both survived these attacks, not by Spitfires at all, Hübner's aircraft recognition was at fault, but the Hurricanes of Wing Commander Beamish and Flying Officer Westmacott of No. 56 Squadron. But the Zerstörer's starboard engine finally ground to a halt and the port engine was hit. It was clear they had to abandon the aircraft, so Franke dived steeply to about 3,000 metres and prepared to bale out. But Hübner had a problem: he was wounded and his canopy would not release, which left them with no option but to attempt a forced-landing.

Gliding down with both engines shot to pieces, Franke made a perfectly-judged belly-landing on Mill Hill Farm, near Rettenden, smashing the port wing against a tree as they slid to a halt amid clouds of dust.

Franke helped Hübner out of the aircraft and applied a field dressing to his wounds before attempting to destroy the aircraft by setting fire to his maps, which he couldn't get to burn. After a while, some troops arrived and Hübner was carried away to hospital while Franke was escorted to a nearby farm. His pockets

A forlorn-looking 'Sharksmouth' of II./ZG 76 on what is obviously a collection field for damaged aircraft, somewhere in France.

were emptied onto the huge farmhouse table as the questions began.

Not understanding a single word of English, Franke gathered that they were trying to ascertain his rank. "Unteroffizier", he barked, inadvertently emphasising the 'offizier'. Not speaking a single word of German, the soldier in charge clearly misunderstood and took Franke to mean that he was an officer and, from his tone that he expected to be treated as such. There was a hurried discussion between the soldiers before one of them helped Franke understand that they wanted his parole, as a German officer and gentleman, that he would not attempt to escape if left at the farm overnight, with an armed guard of course!

It was all so civilised and serious that Franke could barely contain his growing mirth. Of course, he nodded vigorously, straight-faced, you have my parole as an officer - as a non-commissioned officer it's not worth a damn!

So, as dawn broke over the farmhouse the next morning, Franke, an accomplished musician on both piano and violin, hoarse from singing the night away, found himself tinkling away on an ancient piano and sharing a bottle of whisky with his guards. He didn't usually drink, and had never sampled whisky before, but somehow this was a special occasion and after all it was barely four days since his 25th birthday. It had been an excellent evening, an officer-prisoner's life was not at all bad - he could get used to this!

Later that morning, an RAF officer arrived and seemed a little surprised with arrangements. Despite the now insistent pounding behind his eyes, Franke decided to keep up the pretence as long as he could. The officer, who spoke flawless German, offered him a cigarette. They chatted idly for a while, Franke recognising that this fellow knew his business and he must be on his guard.

"Can I just check your name and rank?", the officer asked almost cordially. 'Here goes nothing' thought Franke. "Rudolf Franke, UnterOFFIZIER". This time the inflection was deliberate but it made no difference. The RAF officer masked a smile, "So, UNTERoffizier Franke," he continued, "what height were you flying when you were first intercepted?" Franke, realising that he was rumbled, changed the game. "Somewhere between ground level and 10,000 metres." he replied off-handedly. The officer duly made a note of this gem before his next question, "And what course were you flying?" The pencil hovered, awaiting Franke's reply. "Oh!, somewhere between 0 and 360 degrees." he proffered helpfully. Their eyes met. "We can do this differently, you know," the officer said icily. Franke shrugged as he stubbed out the cigarette, "I understand the terms of the Geneva convention," he replied firmly, "do what you like. Got another cigarette?"

En-route to London, under armed guard, Franke's thoughts were with his parents back in Neukölln, Berlin. They would be worried, but would have to wait for

Zerstörer crew of 2./Erpr. Gr. 210: Pilot Fw. Sommer, left, and Bordfunker Gefr. Schlee. Sommer was killed in action later in the war, Schlee survived.

certain news of him until 13th September when he was confirmed as a prisoner-of-war.

It had been a bad day for the Zerstörers and for their Staffelkapitäne in particular, for yet another, Hauptmann Heinz Nacke of 6./ZG 76, barely made it back to St. Ingelvert. He crash-landed with combat damage so severe that his aircraft, in spite of the shortages, was deemed fit only for scrap. Nacke and his Bordfunker, Stabsfeldwebel Alfred Kühne, were both slightly injured in the landing, but had been lucky to get back at all.

While 6th Staffel toasted their good fortune, there was even more cause for celebration as some of Nacke's pilots had scored, Oberleutnant Wilhelm Herget claiming two victories, a Hurricane and a Spitfire both destroyed south of London. But the Gruppe had lost two Staffelkapitäne, one of them albeit temporarily, so more changes had to be made. Oberleutnant Jabs took over as Staffelführer of 6./ZG 76 pending Nacke's return, and Hauptmann Hans Hoppe was appointed to command 4th Staffel.

It had been a hard-fought day, RAF Fighter Command mounting the largest number of sorties it had yet flown and losing a total of 25 fighters, 9 of the pilots being killed and 5 more badly wounded. Similarly, in their biggest daylight effort since mid-August, the Luftwaffe had lost 40 aircraft, 7 of them Bf 110s, with another 2 Zerstörers being damaged.

This renewed scale of German effort was continued throughout the next day, 31st August, which resulted in the heaviest losses yet to be inflicted on RAF Fighter Command.

Shortly after 8:00 am. that morning, two separate raids on the RAF airfields at Debden and Duxford fought their way through to their targets via the Thames estuary and the Essex coast. These objectives were deep inside British territory, far beyond the effective range of the Bf 109 which, unlike some other Luftwaffe aircraft at this stage in the battle, had not yet been modified to carry auxiliary fuel tanks. So, once again, a strong force of Zerstörers were committed as escort.

Liensberger's V.(Z)/LG 1 accompanied 30 Dornier Do 17s of Major Adolf Fuchs' III./KG 2 bound for Debden, Leutnant Karl-Joachim Eichhorn leading the 8 Bf 110s of 14.(Z)/LG 1 as the Staffelkapitän, Oberleutnant Michel Junge, was not flying on this mission. Immediately to Eichhorn's left in the lead Schwarm flew his Rottenflieger, Feldwebel Gottlob Fritz, flying the Kapitän's machine as his own was unserviceable. Behind them came Leutnant Hugo Adametz with his wing-man Feldwebel Martin Jäckel.

The Staffel was flying at the rear of the Gruppe and as it came in over the Thames estuary Eichhorn recalls, "...the shells of some flak cruisers which were uncomfortable and the whole formation began to 'swim' from side to side."

A simultaneous attack on Duxford, to the north and west, by the Dornier Do 17s of Oberstleutnant Paul Weitkus' II./KG 2 was escorted by Schalk's III./ZG 26. Messerschmitt Bf 109s of 'Schlageter' JG 26, operating at the very extreme of their range, provided additional fighter cover but limited to a quick penetrating sweep of the target area before having to turn back for their bases at Caffiers and Marquise.

Flying in the second Schwarm of Oberleutnant 'Conny' Meyer's 8./ZG 26 en-route to Duxford, Oberleutnant Erich von Bergen, felt distinctly uncomfortable. Earlier in the flight, one after another, the three other Bf 110s in his Schwarm had all been forced to turn back to St. Omer with engine failures or technical problems. Now it was just him flying at the rear all alone.

As the Duxford raid swept inland across Essex, the long-awaited British reaction finally materialised in the shape of 9 Hurricanes. One of the first units ordered up to counter the attack, No. 1 Squadron met the raid as it passed over Chelmsford and immediately went into the attack on a "flock of Me 110s so large that they did not bother to try and count them."

Squadron Leader Pemberton's pilots claimed a number of the Zerstörers probably destroyed and damaged, but lost Sergeant Merchant, whose reserve petrol tank exploded under attack by a Bf 110. Merchant abandoned his blazing Hurricane over Halstead. His was probably the 'Spitfire' claimed by Feldwebel Leonhard Kaufmann of 7./ZG 26, who was the first of Schalk's pilots to score during the action which followed.

Other RAF squadrons soon followed as the two German formations became more committed and their

Sign outside the recreation room for the armourers of 9./ZG 26.

intentions became clear. Up from Fowlmere and led by Flight Lieutenant Clouston, 11 Spitfires of No. 19 Squadron also met the Duxford attack. Clouston took 'B' Flight into the attack on II./KG 2 while 'A' Flight tried unsuccessfully to keep off the 'Horst Wessel' Zerstörers.

No. 19 Squadron was equipped with cannon-armed Spitfires for operational trials and had been experiencing a constant series of problems with the new armament over the preceding weeks. Today was no different, many pilots reporting frustrating stoppages and complaining bitterly that they would have scored better with the old 8 machine guns.

Fighting for their lives, the Spitfires were only able to claim one Bf 110 probably destroyed and another damaged during this action for the loss of 2 Spitfires. Both British pilots baled out, one of them, Flying Officer Coward, being seriously wounded. Another No. 19 Squadron aircraft dropped out of combat and returned to Fowlmere with its hydraulics shot to pieces only to somersault on landing, burst into flames and kill the pilot, Pilot Officer Aeberhardt.

Two of these casualties may well have been the Spitfires claimed in action over Duxford that morning by Oberleutnant Hans Barschel, Gruppenadjutant of Stab, III./ZG 26, and Oberleutnant Sophus Baagoe of 8./ZG 26, notching up his 10th victory.

No. 56 Squadron also suffered badly, mainly at the hands of III./JG 26, during a brisk action over Chelmsford. The 8 Hurricanes had been scrambled from North Weald and vectored onto the enemy formation only to be attacked by Bf 109s before they could complete their attacks.

As he closed on one of the Dorniers, Flying Officer Innes Westmacott exercised commendable caution, "I had a quick look behind and saw a number of 110s belting in from behind on my starboard quarter. I thought I would have time for another attack and turned back in for the Dornier. I think fatigue had affected my judgement, for the enemy had arrived much sooner than I thought fair. I was just pulling up to open fire when, with a tremendous crash, my instrument panel disappeared in fragments, followed immediately by a searing blast of flame as my reserve tank went up in my face."

Possibly Oberleutnant Barschel's second victory on this sortie, Westmacott baled out, landing at Little Baddow badly burned and was admitted to Chelmsford hospital. No. 56 Squadron lost half their number, two pilots baling out and Flight Lieutenant 'Mouse' Weaver killed on the very day that the award of his DFC was announced. The remnants of the squadron were withdrawn from the battle area the following day, moving to Boscombe Down.

Meantime, further to the south and east, the Debden raid was also coming under attack by British fighters. Taking off from Castle Camps, the 9 Hurricanes of No. 111 Squadron, led by Flight Lieutenant Giddings, engaged the Dorniers of III./KG 2 over Hildersham, just north of Debden, as they lined up for their bombing runs. Giddings took his Red Section into the attack as the rest of the squadron tried to keep the Bf 110 escort at bay. A confused action resulted, during which many of the Hurricanes were hit but none too seriously, as the Dorniers dropped their loads and began the withdrawal.

Held in reserve and ordered off late, the 11 Hurricanes of No. 601 Squadron were still gaining height over Debden as the bombers arrived overhead. The British pilots could see the bombs landing on their airfield 7,000 feet below them.

Their attacks over, both German formations turned about heading for home. As they neared the Essex coast, the Zerstörers formed a defensive circle over the Blackwater estuary, intending to cover the final withdrawal of any bombers and attracting elements of 5 British fighter squadrons who were now flooding into the area. Switching their attacks to the German escorts, No. 111 Squadron promptly lost Sergeant Craig who was forced to bale out, just as reinforcements in the shape of a fresh British squadron entered the arena.

Still flying as 'Holzauge', Erich von Bergen spotted 4 British fighters diving from out of the sun and radioed a warning to the rest of the Staffel, who went into a turn, narrowing the angle of attack and forcing the enemy fighters to turn aside. The Bf 110s resumed course, but not for long. As they neared the coast, von Bergen recalls, "The Spitfires came again, but now from below. Though I saw them and warned my unit, they did not react. So I turned against the 4 Spitfires and attacked the last one."

The 'Spitfires' referred to by von Bergen were in fact the Hurricanes of No. 257 Squadron led by Flight Lieutenant Beresford. They had been scrambled late from Martlesham Heath and intercepted the Bf 110s west of Chelmsford, just as the Zerstörers began to form their defensive circle.

Breaking from his isolated position at the rear of the

Hptm. Heinlein, left, in sunglasses, makes a point as Lt. Gerhard Granz, right, listens.

Bf 110 C, 3M + GK, of 2./ZG 2. The only known Zerstörer carrying this code during the battle had the W. Nr. 2134.

An unknown crewman prepares to board a Bf 110 D of Erpr. Gr. 210. Note the factory codes faintly visible behind the unit code 'S9'.

Gruppe to make a solo attack was a bold but dangerous manoeuvre for von Bergen to make, and the outcome was inevitable. Successfully attacking one of the Hurricanes, the Zerstörer was hit by a stunning salvo from Flying Officer Mitchell, leading Green Section of No. 257 Squadron, which exploded the oxygen bottles mounted in the rear fuselage. The force of the explosion tore the rear fuselage apart and the tail unit broke clean away. "The plane could not fly any more, so I gave the order to Becker to jump and I followed immediately."

As they drifted down in their parachutes over the waters of the Colne estuary, a third parachute accompanied them. It carried Pilot Officer Henderson of No. 257 Squadron who also had to abandon his aircraft, after maintaining a stubborn head-on attack to point-blank range on a pair of Bf 110s. No. 257 Squadron still lacked vital combat experience and word had obviously not reached them on the inadvisability of such attacks. He later reported, "...my instruments were shattered. A second or two later, as the second Me 110 appeared, there was a great explosion in my aircraft as my petrol tank was hit, presumably by cannon. The cockpit immediately became a mass of flames and I baled out."

All three were later picked up and landed at Brightlingsea. Von Bergen, threshing about trying to tread water, was rescued by a man in a small boat who pointed a rifle at him and ordered, "Hands up!". Under the circumstances, Erich von Bergen chose to avoid

Lt. Erich von Bergen, pilot of 8./ZG 26, shot down on 31/8/40, spent the rest of the war as a POW.

Oblt. Gerhard Granz of Stab, I./ZG 2.

drowning and declined the invitation, but the humour of it didn't escape him.

Meantime, still far too low to reach III./KG 2 as the Dorniers retired east from Debden, the Hurricanes of No. 601 Squadron encountered the Zerstörers of 14.(Z)/LG 1. Flying as Bordfunker with Feldwebel Fritz, on this their 8th sortie over England, Obergefreiter Karl Döpfer vividly remembers the appalling speed of the attack. One moment they were flying along peacefully, then suddenly the British fighters were there among them. Döpfer barely had time to shout out a warning, "Attack from behind and above!" before they came under fire from Flight Lieutenant Davis. As the Bf 110 reefed hard to port and Döpfer returned fire, he distinctly heard bullet strikes entering the cabin.

Leutnant Eichhorn's experience was similar. "The attack of the Hurricanes was a complete surprise and the only thing I did experience was the crashing of bullets into my cabin and the aircraft. The right engine began to burn at once. Unteroffizier Gröwe was shooting and crying out at the same time. To get away from the attackers, I dived from our flying altitude, 6,000 metres, to sea level. There was some fog and nobody followed me."

He was right, nobody did follow him down but his attacker, Pilot Officer Gilbert, stayed around long enough to witness what followed.

Gröwe had taken the full fury of the attack and was slumped dead in the rear cockpit. Eichhorn flew on at about 20 feet on one engine until, after about 10 minutes, the port engine started to lose power, running progressively slower and slower. He prepared to ditch, releasing the canopy and deploying the dinghy as the aircraft skipped off the waves, but had some trouble getting out of the cockpit in time when the Zerstörer sank like a stone two miles off Foreness.

After many attempts, with his flying boots acting as unwelcome ballast, he collapsed in the dinghy ex-

hausted. Two hours later he was picked up by a fishing boat and landed at Margate where local police took his details even as his head wounds were being bandaged.

Eichhorn's Rottenflieger was in equal trouble. Feldwebel Fritz radioed Döpfer that their port engine was on fire and that he was going to dive to try to extinguish the flames, meantime he should get ready to bale out. Döpfer tried his cabin release handle but nothing happened. The port engine was still burning when the starboard motor started to falter. and Fritz radioed to say that he would try to make the Channel and ditch, meantime Döpfer was to carry on trying to release the canopy. This he did with gusto until, thankfully, it flew off just before they hit the water near the Nore Light. The Zerstörer sank almost immediately and they were unable to release their dinghy, but after about two hours in their life-jackets they were picked up by a shore boat and landed at Margate.

So both raids retired back to their bases in France. The morning had been an unmitigated success for the Luftwaffe, who had hit their targets and inflicted heavy losses on the defending RAF fighters. Messerschmitt Bf 109s claimed to have knocked down 5 British fighters in their brief foray over the target area, while the Zerstörers claimed a further 13 British fighters destroyed.

Oberleutnant Karl Montag's 9./ZG 26 were the highest scorers with 5 victories . 7th Staffel ran them a close second with 4, including the second personal victory for the Staffelkapitän, Oberleutnant Matthes, on his first sortie for 5 days. He claimed a Spitfire east of Southminster.

In fact German claims were fairly close to the truth with a total of 11 British fighters shot down and 3 pilots killed, 6 more pilots being wounded. But whatever the statistics, the escort fighters had done their job well, only two Dornier Do 17s of III./KG 2 returning to Cambrai with any significant damage, and their casualties totalling two crewmen wounded, one of them the Gruppenkommandeur Major Fuchs. 5./KG 2 had one aircraft written-off and one crewman slightly wounded. For such deep penetration raids, remarkably light casualties indeed.

As for the escorts, one Bf 109 had ditched into the Channel, its pilot, Oberleutnant Heinz Ebeling, the Staffelkapitän of 9./JG 26, being rescued unhurt by the Seenotdienst. Three Zerstörers had been lost, as described; another flown by Oberleutnant Georg Christl, Gruppe TO of Stab, III./ZG 26, returning to crash-land at Arques with a wounded Bordfunker on board.

Zerstörers went back into action just after noon, when Erprobungsgruppe 210 struck at Croydon, causing serious damage, but their 2nd Staffel had one Bf 110 shot down and two more damaged by defending fighters. Later that afternoon, 3 more Bf 110s were damaged during an escort sortie for 18 Dornier 17s of KG 76 to Hornchurch by all three Gruppen of ZG 26.

Action throughout the day cost the Luftwaffe 39 aircraft, of which 5 were Zerstörers, 7 more Bf 110s returning to France damaged. The early morning att-

A pilot of 7./ZG 26 is strapped into his Bf 110 by the a member of the ground personnel on the port wing. Although carrying the early style fuselage camouflage, this aircraft also has the white nose introduced in the latter part of the Battle of Britain. Note also the armour plating bolted onto the windscreen, and the spinner tips in the Staffel colour of white. This Staffel, and the rest of its Gruppe, saw action on 31/8/40.

acks on Debden and Duxford had shown that the Zerstörer could still function, most effectively, as a long range escort fighter and refuted the assertion that they could no longer operate without escorts of their own. Certainly, Bf 109s had been present, and in some strength, but only briefly. The fact remains that the Zerstörers had accompanied the bombers deep into enemy territory, protected them well and fought their way out inflicting heavy losses on defending British fighters.

RAF Fighter Command had lost 41 aircraft on the day and suffered their highest losses in the entire battle, even exceeding, by a notable margin, the almost crippling losses of 15th and 18th August. But their losses in pilots were less serious, only 9 killed and 24 wounded, and it was their pilot strength, not aircraft, which was now the critical factor. As an unknown Fighter Command diarist noted, "The month of August saw the beginning of a war of attrition."

Over the next few days the Luftwaffe would maintain its relentless attacks on the British defences and on RAF Fighter Command in particular, with the Bf 110 units continuing to play a significant role.

Every Zerstörer pilot's Flugbuch told the same story, with sortie after sortie, day in and day out. The days merged together, each forming a similar pattern of anxious boredom, nervous anticipation, intense fear, excitement and relief. But experience in the units slowly drained away as old friends and comrades vanished, and new faces came and went. Every Gruppe was now finding it increasingly difficult to sustain operational levels, and aircraft and crews had to be rotated between different Staffeln in an effort to make up numbers.

Shortly before 2:00 pm. on 1st September, Erich Groth's II./ZG 76 were back in the thick of the action, forming part of the escort for the Dornier Do 17s of KG 76 in a major attack on Biggin Hill by over 150 aircraft. Unteroffizier Georg Bierling of 7./ZG 76 was again involved, still fretting about these never-ending close escort sorties, but today his concerns were ill-founded, for the 'Haifisch' Gruppe found itself with a distinct advantage over the British fighters straining to gain height to reach them. In a brisk action over Tunbridge Wells 6th Staffel scored heavily; both Oberleutnant Herget and Oberleutnant Jabs, who was still leading the Staff-

Lt. Seehausen (left) with his Bordfunker, Uffz. Camehl, in a Zerstörer of 7./ZG 26. Part of the Staffel emblem, a penguin holding an umbrella, can be seen.

el in Nacke's absence, each claiming 2 Spitfires and a Hurricane destroyed. The Gruppe retired without loss.

But not every Gruppe had such good fortune. Only two losses were sustained by the Zerstörer units engaged on this mission but both were from Liensberger's V.(Z)/LG 1 in a clash with fighters over Edenbridge. With one engine disabled and his intercom smashed in fighter attacks, 27 year-old Oberfeldwebel Rudolf Kobert of 13.(Z)/LG 1 was unable to raise his Bordfunker and assumed that he was dead or wounded. He dived from 19,000 feet towards the clouds draping the coast and almost made it before he came under further attacks by fighters, including Pilot Officer English of No. 85 Squadron. With both engines out of action, the Zerstörer finally bellied-in at Tarpot Farm, near Bilsington, the victorious Hurricane circling to see Kobert and his Bordfunker, Feldwebel Werner Meinig, both clamber from the aircraft unhurt.

Less fortunate, the Bf 110 of Feldwebel Martin Jäckel of 15th Staffel, probably that attacked by Pilot Officer Mayhew of No. 79 Squadron, plunged deep into Hosey Wood at Brasted where it exploded on impact; the British unable to even ascertain the aircraft type from the wreckage. What little remained of the

A pilot is helped with final preparations as the crew of this Bf 110 of II./ZG 2 prepare to board their aircraft for an escort mission to England.

unfortunate Pomeranian, Jäckel, and his Bordfunker, Flieger Heinz Rösler, was recovered, but defied proper identification and they were eventually buried in nearby St. Martin's Churchyard as 'Unknown Airmen'.

The following day, 2nd September, the Luftwaffe increased the tempo of its offensive, flying almost 1,000 sorties and swamping the defences by the sheer scale of the attacks. Repeating the successful tactics they had developed over preceding days, most German raids now divided into smaller formations on reaching the English coast and fanned out across the southern counties to attack different targets. Tactics which were proving very difficult to counter.

The first major attack of the day developed around 8:00 am. when Hauptmann Erich Rathmann's III./KG 3 targeted airfields on both sides of the Thames; Biggin Hill, Eastchurch, North Weald and Rochford all being hit. Their Dorniers were escorted in over the Thames estuary by the Zerstörers of I. and II./ZG 26 with the Bf 109s of I./JG 51 and I./JG 53 providing top cover.

Stiff opposition came from five British squadrons, some of whom managed to penetrate the fighter escort and get among the bombers. One Dornier was shot down onto Rochford airfield, another three returning to France damaged and with wounded crews, included the Staffelkapitän of 8./KG 3, Hauptmann Jurgen de Lalande.

Maintaining their impressive run of luck, Makrocki's

I./ZG 26 lost a single Bf 110 to No. 72 Squadron's Spitfires, their first casualty since 18th August. Feldwebel Karl Schütz of 2./ZG 26 was attacking one of the Spitfires when he was killed outright by a burst of fire from another flown by Sergeant Rolls. His Bf 110 crashed in White Horse Wood, Birling, after his Bordfunker, Unteroffizier Herbert Stüwe, had baled out unhurt.

Hauptmann Ralph von Rettberg's II. Gruppe was more heavily engaged, getting embroiled with No. 72 Squadron's Spitfires and No. 249 Squadron's Hurricanes. The Hurricanes, who had only moved into North Weald the day before, to relieve No. 56 Squadron, lost five aircraft almost in as many minutes.

Theo Rossiwall's 5th Staffel lost two aircraft in all, one of them struggling all the way back to Wizernes on one engine only to stall on landing and crash onto the airfield from 30 feet. Its wounded pilot, Feldwebel Hans Müller, and his Bordfunker, Unteroffizier Gerhard Gröhl, were both taken to hospital in St. Omer.

The other Zerstörer, after shooting down a No. 249 Squadron Hurricane flown by Pilot Officer Beazley, had both engines shot to pieces, and was forced to ditch in the sea off the Nore. The German pilot, Oberfeldwebel Kurt Rochel, and his Bordfunker, Unteroffizier Willy Schöffler, took to their dinghy and were both later captured unhurt. Theirs was a bitter loss for the Staffel; Rochel and Schöffler being one of their most popular

Crash-landed Zerstörer of 8./ZG 26, 3U + AS. The 'A' would normally be flown by the Staffelkapitän, so this is probably the machine of Oblt. Meyer.

An unknown Unteroffizier stands proudly beside the fin and rudder of this ZG 26 Bf 110, which carries 8 victory bars.

and experienced crews, but remarkably it was the Staffel's only loss during the entire campaign against England.

At 1:00 pm. another raid of some 250 aircraft approached Dover with a massive escort made up of the Bf 110s from Hauptmann Heinlein's I./ZG 2 and Karl-Heinz Lessmann's II./ZG 2 plus the Bf 109s of II. and III./JG 2 and III./JG 54.

Five British squadrons met the attack and, once again, the Spitfires of No. 72 Squadron were among those who tangled with the Zerstörers, losing 4 of their Spitfires in the process.

One of the latest recruits to 2./ZG 2, Leutnant Georg Schipper, fell to Flight Lieutenant Graham. Schipper's Bordfunker, Gefreiter Theo Schockenhoff, baled out and landed unhurt at Alkham, but flying on another couple of miles, Schipper made a good belly-landing at Hougham, near the coast at Dover, and quickly set fire to his aircraft, which was totally destroyed.

Meanwhile the Spitfires continued to worry the rest of the Zerstörers. Feldwebel Lorenz Beil, one of the original pilots of the old 3./ZG 52 (now 6./ZG 2), died instantly when his aircraft simply exploded under attack by Flight Sergeant Steere of No. 72 Squadron. Small pieces of wreckage fluttered down over acres of Vensons Farm, Eastry, where Lorenz Beil and his Bordfunker, Obergefreiter Hans Oehl, both fell dead; the remains of two parachutes being all that was salvaged.

Three Zerstörers were lost in this action, with another machine, flown by the Staffelführer of 2./ZG 2,

Fin and rudder of a 4./ZG 26, Zerstörer. This is probably the machine of Ofw. Fritz Stahl. Of interest is the white outline only swastika.

The remains of Zerstörer, 3M+HK, W. Nr. 3622, of 2./ZG 2, at Hougham, near Dover on 2/9/40. Bordfunker Gefr. Schockenhoff baled out safely; Pilot Lt. Schipper force-landed the aircraft and then succeeded in setting fire to it, destroying the main cockpit area and much of one engine. In spite of that, soldiers still pick inquisitively through the wreckage.

Bf 110 C, 3M + HK of 2./ZG 2. More than one Zerstörer of 2nd Staffel carried this code in 1940, their W. Nrs. being 3515, 3606 and 3622. 3515 was shot down into the Channel on 12/8/40; 3622 was brought down at Hougham, near Dover on 2/9/40.

Oberleutnant Kurt Müller, returning to Berck-sur-Mer with serious damage.

Later that afternoon, all three Gruppen of ZG 26 were back over the Thames estuary forming the escort for Dorniers of KG 76 engaged in an attack on Hornchurch. ZG 26 was now led by Schalk, who had taken over from Huth as Kommodore two days before, Major Karl Kaschka inheriting III./ZG 26.

Yet again, the 'last 100 British fighters' were there to meet them and two 6th Staffel machines returned damaged with badly wounded Bordfunkers aboard. But the 7th Staffel Bordfunkers had a more successful outing. The Staffelkapitän of 7th Staffel, Oberleutnant Matthes, had been forced to return early with one engine shot up and Feldwebel Dibowski later crash-landed back at Arques wounded, his jubilant Bordfunker, Obergefreiter Karl-Heinz Boock, having 'nailed' the Spitfire.

This was a No. 616 Squadron aircraft, one of two which had become separated from their Flight and engaged 'five straggling 110s' of 7th Staffel over the Maidstone area. Flight Lieutenant Gillam latched onto Dibowski's aircraft and opened fire, causing severe damage to both engines despite vigorous return fire from Obergefreiter Boock in the rear cockpit. Flying close alongside Dibowski, Leutnant Konopka saw the danger and cut his throttles, bringing his own Zerstörer sliding back towards Gillam's Spitfire and presenting his own Bordfunker, Unteroffizier Eiberg, with a perfect broadside shot. With both Bordfunker's now riddling his aircraft, Gillam's engine burst into flames and he baled out over Capel, near Tonbridge, to be proudly recorded as a victory by both Bordfunkers.

Maintaining relentless pressure on the British defences, another '250 plus' crossed the Kent coast at around 5:00 pm. and included over 160 Bf 109s and Bf 110s from I./JG 52, III./JG 54 and II. and III./ZG 76. The main formation had reached Ashford before the first full weight of the RAF's reaction was felt, 7 British squadrons engaging the German attack as it forged inland, combats spilling out far across north Kent and over the Thames estuary.

On his second combat sortie of the day, Flight Lieutenant Parnall of No. 249 Squadron attacked one II./ZG 76 Zerstörer, which crashed inverted and burned out on Frith Farm at Laindon. Its pilot, Oberleutnant Karl Wrede, the Gruppe TO, and acting-Gruppenadjutant, was killed along with his Bordfunker, Unteroffizier Richard Kukawka, only recently returned to full flying duties and barely recovered from wounds received on 15th August.

Three more Zerstörers returned holed, two 4th Staffel Bordfunkers being slightly wounded. The third Bf 110, a 5th Staffel machine, landed heavily at Gramont-Abbeville injuring the Bordfunker, Unteroffizier Johann Horst, who was admitted to hospital. But once again, the 'Haifisch' Gruppe had been in the thick of it, the consistent Herget of 6th Staffel claiming another Spitfire destroyed.

So another eventful day for the Zerstörers came to a bloody close. Yet the long-suffering Unteroffizier Georg Bierling of 7./ZG 76, flying his fourth major escort sortie in as many days, simply entered 'heavy fighting' in his daily journal - probably through gritted teeth.

The following day, airfields to the north and east of

London were the targets when, around mid-morning, a formation of about 150 aircraft approached the Thames estuary heading for Debden, North Weald and Hornchurch. Sixteen RAF squadrons were ordered into the air but the controllers stayed their hand too long, leaving the fighters with insufficient height to engage, and allowing the attack on North Weald an almost clear run. Bombing from 15,000 feet, the 30 Dornier Do 17s of II./KG 2 delivered 200 bombs on target, cratering the runway and causing severe damage to hangars and the new operations block.

As the raiders wheeled for home, the first British fighters attacked but were met by determined opposition from the Bf 110s of I./ZG 2 and III./ZG 26, who flew on each side of the bomber formation. The Zerstörers hit the RAF Spitfires and Hurricanes hard and fought a brilliant rearguard action as the bombers retired back towards the Essex coast where I. and II./ZG 26 awaited them. Soon the sky from Chelmsford to Southend was filled with snarling, tumbling aircraft as the German escorts exacted a heavy price on the British.

For once noticeably absent, The Messerschmitt Bf 109s of II./JG 26 were operating in support of this raid, but held themselves over the Essex coast and Thames estuary to provide additional fighter cover for the withdrawal phase of the attack. So, while the Bf 110s

bore the brunt of the British attacks, the Bf 109s certainly added to the growing RAF casualty list.

The harrowing experience of Pilot Officer David Hunt must have been typical of many that morning. Positioning themselves for an attack on the bombers, the 12 Hurricanes of No. 257 Squadron suddenly found themselves on the wrong end of a devastating attack. Whether by Bf 109s or Bf 110s, the effect must have been much the same. In Hunt's own words, "...a dazzling array of multi-coloured light appeared on the starboard side of the cockpit, accompanied by explosive concussions. Immediately flame came through the instrument panel, filling the cockpit and burning my hands, legs and face. The reserve fuel tank had exploded, and I neither gloves nor goggles, which I had pushed over my forehead to get a better view. I then tried to open the hood but found it had jammed. Using both hands on the one side, I managed at last to pull the hood open, undid my Sutton Harness, grabbed my helmet off, and plunged out of the starboard side of the plane." He landed near Brook Farm, Margaretting, and was taken to Billericay Hospital for treatment of his extensive burns. It was to be many months before he returned to duty.

Proving remarkably capable adversaries, the Zerstörers did not escape without losses, particularly I./ZG 2, who lost five aircraft in all. Two of their Bf 110s coll-

Bf 110s of 7./ZG 26 receiving attention from the Staffel mechanics during the later stages of the Battle of Britain.

Soldiers stand guard over the remains of Bf 110 C, M8 + DM, W. Nr. 3226, which crashed at Frith farm, Billericay on 2/9/40. Pilot, Oblt. Wrede (acting-Gruppenadjutant) and Bordfunker, Uffz. Kukawka, were killed.

The partially burnt-out remains of 3M + HL, W. Nr. 2133, of 3./ZG 2 at Rye Hill, near Epping on 3/9/40. The pilot, Oblt. Müller, survived; Bordfunker Uffz. Korn was killed.

British soldiers pose with the port fin and rudder from 3M + HL, which displays 7 victory bars on the fin. Part of the unit code, '3M' can be seen on the fuselage remains in the background.

Another view of the remains of 3M + HL.

ided over Epping; Oberleutnant Kurt Müller, the Staffelführer of 2./ZG 2, and his Rottenflieger, Feldwebel Kurt Wagenbreth, whose starboard wingtip hit the wing and rudder of Müller's aircraft as they both took evasive action to avoid frenzied attacks by the Hurricanes of No. 310 (Czech) Squadron.

Müller, still recovering from his experiences of the previous day, was the only one to survive; his Bordfun-

ker, Unteroffizier Johannes Korn remained in the aircraft which crashed at Rye Hill, Thornwood. Meanwhile, Feldwebel Wagenbreth and Unteroffizier Schubarth had both managed to bale out but were too low and they fell to their deaths at Hubbards Hall, their aircraft plunging into the ground at Hobbs Cross, Harlow, where it later exploded.

But, as the German formation reached the coast and started back across the Thames estuary, more Spitfires joined in the melee. One of them was a No. 54 Squadron aircraft flown by Flight Lieutenant 'Al' Deere, "A few miles east of Hornchurch, and at about 13,000 feet, we met up with the tail end of the escort; about a dozen 110s, all weaving desperately to avoid the bursting AA shells being poured among them from a battery near the Thames."

Breaking from the Stabsschwarm of I./ZG 2, the Gruppe TO, Oberleutnant Reinhold Messner went to the assistance of another Zerstörer which was in trouble and promptly came under attack by a number of the newly-arrived Spitfires, some of which were firing what he thought were heavy calibre weapons.

He was quite right, as he was attacked by Flight Sergeant Unwin of No. 19 Squadron, with cannons working for once, who was soon joined by Pilot Officer Carpenter of No. 222 Squadron. With the Zerstörer starting to disintegrate around them, Messner and his Bordfunker, Unteroffizier Alois Santoni, both baled out

Lt. Gerhard Granz pokes fun at the Iron Cross I. Class of Lt. Reinhold Messner. Messner had been promoted to Oberleutnant by the time he was shot down on 3/9/40 in Bf 110 C-4, 3M + CB. Granz was to follow him into captivity four days later.

over Stowmaries.

During this final stage of the withdrawal, Oberleutnant Siegfried Gottschalk, the Staffelführer of 1./ZG 2, had one engine set alight by Sergeant Scott of No. 222 Squadron, but retired back along the north Kent coast as far as Reculver before he had to abandon his aircraft, breaking his arm in the process. He and his Bordfunker, Unteroffizier Max Hoffmann, were both picked up from the sea and landed at Herne Bay.

Later, the spirited young Bordfunker would try to convince his RAF interrogators that he was on his first war-flight and, as a result, could tell them nothing. But they remained dubious, the Iron Cross ribbon on his tunic suggesting otherwise.

Another 3./ZG 2 machine fell to the Hurricanes and crashed at Canewdon, shot down by Flying Officer Count Czernin and at least two other pilots of No. 17 Squadron; the crew Oberfeldwebel Gerhard Winkler and Gefreiter Oskar Weiler baling out unhurt. Czernin then went on to attack another Zerstörer whose engines were already disabled following attacks by Sub-Lieutenant Carpenter of No. 46 Squadron. This Bf 110 belly-landed at Mundon where the pilot, Leutnant Walther Manhart of 6./ZG 26, and his seriously wounded Bordfunker, Unteroffizier Werner Drews, were both taken prisoner.

As the raid withdrew over the estuary, one more Zerstörer dropped out of combat to crash-land at North Shoebury, riddled from stem to stern in devastating attacks by at least four Spitfires from No. 54 and 222 Squadrons. The crew, Feldwebel Hans Grau and Unteroffizier Günther Uecker, were both badly wounded, the unfortunate Bordfunker, Uecker, dying of his wounds the following day.

Al Deere of No. 54 Squadron was one RAF pilot involved and recalls, "I had singled out a Me 110 and was taking great care to get my opening range accurate - an unusual pleasure afforded by the absence of 109s - when to my amazement a Spitfire, diving vertically from above, opened fire on my intended target which burst into flame and spun away...it was Colin Gray who had beaten me to it. 'He would', I thought angrily, but reluctantly admitting to myself that it was a remarkable piece of shooting."

Feldwebel Grau's aircraft subsequently became subject of a bitter British inter-service dispute when an AA battery laid claim to it. To the RAF pilots' disgust, and as Deere confirms, "In the end, the victory was credited to the guns - much to our annoyance - on the basis that they had done sterling work and needed encouragement. So did we." But no corroboration one way or the other, was forthcoming from Grau for, such was the shattering effect of his experience that he had been rendered stone deaf from post-traumatic shock.

Hauptmann Makrocki's I./ZG 26 continued with their run of luck, suffering a single casualty, a 3./ZG 26 machine wrecked in a heavy crash-landing back at Fontend. This returned minus the Bordfunker, 21 year-old Unteroffizier Horst Klatt, who baled out under fighter attack over the Thames estuary and whose body was later washed ashore at Southend.

Leutnant Joachim Koepsell, flying with 3rd Staffel since his transfer from 1st Staffel on 20th August, recorded this mission as his 25th war flight, a sortie lasting 1 hour and 45 minutes. It was his eighth combat sortie in the last six days.

Nine British fighters were shot down and seven more seriously damaged in this action, from which 5 RAF pilots failed to return and another 6 were badly wounded. III./ZG 26 claimed 12 victories, 8th and 9th Staffeln taking an equal share of the spoils, top-scorer Sophus Baagoe scoring a 'Doppel' to bring his personal tally to 12.

Despite the serious blow to the command structure of I./ZG 2, it had been a singular success for the Zerstörers for as German records show, few British fighters ever reached the bombers before the escorts intervened, a solitary Dornier of 5./KG 2 falling at Langenhoe.

German air superiority over southern England was fast becoming a reality and, for the third time since this phase of the battle commenced, the daily tally of losses swung in favour of the Luftwaffe. But events on the following day, 4th September, would redress this balance and strike another heavy blow at the Zerstörers.

In the morning, sector airfields were again attacked,

Oblt. Hans von Boltenstern, later Hauptmann and second Gruppenkommandeur of Erpr. Gr. 210, killed in action on 4/9/40.

Eastchurch and Lympne both being hit. Then, around lunch-time, a heavy raid of over 300 aircraft crossed the coast between Dover and Beachy Head and fanned-out towards their targets. Aircraft factories were clearly high on the agenda, one formation heading straight for the Short Brothers factory at Rochester, while further west, the Vickers Armstrong works at Weybridge was also targeted for attack by Zerstörers.

Leading the attack were 14 Zerstörers of Erprobungsgruppe 210, now led by Hauptmann Hans von Boltenstern, previously Staffelkapitän of 14.(Z)/LG 1. Close escort was provided by Bf 110s of his old Gruppe, Liensberger's V.(Z)/LG 1, while Vollbracht's Stabsschwarm and Kaldrack's III./ZG 76 gave added fighter protection. Meantime, Groth's 'Haifisch' Gruppe were to fly a freelance sortie, east of the main formation, and cover their withdrawal back over Beachy Head.

As Erprobungsgruppe 210 neared the coast, British fighters appeared below them positioning for an attack. Unaccountably, von Boltenstern attempted to bunt to their level and engage, a dangerous manoeuvre at the height that the Bf 110s were flying. He failed to pull out and simply dived straight into the Channel without a shot being fired. The rest of the Gruppe kept on for the target. Approaching the coast near Brighton, Unteroffizier Adolf Käser of 7./ZG 76 spotted the first

British fighters far off to the west. But holding rigidly to course, the Bf 110s ignored them and carried on. Käser was uneasy; due to losses he had been loaned to 8th Staffel for this mission and was flying with a brand new pilot. It had been common practise within the Gruppe, for some time now, for new crews to be split up on arrival, and paired-off with experienced pilots or Bordfunkers for their first few sorties. It made good sense, but it didn't make him feel any more comfortable.

The British fighters, now recognisable as Spitfires, crossed above and behind them. Then suddenly, one appeared directly behind Willi Schultis' aircraft, which started getting it 'in the neck'. Käser radioed his pilot, Oberleutnant Hans Münich, giving the Spitfire's position, but his call was ignored. Käser had to sit there and watch his friend's Zerstörer slowly drop out of formation with the Spitfire hanging on to its tail, as the rest of the Gruppe maintained station and held course inland. Surviving attacks by Spitfires of No. 234 Squadron, Unteroffizier Schultis bellied his tattered aircraft in at Portway, near Steyning, his bullet-riddled Bordfunker, Unteroffizier Richard Bileck, just barely alive. While, on Coatwood Farm at Wisborough Green, Oberleutnant Raetsch and Obergefreiter Hempel of 9./ZG 76 died in the burning wreckage of their aircraft, picked off by another No. 234 Squadron pilot, Flight Lieutenant Hughes.

Coming under increasingly vicious attacks by British fighters, the pilots of III./ZG 76 did their best to form an Abwehrkreis over Worthing, guarding the western flank of the attacking force's exit route. Intensely bitter fighting erupted when 21 Hurricanes from Tangmere, Nos. 43 and 601 Squadrons, with a top cover of 12 Spitfires from No. 602 Squadron, joined the fray.

With all semblance of cohesion lost, the British and German formations merged, individual combats spilling over the Sussex coast and South Downs. The 'Fighting Cocks' of No. 43 Squadron, led by Squadron Leader 'Caesar' Hull, now joined the Spitfires of No. 234 Squadron in inflicting the worst carnage among the hard-pressed Zerstörer crews.

Käser felt uneasy - not once had he noticed Münich check below them, and watchful as this experienced Bordfunker might be, there was only so much he could do on his own. His worst fears were realised when their starboard engine suddenly burst into flames following attack by Spitfires of Flying Officer Horton and Sergeant Klein of No. 234 Squadron.

Oberleutnant Münich immediately went into a steep dive in an effort to extinguish the sheet of flame which now streamed like a banner back over the wing. Käser, transfixed, watched as his instruments indicated an airspeed in excess of 760 Kms., at which point the port engine started smoking and he called-up to enquire if now might be a good time to bale out?

He pulled the cockpit release handle and braced himself for the sudden rush of air from the slipstream - nothing, the hood was jammed! Standing on his seat and putting his back to the roof, Käser strained against the stubborn canopy using all his strength, but it made

Before and after: two views of Bf 110 C-4, 2N+CN, W. Nr. 3101, of Lt. Münich, pilot, and Bordfunker Uffz. Käser of 8./ZG 76. The individual aircraft letter 'C' can be seen outboard of the starboard wing cross in the crash view at Black Patch Hill, Angmering. Optimistic to the end, Münich and Käser retrieved the dinghy from the aircraft, and set out for the coast 12 miles away. Their escape attempt did not reach fruition, and ultimately they spent the rest of the war as prisoners.

no difference - it was stuck fast.

Thankfully Münich was still up-front and Käser radioed him the bad news. The pilot slowly brought the machine back under control and turned towards the coast, steadily losing height, searching for a place to land. Ironically, as they readied themselves for the landing, the obstinate canopy sprung off, like a cork from a bottle, but by then they were far too low to bale out.

The Zerstörer hit the ground hard, at Black Patch Hill, near Angmering, the port wing taking the full force of the impact and wrenching the engine from its mounting. Käser received a blow on the head and passed out. When he came to, bleeding from a scratch on his temple, an old man was standing alongside the aircraft peering in at him. In spite of the clout on his head, Käser's mind was as clear as a bell, "How far to the coast?", he asked. "Twelve miles", replied the old man, beating a hasty retreat across the field away from the burning machine. It was all that Käser needed to know.

With Münich's help, he dragged the dinghy from its storage point and they set off in the general direction of the coast, humping it between them. All they had to do now, Käser insisted, was reach the coast, hide up and wait for nightfall, then put to sea and paddle to mid-Channel where they would be rescued by the Seenotdienst the following morning - simplicity itself!

With the exploding ammunition in the aircraft crackling away faintly far behind them, they forced their way through some undergrowth and burst into a small, sun-lit clearing. The thoughts of the people enjoying a picnic there are not known, but Münich and Käser, still clutching their dinghy, dived into bushes on the other side of the clearing and were gone, leaving the astonished group to their al-fresco meal.

But before they had gone much further, the sound of heavy vehicles heralded the arrival of a lorry full of armed troops, accompanied by the old man from the crash-site. Accepting the inevitable, Käser hurriedly hid his pistol under a clump of moss before they emerged from hiding and gave themselves up. As they were being driven away, the officer in charge enquired whether they would like a souvenir from their aircraft. 'What a kind gesture', thought Käser, contemplating the dinghy.

Meanwhile, the Bf 110s of Erprobungsgruppe 210 arrived over the target shortly after 1:00 pm. and went straight into their customary well-executed attacks, delivering six 500 Kg. bombs on the Vickers machine shops and assembly sheds. There were 700 casualties, 88 killed, and it took four days to clear the rubble.

As the smoke rose from Weybridge and Erprobungsgruppe 210 turned for the coast, No. 253 Squadron from Kenley, led by the 'B' Flight Commander, Flight Lieutenant Cambridge, were in a shallow dive on the Zerstörers from out of the sun. The 9 Hurricanes slammed into Liensberger's escort Bf 110s, who had formed an Abwehrkreis east of Guildford to cover the withdrawal, and tore into Oberleutnant Michel Junge's 14th Staffel.

Uffz. Balthasar Aretz, pilot with 2./Erpr. Gr. 210, who flew on the raid of 4/9/40 against the Vickers Armstrong works at Weybridge. Aretz flew in the western campaign, the Battle of Britain, on the Russian front and in the Mediterranean, and survived the war - one of the many unsung flyers who served their country.

For once, the Hurricanes had the advantage and they exploited it to the full. Junge's aircraft was one of the first to fall, exploding on Upper Common at Netley, and within minutes, Feldwebel Karl Röhring's Zerstörer screamed out of the combat to crash nearby at West Horsley. A solitary parachute emerged from the turmoil as Röhring's Bordfunker, 26 year-old Unteroffizier Joachim Jäckel, slowly dropped into captivity.

Protecting the eastern flank of the attack, II./ZG 76 had also formed an Abwehrkreis over East Grinstead, where they now came under attack by the Hurricanes of No. 1 (RCAF) Squadron, led by Flight Lieutenant McGregor. Scrambled from Northolt in the middle of a Press visit, the Canadians harried the 'Haifisch' Gruppe south over Uckfield towards Beachy Head, a running fight developing as more British fighters arrived.

The Hurricanes of No. 79 Squadron were among them as Pilot Officer 'Dimsie' Stones recalls, "We succumbed to temptation and went after 15 Me 110s which formed a defensive circle over Beachy Head. We attacked them, hoping to break up their circle, and got one of them in our first attack. I was so close to him before breaking away that I could see a red dragon painted on his nose."

Two 'Haifisch' were brought down in as many min-

On 4/9/40 the last resting place of this Sharksmouth from the Gruppenstab of II./ZG 76, M8+AC, W. Nr. 3602, was the garden of Little Butts Farm, Cousley Wood, near Wadhurst. The crew of Oblt. Weeber, pilot, and Bordfunker Uffz. Michael both survived into captivity. The 'A' in the fuselage code would be in the Gruppenstab colour of green.

utes. Attacked by Pilot Officer Smither of No. 1 (RCAF) Squadron, Oberleutnant Günther Piduhn's Zerstörer exploded over Smarts Hill, Penshurst, giving the hapless crew no chance to escape. A second Bf 110, severely damaged and with its Bordfunker seriously wounded in an attack by another of the Canadian pilots, Flying Officer Nesbitt, spiralled down out of combat to make an impressive belly-landing at Little Butts Farm, Cousley Wood. This was flown by Oberleutnant Hermann Weeber, the Gruppenadjutant, whose Bordfunker, Unteroffizier Max Michael, survived and was taken to the Kent and Sussex Hospital in nearby Tunbridge Wells.

Another was badly damaged by Flying Officer Russell of No. 1 (RCAF) Squadron but managed to reach the coast before coming under attack from some of No. 79 Squadron's Hurricanes, including Flying Officer Peters. With both engines out of action, the 25 year-old pilot, Oberleutnant Ernst-Hartmann Freiherr von Schlotheim, from 'Walti' Borchers 5th Staffel, was determined to get as far away from the English coast as possible before he ditched. He stretched his glide, holding the aircraft close to stalling speed, until 7 miles off Pevensey, when it finally hit the water. Rapidly deploying their dinghy, he and his Bordfunker, Unteroffizier Georg Hommel, struck out energetically for the French coast - a mere 70 miles away. Battling against the tide, they soon realised the futility of it and reluctantly turned back for the nearer coast.

Back over the coast, Stab, III./ZG 76 lost two aircraft to No. 43 Squadron's Hurricanes. One was flown by Oberleutnant Walter Schiller, acting-Staffelkapitän of 7./ZG 76, who abandoned his Bf 110 along with his Bordfunker, Feldwebel Herbert Winkler, following an attack by Pilot Officer Upton. Their Zerstörer crashed and burned out on the downs at High Salvington, near Findon. The other, shot down by Flight Lieutenant Dalton-Morgan, impacted at Church Farm, Washington and exploded with such violence that no trace of the crew, Oberleutnant Helmut Florenz, the Gruppe NO, and his Bordfunker, Gefreiter Rudi Herbert, was found.

Dalton-Morgan then went on to join some other Hurricanes and a Spitfire in chasing another Zerstörer flown by Oberleutnant Wilhelm Schäfer, the Geschwaderadjutant of ZG 2. Forced too low, his damaged port engine labouring, and under attack by four tenacious British fighters, Schäfer had little choice but to make a hurried belly-landing at Mill Hill, high on the downs above Shoreham.

One of the pursuit, Pilot Officer Gilbert of No. 601 Squadron, was scathing, "...in my opinion (he) deliberately, and I consider quite unnecessarily, force-landed about one mile north of Shoreham." An uncharitable view, but probably far less charitable that Oberstleutnant Vollbracht's comments on learning that his Adjutant had failed to return - Schäfer had borrowed the 'old man's' aircraft!

Back at Ligescourt, Unteroffizier Pfaffelhuber of

This page and overleaf: two views of 3M+AA, the Bf 110 C-4 of the Geschwaderkommodore of ZG 2, Obstlt. Friedrich Vollbracht. This Zerstörer was shot down on 4/9/40 with Oblt. Schäfer, Geschwaderadjutant, and Bordfunker Uffz. Bendjus on board. Both survived the landing.

15.(Z)/LG 1 helped his wounded Bordfunker, Willi Banser, from the aircraft. It had been a tough flight, lasting 1¾ hours, and a rougher mission, the 'Tommies' being more than usually pugnacious. So much so, he was convinced that they were equipped with a new type of aircraft and noted in his Flugbuch, "War flight escorting 14 Me 110 bombers to Vickers Wellington Works, Aldershot. There were 30 enemy fighters of latest type, Bristol, probably American. More air fighting at Aldershot when we retired."

Fighting throughout the day cost RAF Fighter Command 17 fighters and 12 pilots; the irrepressible 'Max und Moritz' of 6./ZG 76 continuing their run of successes with Herget claiming a Hurricane south-east of London, while Jabs claimed a Spitfire and a Hurricane.

Total German losses on the day were 28, but a staggering 17 of them were Bf 110s - the Zerstörers having their worst day ever. All but one of these was a result of the Weybridge attack. Liensberger's Gruppe had lost 4 aircraft and crews, all from the same Staffel, and III./ZG 76 had lost six. The still-smoking wreckage of 10 Zerstörers littered the southern counties of England, and prisoners or bodies from two more would come ashore there over the next few days. Three more Zerstörers are presumed to have crashed into the Channel unobserved by either side.

Apart from von Boltenstern's accidental loss, Erprobungsgruppe 210 returned to Calais-Marck unscathed, the target pulverised. The price paid by the Zerstörer escorts had been high, but Erprobungsgruppe 210 would return two days later for a further attack in the area.

Zerstörer activity over the next two days was reduced, as the Luftwaffe made final preparations for the daylight attack on London scheduled for Saturday 7th September. This attack had been planned since 31st August and finally sanctioned by the OKL on 2nd September as a reprisal for the RAF bombing of Berlin. Every available German aircraft was to be used, in what was intended to be the final knock-out blow against RAF Fighter Command, whose last remaining fighters would be brought to battle in defence of their capital and destroyed in the air.

Seated for an outdoor conference are, from left to right: Groth; von Schlotheim; Hohbein; Weber and Jabs. Standing, to the left with his arm in a sling is Nacke. This photograph would date between 30/8/40, when Nacke was wounded in action, and 4/9/40, when von Schlotheim was shot down over England. All are aircrew of II./ZG 76.

LOSS TABLES - AUGUST to 6th SEPTEMBER 1940

Date	Name of crew and rank	Unit	Status	Fate	Aircraft Code & W. Nr.	Damage state	Reason for casualty	Place
06.08.40	Lt. Kurt Prokop Gefr. Herbert Dust	2./Erpr. Gr. 210	P Bf	K K	Bf 110	100%	Crashed during dive-bombing. practise.	Near Denain.
06.08.40	Uffz. Heinrich Schultheis	2./Erpr. Gr. 210	P	K	Bf 110	100%	Lost control and abandoned during high speed manoeuvres on test flight.	Near Denain.
06.08.40	Uffz. Engelbert Mail	3./ZG 26	P	K	Bf 110	100%	Crashed on non-combat flight from Barly.	South-west of Yvrench airfield.
08.08.40	Lt. Günther Beck Uffz. Paul Busch	13.(Z)/ LG 1	P Bf	U W	Bf 110 C-2	40%	Damaged in combat with RAF fighters.	Channel, south of the Isle of Wight.
08.08.40	Fw. Gerhard Jentzsch Uffz. Alfred Dieckmann	13.(Z)/ LG 1	P Bf	K W	Bf 110 C L1 + EH	80%	Damaged in combat with RAF fighters ove the Channel.	Crashed 3 Kms. east of Cherbourg-Theville.
08.08.40	Fw. Alfred Sturm Fw. Helmut Brunner	14.(Z)/ LG 1	P Bf	M M	Bf 110 C-2	100%	Shot down by RAF fighters.	Channel.
08.08.40		V.(Z)/ LG 1	P Bf	U U	Bf 110 C	25%	Damaged in combat with RAF fighters.	Channel, south of the Isle of Wight.
08.08.40		V.(Z)/ LG 1	P Bf	U U	Bf 110 C	70%	Damaged in combat with RAF fighters.	Channel, south of the Isle of Wight.
08.08.40		V.(Z)/ LG 1	P	U U	Bf 110 C	70%	Damaged in combat with RAF fighters.	Channel, south of the Isle of Wight.
08.08.40	Lt. Dziddek	3./ZG 26 3./ZG 26	P Bf	W W	Bf 110	100%	Crashed following collision with Bf 110 of Fw. Döller.	Near Conteville.
08.08.40	Fw. Richard Döller	3./ZG 26 3./ZG 26	P Funk Ofw.	U K	Bf 110 D	100%	Abandoned following collision with Bf 110 of Lt. Dziddek.	Over Conteville.
09.08.40	Uffz. Karl Schock	7./ZG 26	P	W	Ar 66	40%	Crash-landed on local flight.	St. Omer.
09.08.40	Gefr. Franz Weber	7./ZG 26	P	K	Bf 110 C-4	100%	Crashed on non-combat flight. Cause unknown.	Böblingen.
11.08.40	Lt. Kurt Bertram Ogefr. Gerhard Mertins	1./Erpr. Gr. 210	P Bf	K K	Bf 110 C-6	100%	Shot down by RAF fighters over convoy. Crashed in sea.	Off Harwich.
11.08.40	Gefr. Christian Weiss Ogefr. Richard Keilhaupt	1./Erpr. Gr. 210	P Bf	K K	Bf 110 C-6	100%	Shot down by RAF fighters over convoy. Ditched in sea.	Off Harwich.
11.08.40	Oblt. Günther Hensel (Geschwaderadjutant) Oblt. Wilhelm Schäfer	Stab ZG 2 Stab	P Bf	K W	Bf 110 C-2	100%	Shot down by RAF fighters. Crashed in sea. Bordfunker rescued by Seenotdienst.	Off Portland.

Date	Name of crew and rank	Unit	Status	Fate	Aircraft Code & W. Nr.	Damage state	Reason for casualty	Place
11.08.40	Major Ernst Ott (Gruppenkommandeur) Fw. Otto Zimehl	Stab I ZG 2 Stab I	P Bf	K K	Bf 110 C 3M + AB 3078	100%	Shot down by RAF fighters in combat over the Channel.	South of Portland.
11.08.40	Lt. Heinz Jess Gefr. Hans Kossar	1./ZG 2 1./ZG 2	P Bf	K K	Bf 110 C 3M + AH 2127	100%	Shot down by RAF fighters. Crashed in Channel.	South of Portland.
11.08.40	Fw. Erich Teichert Gefr. Erich Kloss	2./ZG 2 2./ZG 2	P Bf	K K	Bf 110 C 3M + LK 3120	100%	Shot down by RAF fighters Crashed in Channel.	South of Portland.
11.08.40	Fw. Rudolf Weis Uffz. Gustav Schwarze	3./ZG 2 3./ZG 2	P Bf	K M	Bf 110 C-4 3M + LL 3123	100%	Shot down by RAF fighters.	Over Portland.
11.08.40		3./ZG 2	P Bf	U U	Bf 110 C	20%	Damaged in combat with RAF fighters. Force-landed at Carquebut.	Off Portland.
11.08.40		I./ZG 2	P Bf	U U	Bf 110 D	10%	Damaged in combat with RAF fighters.	Off Portland.
11.08.40		I./ZG 2	P Bf	U U	Bf 110 C	15%	Damaged in combat with RAF fighters.	Off Portland.
11.08.40		I./ZG 2	P P	U U	Bf 110 C	10%	Damaged in combat with RAF fighters.	Off Portland.
11.08.40	Uffz. Karl-Heinz Hoyer Gefr. Lienhard Dietz	4./ZG 2 4./ZG 2	P Bf	M M	Bf 110 D	100%	Shot down by RAF fighters.	Off Portland.
11.08.40		II./ZG 2	P Bf	U U	Bf 110 D	10%	Damaged in combat with RAF fighters.	Portland area.
11.08.40	Hptm. Johann Kogler (Staffelkapitän) Uffz. Adolf Bauer	1./ZG 26 1./ZG 26	P Bf	W W	Bf 110 D	100%	Shot down by RAF fighters during escort mission for Erpr. Gr. 210. Both crew rescued by Seenotdienst.	Off Felixstowe.
11.08.40	Fw. Erich Puschnerus Uffz. Rudolf Krause	1./ZG 26 1./ZG 26	P Bf	K K	Bf 110	100%	Shot down by RAF fighters during escort mission for Erpr. Gr. 210.	Off Felixstowe.
11.08.40		2./ZG 26	P Bf	U U	Bf 110	20%	Returned to base damaged following combat with RAF fighters during escort mission for Erpr. Gr. 210.	Off Felizstowe.
11.08.40		2./ZG 26	P Bf	U U	Bf 110 C	70%	Crash-landed at St. Omer following combat with RAF fighters during escort mission for Erpr. Gr. 210.	Off Felixstowe.

Date	Name of crew and rank	Unit	Status	Fate	Aircraft Code & W. Nr.	Damage state	Reason for casualty	Place
12.08.40	Ofw. Henniges	4.(F)/ Auf. Gr. 121		W	Bf 110 C-5	30%	Set alight by own AA fire. Force-landed after Bordfunker baled out.	Near Barfleur.
12.08.40	Lt. Erich Beudel Ogefr. Otto Jordan	1./Erpr. Gr. 210	P Bf	U U	Bf 110 S9 + EH	100%	Starboard engine seized following bombing mission to Manston airfield.	Calais-Marck airfield.
12.08.40		I./ZG 2	P Bf	U U	Bf 110 D	35%	Crashed on landing following combat with RAF fighters.	St. Aubin.
12.08.40		I./ZG 2	P Bf	U U	Bf 110 C-4	15%	Returned to base damaged following combat with RAF fighters.	Channel.
12.08.40	Oblt. Siegfried Blume	2./ZG 2 2./ZG 2	P Bf	U M	Bf 110 C 3M + HK 3515	100%	Shot down by RAF fighters. Pilot rescued by Seenot-dienst.	Channel.
12.08.40	Hptm. Hans-Peter Kulbel (Gruppenkommandeur) Uffz. Fritz Budig	Stab I. ZG 2 2./ZG 2	P Bf	K K	Bf 110 D-0 3M + MK 3316	100%	Shot down by RAF fighters during escort mission.	Off Portsmouth.
12.08.40		II./ZG 2	P Bf	U U	Bf 110 D	20%	Returned to St. with damage follow-ing combat with RAF fighters.	Channel.
12.08.40		II./ZG 2	P Bf	U U	Bf 110 D	40%	Returned damaged following combat with RAF fighters.	Channel.
12.08.40	Uffz. Max Schuler Ogefr. Otto Evel	5./ZG 2 5./ZG 2	P Bf	M M	Bf 110 C-2	100%	Shot down by RAF fighters.	South-east of Portland.
12.08.40	Uffz. Heinz Conrad Gefr. Erich Czesny	5./ZG 2 5./ZG 2	P Bf	K M	Bf 110	100%	Shot down by RAF fighters.	Off Portland.
12.08.40		III./ZG 26	P Bf	U U	Bf 110 C	45%	Damaged in combat with RAF fighters. Force-landed at Calais.	Channel.
12.08.40	Hptm. Max Graf Hoyos (Staffelkapitän) Uffz. Siegfried Krommes	8./ZG 76 8./ZG 76	P Bf	K K	Bf 110 C-2	100%	Shot down by RAF fighters.	Off Portland.
12.08.40	Uffz. Rudolf Petersen Ogefr. Martin Heinze	8./ZG 76 8./ZG 76	P Bf	W W	Bf 110 C-2	35%	Damaged in combat with RAF fighters. Force-landed at Caen.	Off Portland.
13.08.40	Lt. Günter Beck Uffz. Karl Hoyer	13.(Z)/ LG 1	P Bf	K M	Bf 110 D	100%	Shot down by RAF fighters.	Channel, west of Bournemouth.
13.08.40	Fw. Georg Klever Uffz. Hugo Weller	13.(Z)/ LG 1	P Bf	W W	Bf 110 D	50%	Damaged in combat with RAF fighters. Force-landed at Condé-sûr-Ifa airfield.	South of Aldershot.

Date	Name of crew and rank	Unit	Status	Fate	Aircraft Code & W. Nr.	Damage state	Reason for casualty	Place
13.08.40	Fw. Hans Datz Uffz. Georg Lämmel	13.(Z)/ LG 1	P Bf	POW K	Bf 110 D	100%	Shot down by RAF fighters.	Channel, west of Bournemouth.
13.08.40	Lt. Horst Werner Gefr. Fritz Klemm	14.(Z)/ Stab V. LG 1	P Bf	M M	Bf 110 C-4	100%	Shot down by RAF fighters.	Channel, 20 Km. west of Bournemouth.
13.08.40	Oblt. Michel Junge Gefr. Alfred Haas	14.(Z)/ LG 1	P Bf	U W	Bf 110 L1+FK 3306	5% known	Returned damaged from combat with RAF fighters.	20 Kms. west of Bournemouth.
13.08.40	Ofw. Heinz Wagner Uffz. Paul Heldt	15.(Z)/ LG 1	P Bf	M M	Bf 110 D	100%	Shot down by RAF fighters.	Channel, west of Bournemouth.
13.08.40	Uffz. Werner Schümichen Ogefr. Otto Giglhuber	15.(Z)/ LG 1	P Bf	POW POW	Bf 110 D L1+FL	100%	Shot down by RAF fighters. Abandoned by crew.	Swalland Farm, Kimmeridge.
13.08.40		V.(Z)/ LG 1	P Bf	U U	Bf 110 D	60%	Damaged in combat with RAF fighters. Belly-landed at Rocquancourt airfield.	Channel.
13.08.40		V.(Z)/ LG 1	P Bf	U U	Bf 110 D	10%	Damaged in combat with RAF fighters.	Channel.
13.08.40		V.(Z)/ LG 1	P Bf	U U	Bf 110 D	100%	Damaged in combat with RAF fighters. Crash-landed at Cherbourg-Theville airfield.	Channel.
13.08.40		7.(F)/ LG 2	P P	U U	Bf 110 C-5	40%	Belly-landed due to engine failure.	Wissant.
13.08.40		I./ZG 2	P Bf	U U	Bf 110 C-4	5%	Damaged in combat with RAF fighters. Force-landed at Le Havre.	Channel.
13.08.40	Uffz. Walter-Ernst Müller	Stab I. Stab I. ZG 2	P Bf	U W	Bf 110 C-4	100%	Abandoned during combat with RAF fighters.	Channel.
13.08.40	Ogefr. Lorenz Maul	3./ZG 2	Bf	W	Bf 110 C-4	Not known	Damaged in combat with RAF fighter.	Winchester.
13.08.40	Lt. Wolfgang Münchmeyer Uffz. Fritz Labusch	1./ZG 2 1./ZG 2	P Bf	POW K	Bf 110 C-4 3M+LH 3201	100%	Shot down by Sgt. Guy of 601 Sqdn. during escort mission.	North Baddesley.
13.08.40		II./ZG 2		W	Bf 110	Not known	Damaged in combat with RAF fighters.	
13.08.40	Lt. Martin Meisel (Gruppe Nachrichtens offizier) Fw. Fritz Fischer	Stab I. Stab I	P Bf	U W	Bf 110 C	100%	Crashed into parked Bf 110 on landing following combat mission.	Clairmarais airfield.
13.08.40	Lt. Joachim Koepsell Uffz. Johann Schmidt	1./ZG 26 1./ZG 26	P Bf	U U	Bf 110 C-4 U8+EH	25%	Became disorient-ated returning from escort sortie. Crash-landed on return.	'sHertogen-bosch.

Date	Name of crew and rank	Unit	Status	Fate	Aircraft Code & W. Nr.	Damage state	Reason for casualty	Place
13.08.40		2./ZG 26	P Bf	U U	Bf 110 D U8+EK 3344	Not known	Damaged in forced-landing following escort mission for Erpr. Gr. 210.	Hunsel/ Mollenbercel.
13.08.40	Oblt. Karl Fuchs Uffz. Willi Ebben	3./ZG 26 3./ZG 26	P Bf	K K	Bf 110 C 3369	100%	Probably that shot down by F/O Weaver of 56 Sqdn. during escort mission for Erpr. Gr. 210. Exploded in mid-air.	Warden Bay, Sheppey.
13.08.40		3./ZG 26			Bf 110 C-4	30%	Bf 110 of Lt. Meisel crashed into aircraft on landing.	Clairmarais airfield.
13.08.40		7./ZG 26	Bf	W	Bf 110	Not known	Force-landed following combat mission.	Amsterdam.
13.08.40		8./ZG 26	P Bf	U U	Bf 110 C	100%	Crash-landed following combat combat mission.	Vlissingen.
13.08.40	Uffz. Erich Schindler Uffz. Arthur Lotz	8./ZG 76 8./ZG 76	P Bf	K M	Bf 110 C	100%	Failed to return from combat mission.	Channel, off Portland.
13.08.40	Uffz. Adalbert Kuhlmann Ogefr. Günther Müller	9./ZG 76 9./ZG 76	P Bf	U U	Bf 110 C	100%	Crashed into the sea. Crew rescued by Seenotdienst.	Channel, off Portland.
14.08.40	Oblt. Werner Weymann	1./Erpr. Gr. 210	P Bf	U U	Bf 110 D	Not known	Damaged by AA fire during bombing attack on Manston airfield. Returned to Calais-Marck on one engine.	Over Manston.
14.08.40	Lt. Heinrich Brinkmann Uffz. Richard Mayer	2./Erpr. Gr. 210	P Bf	K K	Bf 110 D S9+NK	100%	Shot down by AA fire during bombing attack.	Manston airfield.
14.08.40	Uffz. Hans Steding Gefr. Ewald Schank	2./Erpr. Gr. 210	P Bf	K POW	Bf 110 D S9+MK	100%	Shot down by AA fire during bombing attack.	Manston airfield.
14.08.40		2./ZG 26	P Bf	U U	Bf 110 C-4	10%	Force-landed at St. Omer following combat mission.	
15.08.40	Lt. Erich Beudel Ogefr. Otto Jordan	1./Erpr. Gr. 210	P Bf	U U	Bf 110	Not known	Damaged in attack on Martlesham Heath airfield.	Martlesham Heath
15.08.40	Hptm. Walter Rubensdörffer (Gruppenkommandeur) Ogefr. Ludwig Kretzer	Stab Erpr. Gr. 210	P Bf	K K	Bf 110 D S9+AB 3338	100%	Shot down by P/O Duckenfield of 501 Sqdn. following attack on Croydon airfield.	Bletchinglye Farm, Catts Hill, Rotherfield.
15.08.40	Oblt. Horst Fiedler (Gruppenadjutant) (died 18/8/40) Uffz. Johann Werner	Stab Erpr. Gr. 210	P Bf	POW POW	Bf 110 D S9+BB 3374	100%	Shot down by Sgt. Dymond of 111 Sqdn. and Sgt. Pearce of 32 Sqdn..	Redhill aerodrome.

Date	Name of crew and rank	Unit	Status	Fate	Aircraft Code & W. Nr.	Damage state	Reason for casualty	Place
15.08.40	Lt. Karl-Heinz Koch (Gruppe Technical Offizier) Uffz. Rolf Kahl	Stab Erpr. Gr. 210	P — Bf	POW — POW	Bf 110 D S9 + CB 3339	100%	Shot down by F/L Russell of 32 Sqdn. after initial damage over Croydon.	School Farm, Hooe.
15.08.40	Lt. Willi Benedens Uffz. Mass	Stab Erpr. Gr. 210	P — Bf	W — U	Bf 110	Not known	Returned damaged from combat with RAF fighters following atack on Croydon	Over Croydon.
15.08.40	Lt. Erich Beudel Ogefr. Otto Jordan	1./Erpr. Gr. 210	P — Bf	K — K	Bf 110 C-6 S9 + TH	100%	Shot down by F/L Connors and 'Green 2' of 111 Sqdn. following attack on Croydon.	Broadbridge Farm, Smallfield, Horley.
15.08.40	Uffz. Werner Neumann Ogefr. Karl Stoff	1./Erpr. Gr. 210	P — Bf	U — U	Bf 110	Not known	Returned damaged from combat with RAF fighters. following attack on Croydon.	Over Croydon.
15.08.40	Oblt Alfred Habisch Uffz. Ernst Elfner	2./Erpr. Gr. 210	P — Bf	POW — POW	Bf 110 D S9 + CK 3341	100%	Damaged over Croydon; unable to regain French coast.	Hawkhurst.
15.08.40	Lt. Helmut Ortner Ogefr. Bernhard Lohmann	2./Erpr. Gr. 210	P — Bf	POW — K	Bf 110	100%	Shot down by S/Ldr Worrall, F/L Crossley and 'Red 3' of 32 Sqdn. following attack on Croydon.	Ightham.
15.08.40	Fw. Gerhard Jecke Ogefr. Karl Schmergal	14.(Z)/ LG 1	P — Bf	W — W	Bf 110 C	60%	Damaged in combat with RAF fighters. Belly-landed at Cherbourg-West airfield.	North-west of Portland.
15.08.40	Uffz. Hans Saffenreuter	5./ZG 2 5./ZG 2	P — Bf	U — K	Bf 110 C	100%	Shot down by RAF fighters.	Channel.
15.08.40	Oblt. Hans-Jochen Knop Uffz. Jakob Neumayer	Stab ZG 76	P — Bf	K — M	Bf 110 C	100%	Shot down by RAF fighters during escort mission for Ju 88s of LG 1.	Channel, off Isle of Wight.
15.08.40	Hptm. Werner Restemeyer (Gruppenkommandeur) Uffz. Werner Eichert	Stab I. ZG 76 Stab I.	P — Bf	M — M	Bf 110 D M8 + AB	100%	Shot down by RAF fighters during escort mission for He 111s of KG 26.	North Sea, off Newcastle.
15.08.40	Lt. Gustav Loobes (Gruppenadjutant) Uffz. Xaver Brock	Stab I. ZG 76 Stab I.	P — Bf	K — M	Bf 110 D	100%	Shot down by RAF fighters.	North Sea, Off English east coast.
15.08.40	Oblt. Hans-Ulrich Kettling Ogefr. Fritz Volk	1./ZG 76 1./ZG 76	P — Bf	POW — POW	Bf 110 D M8 + CH 3155	100%	Shot down by P/O Bennions of 41 Sqdn. during escort sortie.	Streatlam, near Barnard Castle.
15.08.40	Fw. Klaus Ladwein Ogefr. Karl Lenk	2./ZG 76 2./ZG 76	P — Bf	POW — K	Bf 110 D M8 + EK	100%	Shot down by RAF fighters.	North Sea, off Northumberland coast.

Date	Name of crew and rank	Unit	Status	Fate	Aircraft Code & W. Nr.	Damage state	Reason for casualty	Place
15.08.40	Uffz. Bernhard Richter Uffz. Hans Geishecker	2./ZG 76 2./ZG 76	P Bf	W M	Bf 110 D	100%	Damaged in combat with RAF fighters. Crash-landed at Esbjerg. Bordfunker baled out and lost.	North Sea.
15.08.40	Lt. Heinrich Köhler Uffz. Heinz Oelsner	3./ZG 76 3./ZG 76	P Bf	K K	Bf 110 D	100%	Shot down by RAF fighters.	North Sea, off English east coast.
15.08.40	Ofw. Hans Gröning Ogefr. Helmut Hahn	3./ZG 76 3./ZG 76	P Bf	K M	Bf 110 D	100%	Shot down by RAF fighters.	North Sea.
15.08.40	Oblt. Gordon Gollob (Staffelkapitän) Fw. Friedrich Meyer	3./ZG 76 3./ZG 76	P Bf	U W	Bf 110 D	Not known	Damaged in combat with RAF fighters. Returned to base.	North Sea.
15.08.40	Uffz. Erich Zickler Gefr. Josef Pudlik	3./ZG 76 3./ZG 76	P Bf	U W	Bf 110 D	Not known	Damaged in combat with RAF fighters. Returned to base.	North Sea.
15.08.40	Uffz. Karl-Rudolf Röhrich Uffz. Theodor Neymeyer	Stab II. ZG 76	P Bf	K K	Bf 110 C	100%	Shot down by RAF fighters, probably F/O Edge of 609 Sqdn..	Broadlands, near Romsey.
15.08.40	Lt. Siegfried Hahn (Nachrichtensoffizier) Uffz. Willy Lehner	Stab II. ZG 76 Stab II.	P Bf	W W	Bf 110 C	100%	Damaged in combat with RAF fighters. Crash-landed at Cherbourg-West airfield.	
15.08.40	Oblt. Karl Wrede (Gruppe Technical Offizier) Uffz. Richard Kukawka	Stab II. ZG 76 Stab II.	P Bf	U W	Bf 110 C	100%	Damaged in combat with RAF fighters. Crash-landed at Barneville.	Channel.
15.08.40		II./ZG 76	P Bf	U U	Bf 110 C	100%	Shot down into the Channel by RAF fighters. Crew rescued unhurt.	Channel.
15.08.40	Oblt. Max Wien Uffz. Eugen Diebold	4./ZG 76 4./ZG 76	P Bf	K M	Bf 110 C	100%	Shot down by RAF fighters.	Channel, south of the Isle of Wight.
15.08.40	Oblt. Gerhard Bremer Uffz. Leo Pauli	5./ZG 76 5./ZG 76	P Bf	M K	Bf 110 C-4	100%	Shot down by F/L Barton and probably P/O Meaker of 249 Sqdn..	Farley Road, Slackstead.
15.08.40	Fw. Jakob Birndorfer Uffz. Max Guschewski	6./ZG 76 6./ZG 76	P Bf	K POW	Bf 110 C M8+BP	100%	Shot down by F/O Ostaszewski-Ostoje of 609 Sqdn. and P/O Zurakowski of 234 Sqdn.. Crash-landed on Isle of Wight.	North Ashey Down, Isle of Wight.
15.08.40	Fw. Franz Wagner Uffz. Fritz Spörl	6./ZG 76 6./ZG 76	P Bf	K K	Bf 110 C M8+WP	100%	Believed shot down by F/L McArthur of 609 Sqdn..	Furzley, West Wellow, near Romsey.

Date	Name of crew and rank	Unit	Status	Fate	Aircraft Code & W. Nr.	Damage state	Reason for casualty	Place
15.08.40	Hptm. Friedrich-Karl Dickoré (Gruppenkommandeur) Uffz. Herbert Templin	Stab III. ZG 76 Stab III.	P Bf	Died POW	Bf 110 C 2N + BC	100%	Collided with another aircraft during combat with Hurricanes of 213 Sqdn.. Aircraft abandoned by crew.	Channel. off Weymouth.
15.08.40	Uffz. Herbert Kschamer Uffz. Heinz Voigt	7./ZG 76 7./ZG 76	P Bf	M M	Bf 110 C	100%	Shot down by RAF fighters.	Channel, northwest of Portland.
15.08.40	Uffz. Alois Haas Gefr. Ernst Hoffmann	7./ZG 76 8./ZG 76	P Bf	K K	Bf 110 C 2N + BM	100%	Shot down by RAF fighters.	Channel, northwest of Portland.
15.08.40	Lt. Hans von Miakich Uffz. Paul Tschöpe	9./ZG 76 9./ZG 76	P Bf	K M	Bf 110 C	100%	Shot down by RAF fighters.	Off Portland.
16.08.40	Major Harry Carl (Gruppenkommandeur) Uffz. Wilhelm Maier	Stab II. ZG 2 Stab II.	P Bf	K K	Bf 110 C	100%	Damaged in combat with RAF fighters over the Channel and crashed on landing.	6 Kms. south of Beauzeville.
16.08.40	Oblt. Ernst Hollekamp Fw. Richard Schurk	6./ZG 2 6./ZG 2	P Bf	K K	Bf 110 C A2 + GL	100%	Severely damaged by RAF fighters, possibly F/O Salmon of 1 Sqdn.. Abandoned by crew.	Aldro school, Eastbourne.
16.08.40		Stab ZG 26	P Bf	U U	Bf 110 C-2	80%	Crash-landed following combat combat mission.	St. Omer.
16.08.40	Uffz. Gerhard Drenkhahn Uffz. Josef Frohwein	2./ZG 26 2./ZG 26	P Bf	K K	Bf 110 C	100%	Failed to return from combat mission.	South-east of England.
16.08.40	Lt. Walter Lemmer Ogefr. Josef Lewandowski	5./ZG 76 5./ZG 76	P Bf	M M	Bf 110 C	100%	Shot down by RAF fighters.	Shopwhyke House, near Tangmere.
16.08.40	Lt. Richard Marchfelder (Gruppe Technical Offizier) Ogefr. Herbert Jentzsch	Stab III. ZG 76 Stab III.	P Bf	POW POW	Bf 110 C	100%	Starboard engine set alight by 602 Sqdn. Spitfires, probably S/L Johnstone. Abandoned during return flight.	Droke, near Upwaltham.
16.08.40		III./ZG 76 III./ZG 76	P Bf	U U	Bf 110 C	100%	Shot down by RAF fighters. Crew rescued by Seenotdienst.	Channel, off Brighton.
16.08.40	Oblt. Urban Schlaffer (Staffelkapitän) Ogefr. Franz Obser	9./ZG 76 9./ZG 76	P Bf	POW POW	Bf 110 C 2N + AP	100%	Shot down by 602 Sqdn. Spitfires, possibly P/O Moody.	Lee Farm, Clapham.
18.08.40	Oblt. Arnold Werdin Ofw. Hans Knopf	7.(F)/ LG 2	P Bf	M K	Bf 110 C-5	100%	Shot down by Spitfires of 54 Sqdn..	Thames estuary.
18.08.40	Oblt. Rüdiger Proske (Gruppenadjutant) Uffz. Hans Möbius	Stab I. ZG 26 Stab I.	P Bf	POW POW	Bf 110 C-4 U8 + BB 3102	100%	Shot down by S/Ldr.MacDonnell of 64 Sqdn..	Dering Farm, Lydd.
18.08.40	Uffz. Rudolf Mai Uffz. Josef Gebauer	1./ZG 26 1./ZG 26	P Bf	M M	Bf 110 C-2	100%	Shot down by RAF fighters, probably P/O Flinders of 32 Sqdn..	Rough Common, Harbledown.

Date	Name of crew and rank	Unit	Status	Fate	Aircraft Code & W. Nr.	Damage state	Reason for casualty	Place
18.08.40	Lt. Joachim Koepsell	1./ZG 26	P	U	Bf 110 C-4	10%	Damaged in combat during escort mission for Do 17s of KG 76. Crash-landed at Clairmarais.	Kenley.
	Uffz. Johann Schmidt	1./ZG 26	Bf	U	U8+BH			
18.08.40	Hptm. Herbert Kaminski (Staffelkapitän)	2./ZG 26	P	W	Bf 110 C-2	100%	Ditched following combat with RAF fighters. Rescued by See-notdienst after 4 days.	Channel, off Dunkirk.
	Uffz. Heinrich Strauch	2./ZG 26	Bf	W				
18.08.40		2./ZG 26	P	U	Bf 110 D-0	40%	Damaged in combat with RAF fighters. Crashed on landing at Hermelinghen.	South coast of England.
			Bf	U				
18.08.40	Oblt. Hans-Jürgen Kirchhoff (Staffelkapitän)	3./ZG 26	P	K	Bf 110 D-0	100%	Shot down by RAF fighters.	Off French coast.
	Lt. Berthold Mader (of I./Ln. Rgt. 32)		Bf	K				
18.08.40	Ofw. Willi Stange	3./ZG 26	P	M	Bf 110 C-4	100%	Shot down by F/O Weaver of 56 Sqdn..	Bonnington.
	Uffz. Hans Hesse	3./ZG 26	Bf	M				
18.08.40		2./ZG 26	P	U	Bf 110 D-0	100%	Crashed following combat mission.	Ypres.
			Bf	U				
18.08.40		3./ZG 26	P	U	Bf 110 D-0	100%	Crashed following combat mission.	Le Nieppe.
			Bf	U				
18.08.40	Hptm. Hubert Lüttke (Staffelkapitän)	4./ZG 26	P	K	Bf 110 C	100%	Shot down by P/O Gray of 54 Sqdn..	Clacton.
	Uffz. Herbert Brillo	4./ZG 26	Bf	M	3526			
18.08.40	Fw. Friedhelm Gierga	4./ZG 26	P	POW	Bf 110 C	100%	Shot down by Hurricanes of 85 Sqdn..	Channel, off North Foreland.
	Uffz. Gerhard Baar	4./ZG 26	Bf	M	3U+CM			
18.08.40	Uffz. Heinz Jäckel	4./ZG 26	P	K	Bf 110 C	100%	Severely damag-ed in attacks by RAF fighters, poss-ibly S/L Manton og 56 Sqdn. Crash-landed.	2 miles east of Eastchurch.
	Uffz. Theodor Rütters	4./ZG 26	Bf	POW	3U+AM			
18.08.40		4./ZG 26	P	U	Bf 110 C	30%	Damaged in combat with RAF fighters. Aircraft returned to Wizernes.	Thames estuary.
	Uffz. Willi Völlinger	4./ZG 26	Bf	W (Died same day)				
18.08.40	Oblt. Heinz Hellmuth	6./ZG 26	P	K	Bf 110 C	100%	Shot down by Hurricanes of 56 Sqdn.; final attack by P/O Mounsdon.	Platts Heath, Lenham.
	Fw. Franz Winter	6./ZG 26	Bf	M				
18.08.40	Lt. Hans-Joachim Kästner	6./ZG 26	P	POW	Bf 110 C	100%	Damaged by RAF fighters. Force-landed.	St. Mary's Marsh Blackmanstone. Newchurch.
	Uffz. Walter Kaffenberger	6./ZG 26	Bf	K	3U+EP 3102			
18.08.40	Ofw. Adolf Kiefel	6./ZG 26	P	K	Bf 110 C	100%	Shot down by Sgt. Robinson of 56 Sqdn..	Pluckley.
	Uffz. Josef Hemmersbach	6./ZG 26	Bf	K	3U+IP 3060			

Date	Name of crew and rank	Unit	Status	Fate	Aircraft Code & W. Nr.	Damage state	Reason for casualty	Place
18.08.40	Fw. Herbert Stange Uffz. Gerhard Wollin	6./ZG 26 6./ZG 26	P Bf	POW K	Bf 110 C	100%	Damaged in combat with 56 Sqdn. Hurricanes; finally shot down by P/O Goodman of No. 1 Sqdn..	Channel, off Folkestone.
18.08.40	Fw. Herbert Klare Uffz. Dietrich Brünger	8./ZG 26 8./ZG 26	P Bf	M M	Bf 110 C	100%	Shot down by RAF fighters over Kenley.	Believed near Godstone.
18.08.40		8./ZG 26	P Bf	U U	Bf 110 C	30%	Crashed following combat mission.	Arques.
20.08.40	Fw. Martin Wohlfart Gefr. Albert Dietrich	2/.Erpr. Gr. 210	P Bf	M M	Bf 110 D	100%	Shot down by 'A' Flight of 66 Sqdn..	15 Km. south-east of Aldeburgh.
21.08.40	Uffz. Balthasar Aretz Gefr. Rolf Schilleng	2./Erpr. Gr. 210	P Bf	U U	Bf 110 D-0 S9+EK 3377	10%	Tailwheel collapsed on landing on local flight from Denain.	Calais-Marck airfield.
22.08.40	Uffz. Ernst Glaeske Ogefr. Konrad Schweda	2./Erpr. Gr. 210	P Bf	U U	Bf 110	Not known	Starboard engine damaged by RAF fighters.	Channel.
22.08.40		1./NJG 1	P Bf	U U	Bf 110	60%	Crashed on landing due to brake failure.	Bonninghardt. airfield.
22.08.40	Oblt. Hans-Erich Berger Uffz. Willi Pfeifer	1./NJG 1 1./NJG 1	P Bf	W W	Bf 110	50%	Ground-looped on landing from night mission.	Bonninghardt airfield.
23.08.40		II./ZG 76	P Bf	U U	Bf110 C	40%	Damaged in taxi-ing accident.	Jersey airfield.
24.08.40	Lt. Hofer Two NCOs	Auf. Gr. Ob. der L.	P	K K	Bf 110	100%	Shot down by RAF fighters.	Over Sheerness.
24.08.40	Lt. Jürgen Meyer Fw. Henry Schneider	5./ZG 2 6./ZG 2	P Bf	K W	Bf 110 C-4	100%	Crashed into sea following combat mission. Bord-funker rescued by Seenotdienst.	Channel, 35 Kms. off Cherbourg.
24.08.40	 Gefr. Alfred Trautvetter	8./ZG 26 8./ZG 26	P Bf	U W	Bf 110	Not known	Damaged in combat with RAF fighters. Landed at Arques.	Thames estuary.
25.08.40	Fw. Karl Röhring Ogefr. Herbert Grosse	14.(Z)/ LG 1	P Bf	U W	Bf 110 C-2	100% 100%	Crash-landed at at Roquan-court following combat with RAF fighters.	Warmwell.
25.08.40	Uffz. Alois Pfaffelhuber Uffz. Otto Kramp	15.(Z)/ LG 1	P Bf	U U	Bf 110 C-1 L1+NL	Not known	Force-landed at Barfleur Starboard engine damaged in combat with RAF fighters.	Channel, off Weymouth.
25.08.40	Oblt. Joachim Glienke Uffz. Paul Stuck	13.(Z)/ LG 1	P Bf	M M	Bf 110 C-2	100%	Failed to return from combat mission.	Channel, off Weymouth.
25.08.40	Uffz. Horst Hamann Uffz. Wenzel Maresch	15.(Z)/ LG 1	P Bf	M M	Bf 110 C-4	100%	Failed to return from combat mission.	Channel, off Weymouth.

Date	Name of crew and rank	Unit	Status	Fate	Aircraft Code & W. Nr.	Damage state	Reason for casualty	Place
25.08.40		I./ZG 2	P Bf	U U	Bf 110 C-4	20%	Returned damaged from combat with RAF fighters.	Wareham.
25.08.40	Oblt. Gerard Götz (Staffelkapitän) Uffz. Kurt Haupt	1./ZG 2 1./ZG 2	P Bf	POW POW (Both wounded)	Bf 110 C-4 3M + KM	100%	Probably shot down by Sgt. Feary of 609 Sqdn. during escort mission for Ju 88s of KG 51. Abandoned by crew.	Creech Barrow, near Wareham.
25.08.40	Lt. Karl Westphal Uffz. Josef Brief	1./ZG 2 1./ZG 2	P Bf	K K	Bf 110 C-4 3M + CH 2123	100%	Shot down by S/Ldr. Darley and P/O Tobin of 609 Sqdn. during escort mission for Ju 88s of KG 51.	Winfrith. East Chaldon.
25.08.40	Uffz. Siegfried Becker Ogefr. Walter Wötzel	1./ZG 2 1./ZG 2	P Bf	POW POW (Both wounded)	Bf 110 C-4 3M + KH 3208	100%	Shot down by P/O Agazarian and P/O Gaunt of 609 Sqdn. during escort mission for Ju 88s of KG 51. Abandoned by crew.	Priory Farm, East Holme. Wareham.
25.08.40	Uffz. Karl Horner Uffz. Georg Kirsch	I./ZG 2 I./ZG 2	P Bf	M M	Bf 110 C-4	100%	Failed to return from combat mission.	Over Dorset..
25.08.40		II./ZG 2	P Bf	U U	Bf 110 C-4	25%	Returned damaged from combat with RAF fighters.	Channel.
25.08.40		II./ZG 2	P Bf	U U	Bf 110 C-4	100%	Severely damaged in combat with RAF fighters. Written off on return to base.	Channel.
25.08.40		II./ZG 2	P Bf	U U	Bf 110 D-0	20%	Returned damaged from combat with RAF fighters.	Channel.
25.08.40	Fw. Manfred Dähne Uffz. Fritz Müller	8./ZG 76 8./ZG 76	P Bf	K K	Bf 110 C-4 3532	100%	Shot down by RAF fighters.	Tatton House Farm, Buckland Ripers.
26.08.40		II./ZG 2	P Bf	U U	Bf 110	100%	Damaged in combat with RAF fighters. Force-landed at St. Pierre-Église.	Channel.
26.08.40	Ofw. Kurt Rösler Uffz. Herbert Heinrich	4./ZG 26 4./ZG 26	P Bf	K K	Bf 110 D-0 3U + CM	100%	Shot down by F/L Bruce and F/O Westmacott of 56 Sqdn..	Great Tey.
26.08.40	Fw. Werner Opper Uffz. Paul Nick	9./ZG 26 9./ZG 26	P Bf	K K	Bf 110 C-4 3U + AT	100%	Shot down by P/O Sutton of 56 Sqdn. and 111 Sqdn. Hurricanes.	Crabtree Farm, Great Bentley.
26.08.40	Uffz. Erhart Reinhold Ogefr. Kurt Däumig	9./ZG 26 9./ZG 26	P Bf	K M	Bf 110 C-4 3299	100%	Shot down by RAF fighters.	Thames estuary.

Date	Name of crew and rank	Unit	Status	Fate	Aircraft Code & W. Nr.	Damage state	Reason for casualty	Place
27.08.40		4.(F)/ Auf. Gr. 14	P Bf	U U	Bf 110 C-5	15%	Damaged on landing after running over a bomb.	Cherbourg.
27.08.40		V.(Z)/ LG 1	P Bf	U U	Bf 110 C-2	100%	Severely damaged in taxi-ing accident.	Roquancourt.
29.08.40	Lt. Alfred Thüring	Stab II. ZG 26	P Bf	W U	Bf 110 C-2 3U + CJ	25%	Damaged in combat with RAF fighters.	Over Hastings.
30.08.40	Hptm. Adolf Schuldt (Staffelkapitän) Uffz. Karl Dyroff	5./ZG 2 5./ZG 2	P Bf	K K	Bf 110 D-0 A2 + HK 3315	100%	Severely damaged by F/L Christie of 242 Sqdn.. Crashed and exploded attempting force-landing.	Durrants Road, Ponders End, Enfield.
30.08.40		3./ZG 26 3./ZG 26	P Bf	U U	Bf 110 C-4 U8 + AL 3583	100%	Damaged in combat with RAF fighters. Crash-landed at Cap Gris-Nez.	
30.08.40		I./ZG 26 I./ZG 26	P Bf	U U	Bf 110 C-4 U8 + CX§ 3582	100%	Returned damaged following combat with RAF fighters.	Channel.
30.08.40	Uffz. Franz Lechmann	6./ZG 26	Bf	W	Bf 110 C	Not known	Damaged in combat with RAF fighters.	North of Sudbury.
30.08.40	Uffz. Rudolf Franke Uffz. Willi Hübner	5./ZG 26 5./ZG 26	P Bf	POW POW	Bf 110 C-2 3U + KP* 3496	100%	Shot down by RAF fighters during escort sortie for KG 53.	Mill Hill Farm, Rettenden.
30.08.40	Hptm Heinz Wagner (Staffelkapitän) Stabsfw. Heinrich Schmidt	4./ZG 76 4./ZG 76	P Bf	K K	Bf 110 C M8 + BM 3257	100%	Shot down by P/O McKnight of 242 Sqdn.	Enfield Sewage Farm, Wharf Road, Ponders End, Enfield.
30.08.40	Ofw. Georg Anthony Uffz. Heinrich Nordmeyer	4./ZG 76 4./ZG 76	P Bf	K POW	Bf 110 C M8 + MM 3615	100%	Shot down by F/O Paszkiewicz of 303 Sqdn. and P/O Wicks of 56 Sqdn. Bordfunker baled out.	Barley Beans Farm, Kimpton.
30.08.40	Hptm. Heinz Nacke (Staffelkapitän)	6./ZG 76 6./ZG 76	P Bf	I I	Bf 110 C M8 + KM 3603	100%	Crash-landed at St. Ingelvert with severe damage following combat with RAF fighters.	
30.08.40		7./ZG 76 7./ZG 76	P Bf	U U	Bf 110 C-2 2N + LM 3235	30%	Damaged in combat with RAF fighters. Landed at Calais-Marck on one engine.	
31.08.40	Uffz. Ernst Glaeske Ogefr. Konrad Schweda	2./Erpr. Gr. 210	P Bf	POW K	Bf 110 D-0 S9 + GK 3381	100%	Shot down by RAF fighters following raid on Croydon.	Wrotham Hill, near Stanstead.

§ The fourth character 'X' is not consistent with the method of identifying I. Gruppe aircraft. The correct fourth character for I. Gruppe Stab aircraft would be 'B'; for the three individual Staffeln they would be 'H', 'K' and 'L'.

* 5th Staffel aircrew flying a 6th Staffel aircraft.

Date	Name of crew and rank	Unit	Status	Fate	Aircraft Code & W. Nr.	Damage state	Reason for casualty	Place
31.08.40		2./Erpr. Gr. 210	P Bf	U U	Bf 110 D-0 S9 + DK 3370	30%	Damaged in combat with RAF fighters.	
31.08.40	Uffz. Balthasar Aretz Gefr. Rolf Schilleng	2./Erpr. Gr. 210	P Bf	U U	Bf 110 D-0 S9 + EK 3568	25%	Damaged in combat with RAF fighters.	
31.08.40	Lt. Karl-Joachim Eichhorn Uffz. Richard Growe	14.(Z)/ LG 1	P Bf	POW K	Bf 110	100%	Shot down by RAF fighters.	Off Foreness.
31.08.40	Fw. Gottlob Fritz Ogefr. Karl Döpfer	14.(Z)/ LG 1	P Bf	POW POW	Bf 110 L1 + AK	100%	Ditched in the sea following attack by RAF fighters.	Near the Nore Light, Thames estuary.
31.08.40		3./ZG 2	P Bf	U U	Bf 110 C-2 3M + DL 3083	30%	Crashed on landing on non-combat flight.	Granville.
31.08.40		Stab ZG 26	P Bf	U U	Bf 110 C U8 + JH 3280	15%	Damaged in combat with RAF fighters. Belly-landed at Wizernes.	
31.08.40	Uffz, Georg Leinfelder Uffz. Heinz Lohoff	5./ZG 26	P Bf	U W	Bf 110	Not known	Damaged in combat with RAF fighters.	Over Chelmsford.
31.08.40		6./ZG 26		W	Bf 110	Not known	Damaged in combat with RAF fighters.	Over Chelmsford.
31.08.40	Oblt. Georg Christl (Gruppe Technical Offizier) Flgr. Martin Graf	Stab III. ZG 26 Stab III.	P Bf	U W	Bf 110 C-4 3U + CD 2167	38%	Damaged in combat with RAF fighters. Crash-landed at Arques.	Thames estuary.
31.08.40	Oblt. Erich von Bergen Uffz. Hans Becker	8./ZG 26 8./ZG 26	P Bf	POW POW	Bf 110 D 3U + HS 3396	100%	Shot down into the sea by RAF fighters.	Between Colne Point and East Mersea.
01.09.40		1.(F)/ Auf. Gr. 22	P Bf	U U	Bf 110 C-5 4N + CH 2206	40%	Crash-landed at following reconnaissance mission.	Ostend.
01.09.40	Ofw. Rudolf Kobert Fw. Werner Meinig	13.(Z)/ LG 1	P Bf	POW POW	Bf 110 L1 + OH	100%	Shot down by RAF fighters. in combat south of Croydon. Final attack by P/O English of 85 Sqdn.	Tarpot Farm, Bilsington, Ham Street.
01.09.40	Fw. Martin Jäckel Flgr. Heinz Rösler	15.(Z)/ LG 1	P Bf	K M	Bf 110	100%	Shot down by P/O Mayhew of 79 Sqdn. and F/O F/O Elsdon of 72 Sqdn. over Edenbridge.	Hosey Wood Brasted.
01.09.40	Lt. Ludolf Schmitz	3./NJG 1	P Bf	I U	Bf 110 C G9 + BL 3510	100%	Abandoned by crew due to fuel failure.	Over Lippborg.
02.09.40	Oblt. Kurt Müller (Staffelführer) Uffz. Johannes Korn	2./ZG 2 2./ZG 2	P Bf	U U	Bf 110 D-0 3M + NK 3193	25%	Force-landed on one engine following combat with RAF fighters over south London.	Berck-sur-Mer.

Date	Name of crew and rank	Unit	Status	Fate	Aircraft Code & W. Nr.	Damage state	Reason for casualty	Place
02.09.40	Lt. Georg Schipper Gefr. Theo Schockenhoff	2./ZG 2 2./ZG 2	P Bf	POW POW	Bf 110 C-4 3M + HK 3622	100%	Shot down by Spitfires of 72 Sqdn.	Hougham, near Dover.
02.09.40	Fw. Lorenz Beil Ogefr. Hans Oehl	6./ZG 2 6./ZG 2	P Bf	K K	Bf 110 D-0 A2 + KL 3629	100%	Exploded under attack by F/L Steere of 72 Sqdn..	Vensons Farm, Eastry, near Sandwich.
02.09.40	Uffz. Hermann Deuker Uffz. Ewald Knapp	4./ZG 2 4./ZG 2	P Bf	M M	Bf 110 D-0 A2 + CH 3197	100%	Did not return from combat combat mission.	South of the Thames estuary.
02.09.40	Fw. Karl Schütz Uffz. Herbert Stüwe	2./ZG 26 2./ZG 26	P Bf	K POW	Bf 110 D-1 U8 + DK 3309	100%	Shot down by Sgt. Rolls of 72 Sqdn..	White Horse Wood, Birling, near Maidstone.
02.09.40	Ofw. Kurt Rochel Uffz. Willy Schöffler	5./ZG 26 5./ZG 26	P Bf	POW POW	Bf 110 C-4 3U + GN 3536	100%	Severely damaged by RAF fighters. Ditched in sea.	Off the Nore, Thames estuary.
02.09.40	Fw. Hans Müller Uffz. Gerhard Gröhl	5./ZG 26 5./ZG 26	P Bf	W W	Bf 110 C-4 3U + BN 3045	100%	Damaged in combat with RAF fighters over Thames estuary. Crash-landed due to engine failure.	Wizernes.
02.09.40	Uffz. Otto Brautigam	6./ZG 26 6./ZG 26	P Bf	U W	Bf 110 Bf 110	Not known	Damaged in combat with RAF fighters. Returned to base.	South of London.
02.09.40	Uffz. Walter Duning	6./ZG 26 6./ZG 26	P Bf	U W	Bf 110	Not known	Damaged in combat with RAF fighters. Returned to base.	South-east of London.
02.09.40	Fw. Hermann Dibowski Ogefr. Karl-Heinz Boock	7./ZG 26 7./ZG 26	P Bf	W U	Bf 110 C-4 3U + BR 2191	45%	Crash-landed following combat with RAF fighters.	Arques.
02.09.40	Oblt. Karl Wrede (Gruppe Technical Offizier) Uffz. Richard Kukawka	Stab II. ZG 76 Stab II.	P Bf	K K	Bf 110 C M8 + DM 3226	100%	Shot down by F/L Parnall of 249 Sqdn..	Frith Farm, Laindon Road, Billericay.
02.09.40		7./ZG 76 7./ZG 76	P Bf	U U	Bf 110 C-4 2N + GM 2095	50%	Returned damaged following combat with RAF fighters. Force-landed.	Near Calais.
03.09.40	Oblt. Reinhold Messner (Gruppe Technical Offizier) Uffz. Alois Santoni	Stab I. ZG 2 Stab I.	P Bf	POW POW	Bf 110 C-4 3M + CB 3120	100%	Shot down by RAF fighters during escort sortie for Do 17s. Abandoned by crew.	Edwins Hall, Stowmaries.
03.09.40	Oblt. Siegfried Gottschalt (Staffelführer) Uffz. Max Hoffmann	2./ZG 2 2./ZG 2	P Bf	POW POW	Bf 110 C-4 3M + BK 2146	100%	Shot down in combat with RAF fighters. Crew baled out.	1½ miles off Reculver.
03.09.40	Fw. Kurt Wagenbreth Uffz. Aribert Schubarth	2./ZG 2 2./ZG 2	P Bf	K K	Bf 110 C-4 3M + EK 2065	100%	Collided with Bf 110 of Oblt. Müller during escort mission. Abandoned by crew.	Feltimores, Hobbs Cross, Harlow.

Date	Name of crew and rank	Unit	Status	Fate	Aircraft Code & W. Nr.	Damage state	Reason for casualty	Place
03.09.40	Oblt. Kurt Müller (Staffelführer)	2./ZG 2	P	POW	Bf 110 C-4 3M+HL* 2133	100%	Collided with Bf 110 of Fw. Waggenbreth during escort mission.	Rye Hill, near Epping.
	Uffz. Johannes Korn	2./ZG 2	P	K				
03.09.40	Ofw. Gerhard Winkler	3.ZG 2	P	POW	Bf 110 C-4 3M+EL 3113	100%	Shot down by 17 Sqdn. Hurricanes. Crew baled out.	Pudsey Hall Farm, Canewdon, near Rayleigh.
	Gefr. Oskar Weiler	3./ZG 2	Bf	POW				
03.09.40		3./ZG 26	P	U	Bf 110 C-4 U8+KL 3294	100%	Crash-landed after damage in combat with RAF fighters. Bordfunker baled out into the Channel and killed.	Fontend.
	Uffz. Horst Klatt	3./ZG 26	B	K				
03.09.40	Lt. Walther Manhart	6./ZG 26	P	POW	Bf 110 D 3U+EP 3310	100%	Severely damaged by Sub-Lt. Carpenter of 46 Sqdn.. Force-landed.	Mundon, south of Maldon.
	Uffz. Werner Drews	6./ZG 26	Bf	POW				
03.09.40	Uffz. Rudolf Löhr	6./ZG 26	Bf	W	Bf 110	Not	Damaged in combat with RAF fighters.	Thames estuary.
03.09.40	Fw. Hans Grau (wounded)	7.ZG 26	P	POW	Bf 110 C-2 3U+KR 3225	100%	Shot down by F/O van Mentz of 222 Sqdn. and 54 Sqdn. Spitfires.	North Shoebury House, near Southend.
	Uffz. Günther Uecker (died 4/9/40)	7./ZG 26	Bf	POW				
03.09.40		9./ZG 26	P U		Bf 110 C-2 3U+GT 3578	100%	Crashed on landing following combat with RAF fighters over the Thames estuary.	Wissant.
04.09.40	Oblt. Ellerlage	3.(F)/ Auf. Gr. 10	P	K	Bf 110 C T1+TL 2175	100%	Flew into ground on domestic flight. Cause unknown.	
04.09.40	Hptm. Hans von Boltenstern (Gruppenkommandeur)	Stab Erpr. Gr. 210	P	K	Bf 110 D-0 S9+AB 3390	100%	Crashed into the Channel on combat mission; no RAF fighters involved.	Off Littlehampton.
	Fw. Fritz Schneider		Bf	K				
04.09.40	Oblt. Michel Junge (Staffelkapitän)	14.(Z)/	P	K	Bf 110 D L1+FK 3306	100%	Shot down by 253 Sqdn. Hurricanes.	Upper Common, Netley, near Dorking.
	Uffz. Karl Bremser	LG 1	Bf	K				
04.09.40	Lt. Hans-Heinz Braukmeier	14.(Z)/	P	M	Bf 110 C-2 L1+CK 3541	100%	Did not return from combat mission.	
	Ogefr. Josef Krischewski	LG 1	Bf	K				
04.09.40	Fw. Karl Röhring	14.(Z)/	P	K	Bf 110 D L1+BK 3303	100%	Shot down by 253 Sqdn. Hurricanes.	Waterloo Farm, West Horsley.
	Uffz. Joachim Jäckel (wounded)	LG 1	Bf	POW				
04.09.40	Uffz. Wilhelm Neumann	15.(Z)/	P	K	Bf 110 C-4 L1+FL 2212	100%	Did not return from combat mission.	South of Brooklands.
	Uffz. Walter Speier	LG 1	Bf	M				
04.09.40	Uffz. Alois Pfaffelhuber	15.(Z)/	P	U	Bf 110	Not known	Damaged in combat with RAF fighters. Returned to Caen.	South coast of England.
	Uffz. Wilhelm Banser	LG 1	Bf	W				

* 2nd Staffel crew flying a 3rd Staffel aircraft.

Date	Name of crew and rank	Unit	Status	Fate	Aircraft Code & W. Nr.	Damage state	Reason for casualty	Place
04.09.40	Fw. Walter Pentner Gefr. Johann Crepu-Lafferiere	7./NJG 1 7./NJG 1	P Bf	K K	Bf 110 C-7 1419	100%	Crashed during training flight. flight. Cause unknown.	Erding, near Munich.
04.09.40	Oblt. Wilhelm Schäfer (Geschwaderadjutant) Uffz. Heinz Bendjus	Stab ZG 2 Stab	P Bf	POW POW	Bf 110 C-4 3M + AA 2116	100%	Damaged in combat with F/L Dalton-Morgan of 43 Sqdn.; P/O Gilbert of 601 Sqdn. and P/O Moody of 602 Sqdn. Force-landed.	Mill Hill, Shoreham Downs.
04.09.40	Oblt. Hermann Weeber (Gruppenadjutant) Uffz. Max Michael	Stab II. ZG 76 Stab II.	P Bf	POW POW	Bf 110 C M8 + AC 3602	100%	Damage in combat with 1 (RCAF) fighters. Shot down by F/O Nesbitt.	Little Butts Farm, Cousley Wood, near Wadhurst.
04.09.40	Oblt. Ernst-Hartmann Fr. von Schlotheim Uffz. Georg Hommel	5./ZG 76 5./ZG 76	P Bf	POW POW	Bf 110 C M8 + JN 3287	100%	Damaged by RAF fighters Crashed into the Channel.	7 miles of Pevensey Bay.
04.09.40	Uffz. Paul Neumann	5./ZG 76	Bf	W	Bf 110 C M8 + KN 3229	40%	Force-landed following combat with RAF fighters west of Tonbridge.	Boulogne.
04.09.40	Oblt. Günther Piduhn Gefr. Rudolf Condné	6./ZG 76 6./ZG 76	P Bf	K K	Bf 110 C M8 + CP 2089	100%	Exploded under attack by F/O Smither of 1 (RCAF) Sqdn..	Smarts Hill Penshurst.
04.09.40	Oblt. Helmut Florenz (Gruppe Nachrichtensoffizier and Staffelführer) Gefr. Rudi Hebert	Stab III. ZG 76	P Bf	M M	Bf 110 C-1 2N + DP 2837	100%	Shot down by F/L Dalton-Morgan of 43 Sqdn. Crashed and exploded.	Church Farm, Washington, Pulborough.
04.09.40	Oblt. Walter Schiller (Staffelführer) Fw. Helmut Winkler	7./ZG 76 7./ZG 76	P Bf	POW POW	Bf 110 C-4 2N + BM 3254	100%	Shot down by P/O Upton of 43 Sqdn.. Abandoned by crew.	High Salvington near Findon, Worthing.
04.09.40	Uffz. Wilhelm Schultis Uffz. Richard Bileck (wounded)	7./ZG 76 7./ZG 76	P Bf	POW POW	Bf 110 C-4 2N + HM 3563	100%	Severely damaged in combat with 234 Sqdn. Spitfires. Force-landed.	Portway, Staining.
04.09.40	Ofw. Konrad Daum Uffz. Ferdinand Mayer	7./ZG 76 8./ZG 76	P Bf	K K	Bf 110 C-4 2N + AC 3545	100%	Shot down by RAF fighters.	Channel.
04.09.40	Oblt. Hans Münich Uffz. Adolf Käser	8./ZG 76 7./ZG 76	P Bf	POW POW	Bf 110 C-4 2N + CN 3101	100%	Engine damaged in combat with 234 Sqdn. Spitfires.	Black Patch, near Angmering.
04.09.40	Oblt. Kurt Raetsch Ogefr. Werner Hempel	9./ZG 76 9./ZG 76	P Bf	K K	Bf 110 C-4 2N + KP 2104	100%	Shot down by 234 Sqdn. Spitfires.	Coatwood Farm, Wisborough Green.
06.09.40	Uffz. Gerhard Rüger Uffz. Edmund Ernst	1./Erpr. Gr. 210	P Bf	K POW	Bf 110 D-0 S9 + BH 3373	100%	Shot down by P/O Dibnah of 1 Sqdn.,	Flow Meadow, Foyle Farm, Crowhurst.
06.09.40	Oblt. Friedrich Viertel (Geschwader Technical Offizier) Uffz. Rudolf Roth	Stab ZG 26 Stab	P Bf	POW K	Bf 110 C-4 3U + CA 2145	100%	Engine caught fire due to electrical fault. Abandoned by cew.	Channel, off Dover.

Date	Name of crew and rank	Unit	Status	Fate	Aircraft Code & W. Nr.	Damage state	Reason for casualty	Place
06.09.40	Uffz. Christoph Kiehn	3./ZG 26	P	K	Bf 110 C-4	100%	Shot down by RAF fighters over Kenley. Possibly 111 Sqdn. Hurricanes.	Cannons Hill golf course, near Coulsdon.
	Uffz. Egon Neusz	3./ZG 26	Bf	POW	U8 + CL 2146			
06.09.40	Fw. Leonhard Kaufmann	7./ZG 26	P	K	Bf 110 D-0	100%	Shot down by S/L Hull of 43 Sqdn.	Channel, 4 miles off Bexhill.
	Gefr. Gerhard Schumann	7./ZG 26	Bf	K	3U + HR 3405			

Bf 110 D-0, 3U + HR, W. Nr. 3405, of 7./ZG 26. Fw. Kaufmann, pilot, and Gefr. Schumann were shot down and killed in this aircraft on 6/9/40 over the Channel. Note the light mottle camouflage on the fuselage sides, and the lack of a surround to the individual aircraft letter 'H'.

2N + AN of 8./ZG 76 in its blast pen with engine and gun covers in place.

Two Bf 110 Cs of 3./ZG 26. This photograph shows clearly the simultaneous use of the early style two-tone green upper surface camouflage extending fully down the fuselage sides, on U8+CL, and the later mottled style on U8+FL. U8+CL was shot down on 6/9/40 and crashed at Cannons Hill golf course, near Coulsdon. The pilot, Uffz. Gustav Kiehn, was killed, Bordfunker Uffz. Egon Neusz was wounded, but baled out safely.

CHAPTER 6

SEPTEMBER NEMESIS

Some early sparring took place during the morning of 7th September which resulted in the loss of a reconnaissance Bf 110, two more returning to the continent damaged by fighters. But it was late afternoon before any serious threat materialised, and when it did it was clearly a major effort. Tracked by radar as formation after formation joined up over the French coast, it was the largest Luftwaffe attack yet seen with almost 1,000 aircraft, some 350 bombers with an escort of over 600 Bf 109s and Bf 110s, crossing the Kent coast in two waves, all bound for central London.

Proving yet again the worth of the Zerstörer as a fighting aircraft in its own right, I. Fliegerkorps' operational orders for the attacks were explicit: "Fighter escort will be provided by Jafü 2 in the proportion of one fighter Geschwader for each bomber Geschwader. Fighter escort: JG 26 for KG 30, JG 54 for KG 1, JG 27 for KG 76. In view of the fact that the fighters will be operating at the limit of their endurance, it is essential that direct courses be flown and the attack com

pleted in minimum time. ZG 76 (for this operation under I. Fliegerkorps command) will as from 18:40 (CET) clear the air of enemy fighters over I. Fliegerkorps targets, thereby covering attack and retreat of bomber formations." So, for this attack, I. Fliegerkorps Bf 109s were tied to the bombers while the Zerstörers enjoyed free-range. But not every Bf 110 unit had such freedom, for the Zerstörers of ZG 2 were again detailed as close escort for the Heinkel He 111s of KG 53 in an attack on the oil storage tanks at Thameshaven, III./ZG 26 providing additional fighter protection.

Elements of 16 RAF squadrons rose to meet the attack, the first fighters to engage throwing themselves against the flanks of the towering German formation as it moved towards London. More and more British fighters were flung into the path of the attack in an effort to turn it aside, the massive formation inexorably gaining the southern outskirts of the capital, where the Zerstörers of ZG 76 formed an immense Abwehrkreis over Croydon.

Excellent in-flight view of Zerstörer, 3U + LR of 7./ZG 26. Note that the individual aircraft letter 'L' has no outline, and the starboard engine has a white 'N' stencilled on it, indicating that the aircraft has been fitted with the uprated DB 601 N engines.

Here, they were subjected to ineffectual attacks by 9 Hurricanes of No.111 Squadron defending their home base. But things livened up considerably for the Zerstörers when Douglas Bader's Duxford Wing, Nos. 19, 242 and 310 Squadrons, joined the melee and clashed with ZG 2 to the east of London.

Squadron Leader Brian Lane was leading the Spitfires of No. 19 Squadron, "High above the squadron was the top layer of the fighter escort, Me 110s and 109s. I began to climb up in an endeavour to get at them. As I did so a 110 came screaming down just in front of me, a Hurricane on its tail. As the aircraft passed the Hurricane broke away. Breaking up the squadron into sections I opened the throttle and tore after the Hun with my section. As we closed in behind him, four Hurricanes descended on him as well! Seven to one - most unfair! It didn't take very long, although the German pilot fought us off magnificently, before he and his gunner baled out and their aircraft crashed in flames into a field."

This Zerstörer fell at Park Corner Farm, near Hornchurch, the crew leaving it too late before baling out. The pilot, 22 year-old Berliner Leutnant Kurt Schünemann, Gruppe Technical Offizier of II./ZG 2, baled out too low for his parachute to fully deploy and was killed. His Bordfunker, Unteroffizier Hans Mescheder, was even less fortunate, for his parachute failed completely and he plunged to his death among some cottages at Cranham.

As well as Squadron Leader Lane, they would feature in at least two other British pilots' Combat Reports that evening; Flying Officer Holderness of No. 1 Squadron and Pilot Officer Janough of No. 310 Squadron both laid claim to the destruction of the Zerstörer of Leutnant Schünemann.

Lessmann's II./ZG 2 were to lose three more aircraft in this action, two 4th Staffel machines falling to the Hurricanes of No. 242 Squadron and both crashing within a few miles of Schünemann; Leutnant Karl Stix, the only survivor from all three crews, smashed his leg on landing.

He was taken to Billericay Hospital where some British casualties of the battle were also being treated. Pilot Officer Hunt of No. 257 Squadron, shot down on 3rd September, was one, and his wife recalls, "There was a big air battle on the fourth day. I stood with the nurses at the corridor windows and watched. We were all excited. After a time there was a little crowd in the corridor, looking down at the floor. There was a young German pilot in his pretty blue uniform lying on a stretcher. They put him in the next room to David. Next day we made up a dish of fruit, and I took it in to him. We had a barren conversation in English about his state of health. We grinned at each other over our cramped conversation, and that was that.

"He spent his nights ringing the bell and demanding morphia, when the planes overhead kept him awake. He was taken away in a hurry, and did not pay his visits to the three RAF pilots who were in at the time. He had asked very tentatively if they might let him call on them, and they had all agreed as a matter of course. Certainly none of the RAF pilots bore him malice."

The fourth aircraft lost by II./ZG 2 was a 6th Staffel machine. With both engines crippled and the Bordfunker killed in attacks by Sergeant Furst of No. 310 Squadron, it struggled back as far as Birchington before ditching. The pilot, Oberleutnant Willi Brede, who had been Staffelführer since Heinlein's promotion in mid-August, was picked up by the Margate lifeboat slightly injured.

Flying as Rottenflieger to Hauptmann Heinlein in the Stabsschwarm, Oberleutnant Gerhard Granz, Gruppenadjutant of I./ZG 2, broke formation to flush a Spitfire from one of the Heinkels. With so many British fighters in the vicinity it was a highly risky move and he promptly came under attack from two Hurricanes.

The first was flown by Flying Officer Hardacre of No. 504 Squadron who set the starboard engine of the Bf 110 alight as the second Hurricane closed in and opened fire. This was Pilot Officer Beazley of No. 249 Squadron, presumably keen to even the score after his

tussle with Kurt Rochel five days before.

Now at a serious disadvantage, Granz sought cover in the thick clouds of smoke from the blazing oil tanks at Thameshaven, but the Hurricanes were onto him again before he could reach them. A head-on attack by Sub-Lieutenant Cork of No. 242 Squadron then set both engines on fire, and with bullets scything through the canopy and seemingly passing by both sides of his head, Granz gave the order to his Bordfunker, Feldwebel Willi Schubel, to bale out.

Granz jettisoned the hood, released his straps and yanked the stick back into his belly. At the top of the loop, he dropped out of the seat but his parachute pack caught on the cockpit frame behind him, holding him in. Completing the loop, Granz crashed back into his seat and at less than 500 feet he rolled the aircraft onto its back, fell free and immediately pulled his parachute release.

Even as he left the aircraft it came under final attack from Squadron Leader Beytagh of No. 73 Squadron during which the tail assembly broke away just before it crashed and exploded at Noak Hill, Billericay.

Granz landed, minus boots, in a small garden completely enclosed by hedges. After the frenzy of the last few minutes, it seemed remarkably quiet, apart from the sounds of distant engines and gunfire. Two apprehensive Home Guards eventually appeared beyond the hedge. Not regular troops, Granz noticed. "Good afternoon", he greeted them warmly. "Ah, you're British-

Oblt. Gerhard Granz, Gruppenadjutant of I./ZG 2, left, and his Bordfunker, Fw. Schutel, have fun with a rubber duck in front of their Bf 110 C-4, 3M+BB, W. Nr. 3246. They were shot down in this aircraft on 7/9/40, both surviving into captivity.

Johannes Schalk, above, succeeded Major Huth as Geschwaderkommodore of ZG 26 for the later stages of the Battle of Britain.

they smiled, coming towards him noticeably relieved. "Hell no!", Granz retorted, which stopped them in their tracks and wiped the smiles from their faces. Playtime over, he was bundled into a cell at Billericay Police Station en-route to Cockfosters, where RAF Intelligence gave him plenty to think about with their knowledge of him and his unit - 'most unsettling'.

As the Zerstörers retired back across Kent, 3./ZG 2 were pursued by the Hurricanes of No. 73 Squadron, who caught up with them over Canterbury. Oberfeldwebel Ernst Otterbach's aircraft literally broke up under attack by Sergeant Garton, wreckage littering a housing estate at Eyethorne, near Deal. Although Otterbach and the unfortunate Hauptfeldwebel Fritz Oligschläger, who had come along for the ride, and was acting as Bordfunker on this sortie, both took to their parachutes, neither of them survived.

Unteroffizier Reinhold Dahnke had better luck and baled out safely, surviving attacks by Squadron Leader Robinson and Pilot Officer Langham-Hobart, but his pilot, Leutnant Dietrich Kislinger, died in the aircraft which crashed and burned out at Hoath, near Herne Bay. Theirs was one of 41 Luftwaffe losses on this day, 8 of them Bf 110s which, given the scale of the attack, were relatively modest casualties. But these Bf 110s were all from a Geschwader already seriously depleted by losses, ZG 2, and whose 4th Staffel bore

the brunt. The cumulative effect of such losses in men and materials, when added to those suffered on previous days and sustained over preceding weeks, was fast becoming a serious issue at Staffel level.

In certain Zerstörer units, the ability to gather together sufficient serviceable aircraft and even scratch crews for the next round of sorties had, of late, been proving a distinct headache. But as the last tracks of German aircraft were removed from the plotting room tables, and the Spitfires and Hurricanes landed back at base, fires raged in London and at Thameshaven. It had been the largest daylight raid yet mounted against England and the first attack on London, and after the constant strain of daily combat over previous weeks, it had proved an unnerving experience for many an exhausted British pilot. Expressing the secret thoughts of many, Pilot Officer George Barclay of No. 249 Squadron, confided to his diary, "The odds today have been unbelievable (and we are all really very shaken!)."

Yet, somehow, they came through it and despite their losses on the day, 16 pilots and 25 fighters, RAF Fighter Command had proved that it was still far from being a spent force. British fighter pilots would now, at last, gain some respite as the German attack switched from their airfields to the night bombing of the capital.

7th September witnessed the swansong of Vollbracht's ZG 2, whose survivors were all too soon absorbed into the growing Nachtjagd. Within three weeks, Oberstleutnant Vollbracht himself was gone, to take over as day-fighter leader in Denmark, and Commander of the Zerstörer Ergänzungsgruppe at Vaerlöse, near Copenhagen. His award of the Ritterkreuz was announced on 13th October.

The remaining Zerstörer units would fight on over southern England, taking the battle to the RAF but, as the loss tables show, apart from a few significant attacks, it was never on the same scale as before. So, in early September, as the daylight battle dragged on, the Bf 110 units stood as follows:

I./ZG 26	Hptm. Makrocki	Abbeville, St. Omer
II./ZG 26	Hptm. von Rettberg	Crecy-en-Ponthieu
III./ZG 26	Major Kaschka	Barley, Arques
II./ZG 76	Hptm. Groth	Le Mans, Abbeville
III./ZG 76	Hptm. Kaldrack	Laval
V.(Z)/LG 1	Hptm. Liensberger	Ligescourt, Alençon
Erpr. Gr. 210	Hptm. Lutz	Denain

Fatigue and bad weather reduced the level of activity over the next few days, during which Göring decided to extend attacks on London by day and by night. It was a serious tactical blunder. Had the Luftwaffe, with air superiority over southern England already effectively in its grasp, maintained attacks on RAF Fighter Command's sector airfields for a few more days, the outcome of the battle may well have been different.

In the early evening of 9th September, another large raid on the capital by Junkers Ju 88s of KG 30 and Heinkel He 111s of KG 53 was repulsed by RAF fighters. Zerstörer escorts of V.(Z)/LG 1 and III./ZG 76 lost four aircraft between them, another Bf 110 crash-landing at Quoeux.

A report from the OKL on this date confirmed, "The

maintaining of the attack against London is intended to take place by day through Luftflotte 2 with strong fighter *and destroyer units*; by night Luftflotte 3 will carry out attacks with the object of destroying harbour areas, the supply and power sources of the city." Clearly, the Luftwaffe High Command still considered the Zerstörer capable of the role for which it was originally intended.

During this period of unsettled weather, as Hitler wrestled with the decision on a final date for the invasion of England, day attacks on London were renewed in earnest. A heavy attack on 11th September was a mere prelude to the planned major assault on the city, which was to herald the launch of the invasion and lead to the final, irrevocable defeat of England.

By mid-afternoon that day, the weather had improved sufficiently for the attack on London to proceed, with simultaneous raids on Portsmouth, and the first major attack on the Spitfire works at Southampton by Erprobungsgruppe 210. Heinkel He 111s of KG 1 and KG 26 aimed for London docks with a strong fighter escort including Bf 110s, mainly from 'Horst Wessel' ZG 26, although elements of other Zerstörer units, including V.(Z)/LG 1, and II. and III./ZG 76, were also involved.

Twenty Bf 110s of I./ZG 2 supported the Portsmouth attack and clashed with No. 213 Squadron's Hurricanes over Selsey Bill. Vollbracht's unit lost its last Zerstörer in the campaign against England, another Bf 110 returning with serious damage. Two Hurricanes also failed to return to base, one of the pilots being killed.

At Clairmarais, Feldwebel Hermann Brinkmann of 2./ZG 26, briefed for the escort sortie for KG 26, couldn't coax his aircraft to start and asked the chief mechanic if there was a spare. Amazingly there was, but he had to understand that it was a bit of a 'hack' and only made airworthy with spares cannibalised from other damaged machines. Keen to fly, Brinkmann took it, but at 13,000 feet, just short of the target area, he started having second thoughts when one engine abruptly ground to a halt.

Brinkmann dropped out of formation and moved towards the slower bombers hoping to gain some protection from their guns. But he was spotted and almost immediately attacked by British fighters, during which the good engine was hit. He dived away, heading for the coast, hoping to reach the Channel where they could ditch. This, at least, would give them an even chance of being picked-up by their own side.

But it soon became obvious that the coast was too far away, so Brinkmann lost more height and prepared for a belly-landing. But as they neared the ground, they were attacked by another British fighter, which shattered the canopy, destroyed the radio and wounded Brinkmann's Bordfunker, Unteroffizier Krüsphow, in the thigh.

Skimming over a lorry strategically parked in the middle of the very field he had picked out for their landing, Brinkmann barely cleared a small wood and

Fw. Hermann Brinkmann of 2./ZG 26, who was shot down into captivity on 11/9/40.

dropped the aircraft into a field at Cobham Farm, Charing. Jerking to a halt after a short run, they clambered from the aircraft watched by a soldier and a farm labourer, who was armed with the statutory pitchfork. They walked across to the soldier, who threw them a very impressive salute, and accepted their surrender with as much enthusiasm as he later accepted their flying badges, which they quickly bartered for cigarettes - after all, it was going to be a long captivity.

Meantime, the Zerstörers formed an Abwehrkreis over the Isle of Sheppey, where they attracted some of the 20 British squadrons opposing this raid.

II./ZG 26 were the hardest hit, losing three aircraft and crews in the sea off Margate. Squadron Leader Brian Lane of No. 19 Squadron describes the final moments of one, "Two Me 110s swam into view and joined up one on each side of the bombers, one of them...dropping back behind the Heinkels. I closed in and fired at him from dead astern. I hit him with the first burst, a shower of pieces flying off from his starboard engine as the aircrew stopped. He made no attempt to avoid my fire, he just flew straight on. Puzzled, I broke away as I overshot him and turned to come back in again. Taking a sight on the port engine,

Uffz. Josef Radlmair, Bordfunker with Stab, II./ZG 26, killed in action on 11/9/40.

Uffz. Hermann Klaiber of 4./ZG 26, killed in action on 11/9/40.

I opened fire again. At the second burst a huge cloud of smoke and flame belched out and the aircraft slowly went down in a dive. Breaking away, I glanced down but he was lost from view."

Another, flown by Oberleutnant Walter Henken, Gruppenadjutant of II./ZG 26, with his Bordfunker, Feldwebel Josef Radlmair, also dropped into the sea off Margate brought down by the Hurricanes of Flight Lieutenant Bayne and Flying Officer Count Czernin of No. 17 Squadron.

In all, 5 'Horst Wessel' Zerstörers failed to return from this sortie, Wilhelm Speiss of 1st Staffel limping back to Calais-Marck with heavy damage and his Bordfunker, Unteroffizier Josef Haschke, slumped in the cockpit behind him, dead.

Leutnant Joachim Koepsell also returned with hits in his aircraft, but was well-satisfied, having flushed a Spitfire from Schön's tail - one of two claims he was to file following this sortie. Meantime, pilots in the other Gruppen had also scored, Oberleutnant Otto Weckeiser of 15.(Z)/LG 1 among them. Herget of 6./ZG 76 claimed a Spitfire south-east of London, and Jabs an-

other, while Leutnant Botho Sommer, Gruppenadjutant of III./ZG 26, gained his 7th victory with a Spitfire south of Hastings.

Further west, Erprobungsgruppe 210's attack on the Spitfire works at Woolston, Southampton did not go quite as planned. True, they demolished a factory, but it was the Cunliffe-Owen factory, not the Supermarine works. All of their aircraft returned to Cherbourg-Ost. They would have to return more than once in an attempt to finish the job.

RAF Fighter Command lost 25 aircraft in action during the afternoon attacks, 11 of the pilots being killed. 12 more of their fighters were damaged and 11 pilots wounded. Another heavy attack on London had been countered, but with total aircraft losses for the day the same on both sides of the Channel, the battle was hanging by a thread.

The Zerstörer units suffered no further losses until 15th September, when they flew in support of the next phase of massed attacks on London.

Following sporadic raids throughout the previous night, Bf 109 Jabos of II./LG 2 hit the city just before noon, and were followed by 25 Dornier Do 17s of I. and III./KG 76, heavily escorted by fighters, including Bf 109s of I./JG 27, I./JG 52 and I./JG 53. The bombers were aiming for rail targets around Battersea and crossed the English coast at Dungeness, heading directly for London, where they were met by 22 RAF fighter squadrons, many of them now operating in pairs.

Zerstörers were not involved until mid-afternoon when, preceded by a fighter sweep over Kent by Bf 109s of III./JG 51, they escorted another heavy raid by over 100 bombers from II. and III./KG 2, II./KG 3., I. and II./KG 26 and I. and II./KG 53 headed for the Lon-

Feldmarschall Albert Kesselring with aircrew of V.(Z)/LG 1 following the award of the Iron Cross, Second Class. From left: Kesselring; Lt. Hugo Adametz, 14th Staffel, killed in action 15/9/40; Uffz. Köpge, Gruppenstab, killed in action 27/9/40; Uffz. Brüggow, 15th Staffel, POW 15/9/40 and Uffz. Seufert, 13th Staffel.

don docklands. Hampered by clouds, they diverted to bomb alternative targets.

The bombers were heavily escorted by Bf 109s from I./JG 3, I./JG 77 and I./LG 2, as well as Zerstörers of V.(Z)/LG 1 and the 'Horst Wessel' Geschwader: I./ZG 26 flying close support for the Heinkel He 111s of KG 26. This raid was bitterly contested all the way inland across Kent and Surrey by fighters from 31 RAF squadrons who sortied to oppose it.

Liensberger's V.(Z)/LG 1 was the only Zerstörer unit to suffer any casualties, not only on this sortie, but throughout the whole day, their 13th Staffel losing two Bf 110s, One, the Staffelkapitän, Oberleutnant Helmut Müller, was shot down by Sergeant O'Manney of No. 229 Squadron. The Zerstörer dived into the ground at Hothfield, its 27 year-old pilot killed but his Bordfunker, Feldwebel Andreas Hoffmann, surviving the crash only to die of his injuries later that day. The Bf 110 of Leutnant Ernst Gorisch, from Allenstein, also failed to return.

The Gruppe lost a third aircraft and crew, from 14th Staffel, currently being led by the Gruppenadjutant, Oberleutnant Ernst Zobel. This Bf 110 was piloted by the young Austrian, 19 year-old Leutnant Hugo Ademetz, who was reported missing along with his Bordfunker, Obergefreiter Rudi Stief.

As British fighters were re-arming and re-fuelling, and in an effort to confuse and split the defences, the attack switched to the west. 26 Heinkel He 111s of I. and III./KG 55 attacked the Royal Naval dockyards at Portland and, shortly afterwards, 10 Bf 110s and 3 Bf 109s of Erprobungsgruppe 210 headed for the Supermarine Works at Woolston, Hampered by AA fire they failed once again to hit their target.

Within an hour of landing back at Clairmarais, I./ZG 26 were off on their second sortie of the day, acting as escort for the Heinkels of KG 53. They were joined by II./ZG 26 from St. Omer, but the formation was recalled, and returned without incident.

By the end of the day on 15th September it was clear that, failing in its expectations, the Luftwaffe had suffered their highest losses since 18th August, with 56 aircraft lost and 23 more damaged in action. While significantly less than the '185 destroyed' reported by the British press it was, nonetheless, a miserable result which provoked angry recriminations from Göring against the German fighter units.

Zerstörers had played relatively little part in the day's action, only about half of the 90 serviceable Bf 110s in Luftflotte 2 actually flying sorties. This was reflected in their losses.

RAF Fighter Command had lost 29 aircraft, 12 of

Bf 110 C, 3U + AR of 7./ZG 26. This aircraft was shot down on 26/9/40 with the crew of Lt. Kuno-Adalbert Konopka, pilot, and Uffz. Rudolf Elberg, Bordfunker, on board. Both were killed.

Aircrew of 7./ZG 26. From left: Uffz. Heinz Golisch; Ofw. Franz Santel and Uffz. Karl-Heinz Boock.

Oblt. Ernst Matthes, Staffelkapitän of 7./ZG 26. The Staffel emblem of a penguin carrying an umbrella can be clearly seen.

Officers of 7./ZG 26. From left: Oblt. Matthes; Lt. Konopka; Lt. Seehausen and unknown behind Seehausen.

their pilots being killed, and a further 27 fighters had been damaged in combat, with 14 pilots wounded. It had been a significant day, and saw the turning point in the battle, which was a fact not recognised by either side at the time.

Over the following weeks, with the scale of Luftwaffe operations significantly reduced, Zerstörer activity was correspondingly less. The need for daily close escort sorties for massive daylight bomber attacks, fighting their way in to and back from the target, was past. Those Bf 110 units still based on the Channel coast took the opportunity to make good their losses and reorganise. But the campaign against Britain still carried on and there were to be exceptional days.

On the morning of 25th September, Oberleutnant Ernst Matthes, Staffelkapitän of 7./ZG 26, was chatting with his crews alongside their aircraft at Cherbourg. They had flown-in from St. Aubin earlier that morning and re-fuelled, and now sat around waiting for final orders to take off.

Matthes found himself reflecting on the losses they had suffered since the opening of the western campaign, which seemed a lifetime ago. In France the

Gruppe had lost 27 killed, 6 missing and 17 wounded, including Oberleutnant Heinrich, the original Staffelkapitän of 7th Staffel, who died of wounds received in action over Beauvais on 20th May. But during the same period, they had destroyed 70 aircraft in combat and another 7 on the ground. Not a bad tally!

At last their orders came through: 'Bomber escort to Bristol, main target the Spitfire works at Yeovil. As far as possible, the bomber units must reach their targets unhindered. Combat with English fighters only as a defensive measure.' The Zerstörer crews exchanged glances. Matthes shared their thoughts: no attacks, no opportunity for combat, only the same old diet of strict discipline and duty - protecting the bombers from attack by British fighters.

They were to accompany 64 Heinkel He 111s of KG 55 on this attack, aiming for the Bristol Aeroplane works at Filton, ZG 26's 50 Bf 110s flying close escort to the bombers all the way there and back. They would be supported by 50 Bf 109s of I. and II./JG 2 and II./JG 53, who would accompany the formation as far as the English coast. Also flying with the main formation, 11 Bf 110s of Erprobungsgruppe 210 were to

L1 + KK of 14.(Z)/LG 1 in the classic 'Fliegerdenkmal' position.

separate on nearing the English coast to attack Portland.

Further west, a feint against Plymouth by Junkers Ju 88s of KG 51 would divert attention from the main attack, while to the east, a feint against Portsmouth by Junkers Ju 88s of KG 54, would add to the confusion.

Robert Götz, a gunner serving with I./KG 55 based at Dreux, wrote of this, his 7th war flight, "Attack on an aircraft factory at Filton. And three Me 110 fighter groups have been announced as heavy fighter protection. Over Cherbourg, they in fact suddenly appear above us. It is a very reassuring feeling to see so many big two-engine fighters up there, with their shark's teeth and similar symbols painted on them. And these can accompany us much further inland than the single-engined Me 109, and are supposed to have terrifying fire-power. But there have been rumours that they are by no means all that fast, as the circumstances would urgently require. However that may be, there they were as guardian angels and would soon show their teeth."

III./ZG 26, led by Major Kaschka, took-off at 10:40 am. for their rendezvous with the bombers over Cher-

bourg, the Bf 110s flying between 500-600 feet above the Heinkels. Over England, small formations of British fighters approached them but were soon beaten off. Then it started getting livelier, with heavy AA fire and larger groups of fighters making determined attacks which cut through the German formation.

Götz again, "Up there, above Portsmouth the Spitfires are already appearing again, and attacking savagely. And no counter-action by our fighters is to be seen. With consternation, I see an Me 110 flying quite low and slowly over a clear area, where it pulls up sharply. And equally slow, behind it, is a Spitfire which one can almost see being shaken by the bursts of fire that it is pouring into the body of the battered Zerstörer. And above us is flying the main body of our vaunted guardian angels, still in unbroken formation. But I hadn't seen them in action, whatever others had done. Perhaps, because of their alleged limited capacities, they had been ordered only to give us some degree of protection. They obviously had to look after themselves as well. But in that case, goodbye to daytime attacks on England."

Finally reaching the target, the bombers dropped

Two views Bf 110 C, L2 + ER, W. Nr. 2185, of 7.(F)/LG 2, which finally came to rest in a hedge in Beeneys Lane, north of Hastings on 25/9/40. The crew of Oblt. Weyergang, pilot, and Bordfunker Fw. Nelson did not survive the crash.

their loads and turned on a reciprocal heading for home. Several of them had already been hit, engines burning, staining the sky with their smoke. Oberleutnant Matthes recalls, "During the bombing run, we tried to hold a partial defensive circle above the bombers but were again and again turned in combat, mainly by Spitfires. They attacked from all sides, above and below - it was a crazy carousel!"

Squadron Leader Darley, leading the Spitfires of No. 609 Squadron from Warmwell, recalls, "There were three large arrowhead formations of about 60 aircraft each, and above this lot about 30 Me 110s. As we were the only squadron on the scene, the odds were about 20 to 1. Being the first in, I had a most uneasy feeling that at least 200 rear gunners were firing at me! After our first attack, the AA opened up, so the amount of lead whistling about the sky was prodigious. The next thing was a realisation that three Me 110s were on my tail, and I had quite a tussle with them until I ran out of ammo. As far as I can recall, we all got back safely, but how on earth we all escaped being shot down is still a mystery!"

Matthes was doing his best, claiming his 3rd victory south-west of Bristol. "Ahead of me a Spitfire was attacking our formation. I cut in behind him and opened fire with all weapons, the Englishman dropped away dragging a heavy plume of smoke. Unfortunately, my usual Rottenflieger had been shot down by naval AA fire over the Thames estuary and my new wingman was not covering my tail so well, so I came under fire from another Spitfire which damaged my starboard engine and wing.

Previous page: Two views of Bf 110 C, 3U + JR, of Oblt. Ernst Matthes, Staffelkapitän of 7./ZG 26 as it moves out for another flight. Above: the same aircraft after force-landing back at Cherbourg following an escort mission for He 111s of KG 55 on 25/9/40. Two victory bars adorn the fin. Note that the white tactical marking on the nose is rather weather-beaten.

"My Bf 110 started smoking badly, hopefully she wouldn't start burning - so what now? I was separated from my unit and couldn't expect any protection from them as they were still engaged in combat with Spitfires. So I shut down the damaged engine and closed up on the returning bombers below me for some protection. The idea seemed good in theory, but to think that my smoking engine and low speed wouldn't eventually attract the attention of British fighters was, in reality, a nonsense. So I stood the aircraft on its nose and dived to within 600 feet of the ground.

"This reduced the smoke from my damaged engine, and it occurred to me that a forced-landing might be a possibility, although the Bordfunker and I were both unhurt and with our parachutes intact. Unlike the time over Rheims when my aircraft had been hit by over 100 bullets and a bale-out made impossible with my parachute shot to ribbons. On that occasion, I had force-landed at Moselbergland. Now, if we were attacked by fighters again on this flight, I decided that a parachute drop, to a prison camp, was the only alternative.

"But, fortunately, the fighters were still occupied with the bombers above us, as we scuttled back across England on one engine. I got worried when we neared the coast for, I knew from experience, that was where British fighters often waited to catch returning aircraft. If I could gain some height, I determined to try to get as far as the Isle of Wight before deciding whether to force-land or attempt the Channel crossing."

Feldwebel Walter Scherer of 8./ZG 26 had no such options. His port engine was on fire following attacks by Pilot Officer Williams of No. 152 Squadron and Pilot Officer Mayers of No. 601 Squadron, and he knew that his badly wounded Bordfunker, 20 year-old Gefreiter Heinz Schumacher, probably wouldn't survive the return flight. So Scherer came in for a heavy forced-landing near Greatridge Wood, Boyton, suffering a fractured skull and head wounds, as well as two crushed ribs, a broken left leg and a badly bruised spine.

As he was being loaded into the car which was to take him to hospital in Warminster, Scherer saw soldiers lifting Schumacher's body from the cockpit and covering him with his parachute. He had probably been killed outright in the first British fighter attack.

Meanwhile Matthes was still trying to avoid a similar fate. "Our luck held, we weren't attacked again by either AA or fighters. We both fired off all our ammunition, probably saving the minimum of weight, but the port engine, with careful handling, was doing its job. We weren't losing much height, and I worked out that if nothing else happened, we might still make it back to the French coast. Also, I told myself that if the worst happened, there was always the life-rafts moored at regular intervals across the Channel, and on big missions like this the Seenotdienst, as well as the Royal Navy and fishing boats, looked out for crews who ditched in the sea along the way.

"We were gradually losing height and getting perilously close to the water, seeing not a single life-raft nor any sign of a helpful sailor. But, after what seemed an eternity, the French coast appeared on the horizon, and I gratefully set the aircraft down at the edge of Cherbourg airfield, turning-in with the last drops of petrol in the tank and settling her down gently on her belly. It had been my 21st war-flight over England, my 52nd combat sortie and my second forced-landing of the war. Three days later, we were back in action with a new machine."

III./ZG 26 lost two Bf 110s on this sortie, one crew ditching in the sea off Weymouth during the return flight but picked-up unhurt by the Seenotdienst. Two Zerstörers returned damaged, for in addition to Matthes, another Bf 110 crashed on landing at Theville and was completely wrecked. Given the scale of the RAF's

reaction, the escorts had done their job well, for only four Heinkels failed to return, another landing at Caen damaged.

Pilot Officer David Crook of No. 609 Squadron had not been involved in this action, but in his view, "...the Germans suffered fairly heavy losses, though I think on the whole they could claim it as a moderately satisfactory raid."

Two of No. 152 Squadron's Spitfires had been shot down, one of the pilots killed, another two of their aircraft returning to Warmwell slightly damaged. Another Spitfire from No. 609 Squadron had force-landed near Glastonbury, while two Hurricanes of No. 238 Squadron had also suffered combat damage; one of them crashing while attempting a forced-landing at Charmy Down.

In a running battle with British fighters far beyond the English coast and deep into enemy territory, the Zerstörers had shown that, even at this stage in the battle, they could still hold their own. But two days later, attempting to repeat their success, they were to experience a very different result.

On 27th September, mid-morning raids on the southern suburbs of London by Bf 110 fighter-bombers, escorted by Bf 109s, provoked a heavy reaction from British fighters. Such was the defence's response

Another view of the Bf 110 C, 3U + JR of Oblt. Ernst Matthes, Staffelkapitän of 7./ZG 26 after his force-landing at Cherbourg on 25/9/40. This closer view shows that the port wing root has been wrenched away from its fuselage mounting point.

Hptm. Horst Liensberger, Gruppenkommandeur of V.(Z)/LG 1, killed in action on 27/9/40.

that the German fighters were simply overwhelmed and suffered appalling losses in a series of running battles and bitterly contested combats high above the Surrey/Sussex borders.

Intercepted at 19,000 feet by British fighters, Liensberger's V.(Z)/LG 1 suffered severe losses in action over Redhill. Chased south by a Hurricane at tree-top height, Hauptmann Horst Liensberger, Gruppenkommandeur of V.(Z)/LG 1, could not shake off his pursuer, Pilot Officer Percy Burton of No. 249 Squadron. Over Hailsham, the Gruppe heard the Kommandeur's last radio message, 'Both engines are hit...am trying to turn...it's impossible...I will try to land.' Then nothing more.

His Zerstörer crashed near Hamlins Mill, minus its tail unit, which had been severed from the fuselage in a collision with the Hurricane. Many witnesses later attested that the Hurricane, presumably out of ammunition, had deliberately rammed the Bf 110. None of the three combatants survived.

On 22nd October, Major beim Stabe, Hauptmann 'Papa' Haarman, confided to a personal chronicle, "The 27th September was a black day for the outfit. I regarded Horst Liensberger highly as my commander and as a human being and, despite the age difference, I venerated him. I am sure he will come back after the war." Tragically, it would be so, but not as Haarman intended, for Liensberger's death was later confirmed vie the International Red Cross in Geneva. His remains were buried at Hailsham cemetery and repatriated to his home town, Innsbruck, for re-burial in the family plot in 1962.

His was not the only loss, however, for 7 of the 13 Bf 110s of V.(Z)/LG 1 which flew on this mission failed to return. Two 13th Staffel aircraft were lost. Feldwebel Adolf Bruns and Gefreiter Franz Gröbl killed in their aircraft which crashed at Chelwood Gate, in the Ashdown Forest, overwhelmed by repeated attacks by at least five Hurricanes: Squadron Leader McNab and Flying Officer Russell of No. 1 (RCAF) Squadron; Pilot Officer Currant of No. 605 Squadron and probably also Flight Lieutenants Strickland and Sing of No. 213 Squadron.

The Bf 110 of Gefreiter Hans Swietlik of 13th Staffel, with both engines disabled in attacks by Sergeant Wright of No. 605 Squadron, fell into the Channel off Folkestone. The body of his Bordfunker, Gefreiter Heinz Welz, was washed ashore at Sandwich on 25th October.

Another of Liensberger's Gruppe, a 14th Staffel machine flown by Feldwebel Friedrich Lindemann, exploded under attack by Flying Officer Eckford of No. 253 Squadron and fell over Dallington, near Heathfield. Both Lindemann and his Bordfunker, Obergefreiter Artur Hübner, being killed, one falling from the machine with an unopened parachute.

Although of poor quality, this is the only known photograph of Fw. Lindemann, pilot, right, and Ogefr. Hübner, Bordfunker, of 14.(Z)/LG 1. Both were killed in action on 27/9/40 in Bf 110 C-2, L1 + CK. Lindemann sports a moustache, a less prevalent occurence in the Luftwaffe than with their RAF counterparts.

The wreckage of Hptm. Horst Liensberger's Bf 110 C-2, L1+XB, near Hamlins Mill, Hailsham. The tail unit, detached from the airframe, landed relatively intact. On the port fin, roundels are used to denote victories, rather than the more usual bars.

Socketts Manor, Oxted, 27/9/40. Oblt. Weckeiser force-landed his Bf 110 C-2, L1+LL, W. Nr. 3533 following repeated attacks by RAF fighters. Weckeiser and his Bordfunker, Gefr. Brügow, entered British captivity as a result. Of interest is the early-style solid camouflage down the fuselage sides, the non-standard (for the time) thinner white outline to the fuselage cross, and the white nose. Four victory bars adorn the fin.

Close-up view of the port fin and rudder of Weckeiser's Bf 110 C-2. The four victory bars on the fin carried the dates 13.8, 15.8, 15.8, and 11.9 beneath them.

Uffz. Hans Bechthold, pilot with 15.(Z)/LG 1, who became a prisoner-of-war on 27/9/40, when shot down in Bf 110 C-2, L1+GL.

Three of 15th Staffel's aircraft also remained in England. The Staffelkapitän, 26 year-old Oberleutnant Ulrich Freiherr von Gravenruth, from Affing in Augsburg, and his Bordfunker, Feldwebel Otto Reinhold, were both killed. Their crippled Zerstörer was chased south by four RAF fighters and blundered over Gatwick, where it was finally engaged by the aerodrome defences and blown to pieces.

Unteroffizier Hans Bechthold abandoned his Bf 110 under attack by five RAF fighters when his starboard engine was set alight and his Bordfunker, Unteroffizier Hans Koch, killed. His aircraft crashed and burned out at Horham Manor Farm, at Horam.

With British fighters swarming all over them, only one of V.(Z)/LG 1's Zerstörers managed a forced-landing, putting down at Socketts Manor, near Oxted. This was attacked by at least 8 British fighters and the fortunate pilot, Oberleutnant Otto Weckeiser, miraculously escaped injury, but his Berliner Bordfunker, Gefreiter Horst Brüggow, was captured wounded.

It was the end for Liensberger's Gruppe, which was unable to sustain such losses on top of the many casualties they had suffered over previous weeks. It was a bitter outcome, but within 48 hours, the exhausted remnants of the Gruppe, under the temporary command of Oberleutnant Hellmut Peters, were dis-

banded and withdrawn to Bavaria, where they would remuster to form the nucleus of I./NJG 3.

However, misery for the Zerstörers did not end there for, later that morning at 11:45 am., in a repeat of the tactics adopted two days before, two simultaneous raids attempted to divide and confuse the defences. One, a large raid of 300 aircraft aimed for London, was prevented from reaching the capital by determined British fighter opposition.

Further west, 10 Bf 110s of Erprobungsgruppe 210 took off from Cherbourg-Ost and headed for the Parnall Aircraft factory at Yate, led by Hauptmann Martin Lutz. They flew as two extended Schwärme of 5 aircraft each, one made up of 1st Staffel aircraft led by Lutz, the other, 2nd Staffel machines led by their Staffelkapitän, Oberleutnant Wilhelm-Richard Roßiger. Partway across the Channel, Leutnant Wolfgang Schenck of 1st Staffel turned back for France due to continuing engine trouble, reducing the attackers to 9.

They were escorted by 42 Bf 110s of 'Horst Wessel' ZG 26. Flying with Oberleutnant Montag's 9th

U8 + GL, W. Nr. 3353, of Lt. Joachim Koepsell, pilot, and Bordfunker Uffz. Johann Schmidt, shot down over south-west England on 27/9/40, Koepsell surviving, Schmidt being killed. This Bf 110 carries the white tactical nose, and also a small white band around the rear fuselage, common to aircraft of ZG 26 in the later stages of the Battle of Britain.

Staffel, 20 year-old Gefreiter Georg Jakstadt recalls, "Our Gruppe took off shortly before 10:00 am. and formed up at about 1,500 feet, climbing to 2,500 feet behind Cherbourg to rendezvous with the bombers (whose) target was the Bristol aircraft works, our mission to escort them."

Eleven Bf 109s of II./JG 2 flew ahead of the formation, and to cover their return, more Bf 109s of I. and III./JG 2, together with elements of JG 53, would meet them over Swanage.

Although four RAF squadrons were scrambled to meet the raid, the sector controller was hesitant which allowed the German formation to avoid the defending fighters as it crossed the coast east of Portland. At this point, the Bf 110s of II. and III./ZG 26 broke away to form two Abwehrkreis over Warmwell and Portland. Erprobungsgruppe 210, with their close escort of Makrocki's I./ZG 26, continued direct for the target, going into a shallow dive.

Directly ahead of them, the Hurricanes of No 504 Squadron took-off from Filton, led by Flight Lieutenant Barrington Royce, and were climbing hard to reach the Bf 110s height. The two formations met head-on as Lutz's aircraft dived on their target. The Hurricanes broke up the attack and the Bf 110s veered away south-east, jettisoning their bombs, as the escorts of I./ZG 26 manoeuvred to intervene, all in the teeth of heavy AA fire.

Leutnant Joachim Koepsell of 3./ZG 26 recalls, "We pulled up into a climbing turn to position for an at-

tack...zooming to gain height quickly. We continued our turn but as I looked around I saw, much to my surprise, that they were coming at us head-on at the same height. I believed our speed. in the dive should have given us the better rate of climb, but the British fighters climbed faster than I had anticipated. I had made a serious mistake and the enemy aircraft were quickly upon us."

No. 504 Squadron's attack had been decisive and the Zerstörers now had a running fight on their hands in order to reach the sanctuary of the coast. There, the waiting escorts were already coming under attack from the British fighters scrambled earlier.

Probably hit and damaged by Pilot Officer Murray Frisby in the initial head-on clash over Filton, Hauptmann Lutz's aircraft had broken away diving for Swanage and had probably been attacked by Flight Lieutenant Rook, also of No 504 Squadron. The crippled Zerstörer's engines burst into flames and it went into a vertical dive wreathed in smoke. It ploughed into trees and crashed at Bussey Stool Farm, Cranbourne Chase, from where the bodies of Lutz and his Bordfunker, Unteroffizier Anton Schön, were later recovered.

The loss of Martin Lutz was another severe blow to Erprobungsgruppe 210. He was the unit's third Gruppenkommandeur to be lost in action against England since their formation in July. Oberleutnant Werner Weymann, Staffelkapitän of 1st Staffel took temporary command of the Gruppe on their return to Denain later that day. Lutz was to be posthumously awarded the

U8+FK of Ofw. Tiepelt, pilot, and Uffz. Brosig, Bordfunker, of 2./ZG 26. This aircraft was shot down over Bristol on 27/9/40 during an escort mission for Erpr. Gr. 210, Tiepelt and Brosig being killed.

Part of the wreckage of U8+FK following its demise on 27/9/40.

Ritterkreuz four days later.

Meantime, I./ZG 26's Zerstörers were in fierce combat with No. 504 Squadron's Hurricanes as the German formation attempted to retire south-east. One, a 2nd Staffel machine, had both engines set alight in an attack by Flying Officer Royce and broke up in a dive, the main wreckage falling at the Stapleton Institution, Bristol. Its pilot, Oberfeldwebel Hans Tiepelt, and his Bordfunker, Unteroffizier Herbert Brosig, were both killed.

Fighting for his life, Joachim Koepsell was engaged by Sergeant Jones of No. 504 squadron whose head-on attack set his fuel tank ablaze. "My aircraft was badly damaged in this first encounter - the starboard forward petrol tank caught fire, my windscreen was shot up and from my comrade Schmidt, in the back, I heard a rattle from his throat over the intercom." Unteroffizier Johann Schmidt was hit in the throat by machine gun fire and probably died instantly.

"The state of my aircraft ruled out any chance of getting home or of even making a forced-landing - the forward petrol tank was now burning fiercely while the large tank situated behind it could explode at any mom-

Lt. Joachim Koepsell in front of his Bf 110, which carried the coat-of-arms of his home city, Lübeck, on the nose. Koepsell became a POW on 27/9/40 after flying throughout the Battle of Britain with 1. and 3./ZG 26.

ent." Koepsell eventually abandoned the aircraft over Radstock, pulling his parachute release after a delay drop of about 5 seconds, taking him far below the battle raging above. He landed unhurt at Terry Hill, his aircraft crashing on Haydon Farm, where it exploded on impact. Unteroffizier Schmidt fell from the aircraft as it broke up, losing its tail, and landed dead with an unopened parachute near the Kilmersdon Colliery railway.

More British fighters engaged as the German formation retreated back across Dorset towards the coast, where their waiting escorts were now coming under heavy attack.

Pilot Officer Constable-Maxwell of No. 56 Squadron had to return to Boscombe Down due to a problem with his oxygen system, but had taken off again and was flying alone. He later recorded, "There are twenty five to thirty Dorniers (sic) in open formation and I do a stern attack on the rear aircraft. Tracer comes back and a piece of junk falls from the left side of the cockpit...but the rear gunner continues to fire back. I close up slightly and fire another burst at the port engine. Part of the cowling comes off. I break away hard to the left. On turning right again I see the machine diving down with a cloud of black smoke coming from the port engine."

The 'Dornier' attacked by the young, inexperienced British pilot was a 2./Erpr. Gr. 210 Zerstörer piloted by Feldwebel Friedrich Ebner, one of the ex-Stuka pilots from 3./StG 77 who had been absorbed into the unit on its formation. With his port engine well alight, Ebner dived from 12,000 to 4,000 feet to avoid further attack, his Bordfunker, 20 year-old Gefreiter Werner Zwick, maintaining a spirited defence until he was severely wounded in the stomach and lost consciousness.

Constable-Maxwell continues, "Another Hurricane (Flight Lieutenant Rook of No. 504 Squadron) gives it a burst as it goes down - I think he might have gone for one of his own. I follow down in a steep dive. They manoeuvre for position. I try to do a head-on attack, but at the last moment he turns away. I follow round and get in a long burst from 100 to 70 yards from the inside of the circle. The Dornier (sic) then dives right away down - I follow and suddenly feel almost sick.

No one has got out and it appears to be going to dive into the ground. He pulls out, however, and circles slowly - I notice that his port engine has stopped. I am just going to give him another shot when I realise that he is just trying to land.

"For five minutes I watch him from a vantage point of some 500 feet above and on his right. The other Hurricane does the same just behind me. The EA tries

213

Zerstörer fighter-bomber of 2./Erpr. Gr. 210, whose Staffelkapitän, Oblt. Roßiger, was killed on 27/9/40.

Lt. Gerhard Schmidt, pilot of 1./Erpr. Gr. 210, killed in action on 27/9/40.

to land in a field ahead of him, but overshoots and opens up his one good engine. There are trees in front - I could not desire a friend to clear those trees more than that German. He gets over and I am delighted. On we go at 140 mph.. Suddenly he slows up - I do so too and nearly stall. I lose him for a second - there is a hill in front of him but he had not cleared it. I turn and see a huge great silver thing lying broken on a grassy bank between two woods. There is a black hole to one side where it must have hit the ground. The nose is askew - broken at the base - the whole plane is steaming but is not on fire - it is on its belly but seems otherwise alright. No one gets out."

The Bf 110 crash-landed at Preston Hill, near Iwerne Minster, the seriously-wounded Zwick being rushed to Shaftesbury Hospital. RAF Intelligence later caught up with him there, describing him as 'nearly dead'. Despite his horrendous wounds, Zwick would survive and was repatriated back to Germany through Sweden in October 1943.

As they neared the coast, another of Lutz's formation, piloted by Leutnant Gerhard Schmidt of 1st Staffel, dived vertically into the ground at Kimmeridge, probably shot down by Pilot Officer White of No. 504 Squadron. Both Schmidt and his Bordfunker, Feldwebel Gerhard Richter, were killed. Schmidt had been one of the original pilots on complement with 1./ZG 1 when the western campaign commenced in May.

Personnel of 9./ZG 26 relax with drinks on an airfield in France. In the background can be seen 3U + FT, the aircraft of Gefr. Georg Jakstadt, pilot, and Gefr. Emil Liedtke, Bordfunker. They flew this aircraft on 27/9/40 and collided with the Spitfire of P/O Miller of No. 609 Sqdn., Jakstadt being the only survivor.

Meantime, the Spitfires of No. 609 Squadron, led by Pilot Officer Miller, met the Zerstörers of III./ZG 26 over the coast. Pilot Officer David Crook recalls, "...we saw a squadron of Me 110s circling over Swanage at 25,000 feet, waiting to protect their bombers on their return. We immediately turned towards the enemy fighters and started to climb above them.

"They had formed one of their defensive circles, going round and round on each other's tails - altogether quite a tough nut to crack. There were fifteen of them and twelve of us, and we made the most of it."

George Jakstadt of 9th Staffel remembers, "Shortly after crossing the English coast we were attacked by 12-15 Spitfires who dived on us with great speed. We immediately started to form a defensive circle but suddenly my aircraft took a number of hits.

"The Spitfire which attacked me swept past above and ahead of me, so I broke formation and followed it firing short bursts. But it was much more manoeuvrable than my heavy Bf 110 and it quickly turned and came in for another attack at the same height. We attacked each other head-on firing continuously and we must have both received a large number of hits."

As the Spitfires manoeuvred for attack, Crook was

Gefr. Georg Jakstadt, left, and Gefr. Emil Liedtke, of 9./ZG 26, both involved in the collision with P/O Miller of 609 Sqdn. on 27/9/40.

flying close behind his leader. "I was flying just behind Mick and he turned slightly left to attack an Me 110 which was coming towards him. But the German was as determined as Mick, and refused to give way or alter course to avoid this head-on attack. Their aggregate speed of closing was at least 600 mph. and an instant later they collided."

Holding course, Gefreiter Jakstadt had already decided his next move. "As we closed on each other, I decided to pull-up at the last second, passing over the Spitfire and away behind it. Regrettably, my opponent decided to do exactly the same thing which resulted in a head-on collision.

"There was a terrific bang, my right wing folded up and the aircraft caught fire, going into a flat spin. My Bordfunker, Liedtke, screamed aloud just before the impact but I heard nothing more from him afterwards."

Crook watched in horror, "There was a terrific explosion and a sheet of flame and black smoke seemed to hang in the air like a great ball of fire. Many little shattered fragments fluttered down and that was all."
Pilot Officer Keith Ogilvie of No 609 Squadron was another witness. He later confided to his diary, "The 110 turned out to get his cannons working on Mick, and they hit head-on. There was a terrific explosion, a sheet of flame and a column of black smoke. I glimpsed a Spitfire wing fluttering out and the white of a parachute with something on the end. It was ghastly."

Miller was killed instantly, the wreckage of his Spitfire falling in pieces over Chesilbourne. Meanwhile Jakstadt tried to jettison his shattered cockpit hood but it was buckled and would not budge. So, using all his strength, he smashed out the side panels, which he managed, but only with great difficulty. Everything around him was on fire, and in spite of his thick flying suit, he somehow forced himself through the opening, realising too late that his parachute pack would not go through the gap. With strength born of desperation, Jakstadt clawed at the cabin frame trying to force it apart with his bare hands, but in spite of his frantic efforts, it was no use.

"I was on the point of giving up and thinking, 'one more crash like the one just now and it's goodbye!', when everything around me was suddenly peaceful and still. The violent flat spin had created a centrifugal force which threw me out and away from the machine. It was as if I was laying on a giant pillow - I was clear of the aircraft."

As his Bf 110 started to break up over Piddletrenthide, with Gefreiter Emil Liedtke still strapped in the rear cockpit, Jakstadt fell clear. "I hurriedly pulled the release handle, my parachute opening when I was only about 1,000 feet above the ground. As I hit the ground I toppled forward onto my face, literally kissing the earth. A Spitfire circled me at about 300 feet as some men came running up to me. 'Hands up!' Thank

With the pilot in the cockpit and ground crew on the port wing root, this Bf 110 of 4./ZG 26 in pristine condition appears to be ready to move out of its blast pen. The slight contrast between the two upper surface camouflage colours of dark green and black green, and the curved demarcation line between the upper and lower camouflage from wing root to nose are noteworthy. Spinner tips are in the Staffel colour of white. No Staffel or Gruppe emblem has been applied to this machine.

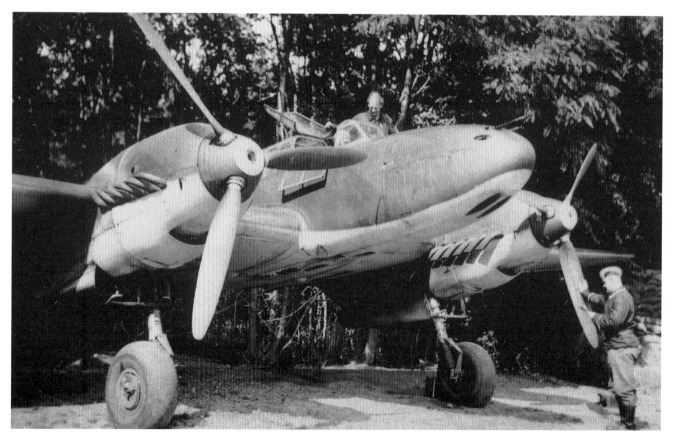

Oblt. Arthur Niebuhr, pilot of 4./ZG 26. Niebuhr was killed in action on 27/9/40 flying Zerstörer, 3U + IM.

God I was carrying no weapon, apart from a clasp knife, which every airman carried. A big man stepped up to me, laid his hand on my shoulder and said 'You are safe until the end of this war!'

"A policeman appeared and drove me away to his house, my parachute in my lap, where his wife tended my burned face and applied a temporary dressing. I was kept there overnight, in a cell, and the following morning taken to hospital, I think in Dorchester, where my thickly-bandaged face was treated by a doctor with some wonderful burn ointment, 'Tannifax'. After two days there, I was escorted to London by two armed soldiers."

Stunned, the rest of No. 609 Squadron's Spitfires were then joined by some Spitfires of No. 152 Squadron who had already engaged the Zerstörers of II./ZG 26 a little further to the west.

With both engines disabled in attacks by Pilot Officer Staples of No. 609 Squadron, one Bf 110 exploded over Middle Bere Farm, near Arne, after further attacks by Pilot Officer Watson of No. 152 Squadron. Oberleutnant Artur Niebuhr, Staffelkapitän of 4./ZG 26, and his Bordfunker, Unteroffizier Klaus Thiesen, were both killed instantly; the violence of the explosion such that it was locally reported that the aircraft had received a direct hit by AA fire.

Another Zerstörer also fell out of this combat, Unteroffizier Fritz Schupp of 8./ZG 26 force-landing at Kimmeridge, his port engine ablaze following attack by Pilot Officer Watson of No. 152 Squadron. Schupp

Gefr. Karl Nechwatal and Uffz. Fritz Schupp of 8./ZG 26 seen at Arques during the Battle of Britain. As a crew they were shot down on 27/9/40.

Bf 110 C-4, 3U+DS, W. Nr. 3290, of Uffz. Fritz Schupp and Gefr. Karl Nechwatal at Wareham, near Kimmeridge on 27/9/40. Three white victory bars can be seen on the starboard rudder.

Pilot Uffz. Fritz Schupp at the controls of his Bf 110.

Below, Oblt. Wilhelm-Richard Rößiger, Staffelkapitän of 2./Erpr. Gr. 210, missing in action, 27/9/40.

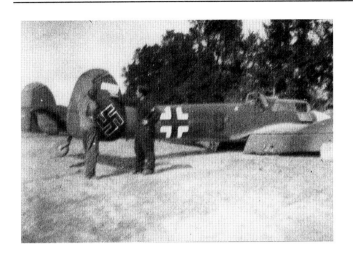

Bf 110 D flown by Ofw. Saleker of 4./ZG 26, crash-landed at Cherbourg on 30/9/40 after being damaged in combat with RAF fighters over the Channel in which Saleker and his unknown Bordfunker were wounded. Note the array of victory bars on the fin. This aircraft was normally the mount of Lt. Sommer, the Nachtrichtensoffizier of III./ZG 26.

and his Bordfunker, Gefreiter Karl Nechwatal, were both captured slightly wounded. Two miles to the east, another Bf 110 which plunged deep into the ground defied any identification.

One Bf 110 of III./ZG 26 force-landed at Cherbourg on return and two more Bf 110s fell into the sea as the running battle crossed the Dorset coast and headed back across the Channel. One was the Staffelkapitän of 2nd Staffel, Erprobungsgruppe 210, Oberleutnant Wilhelm-Richard Roßiger, whose aircraft dived into the sea and was possibly that shared by Pilot Officers Crook and Bisdee of No. 609 Squadron 60 miles off the coast. No trace of 26 year-old Roßiger or his Bordfunker, Oberfeldwebel Hans Marx, was ever found. He was awarded a posthumous Ritterkreuz on the same day as his Kommandeur, Lutz, also lost on this raid.

It had been another epic day. RAF Fighter Command losing a total of 28 aircraft, with 32 more damaged in action. Twenty British pilots had been killed and seven more wounded, but serious as these losses were, it had been a truly disastrous day for the Zerstörers - the worst in their operational history to date. Of the 57 aircraft lost by the Luftwaffe in action on this day, a third of them, 19 in all, had been Bf 110s - one more returning with serious damage.

Representative of the changing mood of the times for the Luftwaffe is the following letter dated 10th October from ground mechanic Willi Peele to his friend, Erwin Landgraf, who flew with 4./ZG 26 and was shot down and wounded on 18th May.

"Dear Erwin,
I received your welcome letter of the 14.9 yesterday. I am so pleased to hear from you again. I, myself am very well - how is your own health? I see you are still in hospital. Yes, dear Erwin, war brings with it some terrible things, don't you think? Gerhard Wohl, once with us, astounded

us. He did damn well everything with us - he's still fighting the English. He's already won the Iron Cross I and II. It's a pity you can't be here with us too. In our Staffel there have been many changes lately. Oblt. Niebuhr was our last Staffelkapitän - unfortunately the great fellow passed on on 27.9 - and who knows who will be next. Yes, Fritz Stahl and Erwin Gensler also didn't return from an attack - can you believe it? Fritz was promoted to Oberfeldwebel on 1.10. I can't tell you everything in a letter - you understand, don't you. Most of the old foxes have gone. Kurt Saleker is in hospital at the moment, he was wounded in an air battle. We are, at present, in a cold place - our quarters are about 10 Kms. from the airfield. The quarters, themselves, are very nice, it is a large castle. Congratulations, by the way, on your promotion. When do you think the war will end? Tommy won't be able to stand the bombing attacks for long. Our personnel location is now Feldpostamt Paris. Now I must finish my letter - duty calls again.

Hauptfeldwebel Prell says he'd like to hear from you, eh? Now, dear Gerhard (sic) I wish you a good recovery for the future. To your dear wife also go my best wishes.

Please excuse the writing, done in haste. Herbert Stange and Friedl Gierga send greetings from English captivity via the International Red Cross. Hopefully we'll see them soon, eh?"

Heil Hitler!

Your comrade, Willi Peele

The indefatigable Erprobungsgruppe 210 ventured over England again on 5th October, led by acting-Gruppenkommandeur Oberleutnant Werner Weymann, but met stiff resistance from defending RAF fighters. Weymann, who only joined the unit in early August, was flying one of two Bf 110s lost on this mission, another two aircraft returning to France damaged.

In what transpired to be the last major action of Bf 110s over southern England on 7th October, II. and III./ZG 26 were hard hit when they escorted Junkers Ju 88s of II./KG 51 on an attack on the Westland Aircraft works at Yeovil. II. Gruppe lost three and III. Gruppe lost four Bf 110s to the defending fighters, 9th Staffel being hardest hit, losing three Zerstörers.

Rounding the year off, Erprobungsgruppe 210 returned to their former hunting ground in force on 17th November: the south-east coastal area of England. They were intercepted before they could attack their intended target, Wattisham airfield, and ultimately lost three further Bf 110s.

Never again would the Zerstörers venture against Britain in any significant numbers. Although the Bf 110 would still sortie over England in the forthcoming months, it must be said that 27th September had been a turning point - the nadir of the operational history of the Zerstörer in 1940.

Hptm. Schön, pilot, and Fw. Meyer, Bordfunker, on a Bf 110 E of ZG 2. Note the capped spinners.

Below, two views of (left) the burial ceremony for Lt. Scharnhorst and Ogefr. Stephan of I./ZG 26, shot down into the Channel on 1/10/40 and, (right) the grave of Ogefr Stephan.

Bf 110 C, 3U + GR, of 7./ZG 26 carrying the white tactical nose marking used by ZG 26 in the final stages of the Battle of Britain.

Kesselring (extreme right) chats to Hptm. Groth with his personal aircraft standing ready to board, and a 'Haifisch' in the background parked among trees.

Le Mans, 1st October. Following the award of the Knights Cross of the Iron Cross to Hptm. Erich groth and Oblt. Hans-Joachim Jabs, Groth, the Gruppenkommandeur of II. Gruppe parades before the men of 4th and 6th Staffeln, with Hptm. Hans Hoppe, far left, and Oblt. Jabs, Gruppenadjutant, behind him.

Hptm. Groth, left and Oblt. Jabs stand proudly before a Sharksmouth displaying their 'Ritterkreuz' on 1/10/40.

Unusual head-on view of Uffz. Paul Wenke and Ogefr. Hans Heinrich in the cockpit of M8 + HM of 4./ZG 76.

M8 + HM of Uffz. Paul Wenke, pilot, and Ogefr. Hans Heinrich of 4./ZG 76. Wenke and Heinrich flew missions throughout the Battle of Britain and were one of the many unsung Bf 110 crews who gave as much unstinting service in 1940 as the more illustrious names. The writing and signature on the photograph is that of Hans Heinrich.

Left: Gefr. Bernhard Demmig, Bordfunker of 9./ZG 26, POW on 7/10/40.

Above: Three 'Ritterkreuzträger' of II./ZG 76. From left, Hptm. Nacke; Hptm. Groth and Oblt. Jabs.

Below: This 'Sharksmouth' of 4./ZG 76 was spectacularly 'pranged' by Hptm. Hoppe on 28/10/40. Points of interest are the W. Nr., 3429 on the canopy, and the airframe number '5' on the fuselage.

Two views of 2N+EP being examined at Farnborough Royal Aircraft Establishment (RAE). Note the tubes in the raised cowling which fitted over the machine gun muzzles.

Two views of a Bf 110 receiving attention to its machine guns. The significance of the number 12 on the nose is not known.

Winter 1940. 3U + AR of Oblt. Ernst Matthes, Staffelkapitän of 7./ZG 26, being manhandled by a cluster of groundcrew. Matthes flew this aircraft after his earlier mount, 3U + JR, had been damaged in combat and a force-landing on 25/9/40

Another view of 3U + AR, being taxied by Matthes in the winter snow.

The ultimate fate of many Zerstörer crews was residence at a POW camp in Canada. Far left - Fw. Ludwig Obermeier, 9./ZG 26; 3rd from left - Uffz. Karl Nechwatal, 8./ZG 26; 5th from left - Uffz. Bernhard Demmig, 9./ZG 26; 6th from left - Ofw. Walter Scherer, 8./ZG 26; 6th from right - Uffz. Karl Stoff, 1./Erpr. Gr. 210; 5th from right - Uffz. Werner Neumann, 1./Erpr. Gr. 210; 3rd from right - Uffz. Oskar Weiler, 3./ZG 2.

¤¤

ZERSTÖRER STAFFELHUNDE

A feature of all airforces is the pets which they surround themselves with. In this respect the Luftwaffe was no different than any other, and within the Luftwaffe, the Zerstörer units had their share of pets. The most popular pet was undoubtedly the 'Hund', and it will never be known exactly how many true missions Luftwaffe 'Hunde' flew on. This small section is therefore dedicated to those faithful companions of Zerstörer crews who were always on hand awaiting their safe return. They provided some measure of sanity during a very intense period of young men's lives.

Above: 'Bobby' of 7th Staffel, Zerstörergeschwader 26 with his Staffel on parade behind him for a photo-call. Back row, left to right: Uffz. Heinz Golisch (Bf); Uffz, Heinz Camehl (Bf); unknown; Uffz. Heinz Krauss (Bf) and Uffz. Georg Stirnweiss (Bf). Middle row, left to right: unknown; Ofw. Franz Santel (Bf); Fw. Franz Sander (P); Fw. Herbert Lange (P) and Fw. Helmut Haugk (P) (on wall). Front row, left to right: Uffz. Karl-Heinz Boock (Bf) and Ofw. Bracun (P).

Previous page, left: 'Grog', a Schnauzer attached to the Gruppenstab of Erprobungsgruppe 210, seen here relaxing in the standard furniture of high summ-er 1940. Grog was the pet of the Gruppe Technical Offi-cer, Leutnant Karl-Heinz Koch, and when Koch was shot down on 15/8/40, Grog transferred to 3rd Staffel, where he was looked after by the Staffelkapitän, Ober-leutnant Otto Hintze.

Previous page, right: 'Bourchi' Victor Mölders' dog leaps playfully with a tyre around its waist, no mean feat for such a small dog! Mölders holds a bottle, with Bf 110 2N + GH forming a backdrop.

Right: The redoubtable 'Puck' with one of the many hedgehogs which appeared frequently on Stavanger-Sola airfield. Puck's treatment of hedgehogs who would not play is fully described in the main body of the text.

LOSS TABLES - 7th SEPTEMBER TO DECEMBER 1940

Date	Name of crew and rank	Unit	Status	Fate	Aircraft Code & W. Nr.	Damage state	Reason for casualty	Place
07.09.40	Lt. Hans Gödsche Oblt. Gerhard Russel	4.(F)/ Auf. Gr. 14	P Bb	K K	Bf 110 C-5 5F+MM 2208	100%	Shot down by 602 Sqdn. Spitfires.	Channel.
07.09.40	Lt. Franz Felix	4.(F)/ Auf. Gr. 14	Bb	W	Bf 110 C-5 2211	20%	Damaged by F/L Christie and P/O Beaumont of 152 Sqdn..	Cherbourg.
07.09.40	Fw. Richard Schütze	1.(F)/ Auf. Gr. 22	Bf	W	Bf 110 C 4N+DH 2207	35%	Damaged by 222 Sqdn. Spitfires. Force-landed	30 Kms. north-west of Vlissingen.
07.09.40	Oblt. Gerhard Granz (Gruppenadjutant) Fw. Willi Schubel	Stab I. ZG 2 Stab I.	P Bf	POW POW	Bf 110 C-4 3M+BB 3246	100%	Shot down by F/O Hardacre and P/O Beazley of 249 Sqdn.	Noak Hill, Billericay.
07.09.40	Lt. Dietrich Kislinger Uffz. Reinhold Dahnke	3./ZG 2 3./ZG 2	P Bf	K POW	Bf 110 C-4 3M+LL 2216	100%	Shot down by S/L Robinson and P/O Langham-Hobart of 73 Sqdn.	Old Tree Farm, Hoath, near Herne Bay.
07.09.40	Hptfw. Fritz Oligschläger Ofw. Ernst Otterbach	3./ZG 2 3./ZG 2	P Bf	K K	Bf 110 C-4 3M+FL 3117	100%	Broke up under attack by Sgt. Garton of 73 Sqdn.	Eythorne, near Deal.
07.09.40	Lt. Hans Dietrich Albert Uffz. Hans Scharf	4./ZG 2 4./ZG 2	P Bf	K K	Bf 110 D-0 A2+BH 3185	100%	Shot down by S/L Bader and Sub-Lt. Cork of 242 Sqdn.	Swan Lane, Downham Hall, near Wickford.
07.09.40	Lt. Karl Stix Gefr. Heinrich Hetz	4./ZG 2 4./ZG 2	P Bf	POW K	Bf 110 D-0 A2+JH 3328	100%	Shot down by P/O Crowley-Milling and Sub-Lt. Gardner of 242 Sqdn.	Bullers Farm, Little Burstead.
07.09.40	Lt. Kurt Schünemann (Gruppe Technical Offizier) Uffz. Hans Mescheder	Stab II. ZG 2 Stab II.	P Bf	K K	Bf 110 D-0 A2+NH 3334	100%	Shot down by F/O Holderness of 1 Sqdn., P/O Janouch of 310 Sqdn. and F/L Lane of 19 Sqdn. Abandoned by crew.	Park Corner Farm, Hacton Lane, Hornchurch.
07.09.40	Oblt. Willi Brede (Staffelführer) Uffz. August Galla	6./ZG 2 6./ZG 2	P Bf	POW K	Bf 110 C-4 A2+ML 3570	100%	Severely damaged by Sgt. Furst of 310 Sqdn. Ditched in sea.	Channel, off Birchington.
09.09.40	Uffz. Alois Pfafflhuber Uffz. Otto Kramp	15.(Z)/ LG 1	P Bf	K K	Bf 110 C-4 L1+DL 3298	100%	Exploded following attack by P/O Tamblyn of 242 Sqdn. and 310 Sqdn. Hurricanes.	Maori Sports Club, Old Malden Lane, Worcester Park.
09.09.40	Uffz. Helmut Mütschele Uffz. Herbert Mosel	4./NJG 1 4./NJG 1	P Bf	K K	Bf 110 D 3136	100%	Crashed on routine ferry flight due to mechanical failure.	Manching, near Ingolstadt.
09.09.40	Uffz. Georg Bierling Uffz. Friedrich Kurella	7./ZG 76 7./ZG 76	P Bf	K K	Bf 110 C-4 2N+FM 2137	100%	Shot down by AA fire.	Borden, near Sittingbourne.

Date	Name of crew and rank	Unit	Status	Fate	Aircraft Code & W. Nr.	Damage state	Reason for casualty	Place
09.09.40	Fw. Hermann Koops Uffz. Christian Weiher	9./ZG 76 7./ZG 76	P Bf	POW K	Bf 110 C 2N+EP* 3108	100%	Severely damaged by RAF fighters. Ditched in sea on return flight.	Channel, 5 miles off Newhaven.
09.09.40	Fw. Eduard Ostermünchner Gefr. Werner Zimmermann	9./ZG 76 9./ZG 76	P Bf	K K	Bf 110 C 2N+EP* 3207	100%	Rammed by F/O Boulton of 310 Sqdn.	Woodcote Park Avenue, Woodmanstern.
09.09.40		9./ZG 76 9./ZG 76	P Bf	U U	Bf 110 C 2N+CP 2081	Not known	Damaged in combat with RAF fighters over Croydon. Crash-landed.	Quoeux airfield.
11.09.40	Gefr. Erich Kling Gefr. Waldemar Sossna	2./ZG 2 2./ZG 2	P Bf	M M	Bf 110 C-4 A2+MH**§ 3376	100%	Did not return from escort mission.	Portsmouth.
11.09.40		I./ZG 2	P Bf	U U	Bf 110 C-4 3M+LH 3623	50%	Damaged in combat with RAF fighters over Portsmouth. Crash-landed.	St. Aubin.
11.09.40	Oblt. Wilhelm Spies (Staffelkapitän) Uffz. Josef Haschke	1./ZG 26 1./ZG 26	P Bf	U K	Bf 110 C-4 U8+KH 2190	20%	Damaged in combat with RAF fighters. Crash-landed.	Calais-Marck airfield.
11.09.40	Fw. Hermann Brinkmann Uffz. Erwin Grüschow	2./ZG 26 2./ZG 26	P Bf	POW POW	Bf 110 C-3 U8+HL*** 1372	100%	Developed engine trouble, then attacked by RAF fighters. Force-landed.	Cobham Farm, Charing.
11.09.40	Oblt. Walter Henken (Gruppenadjutant) Fw. Josef Radlmair	Stab II. ZG 26 Stab II.	P Bf	K K	Bf 110 C-4 3U+HM 3625	100%	Shot down by RAF fighters.	Channel, 3 miles off Margate.
11.09.40	Oblt. Randoald Birkner Uffz. Hermann Klaiber	.4./ZG 26 4./ZG 26	P Bf	M K	Bf 110 D-2§ 3U+DM 3392	100%	Did not return from combat mission. Crashed into the sea.	Thames estuary.
11.09.40	Lt. Rudolf Volck Ogefr. Ernst Hofmann	6./ZG 26 6./ZG 26	P Bf	M K	Bf 110 D-2§ 3U+HP 3400	100%	Shot down by RAF fighters. Crashed into the sea.	Thames estuary.
11.09.40	Oblt. Joachim Junghans Gefr. Paul Eckert	9./ZG 26 9./ZG 26	P Bf	K M	Bf 110 C-4 3U+LT 3231	100%	Believed shot down by Sgt. Jennings of 19 Sqdn.	Barnes Cote, Harvel.
11.09.40		II./ZG 76	P Bf	U U	Bf 110 C M8+KC 3285	100%	Damaged by RAF fighters. Ditched in the Channel; crew rescued by Seenotdienst.	Channel.
12.09.40		9./ZG 26	P Bf	U U	Bf 110 C-4 3628	15%	Force-landed during routine flight. Cause unknown.	Teutoburger Wald.

* It is unlikely that two aircraft from the same Staffel would carry the same fuselage code on the same day. This is likely to be an entry error in Luftwaffe records.
** I. Gruppe crew flying a 4th Staffel aircraft.
*** 2nd Staffel crew flying a 3rd Staffel aircraft.
§ The 'D-2' was the Dackelbauch version of the Bf 110. It is unlikely that ZG 26 operated these aircraft, as the only known unit to use them was I./ZG 76.

Date	Name of crew and rank	Unit	Status	Fate	Aircraft Code & W. Nr.	Damage state	Reason for casualty	Place
12.09.40		II./ZG 76	P Bf	U U	Bf 110 C M8+MN 0361	100%	Crashed during local flight. cause unknown.	Cambrai.
15.09.40	Oblt. Helmut Müller (Staffelkapitän) Fw. Andreas Hoffmann	13.(Z)/ LG 1	P Bf	K K	Bf 110 C-3 L1+IH 3802	100%	Shot down by RAF fighters south of London.	Hothfield Farm, Hothfield, near Ashford.
15.09.40	Lt. Ernst Gorisch Uffz. Walter Gerigk	13.(Z)/ LG 1	P Bf	M M	Bf 110 C-3	100%	Severely damaged in combat south of London. Crashed on return flight.	Channel
15.09.40	Lt. Hugo Adametz Ogefr. Rudi Stief	14.(Z)/ LG 1	P Bf	M M	Bf 110 C-3	100%	Severely damaged in combat south of London. Crashed on return flight.	Channel.
17.09.40		III./ZG 76	P Bf	U U	Bf 110 C 2N+HN 3513	60%	Crashed on landing due to mechanical failure.	Laval airfield.
22.09.40		2.(F)/ Auf. Gr. 11	P Bf	U U	Bf 110 C-5 MJ+ZE 2231	15%	Damaged by own AA fire during reconnaissance mission. Force-landed.	Near Mardyck.
24.09.40	Lt. Ulrich Fr. von der Horst Ogefr. Franz Öllers	1./Erpr. Gr. 210	P Bf	M M	Bf 110 D-0 S9+HH 3384	100%	Shot down by AA fire over Southampton	Channel, off Southampton.
24.09.40	Lt. Hans Calame	4./ZG 76	P	W	Bf 110 C-4 2159	10%	Returned damaged by AA fire on combat mission.	Over Southampton.
24.09.40	 Uffz. Otto Kühn	4./ZG 76 4./ZG 76	P Bf	U W	Bf 110 C-2 2638	10%	Returned damaged by AA fire on combat mission.	Over Southampton.
24.09.40	Uffz. Rudolf Sichel	8./ZG 76	P Bf	W U	Bf 110 C-4 3251	100%	Shot down by AA fire on combat mission. Crew rescued by Seenotdienst.	Channel, off Southampton.
24.09.40	Uffz. Alfred Helwig Uffz. Egon Mirow	8./ZG 76 8./ZG 76	P Bf	M M	Bf 110 C-4 2N+DN 3534	100%	Shot down by AA fire on combat mission.	Channel, off Southampton.
25.09.40	Oblt. Eberhard Weyergang Fw. Gustav Nelson (died same day)	7.(F)/ LG 2	P Bf	K W	Bf 110 C L2+ER 2185	100%	Engine damaged in attack by P/O Dewar of 229 Sqdn.	Beeneys Lane, Baldslaw, north of Hastings.
25.09.40	Oblt. Ernst Matthes (Staffelkapitän) Ofw. Franz Santel	7./ZG 26 7./ZG 26	P Bf	U U	Bf 110 C-4 3U+JR 2130	20%	Damaged in combat with Spitfire. Force-landed on one engine.	Cherbourg.
25.09.40	Fw. Walter Scherer (wounded) Gefr. Heinz Schumacher	8./ZG 26 8./ZG 26	P Bf	POW K	Bf 110 C-4 3U+GS 3591	100%	Shot down by P/O Williams and P/O Mayers of 601 Sqdn. Force-landed.	Well Bottom, near Boyton.
25.09.40		III./ZG 26	P Bf	U U	Bf 110 C 3263	100%	Shot down by RAF fighters. Crew rescued by Seenotdienst.	Channel, off Weymouth.

Date	Name of crew and rank	Unit	Status	Fate	Aircraft Code & W. Nr.	Damage state	Reason for casualty	Place
25.09.40		III./ZG 26	P Bf	U U	Bf 110 C-4 2194	100%	Crashed-on landing following combat with RAF fighters.	Theville.
25.09.40	Lt. Werner Pistor	Stab II. ZG 76	P	K	Bf 110 C-2 3111	100%	Crashed during cross-country flight from Nürnberg to Giessen in bad weather.	Erbach, near Wurzburg.
26.09.40	Lt. Wilhelm Panek Uffz. Walter Schmidt	4.(F)/ Auf.	P Bf	K K	Bf 110 C-5 5F + CM 2187	100%	Believed shot down by F/L Blackadder of 607 Sqdn. during reconnaissance mission.	South Mead Ledge, west of Cowes, Isle of Wight.
26.09.40	Fw. Hubert Rohde Fw. Ernst Feder	1./ZG 26 1./ZG 26	P Bf	POW POW	Bf 110 C-4 U8 + HH 3028	100%	Damaged by AA fire over Southampton, Shot down by P/O Urwin-Mann of 238 Sqdn.	Bleak Down, Newport, Isle of Wight.
26.09.40	Lt. Kuno-Adalbert Konopka Uffz. Rudolf Eiberg	7./ZG 26 7./ZG 26	P Bf	K K	Bf 110 C-4 3U + AR 3094	100%	Shot down by P/O Wigglesworth of 238 Sqdn.	Tapnell Farm, Freshwater. Isle of Wight.
27.09.40	Hptm. Martin Lutz (Gruppenkommandeur) Uffz. Anton Schon	Stab Erpr. Gr. 210	P Bf	K K	Bf 110 D-3 S9 + DH 3378	100%	Shot down by Hurricane(s) of 504 Sqdn..	Bussey Stool Farm, Tarrant Gunville. Cranbourne Chase
27.09.40	Lt. Gerhard Schmidt Fw. Gerhard Richter	1./Erpr. Gr. 210	P Bf	K K	Bf 110 D-3 S9 + JH 3888	100%	Shot down by RAF fighters.	Kimmeridge.
27.09.40	Oblt. Wilhelm-Richard Rößiger (Staffelkapitän) Ofw. Hans Marx	2./Erpr. Gr. 210	P Bf	M M	Bf 110 D-0 S9 + GK 2248	100%	Shot down by RAF fighters.	Channel.
27.09.40	Fw. Fritz Ebner Gefr. Werner Zwick (Wounded)	2./Erpr. Gr. 210	P Bf	POW POW	Bf 110 D-0 S9 + DK 4270	100%	Shot down by F/L Rook of 504 Sqdn. and F/O Constable-Maxwell of 56 Sqdn.. Force-landed.	The Beeches. Preston Hill, Iwerne Minster.
27.09.40	Hptm. Horst Liensberger (Gruppenkommandeur) Uffz. Albert Köpge	Stab V.(Z)/ LG 1	P Bf	K K	Bf 110 C-2 L1 + XB 3560	100%	Rammed by F/O Burton of 249 Sqdn..	Simmons Field near Hamlins Mill near Hailsham.
27.09.40	Gefr. Hans Swietlik Gefr. Heinz Welz	13.(Z)/ LG 1	P Bf	K K	Bf 110 D-0 L1 + BH 3333	100%	Believed shot down by Sgt. Wright of 605 Sqdn..	Channel, off Folkestone.
27.09.40	Fw. Adolf Bruns Gefr. Franz Gröbl	13.(Z)/ LG 1	P Bf	K K	Bf 110 D-0 L1 + CH 3304	100%	Shot down by S/L McNab and F/O Russell of 1 (RCAF) and P/O Currant of 605 Sqdn. and 213 Sqdn. Hurricanes.	Chelwood Gate, Ashdown Forest, near East Grinstead.
27.09.40	Fw. Friedrich Lindemann Ogefr. Artur Hübner	14.(Z)/ LG 1	P Bf	K K	Bf 110 C-2 L1 + CK 3548	100%	Believed shot down by F/O Eckford of 253 Sqdn. Exploded following attack.	Coppice Farm, Three Cups, Dallington, near Heathfield.

Date	Name of crew and rank	Unit	Status	Fate	Aircraft Code & W. Nr.	Damage state	Reason for casualty	Place
27.09.40	Uffz. Hans Bechthold Uffz. Hans Koch	14.(Z)/ LG 1	P Bf	POW K	Bf 110 C-2 L1+GL* 3849	100%	Shot down by RAF fighters. Force-landed.	Horam Manor, Farm, north of Hailsham.
27.09.40	Oblt. Ulrich Fr. von Gravenreuth (Staffelkapitän) Fw. Otto Reinhold	15.(Z)/ LG 1 15.(Z)/	P Bf	K K	Bf 110 D-0 L1+BL 3147	100%	Shot down by AA fire and RAF fighters.	Near Gatwick aerodrome.
27.09.40	Oblt. Otto Weckeiser Uffz. Horst Brüsgow	15.(Z)/ LG 1	P Bf	POW POW	Bf 110 C-2 L1+LL 3533	100%	Shot down by RAF fighters. Force-landed.	Socketts Manor Oxted.
27.09.40	Ofw. Hans Tiepelt Uffz. Herbert Brosig	2./ZG 26 2./ZG 26	P Bf	K K	Bf 110 C-4 U8+FK 2162	100%	Shot down by F/O Royce of 504 Sqdn..	Stapleton Institution, Fishponds, Bristol.
27.09.40	Lt. Joachim Koepsell Uffz. Johann Schmidt	3./ZG 26 3./ZG 26	P Bf	POW K	Bf 110 C U8+GL 3352	100%	Shot down by Sgt. Jones of 504 Sqdn..	Haydon, near Radstock.
27.09.40	Oblt. Arthur Niebuhr (Staffelkapitän) Uffz.. Klaus Theisen	4./ZG 26 4./ZG 26	P Bf	K K	Bf 110 C-4 3U+IM 3629	100%	Shot down by RAF fighters.	Salters Wood, Middle Bere, Farm, near Arne.
27.09.40	Oblt. Hans Barschel (Gruppenadjutant) Uffz. Hans Klose	Stab III. ZG 26 Stab III.	P Bf	M M	Bf 110 C-4 3U+BD 2168	100%	Shot down by RAF fighters.	Channel, off Dorset coast.
27.09.40	Uffz. Fritz Schupp Gefr. Karl Nechwatal	8./ZG 26 8./ZG 26	P Bf	POW POW	Bf 110 C-4 3U+DS 3290	100%	Shot down by Spitfires of 152 Sqdn. Force-landed.	Kimmeridge.
27.09.40	Gefr. Georg Jakstadt Gefr. Emil Liedtke	9./ZG 26 9./ZG 26	P Bf	POW K	Bf 110 C-4 3U+FT 3297	100%	Collided with Spitfire of P/O Miller of 609 Sqdn. in combat over Warmwell.	Dole Ash Farm, Piddletrenthide.
27.09.40		III./ZG 26	P Bf	U U	Bf 110 C-4 3098	40%	Damaged in combat with RAF fighters. Force-landed	Cherbourg.
27.09.40	Oblt. Wilfried von Eichhorn (Gruppenadjutant) Uffz. Erich Bartmuss	Stab II. ZG 76 Stab II.	P Bf	POW K	Bf 110 D-3 M8+XE 4215	100%	Believed shot down by P/O Worrall and Sgt. Palliser of 249 Sqdn..	Channel, off Hastings.
27.09.40	Fw. Hans Peterburs	9./ZG 76	P Bf	W U	Bf 110 D 2N+DP 3584	100%	Damaged in combat with RAF fighters. Force-landed	Near Dieppe.
28.09.40	Hptm. Eberhard Heinlein (Gruppenkommandeur) Fw. Paul Lösche (died 12.10.40)	I./ZG 2 I./ZG 2	P 1. Wart	K I	Bf 110	100%	Crashed in bad weather during ferry flight from Toussus -le-Noble to Augsburg.	Near Tuttlingen.
29.09.40		III./ZG 76	P Bf	U U	Bf 110 C 3422	100%	Crashed during local flight. Cause not known.	St. Aubin airfield.
30.09.40	Ofw. Kurt Saleker Uffz. Siegfried Jäger	4./ZG 26 4./ZG 26	P Bf	W W	Bf 110 D-0	100%	Damaged in combat with RAF fighters over the Channel.	Theville.

* 14th Staffel crew flying a 15th Staffel aircraft

234

Date	Name of crew and rank	Unit	Status	Fate	Aircraft Code & W. Nr.	Damage state	Reason for casualty	Place
01.10.40	Lt. Artur Scharnhorst (died 02.10.40)	3./ZG 26	P	W	Bf 110 D	100%	Shot down by RAF fighters over the Channel, off Swanage. Crashed in the sea.	Cherbourg.
	Ogefr. Martin Stephan	3./ZG 26	Bf	K	4212			
02.10.40	Oblt. Eckert	7.(F)/ LG 2	P Bf	K K	Bf 110 C-5 L2 + DR 2263	100%	Collided with Bf 110, L2 + FR, on non-combat flight.	Near Brussels.
02.10.40		7.(F)/ LG 2	P Bf	U U	Bf 110 C-5 L2 + FR 2188	100%	Collided with Bf 110, L2 + DR, on non-combat flight. Abandoned by crew.	Near Brussels.
05.10.40	Oblt Werner Weymann (Acting-Gruppenkommandeur)	1./Erpr. Gr. 210	P	M	Bf 110 D-3 S9 + FH 3382	100%	Shot down by RAF fighters. Crashed in sea.	Channel.
	Uffz. Erwin Hübner		Bf	M				
05.10.40	Fw. Fritz Duensing Fw. Helmut Krappatsch	1./Erpr. Gr. 210	P Bf	K K	Bf 110 D-3 S9 + GH 3383	100%	Shot down by S/L Hogan of 501 Sqdn..	Millbank Place, Kingsnorth. Near Ashford.
05.10.40	Ofw. Robert Schulze	1./Erpr. Gr. 210	P Bf	U W	Bf 110 D-0 S9 + EH 3598	15%	Damaged in combat with RAF fighters. Force-landed.	Calais.
05.10.40	Uffz. Balthasar Aretz Gefr. Rolf Schilleng	2./Erpr. Gr. 210	P Bf	W	Bf 110 E-2 S9 + EK 4209	40%	Damaged in combat by P/O Lund of 92 Sqdn..	South of London.
06.10.40	Hptm. Heinrich Graf von Stillgried und Rattonitz (Gruppenkommandeur)	II./NJG 1	P	K	Bf 110 D-0 G9 + CC 3174	100%	Crashed due to engine catching fire on non-combat mission.	Near Lienen, 40 Kms. north-east of Koenen.
	Uffz. Herbert Lemke	II./NJG 1	Bf	K				
07.10.40		9./NJG 1	P Bf	U U	Bf 110 D-1 G9 + GT 3308	80%	Crashed on take-off due to engine failure.	Stendal.
07.10.40	Ofw. Erwin Gensler Uffz. Franz Häfner	4./ZG 26 4./ZG 26	P Bf	POW POW	Bf 110 E-1 3U + FM 3427	100%	Believed shot down by P/O Marrs of 152 Sqdn. Crashed in sea.	Channel, off Ringstead Bay.
07.10.40	Ofw. Fritz Stahl Uffz. Ernst Mauer	4./ZG 26 4./ZG 26	P Bf	M M	Bf 110 D-2* 3U + HN§ 3416	100%	Shot down by RAF fighters.	South of Portland.
07.10.40	Ofw. Karl Herzog Ogefr. Herbert Schilling	6./ZG 26 6./ZG 26	P Bf	K K	Bf 110 C-7 3U + JP 3418	100%	Shot down by F/L Robinson of 609 Sqdn.	Long Bredy, near Dorchester.
07.10.40	Lt. Botho Sommer Gruppenadjutant)	Stab III. ZG 26	P	POW	Bf 110 E-1 3U + DD 3421	100%	Shot down by RAF fighters over Dorchester.	Channel, Weymouth Bay.
	Uffz. Paul Preuler	Stab III.	Bf	POW				
07.10.40	Lt. Kurt Sidow Gefr. Josef Repik	9./ZG 26 9./ZG 26	P Bf	K K	Bf 110 C-4 3U + BT 3283	100%	Believed shot down by F/O Dundas of 609 Sqdn.	Hart Hill, Stoborough, near Wareham.
07.10.40	Oblt. Hubert Grisslich Uffz. Ludwig Obermeier	9./ZG 26 9./ZG 26	P Bf	POW POW	Bf 110 C-4 3U + GT 3640	100%	Shot down by RAF fighters.	Channel, off Weymouth.

* The 'D-2' was the Dackelbauch version of the Bf 110. It is unlikely that ZG 26 operated these aircraft, as the only known unit to use them was I./ZG 76.
§ 4th Staffel crew flying a 5th Staffel aircraft

Date	Name of crew and rank	Unit	Status	Fate	Aircraft Code & W. Nr.	Damage state	Reason for casualty	Place
07.10.40	Gefr. Bernhard Demmig Ogefr. Josef Bachmann	8./ZG 26 8./ZG 26	P Bf	POW K	Bf 110 C-4 3U + JT* 3564	100%	Shot down by F/L Robinson of 609 Sqdn. and F/O Brooker of 56 Sqdn. over Dorchester.	Near Corfe Castle.
08.10.40		I./ZG 26	P Bf	U U	Bf 110 C-3 1373	Not known	Damaged in taxi-ing accident.	Trecquile airfield.
09.10.40		Stab NJG 1	P Bf	U U	Bf 110 D-0 G9 + CA 3360	45%	Collided with Ju 88 of KG 1 while taxi-ing.	Handorf airfield.
09.10.40		7./ZG 76	P Bf	U U	Bf 110 D-0 2N + EM 3330	10%	Damaged in taxi-ing accident.	Laval airfield
12.10.40	Oblt. Leopold Doffek Uffz. Heinrich Ott	4.(F)/ Auf. Gr. 14	Bb P	K K	Bf 110 C-5 5F + MM 2243	100%	Crashed shortly after take-off on reconnaissance mission; cause unknown.	Periers-sur-le Dar near Caen.
13.10.40	II./ZG 26				Bf 110 D 3401	25%	Force-landed on non-combat flight.	Le Cateau.
15.10.40	Lt. Hans-Georg Mangersdorf Uffz. Hubert Winter	2./NJG 1 2./NJG 1	P Bf	K K	Bf 110 D G9 + FK 3620	100% 100%	Shot down by return fire from RAF night bomber.	12 Kms. west of Gaedelegen.
15.10.40		4./NJG 2	P Bf	U U	Bf 110 D 2A + BL 3812	100%	Hit by return fire from RAF bomber. Abandoned by crew.	Holland.
16.10.40		7./NJG 1	P Bf	U U	Bf 110 C G9 + FR 2634	100%	Crash-landed due to mechanical failure on combat mission.	Near Mecheln.
16.10.40	Fw. Pülke Fw. Wehner	1.(H)/ Auf. Gr.	P Bf	I I	Bf 110 E-1 6300	60%	Crashed during local flight, Cause unknown.	Bergen-op-Zoom.
16.10.40	Oblt. Ernst Zobel Uffz. Robert Pellnat	2./NJG 3 2./NJG 3	P Bf	W W	Bf 110 D-1 L1 + AK 3302	100%	Crashed attempting to land in poor weather on non-combat flight.	Perleberg.
17.10.40		III./ZG 76	P Bf	U U	Bf 110 D-2 3391	20%	Damaged on combat mission. Force-landed.	St. Aubin.
17.10.40	Oblt. Paul Zimmermann Gefr. Walter Makowski	4./NJG 2 4./NJG 2	P Bf	K K	Bf 110 D 3M + AH 3385	100%	Crashed following combat sortie.	Dongen.
18.10.40		III./NJG 1	P Bf	U U	Bf 110 C 0973	60%	Crashed on landing following combat mission.	Stendal.
18.10.40		II./ZG 2	P Bf	U U	Bf 110 3637	30%	Landing accident on non-combat flight.	The Hague.
20.10.40	Oblt. Roland Semmerich Uffz. Rudolf Ebeling	7.(F)/ LG 2	P Bf	POW K	Bf 110 C-5 L2 + MR 2228	100%	Shot down by Spitfires of 92 Sqdn. on photo-reconnaissance mission.	Bockingfod, Horsmonden.

* 8th Staffel crew flying a 9th Staffel aircraft.

Date	Name of crew and rank	Unit	Status	Fate	Aircraft Code & W. Nr.	Damage state	Reason for casualty	Place
21.10.40	Uffz. Werner Hesse Uffz. Stephan Stadler	2./Erpr. Gr. 210	P Bf	W W	Bf 110 D-0 3367	100%	Crashed on local flight due to control failure.	West of Trith-St. Leger.
21.10.40	Oblt. Arno Walther (Staffelkapitän) Uffz. Horst Hoffmann	8./NJG 1 8./NJG 1	P Bf	K K	Bf 110 D 3143	100%	Crashed on take-off, believed due to engine failure.	Stendal.
25.10.40	Lt. Conrad Wacker Gefr. Gerhard Gneist	2.(F)/ Auf. Gr. 122	P Bf	POW K	Bf 110 C-5 F6+MK 2257	100%	Shot down by P/O Norfolk of 72 Sqdn. during photo-reconnaissance mission to Derby.	North Sea, off Great Yarmouth.
25.10.40		II./ZG 26	P	U	Bf 110 C-7 3630	100%	Crashed on non-combat flight. Cause unknown.	St. Aubin.
26.10.40		I./NJG 1	P Bf	U U	Bf 110 C-2 3599	35%	Collided with Bf 110 of II./NJG 1.	Schipol airfield.
26.10.40		II./NJG 1	P Bf	U U	Bf 110 C-2 3538	35%	Collided with Bf 110 of I./NJG 1.	Schiphol airfield.
27.10.40		Erg. St. ZG 26	P Bf	U U	Bf 110 C-4 3625	20%	Damaged in taxi-ing accident.	Guyancourt airfield.
28.10.40	Major Hans-Günther von Obernitz Hptm. Georg Dechant	2.(F)/ Auf. Gr 123 Fk. Reg Bb I/19	P Bb	I I	Bf 110 C-5 4U+ZK 2241	60%	Crashed on take-off on ferry flight to Jersey.	Saarbrücken.
28.10.40	Uffz. Karl Bertram Ofw. Kurt Lorenz	9./NJG 1 7./NJG 1	P Bf	K K	Bf 110 D 3356	100%	Crashed in flames on night combat mission.	4 Kms. north of Tellingstedt, near Rendberg.
28.10.40	Hptm. Hans Hoppe (Staffelkapitän)	4./ZG 76	P	I	Bf 110 C M8+AM 3429	100%	Crashed on take-off due to mechanical failure.	Jever.
29.10.40	Fw. Siegfried Tröppl (died 30/10/40) Uffz. Otto Büttner	2./Erpr. Gr. 210	P Bf	W K	Bf 110 D 3655	100%	Damaged by Spitfires of 92 Sqdn.south of London. Crashed when engines failed.	St Ingelvert.
29.10.40	Fw. Leo Hocheder Ogefr. Helmut Sengbusch	8./ZG 76 8./ZG 76	P Bf	K K	Bf 110 D-3 4218	100%	Crashed on landing on ferry flight. Cause unknown.	Denain.
01.11.40	Fw. Paul Kröplin Gefr. Helmut Hartmann	1.(F)/ Auf. Gr. 22	P Bf	W W	Bf 110 C-5 2203	30%	Damaged by Spitfires of 92 Sqdn. over Thames. Force-landed.	Calais.
05.11.40	Fw. Arthur Hering Gefr. Heinz Ulrich	4./ZG 76 4./ZG 76	P Bf	K M	Bf 110 C-4 M8+GM 3443	100%	Shot down by return fire from 206 Sqdn. Hudson. Crashed into the sea.	Off Terschelling.
07.11.40	Oblt. Herbert Kopetsch Lt. Helmut Veil	3.(F)/ Auf. Gr. 11	P Bf	M M	Bf 110 C-5 M1+ZC 2229	100%	Shot down by Spitfires of 603 Sqdn..	Off Ramsgate.
14.11.40	Hptm. Kurt Holler (Staffelkapitän) Uffz. Robert Gotha Uffz. Hermann Möller	9./NJG 1 9./NJG 1 9./NJG 1	P Bf 1. Wart	W W K	Bf 110 D 3357	60%	Force-landed on ferry flight from Schleswig to Rhein.	Hamburg-Stade.

Date	Name of crew and rank	Unit	Status	Fate	Aircraft Code & W. Nr.	Damage state	Reason for casualty	Place
15.11.40		III./NJG 1	P Bf	U U	Bf 110 D 3140	50%	Taxi-ing accident.	Rhein airfield.
15.11.40	Uffz. Paul Wenke Uffz. Nikolaus Gebler	4./ZG 76 4./ZG 76	P Bf	W K	Bf 110 M8+HM 2284	100%	Collision with Bf 110 (3432) during non-combat flight. Abandoned by crew.	Moorhausen, near Jever.
15.11.40		4./ZG 76	P Bf	U U	Bf 110 3432	100%	Collision with Bf 110 (2284) during non-combat flight. Abandoned by crew.	Moorhausen, Near Jever.
15.11.40	Fw. Otto Kaiser Ogefr. Heinrich von der Sande	1.(F)/ Auf. Gr. 22	P Bf	M M	Bf 110 C-5 4N+DH 2242	100%	Shot down by Spitfires of 19 Sqdn.. Crashed into the sea.	Channel, 20 miles off Deal.
15.11.40	Lt. Heinz Venjakob Uffz. Jonny Boschen	1.(F)/ Auf. Gr. 22	P Bf	K K	Bf 110 C-5 4N+BH 2205	100%	Shot down by Spitfires of 19 Sqdn.. Crashed into the sea.	Thames estuary, off Southend.
16.11.40		Erpr. Gr. 210	P Bf	U U	Bf 110 3462	30%	Taxi-ing accident.	Merville.
16.11.40		1.(F)/ Auf. Gr. 122	P Bf	U U	Bf 110 C-5 2262	70%	Crash-landed. Cause not known.	St. Omer.
16.11.40	Lt. Reinhold Nacke	2./NJG 1 2./NJG 1	P Bf	W U	Bf 110 C-4 3004	25%	Damaged by return fire during attack on 44 Sqdn. Hampden.	Bremerhaven.
17.11.40	Uffz. Werner Neumann Ogefr. Karl Stoff	1./Erpr. Gr. 210	P Bf	POW POW	Bf 110 D-3 S9+MH 3659	100%	Shot down by Hurricanes of 17 Sqdn. during convoy attack.	Off Harwich.
17.11.40	Uffz. Hermann Strobel Ogefr. Willi Rademacher	2./Erpr. Gr. 210	P Bf	M K	Bf 110 E-2 S9+LK 3465	100%	Shot down by Hurricanes of 17 Sqdn. during convoy attack.	Off Dunkirk.
17.11.40	Uffz. Johannes Kowatsch Uffz. Hans-Georg Bade	2./Erpr. Gr. 210	P Bf	M K	Bf 110 C-4 S9+JK 3648	100%	Shot down by Hurricanes of 17 Sqdn. during convoy attack.	Off Noordwijk.
17.11.40	Ofw. Robert Straitz Lt. Helmut Fischer	4.(F)/ Auf. Gr. 14	P Bb	M M	Bf 110 C-5 5F+QN* 2264	100%	Failed to return from weather reconnaissance flight. Crashed into Channel.	Hastings.
20.11.40		III./NJG 1	P Bf	U U	Bf 110 D 1360	20%	Force-landed during non-combat flight due to technical fault.	Krefeld.
22.11.40	Fw. Friedrich-Karl Straßweg Uffz. Willi Kerwel	1./NJG 3 1./NJG 3	P Bf	K K	Bf 110 D-2 3361	100%	Crashed during practise attacks Cause not known.	Stuttgart-Degerloch.
22.11.40	Gefr Walter Maerz Stabsfw. Alfred Kühne	6./ZG 76 6./ZG 76	P Bf	K M	Bf 110 M8+MP 3646	100%	Crashed on landing on combat sortie.	Moorhausen, near Jever.

* 4th Staffel crew flying 5th Staffel aircraft.

Date	Name of crew and rank	Unit	Status	Fate	Aircraft Code & W. Nr.	Damage state	Reason for casualty	Place
23.11.40		6./ZG 76	P Bf	U U	Bf 110 C-4 3650	20%	Damaged due to undercarriage failure.	Leeuwarden.
24.11.40	Lt. Friedrich Lugger (Gruppe Nachrichtens-offizier)	Stab ZG 26	P	K	Bf 110 3636	100%	Collided with Bf 110 (3173) during routine flight.	Caen-Carpiquet.
24.11.40	Lt. Günter Grass Uffz. Albert Schaupp	7./ZG 26 7./ZG 26	P Bf	K K	Bf 110 3173	100%	Collided with Bf 110 (3636) during routine flight.	Caen-Carpiquet.
26.11.40	Uffz. Walter Volkhardt Uffz. Eduard Euler	8./ZG 26 8./ZG 26	P Bf	M M	Bf 110 3U+GS 3409	100%	Shot down by Spitfires of 92 Sqdn.. Crashed into the sea.	Off Eastchurch.
28.11.40	Lt. Walter Burmeister Oblt. Alexander von Brixen	3.(F)/ Auf. Gr. 31	P Bf	M M	Bf 110 C-5 5D+SL 2201	100%	Shot down by P/O Hancock of of 152 Sqdn.. Crashed into the sea.	Channel, off Southampton.
29.11.40	Oblt. Rudolf Pytlik Oblt. Tankred Freyer	Stab StG. 1	P Bb	K M	Bf 110 A5+AA 2301	100%	Shot down by Spitfires of 603 Sqdn.. Crashed into the sea.	Off Ramsgate.
29.11.40		I./NJG 1	P Bf	U U	Bf 110 2058	60%	Crashed due to engine failure on routine flight.	Stade.
30.11.40		I./ZG 76	P Bf	U U	Bf 110 D-2 3341	100%	Crashed due to engine failure. Possibly attacked by P/O Edwards of 234 Sqdn. off Plymouth.	Bernay.
30.11.40		2.(F)/ Auf. Gr. 122	P Bf	U U	Bf 110 C-5 2236	50%	Force-landed following engine failure.	Dixmuiden.
03.12.40		III./ZG 26	P Bf	U U	Bf 110 D-2 3403	100%	Crashed following engine failure during routine flight.	Bernay.
08.12.40	Fw. Otto Mercier Ofw. Adolf-Josef Schönewald	4.(F)/ Auf. Gr. 14	P Bf	M M	Bf 110 C-5 5F+DM 2256	100%	Shot down by F/L Olive of 65 Sqdn. on reconn-aissance flight.	Channel, off Portsmouth.
09.12.40	Gefr. Gerhard Lobedann Uffz. Heinz Wittig	7./ZG 76 7./ZG 76	P Flg. Mech.	K K	Bf 110 969	100%	Crashed during routine flight. Cause unknown.	Parchim.
11.12.40		Erpr. Gr. 210	P Bf	U U	Bf 110 3435	5%	Damaged by AA fire during shipping attack.	North Sea.
11.12.40		6./NJG 1	P Bf	U U	Bf 110 4221	20%	Damaged. Circum-stances not known.	Deelen.
13.12.40	Uffz. Heinrich Horstmann	9./ZG 76	P	K	Bf 110 D-0 3162	100%	Crashed following collision during routine flight.	Kristiansund-Kjewik.
14.12.40		Erg. St. NJG 1	P Bf	U K	Bf 110 D 4208	100%	Abandoned during training flight. Cause unknown.	Neuburg.

Date	Name of crew and rank	Unit	Status	Fate	Aircraft Code & W. Nr.	Damage state	Reason for casualty	Place
15.12.40	Fw. Hans Rasper	4./NJG 1 4./NJG 1	P Bf	U U	Bf 110 EG + FM	20%	Damaged by return fire during attack on RAF Wellington.	Petten.
18.12.40		3.(F)/ Auf. Gr. 11	P Bf	U U	Bf 110 C-5 2287	35%	Belly-landed at Calais following damage by 421 Flight Spitfires during reconnaissance sortie.	Off Ramsgate.
19.12.40		I./StG 3			Bf 110 C-2 3056	70%	Crash-landed. Cause unknown.	Ostend.
20.12.40	Oblt. Heinrich Griese (Staffelkapitän) Uffz. Albert Baukenrodt	1./NJG 1 1./NJG 1	P Bf	W K	Bf 110 C-4 2279	100%	Abandoned by crew during routine flight. Cause unknown.	Rhinow gliding field.
22.12.40		7./NJG 1	P Bf	U U	Bf 110 0962	20%	Damaged. Circumstances not known.	Leeuwarden.

The loss tables in this work are drawn from two main sources: the Luftwaffe Quartermaster's returns from which replacement aircraft requirements were calculated, and the 'Namentliche Verlustmeldungen', which were the returns made at unit level for personnel losses, or wounds/injuries, and were used by Headquarters for the notification of next-of-kin and provision of replacement personnel. There were many inaccuracies in the original loss returns, and where these have been identified, they have been corrected. However, the lists in this work cannot claim to be 100%, since, on occasions, aircraft might have suffered damage which was repairable at unit level, and therefore no return would have been made at unit level.

Force-landed Bf 110 C-5 of 7.(F)/LG 2. Note the white spinner tip and the unit emblem on the nose.

APPENDICES

APPENDIX 1 MESSERSCHMITT 110 TYPES USED IN 1940

APPENDIX 2 MESSERSCHMITT 110 SPECIFICATION

APPENDIX 3 EXAMINATION OF MESSERSCHMITT 110 BY THE ROYAL
AIRCRAFT ESTABLISHMENT, FARNBOROUGH

APPENDIX 4 WALTER RUBENSDÖRFFER - FIRST 'ZERSTÖRER'
RITTERKREUZTRÄGER

**Air-to-air view of Messerschmitt 110 Cs of 2nd Staffel, Zerstörergeschwader 76. Staffelkapitän Wolfgang
Falck leads in M8 + GK.**

APPENDIX 1

MESSERSCHMITT 110 TYPES USED IN 1940

Like all aircraft of the Luftwaffe, the Messerschmitt 110 had its major variants identified by a letter. The following table gives details of the types flown in 1940, and the various changes made within each variant, which were identified by a sub-number. At this period of the war the abbreviation used was 'Bf', which abbreviation will be used for the purposes of this appendix.

Bf 110 C

C-0	Pre-production model powered by DB 601 A engines and with a revised radiator arrangement.
C-1	Production version of C-0
C-2	FuG 10 replaced FuG IIIaU; improvements made to Bordfunker's position.
C-3	Improved MG-FF 20 mm cannon.
C-4	Minor modifications, including the provision of armour protection for pilot and Bordfunker for the first time.
C-4/B	Fighter-bomber version of the 'C-4'. Fitted with paired ETC 250 bomb-racks under centre section of fuselage, to carry two bombs, and normally fitted with the uprated DB 601 N engines.
C-5	Reconnaissance version. The two 20 mm cannon were removed and replace by a single Rb 50/30 camera, mounted above an aperture in the floor of the cockpit.
C-5/N	Reconnaissance version fitted with uprated DB 601 N engines.
C-6	The two 20 mm. cannon were replaced by a single 30 mm. MG 101 cannon. This version was operated exclusively by Erprobungsgruppe 210.
C-7	Fighter-bomber version with paired ETC 500 bomb-racks, DB 601 N engines fitted as standard, and with strengthened undercarriage.

Bf 110 D

D-0	Pre-production long-range version with centrally-mounted 'Dackelbauch', or basset-belly fuel tank which held 264 Imp. gallons of fuel.
D-1/R-1	Production version of 'D-0'.
D-1/R-2	'Dackelbauch' replaced by two underwing 198 Imp. gallon fuel tanks.
D-1/U-1	Night-fighters fitted with 'Spanner I and II', an infra-red device intended to pick up on bomber's exhaust gases.
D-2	Had option of carrying 'Dackelbauch' or bombs.
D-3	Fighter-bomber version, with extended fuselage for dinghy stowage. Also identified by Luftwaffe as 'Bf 110 D 0-B'.

Bf 110 E

E-0	Pre-production version with DB 601 A engines and four ETC 50 bomb-racks under the wings. Also fitted was a small air inlet on the machine gun cowling.
E-1	Production version of 'E-0'.
E-1/R-2	Wing bomb-racks deleted in favour of twin ETC 1000 bomb-racks mounted under the fuselage.
E-2	Standard production version of fighter-bomber.

APPENDIX 2

MESSERSCHMITT 110 SPECIFICATION

In spite of the military need to ensure security in all matters, Luftwaffe aircrew in 1940 carried a multitude of information with them on missions over England, and this information was gratefully accepted by RAF Intelligence, desperate for even the tiniest scrap of information to help build as complete a picture as possible of their adversaries. One of the documents which fell into British hands was the complete specifications of Messerschmitt 110 C-4, M8+AC, which came to ground on 4th September. The full details, reproduced exactly from the original document, are as follows:

Type: Bf 110 C-4 (Class B2. H5K *See note).
Works No: 3602
Date of Manufacture: 11.4.40
Date of Acceptance tests: 22.7.40
Manufacturer's Markings: TD+GD
Manufacturer: MIAG Mecklenberg & Industrie A-G Braunschweig
Tanks, Petrol: 4, total capacity 1,270 litres
Tanks, Oil   2,   "   "   70 litres
Maximum Flying Weight: 6950 Kg.
Maximum Landing   "   6750 Kg.
Crew: two, or in exceptional circumstances & with special loading plan, 3.
Speeds:

Horizontal flight at ground level:	475 k.p.h.
Gliding or diving:	700 k.p.h.
Operate landing flaps:	250 k.p.h.

Engine Particulars

Type	DB 601/A	DB 601/A
Series	1	1
Works No.:	64599	65121
Manufacturer	Daimler Benz	Daimler Benz
	Genshagen	Genshagen
Place and date of test:	" 6.6.40	" 4.6.40

Both tested after 2½ running hours, next test to take place after 250 hours (not carried out).
(A set of engine and air frame cards found in Me. 110 M8+AC)

The 'H5K' is a classification for the fitness for aerobatics. The lowest classification is H1K and small civil aircraft are usually H2K. Classification 5 denotes that the aircraft is capable of performing all forms of aerobatics, but the air frame record has an endorsement: "The engines, etc., of this a/c are not suited for carrying out upside down flying. However they are capable of performing aerobatics of other types where upside down flying of a short duration only is necessary in connection with other movements"

A further Intelligence note referring to the comment concerning a crew of 3 was made as follows:

"...reference was made to the possibility of Me 110 carrying three people with a special load distribution. There is now further confirmation of this: on 6.9.40 the Me 110 U8+HL made a flight ST. OMER - DORTMUND - HANOVER and back carrying a crew of three.

APPENDIX 3

EXAMINATION OF MESSERSCHMITT 110
BY THE
ROYAL AIRCRAFT ESTABLISHMENT,
FARNBOROUGH

ENEMY AIRCRAFT - MESSERSCHMITT 110

A brief survey of the following aspects of the Me.110

1. Cockpit arrangements
2. Handling characteristics
3. Design for ease of production
4. Maintenance provisions

---

1.   Introduction.   The Me 110 is a small fast long range twin-engined two seater fighter which can also be converted to a light bomber. The D.B.601.A engines drive 3-blade V.D.M. electrically controlled airscrews.

The armament consists of four machine guns in the nose, two 20 mm. guns in the bottom of the fuselage, and one machine gun on a hand operated mounting in the rear cockpit.

A full range of blind flying and radio equipment is carried, including D.F. and blind approach sets.

2.   Cockpit Arrangements.

2.1 General. The cockpit is more comfortable than the Me 109 and has ample headroom but is nevertheless too small for a big man. The pilot's seat is slightly more upright than that in the Me 109 but since it is difficult to put very high accelerations on this aeroplane the seating position is satisfactory from the point of view of blacking out. The harness straps are clumsy and not very efficient. A plug for heated clothing is provided as there is no hot air system in this machine.

2.2 Flying Controls. The control column is well positioned and similar to that used in the Me 109, with an offset grip. Fore and aft adjustment is provided on the rudder pedals and is independent on port and starboard pedals. The seat is adjustable for height and its weight is balanced by springs.

2.3 Trimming and flap controls. Trimming tabs are provided on elevator and rudder. The elevator trimmer control is a vertical wheel on the left of the pilot; the rudder trimmer control is a lever moving over a notched quadrant on a horizontal panel on the pilot's right.

The flaps are hydraulically operated by two knobs marked "In" and "Out" on the left hand side of the instrument panel. A mechanical connection is provided to the moveable tailplane so that the change of trim to flaps fully down is small. Emergency lowering of the undercarriage is effected by compressed air. The flaps cannot be raised by the emergency system. If an attempt is made to lower the flaps while the undercarriage is up, or before it is fully down, a hooter sounds and continues to sound until the flaps are raised or the undercarriage lowered. The position of the flaps is shown on a mechanical indicator, having a straight scale graduated from 0° to 50° on the left of the pilot.

2.4 Engine controls. The mixture strength and boost are controlled automatically by capsule regulation.

The airscrews are fully feathering variable pitch and are controlled by two switches on the left of the instrument panel.

The coolant radiator flaps are controlled by two nine-position switches at the bottom centre of the dashboard. The positions of the flaps are indicated by rods projecting vertically from the upper surface of the wing.

The oil cooler flaps are operated by two five-position levers on the left of the pilot's seat.

The ignition can be retarded in order to clean the plugs by pulling two handles on the right of the pilot.

2.5 Brakes. The brakes are applied by toe pressure on the rudder pedals and are effective but not very sensitive. No parking brake is provided.

2.6 <u>Instruments</u>. The instruments are well grouped with flying instruments in the top centre, the main engine instruments on the right and temperature gauges at the bottom centre. As on the Me 109, no direct gyro is fitted although space is provided for one on the instrument panel. This space is blanked off but mounted on the blanking off plate is a hand control for setting the outer scale of the repeater compass against the lubber mark.

An airscrew pitch indicator, oil inlet and outlet temperature gauges and a combined fuel and oil pressure gauge are mounted on the inboard side of each engine nacelle.

2.7 <u>View</u>. The view during flight and when taxying is good but, due to the rather cramped cockpit, it is impossible to see the tailplane and no rear view mirrors are fitted.

The cockpit hood opens in three parts, the top part hinging upwards along its rear edge and the two sides hinging outwards and downwards. The hood, therefore, cannot be opened in flight or when taxying or running up.

A direct vision panel is fitted but it is not well positioned so that it is difficult to see straight ahead through the panel.

2.8 <u>Entrance and escape</u>. The cockpit is entered from the port side. A ladder is provided which is normally housed inside the fuselage just aft of the port trailing edge. By pressing a button, the ladder is released and can be pulled down into position. It is pushed in after use. Several hand grips are provided but it has been found that due to the metal surfaces of the wing becoming worn smooth, considerable difficulty may be experienced in reaching the front cockpit.

In an emergency the pilot uses the normal means of exit which gives plenty of for escape with a parachute. The cover of the rear cockpit can be jettisoned by pulling one of two handles, either at the rear or at the front. The tailplane may form rather a dangerous obstruction when baling out, especially from the rear cockpit, due to the low position of the tailplane.

3. <u>Handling characteristics</u>.

3.1 <u>General.</u> In the version flown in this country, the all up weight was 13,800 lb. giving a wing loading of 33 lb/sq.ft. Later versions are flying at a slightly higher wing loading.

The aeroplane is very clean. Performance tests have been made with and without the "N" type blower. Changing to the "N" type supercharger increases the absolute ceiling from 31,800 ft. to 34,500 ft.. Top level speed is about 340 m.p.h.. Rate of climb at sea level is about 2,200 ft/min..

3.2 <u>Aerodynamic features</u>. Aerodynamically the aeroplane has much in common with the Me 109 E, main points of interest being:-

1. Slotted flaps, slotted ailerons and automatic wing tip slats are fitted. The ailerons are drooped 10° when the flaps are lowered.

2. The fabric covered control surfaces are massed balanced.

3. Trimming and balance tabs are fitted on the elevator and trimming tabs alone on the rudder. No means are provided for trimming the ailerons in flight.

4. The tailplane incidence is automatically increased by a mechanical interconnection when the flaps are lowered, to counteract any change of trim.

5. As on the Me 109 E, the slotted flap just behind the radiator is deepened to form a fairing to prevent the radiator flap stalling.

3.3 Points in regard to handling are detailed below.

3.31 <u>Take-off.</u> It is not necessary to use flaps for take-off. The tail is fairly heavy and takes some time to rise, even with the stick held well forward. The take-off run is much longer than that of the Me 109 E and directional control is poor until a speed of about 120 m.p.h. is reached. Fairly coarse use of the rudder is necessary to keep the aeroplane straight at low speeds. The initial climb is good.

3.32 <u>Flying Controls</u>. The controls are fairly light and effective up to 250 m.p.h.. Above this speed they become increasingly heavy but not unduly so for a twin-engined aircraft. At 400 m.p.h. the ailerons are lighter than those of the Me 109 E, the elevators heavier. Owing to the heaviness of the elevators at high speeds, plenty of height must be allowed for recovery from dives.

3.33 <u>Landing</u>. The undercarriage should be lowered before lowering the flaps. Notwithstanding the automatic adjustment of the tailplane incidence, at the commencement of lowering the flaps, the nose rises and a fairly large forward force on the elevators is required to counteract it. Towards the end of the flap movement the nose starts to sink and a backward movement of the elevator control is required. The eventual change of trim when the flaps are fully extended is very small. The ailerons are depressed at the same time as the flaps and a sudden lightening of their control is noticed but there is no marked decrease in their effectiveness.

The approach is made at a speed of 95-100 m.p.h. and is straightforward. The landing is normal and far easier than on the Me 109 E, there being little tendency for a wing to drop. The ground run is about 600 yards.

3.34 <u>Single engine approach</u>. Single engine performance is good as the airscrew of the dead engine can be fully feathered and at light load the machine is capable of climbing on one engine if the other engine should cut out at take-off. Great care must be taken when landing on one engine since if the good engine is opened up at low speeds violent swing and bank occur. Lowering the flaps accentuates this tendency and not more than 25° of flap should be used if a landing has to be made on one engine.

3.35 <u>Slats</u> As on the Me 109 E, opening of the slats is accompanied by violent aileron snatching. The vibration ceases when the slats are fully open.

4. <u>Design for ease of production</u>.

4.1 <u>General</u>. In this aircraft, as in most other German types, the use of extrusions is limited to those parts which cannot be formed from strip. The advantage of this is evident as strip is much easier to produce than extruded sections.

Interchangeability troubles are avoided to a large extent by the methods used for sub-assemblies which are described later, and very accurate jigging is unnecessary. These methods of attachment of sub-assemblies at the same time facilitate initial assembly and maintenance.

Protective treatment against corrosion is used to a less extent than in British aircraft and it has been found that corrosion in the presence of sea water takes place very rapidly, particularly as extensive use is made of magnesium rich alloys in parts of the structure.

4.2 <u>Wings</u>. The wings are of modern stressed skin design, having a single spar with heavy concentration flanges, the wing skin taking torsion and drag loads. The spar flanges are built up of extruded angle sections placed back to back with additional flange plates riveted to the outside. The plate web is sandwiched between the angled sections, and the skin is riveted direct to the spar flange. The use of such simple sections as angles in the spar flange is a production advantage, although the large amount of riveting would tend to offset this advantage and might result in a larger section than would be adopted for a solid drawn flange.

Top hat section spanwise stringers, stepped down in size from root to tip, are used. In the inner wing, these are joined over the top of the chordwise stiffeners by gusset plates, but in the outer wing are continuous, the chordwise stiffeners and rib booms being joggled over them. The chordwise stiffeners and rib booms are mainly of Z-section.

4.3 <u>Wing attachment</u>. The wings are attached at the side of the fuselage in an unorthodox manner. The bottom boom has a horizontal pin but the top boom ends in a threaded spigot. This passes through a fitting in the fuselage and a nut is screwed on inside. This necessitates a slight vertical offset of the top flange of the centre section to enable the nut to be used. There are two other attachment points near the leading and trailing edges, both being horizontal pin joints.

4.4 <u>Fuselage</u>. The fuselage is rather unusual in design. There are sixteen continuous top hat section stringers attached to the skin by a single row of rivets through the top. The skin and frames, .006″ thick, are integral, the two transverse edges of alternate panels being bent up to form Z-section flanges on the inside of the fuselage. These sheets are also joggled so that flush skin laps can be formed with the alternating plain sheet panels. The fuselage is built in two halves with a longitudinal seam in the vertical plane. The two halves are joined along the top and bottom by two wide hat section stringers using two rows of rivets so that a butt joint is formed. The other stringers pass through clearance holes in the integral formers but there are no gussets between the stringers and formers. The plating-former combination is evidently a pressing and to combine such fabrication in one operation is of considerable advantage for large scale production.

4.5 <u>Tail unit</u>. The tail plane is constructed in two pressed half shells, the leading and trailing edge members, main spar and ribs also being split along the chordal plane. When the tail plane is assembled the two halves of the spar and the ribs are joined by bolts which are inserted through holes in the outer skin. The holes are afterwards covered by fabric patches. The leading and trailing edge members, being still accessible, are joined by rivets. The assembly is finished off at the leading edge with a 3 mm. thick half round section, fixed by screws.

4.6 <u>Fuel tanks</u>. Two fuel tanks are carried in each wing, one on each side of the spar, and the tanks are tapered to fit the contour of the wing. The tanks are of the normal German type consisting of a braced fibre shell with a self sealing covering of leather and rubber layers. The tanks are slung from a fibre frame which is belted to six brackets attached to the spars. Two webbing straps pass under each tank parallel to the fuselage and swinging of the tanks is prevented by two thinner webbing straps at the fuselage end of each tank.

4.7 <u>Engine mountings</u>. The usual type of German in-line engine mounting is used in this aircraft. This consists of two massive forged magnesium alloy bearers projecting horizontally forward from two Junkers type ball joint attachments at the top of the engine bulkhead. The horizontal members are each braced by a forged magnesium alloy strut to a point lower down on the bulkhead.

This bracing strut is pin jointed at the top end and has the Junkers type ball joint at the lower end.

A small ball jointed tubular strut connects a point half-way up the inboard bracing strut to a point on the leading edge of the next inboard complete wing rib to afford lateral stab-ility to the engine mounting. Each bearer carries the engine at two points which have anti-vibration rubber bushings.

4.8 <u>Undercarriage</u>. The undercarriage is simple and well designed, each unit consisting of a single cantilever type shock absorber strut with wheel and tyre located on the outboard side of the strut. Two side stays and one back stay are used to brace the strut. The back stay is pin jointed at its upper end to a bracket on the bottom flange of the main spar. The backstay is folded upwards by a single hydraulic jack in each nacelle thus causing the main oleo-pneumatic strut to retract backwards.

5. <u>Maintenance Provisions</u>.

5.1 <u>General</u>. In this machine as in all German aircraft, the design from the point of view of ease of maintenance is well thought out.

5.2 <u>Inspection doors and cowling</u>. Large numbers of quickly detachable inspection covers are provided in the wings and fuselage and there are plenty of detachable panels of all sizes fixed by screws. Most of the inspection covers can be released without tools by a spring loaded push button fastener. The engine cowling is quickly removable and interchangeability is guaranteed by the type of fasteners used, the cowling being drawn tightly into position as the fasteners are engaged. These fasteners are also adjustable for position in one direction by means of a screw thread and locknut on one half of the fas-tener.

5.3 <u>Removal of sub-assemblies</u>. Removal of wings, fins and tail plane is easy on this machine, all the joints, control rods, piping and electrical connections being readily accessible after removing the fillets (which are fixed by screws) in the case of the wings and tailplane, and after removing three fabric patches in the case of the fins.

All these major components are made readily interchangeable by the methods of attachment used. The wing attachment has already been described. The tail plane is attached at three points, there being two horizontal coaxial pins at the main spar about which the tail plane can hinge and a further pin joint near the leading edge which is adjustable vertically. The fins are similarly attached by three pins which are so disposed as to allow the maximum amount of tolerance in manufacture.

5.4 <u>Fuel tanks and accessories</u>. The ease with which the fuel tanks can be removed and replaced is outstanding. A fuel tank can be removed in less than four man hours. Fuel tank accessories such as the immersed pump and contents gauge float unit are situated at the top of the tank and can easily be withdrawn through covers in the top wing surface without removing or draining the tank. No self sealing piping or pipe couplings are used. The filters are situated inside the undercarriage nacelles and are readily accessible.

5.5 <u>Engines</u>. The engines are removed complete with engine mountings. All connections for fuel, oil and cooling systems and all electrical connections are arranged on the bulkhead. All disconnecting points are given distinguishing marks and comprise:

On both engines:	5 mounting connections	(hexagonal nuts)
	10 pipe connections	(" ")
	1 throttle connection	(" ")
	1 oil cooler flap control	(" ")
	2 wire controls	(snap hooks)
	29 electrical cable connections	(screwed terminals)
	2 electric pin plugs	
On the port engine:	1 air intake	(clipped flexible pipe)
	1 vacuum pump suction	(hexagonal nut)
On the starboard engine:	2 hydraulic pump connections (hexagonal nuts)	

The sparking plugs are very accessible being all situated on the outside of the cylinder banks.

The airscrews are attached to the shaft as in all German aircraft by Hirth couplings with facially serrated flanges. The V.D.M. spinners are easily removable by inserting a special tool through a slot at the rear edge of the spinner and turning it to free a spring loaded toggle lock. The spinner can then be turned to release a number of grooved locking pegs and then drawn forward.

5.6 <u>Jacking points</u>. Two jacking points are provided under the centre section spar just inboard of the wing joints and a hole is provided passing right through the rear end of the fuselage through which a bar may be passed for jacking and holding down.

5.7 <u>Rigging marks</u>. Rigging points are marked on the fuselage by flat head rivets which stand proud from the fuselage and cockpit surround and are coloured red.

5.8 <u>Hydraulic system</u>. The header tank is located in the starboard engine nacelle and a pump and filter are mounted on this engine. A disadvantage of the compressed air emergency system of under-carriage and flap operations is that the hydraulic system must be completely drained and refilled after each emergency operation. The reservoirs for the master cylinders for the brakes incorporated a non-return valve at the filling point, which necessitates the use of a syringe in refilling.

5.9 <u>Refuelling</u>. The four fuel tanks are filled at points on the top surface of the wing and provision is made to prevent fuel entering the wing itself. The covers are provided with push-button fasteners. A graduated dipstick is provided at each filling point.

5.10 <u>Air and oxygen replenishment</u>. The air and oxygen systems both have refilling points on the side of the fuselage, that for the oxygen system being just aft of the wing trailing edge as the bottles are situated near the tail, and that for the compressed air system being just forward of the leading edge as the bottles which provide air for emergency operation of the hydraulic system are also used for gun cocking.

5.11 <u>Greasing</u>. Tecalemit grease nipples are provided throughout the machine. These are painted red.

5.12 <u>Pipe lines</u>. The standard German colour code for pipe lines is used in this aeroplane. All pipe lines are painted throughout their length with one colour to indicate roughly the fluid in them, thus:

Oil	-brown.
Fuel	-yellow.
Coolant	-green.
Air	-blue.

In addition at intervals along the pipe may be painted bands of a different colour to indicate the particular service in which it is employed.

5.13 <u>Armament</u>. The fixed guns are very accessible. The top of the nose fairing can be removed complete and the four machine guns can then be removed from the aircraft in a very short time. The accessories however, are complicated and the electrical gear elaborate. Ammunition for these guns is contained in boxes which slide into the nose of the fuselage and are held in place by a door with a single fastener. The magazines for the 20 mm. guns can be changed in flight as they are accessible to the occupant of the rear cockpit.

5.14 <u>Electrical system</u>. No fuses are used, their place being taken by thermal circuit breaker switches. Tripping of the circuit breaker is revealed by the position of a red button and they can be instantly re-set

Engine starting is independent of any external electrical supply. Inertia type starters are used and these can be operated either from an external supply or from the aircraft battery or by hand.

All wiring is numbered, making the tracing of circuits easy.

APPENDIX 4

WALTER RUBENSDÖRFFER
FIRST 'ZERSTÖRER' RITTERKREUZTRÄGER

Walter Rubensdörffer was born on 1st August 1910, the first of two sons to Paul and Anne Rubensdörffer, in Basle, Switzerland. In 1912 the family moved to Pforzheim, where Paul Rubensdörffer had previously lived. All of Walter's schooldays were spent in Pforzheim, and in Easter 1928 he passed his 'Abitur' at the Oberrealschule in Pforzheim. During his schooldays he became an enthusiastic skier and mountain climber, obviously having a penchant for the outdoor life. In 1928 he attended the Hanseatic Yachting School, and received training on the ships 'Deutschland' and 'Niobe'.

Sometime in 1932 he undertook a trip to Moscow, and with the emergence of the German armed forces again, he enlisted in the Luftwaffe and was granted a Commission. For a time he worked in the Luftfahrtministerium, and with the possibility of hostilities starting with the reoccupation of the Rhineland in early 1936, Walter Rubensdörffer was appointed Staffelkapitän of 3./StG 165. As the youngest Hauptmann in the Luftwaffe he was to have a spell with the 'Legion Condor', scoring a sole victory on 2nd May 1939 while with the Stab section of Jagdgruppe J/88. Little is known of his activities upon his return to Germany, but it is likely that he spent further time at the Air Ministry.

Upon the outbreak of war in 1939, he joined a flying unit, but was not fully released from duties by the Air Ministry, and therefore flew only a small number of missions against Poland. On 1st July 1940 he was given command of Erprobungsgruppe 210. He was a well-liked and respected leader, and shortly after taking command, on 19th July 1940, he was awarded the Iron Cross, First Class, for "courageous leadership of your Gruppe".

Hauptmann Walter Rubensdörffer led Erprobungsgruppe 210 through the first phase of the Battle of Britain, the attacks on shipping around the south and south-east coast of England. When the Luftwaffe began to attack targets on the English mainland, Erprobungsgruppe 210 found themselves in the forefront of that phase also, and it was during such a land-based raid in the early evening of 15th August 1940 that Walter Rubensdörffer lost his life while leading his Gruppe. Many have speculated as to why Rubensdörffer led Erprobungsgruppe 210 in to attack Croydon, and not the allotted target of Kenley. Only one man has the answer - Walter Rubensdörffer.

Four days after his death, Walter Rubensdörffer was awarded the Ritterkreuz. He was only the 5th 'Jagdflieger' to receive it, and the first 'Zerstörer' pilot. Walter Rubensdörffer was originally buried at Tunbridge Wells cemetery with his Bordfunker, Ludwig Kretzer, but both were re-interred in the German Soldatenfriedhof in Cannock Chase.

BIBLIOGRAPHY

PUBLISHED SOURCES

Aders, Gebhard. History of the German Night Fighter Force, 1917-1945. Jane's, 1979.

Barclay, George. Fighter Pilot. William Kimber, 1976.

Beedle J.. 43 Squadron. Beaumont, 1966.

Bekker, Cajus. The Luftwaffe War Diaries. Macdonald, 1966.

Bolitho, Hector. Combat Report. Batsford, 1943.

Collier, Basil. The Defence of the United Kingdom. HMSO, 1957.

Collier, Richard. Eagle day. Hodder and Stoughton, 1966.

Crook, Flight Lieutenant D.M.. Spitfire Pilot. Faber and Faber, 1942.

Deere, Alan C.. Nine Lives. Hodder and Stoughton, 1959.

Deighton, Len. Fighter. Jonathan Cape, 1977.

Ellan, Squadron Leader B.J.. Spitfire! John Murray, 1942.

Foreman, John. Battle of Britain - The Forgotten Months. Air Research, 1988.

Forrester, Larry. Fly For Your Life. Muller, 1956.

Franks, Norman. Double Mission. William Kimber, 1976.

Franks, Norman. Fighter Leader. William Kimber, 1978.

Gleed, Ian. Arise to Conquer. Victor Gollancz, 1942.

Johnstone, Air Vice Marshal Sandy. Enemy in the Sky. William Kimber, 1976.

Jullian, Marcel. The Battle of Britain. Jonathan Cape, 1967.

MacMillan, Wing Commander Norman. The Royal Air Force in the World War. George Harrap, 1942-1944.

McKee, Alexander. The Coal-Scuttle Brigade. Souvenir Press, 1957.

McKee, Alexander. Strike from the Sky. Souvenir Press, 1960.

Mason, Francis K.. Battle over Britain. McWhirter Twins, 1969.

Masters, David. "So Few". Eyre and Spottiswoode, 1941.

Mohlenbeck and Leihse. Ferne Nacht Jagd. Motorbuch Verlag, 1976.

Moulson, Tom. The Flying Sword. Macdonald, 1964.

Neil, Wing Commander Tom. Gun Button to 'Fire'. William Kimber, 1987.

Obermeier, Ernst. Die Ritterkreuzträger der Luftwaffe, 1939-1945, Band I, Jagdflieger. Verlag Dieter Hoffmann, 1989.

Page, Geoffrey. Tale of a Guinea Pig. Pelham Books, 1981.

Price, Alfred. The Hardest Day. Macdonald and Jane's, 1979.

Price, Alfred. Battle of Britain Day - 15 September 1940. Sidgwick and Jackson, 1990.

Ramsey, Winston G.. The Battle of Britain - Then and Now. After the Battle, 1980.

Ramsey, Winston G.. The Blitz - Then and Now, Vols. 1-2. After the Battle, 1987-1988.

Rayner, Geoff. One Hurricane - One Raid. Airlife, 1990.

Reis, Karl and Ring, Hans. The Legion Condor. Schiffer Military History, 1992.

Revell, Alex. The Vivid Air. William Kimber, 1978.

Richey, Paul. Fighter Pilot. Batsford, 1941.

Shaw, Michael. Twice Vertical. Macdonald, 1971.

Stones, Donald. Dimsie. Wingham Press, 1991.

Townsend, Peter. Duel of Eagles. Weidenfeld and Nicolson, 1971.

Vasco, John. Bombsights Over England. JAC Publications, 1990.

Wakefield, Kenneth. Luftwaffe Encore. William Kimber, 1979.

Wallace, Graham. RAF Biggin Hill. Putnam, 1957.

Wood, Derek and Dempster, Derek. The Narrow Margin. Hutchinson, 1961.

Wood, Tony and Gunston, Bill. Hitler's Luftwaffe. Salamander, 1977.

Wright, Esther Terry. Pilot's Wife's Tale. John Lane the Bodley Head, 1942.

Wundshammer, Benno. Flieger-Ritter-Helden. C. Bertelsmann Verlag, 1942.

Ziegler, Frank. The Story of 609 Squadron. Macdonald, 1971.

OTHER DOCUMENTARY SOURCES

Air Ministry Pamphlet. The Rise and Fall of the German Air Force (1933-1945). ACAS(I), 1948.
Air Pictorial. Various editions, 1963-1969.
Aircraft Illustrated. Various editions, 1969-1971.
Dörr, Manfred. Die Geschichte der III./ZG 26 Horst Wessel. Jägerblatt, Various editions, Gemeinschaft der Jagdflieger EV.
Marchfelder, Richard. Most Pilots are Gentlemen. Unpublished Manuscript, 1984.
Namentliche Verlustmeldungen. Various units, 1940.
Ob. d. L. Genst. Qu./6 Abteilung loss returns, 1940. Deutsche Dienststelle (WASt), Berlin.
RAF Flying Review. Various editions, 1961-1967.
RAF Squadron Operations Record Books (Forms 540). Various, 1940.
RAF Combat Reports (Forms 'F'). Various, 1940.

EYE WITNESSES

We are most grateful for the valuable assistance of many Bf 110 pilots and Bordfunkers whose personal memories and wartime experiences form an important element of this book. They were all most generous in their hospitality and their time in responding to our queries. We hope that they feel that we have done their stories justice.

Unteroffizier Siegfried Becker, pilot of 1./ZG 2.
Oberleutnant Erich von Bergen, pilot of 8./ZG 26.
Obergefreiter Karl-Heinz Boock, Bordfunker of 7./ZG 26.
Feldwebel Hermann Brinkmann, pilot of 2./ZG 26.
Obergefreiter Karl Döpfer, Bordfunker of 14.(Z)/LG 1.
Oberleutnant Wilfried von Eichborn, pilot and Gruppenadjutant of II./ZG 76.
Leutnant Karl-Joachim Eichhorn, pilot of 14.(Z)/LG 1.
Hauptmann Eberhard d'Elsla, pilot and Staffelkapitän of 5./ZG 26.
Hauptmann Wolfgang Falck, pilot, 2./ZG 76, Gruppenkommandeur of I./ZG 1 and Geschwaderkommodore of NJG 1.
Unteroffizier Rudolf Franke, pilot of 5./ZG 26.
Oberleutnant Gerhard Granz, pilot and Gruppenadjutant of I./ZG 2.
Feldwebel Hans Grau, pilot of 7./ZG 26.
Gefreiter Hans Heinrich, Bordfunker of 4./ZG 76.
Feldwebel Erich Hermanski, Bordfunker of 4./ZG 1 and 7./ZG 76.
Oberleutnant Hans-Joachim Jabs, pilot and Staffelkapitän of 6./ZG 76.
Gefreiter Georg Jakstadt, pilot of 9./ZG 26.
Oberleutnant Hans Jäger, pilot and Gruppenadjutant of I./ZG 76.
Oberleutnant Gerhard Kadow, pilot and Staffelkapitän of 6./ZG 1 and 9./ZG 76.
Unteroffizier Adolf Käser, Bordfunker of 8./ZG 76.
Oberleutnant Hans-Ulrich Kettling, pilot of 1./ZG 76.
Obergefreiter Herbert Klinke, Bordfunker of 5./ZG 1.
Leutnant Joachim Koepsell, ,pilot of 1. and 3./ZG 26.
Hauptmann Hans Kogler, pilot and Staffelkapitän of 1./ZG 26.
Unteroffizier Erwin Landgraf, pilot of 4./ZG 26.
Leutnant Richard Marchfelder, pilot and Gruppe TO of II./ZG 1 and III./ZG 76.
Oberleutnant Ernst Matthes, pilot and Staffelkapitän of 7./ZG 26.
Oberleutnant Victor Mölders, pilot of 1./ZG 1 and Staffelkapitän of 1./NJG 1.
Leutnant Wolf Münchmeyer, pilot of 1./ZG 2.
Gefreiter Karl Nechwatal, Bordfunker of 8./ZG 26.
Oberleutnant Rüdiger Proske, pilot and Gruppenadjutant of I./ZG 26.
Unteroffizier Theodor Rütters, Bordfunker of 4./ZG 26.
Obergefreiter Fritz Volk, Bordfunker of 1./ZG 76.
Leutnant Ernst-August Wörner, pilot of I./ZG 26.

A similar debt of gratitude is owed to the relatives of many of those who did not survive the events described, or who died post-war. For allowing us privileged access to family documents and photographs of the period, we are most grateful to the relatives of those aircrew shown below. We hope that this book will act as a small but lasting tribute to the memory of those who did not return.

Feldwebel Jakob Birndorfer, pilot of 6./ZG 76.

Unteroffizier Rudolf Condné, Bordfunker of 6./ZG 76.

Feldwebel Hans Datz, pilot of 13.(Z)/LG 1.

Hauptmann Friedrich-Karl Dickoré, pilot and Gruppenkommandeur of II./ZG 1 and III./ZG 76.

Unteroffizier Eugen Dibold, Bordfunker of 4./ZG 76.

Unteroffizier Alois Haas, pilot of 4./ZG 1 and 7./ZG 76.

Hauptmann Eberhardt Heinlein, pilot and Gruppenkommandeur of I./ZG 2.

Oberleutnant Joachim Junghans, pilot of 9./ZG 26.

Unteroffizier Rudolf Krause, Bordfunker of 1./ZG 26.

Hauptmann Horst Liensberger, pilot and Gruppenkommandeur of V.(Z)/LG 1.

Leutnant Horst Marx, pilot of 1./ZG 1.

Feldwebel Josef Radlmair, Bordfunker of Stab, II./ZG 26.

Unteroffizier Erhart Reinhold, pilot of 9./ZG 26.

Unteroffizier Otto Schamberger, Bordfunker of Stab, I./ZG 1.

Oberfeldwebel Fritz Stahl, pilot of 4./ZG 26.

Feldwebel Franz Winter, Bordfunker of 6./ZG 26.

Acknowledgements

A book of this nature relies on the co-operation and assistance of a great many people, most of whom are acknowledged separately. The following also made material contributions for which we are equally grateful: Horst Amberg, Peter Grimm, Knut Maesel, Ludwig von Eimannsberger, Oskar Fath, Horst Diener, Hans Rasper, Karl-Fritz Schröder and Herbert Thomas.

Those indefatigable researchers, John Foreman and Chris Goss, were both free with access to their impressive archive records of the period. They provide excellent models that many an official depository could do well to duplicate, and we thank them for their abiding interest and dedication in documenting events long past, and for opening their files to us so readily. On the European continent, excellent help was received from Eric Mombeek and Jean-Loius Roba.

Thanks also to my good friend, editor and publisher, John Vasco, whose drive and enthusiasm got us off the ground, navigated us through an often difficult flight and brought us in to a safe landing - Beinbruch! For organising our joint forays throughout Germany, and for his easy companionship, endurance, patience and humour along the way I am particularly grateful. We mined a rich vein of personal memories and in the doing, created a good few of our own. Es war ein 'Stück Puch!'.

PETER CORNWELL
GIRTON, CAMBRIDGESHIRE
DECEMBER 1994

The idea for this book first surfaced when I was considering a further research project to follow the Erprobungsgruppe 210 work, and asked Peter what he thought. His enthusiasm for a work on the Messerschmitt 110 in 1940 was such that it was immediately agreed that it should be a joint venture. I am, in turn, indebted to Peter for bringing years of research experience to bear, and for being such an entertaining companion on the treks across Germany and Austria to visit former aircrew in their homes. Peter's command of German came in handy on more than one occasion. His contribution to the history of the Battle of Britain cannot be underestimated, and I could not have had a more knowledgeable researcher on board for the duration of the research. My gratitude is extended to him for his eternal patience in answering the multitudinous queries I placed with him, and for his meticulous attention to detail. Finally, thanks to Anne, Jamie and Claire who have endured years of living with the subject; their patience and understanding is humbly acknowledged.

JOHN VASCO
NORWICH, NORFOLK
DECEMBER 1994

INDEX

This index does not include appendices, captions to photographs or entries in the loss tables

* *

The Messerschmitt 110 went on to reach its pinnacle of achievement after 1940 in the night-fighting role.